PSYCHOLOGICAL COMMENTARIES

VOLUME TWO

PSYCHOLOGICAL COMMENTARIES

On the Teaching of

G. I. GURDJIEFF

AND

P. D. OUSPENSKY

by

Maurice Nicoll

WATKINS · LONDON

Publishers & Booksellers

First public edition 1952
Reprinted several times

This edition © 1980 Watkins Publishing

ISBN Vol 1: 0 7224 0182 5
Vol 2: 0183 3. Vol 3: 0184 1

Printed in Great Britain
by A Wheaton & Co Ltd, Exeter

CONTENTS

Birdlip, 1944

Birdlip, 1945

Quaremead, Ugley, 1945

NOTE ON THE STUDY OF LOSS OF FORCE

The conception of force is an essential idea in the Work. In order to awaken a man must have force: without force he cannot awaken. The conception of force can be best understood if it is studied from two angles. The Work says that a man *loses* force in a great many specific ways which it mentions, that he *gains* force by work on them, and that he *creates* force by the act of Self-Remembering.

Let us study *loss of force*. We are told that we can only begin to awaken after much effort and long struggle; and that this is due to the fact that life wants us to stay asleep for its own reasons. This means that life prevents us from conserving force, or, put the other way, life takes our force. Since we are nothing but a mass of habits, life forms very early in us various habits of losing force, sometimes very complex ones. So we lose force mechanically, just as we do everything else mechanically. It is very difficult to see how we lose force. We have to view ourselves in the light of new knowledge—to exchange our old ideas for new—in order to realize what is continually happening. A person may lose force in a flash, just because of touching a negative emotion. In the Work, which is long, we begin to realize that we are faced by this mass of habits, *that is not us*. This is a painful experience and it is unnecessary to enter into it unless one is convinced that there is something to reach.

Now, to awaken, anything anti-mechanical may help. *Self-observation* is anti-mechanical and must come before everything else. But it is in *non-identifying* that the main key lies to preventing *loss of force*. Every act of non-identifying saves force. We are speaking of force necessary for awakening. If we identify with everything, inner and outer, we cannot have force for doing or understanding the Work. The Work will remain far away as a vague cloud. After a time one begins to notice that one is asleep. That is, one begins to notice that one has lost force. At the same time one notices that the Work and its ideas seem very far away. When one begins to have a barometer of this kind, it is possible to study in more detail what it is that causes loss of force. Although the causes of loss of force can be arranged in general categories, that apply to everyone, such as negative states, each person has particular causes that must be observed personally in the greatest detail and reflected upon with the greatest care in the light of the new understanding that the Work gives. Otherwise there is no sincerity with oneself, upon which alone can anything be built within oneself. Nor can there be any centre of gravity established by the influence of the Work, and so nothing will reach us that belongs to Real 'I'.

All this belongs to the necessity of valuation that is frequently spoken of. Without valuation of the Work there can be no sincerity with it, nor can there be a definite inner perception of loss of force. That is, a person will not notice distinctly that he is asleep, although he may notice that the Work seems far away. It is very interesting to begin to notice the sources of loss of force and the conditions connected with them. There are certain trains of thought, for instance, that cause loss of force, and it may take some years before you see why. And it often happens that things you thought quite harmless and even admirable cause loss of force.

Now to recall briefly that other angle—what *creates* force. It is the act of Self-Remembering that creates force. The opening of the mind to the act and the meaning and significance of Self-Remembering and the accompanying separation from all one's usual ideas of oneself, from one's usual small feelings and internal considerings—this actually creates force. So one *gains* force by every act of non-identifying because one prevents its loss, and one *creates* force by Self-Remembering.

Now you will see that it is necessary to isolate oneself from the action of life. But to understand what this means in a general sense, and what it means for each of you in a particular sense, is not something given us ready-made. It is only gradually that one begins to see. How impatient some people are about the Work. I sometimes marvel at people expecting to reach in a short time states that demand a life-time of work before they can be attained. There is always something outside and something inside that a person should try to isolate himself from. What does it mean to isolate oneself? You can say "insulate" if you like. If life takes all force and keeps us asleep it is necessary to isolate oneself from at least some of its various powers over us. Some people are always upset about something or other—about something that they think very wrong. Let us say they are politically upset, or morally upset, or religiously upset, or hygienically upset, or, simply, just always upset by everything. They lose force. That is, in these ways life robs them of all force for awakening. They think, however, that they are doing right. This is not a good thing to think mechanically. When you feel you are right you may be sure you are asleep. But of course life robs us of force in many other ways. We are not important in the Ray of Creation. We are living on a mere point in the Milky Way which is billion-sunned and there are billions of Milky Ways. Yes, we are very small. But there is a chance. To have this double-feeling is a form of Self-Remembering.

Now as regards Self-Remembering, which is the means of actually creating force—you remember the First Conscious Shock and the energies resulting?—there are many ways of Self-Remembering. But they all depend on the feeling that there is something else, that this life on this extremely bad planet is not explicable in terms of itself. There is something else. We then meditate on the Octave from the Sun, until it becomes a living thing in our mind, and speaks to us. Then perhaps we begin to see what "isolation" means. However, we have moments in which we feel that the *future* will surely be better. But there are two futures, one in time and one in scale, one horizontal

374

—the other vertical and always there, just above our present state. There are many forms of Self-Remembering. You have to get out of your own way, to get out of your own light. Since we are different at different moments, Self-Remembering is different at different times. The "Sly Man" knows this. He does not always practise the same method. To do so is to make it mechanical. What is mechanical is useless for the Work. He moves, as it were, forward and then backward and then forward, and so on. In any case he experiments. He notices what was and is no longer useful and invents some other way—and so on. Some time we will speak of "Sly Man". But everyone should above all things think of and study and try to self-remember each day. Try· to get out of your own way. Try to let something get in that cannot because *you* are in the way. Can you stop the noise of yourself for even a moment? Can you get out of the ordinary feeling of yourself? Can you become *no one* for a moment to yourself? Or, by contrast, can you feel the intense reality of yourself? Can you feel *I* in all you have to do, for a time? All these are different ways of remembering oneself. There are many other ways, but try to discover *one* for yourself, to begin with, and get to know the taste of it. Then you will know more distinctly when you are asleep. We are trying to awaken to another *level* of life. We believe this is the real meaning of our existence. But to awaken we must have force. Whatever we do consciously remains: whatever we do mechanically is lost to us. So we have to learn how to live in life and not be eaten by life. Identify with life and give all your force to life and you cannot awaken, just as you cannot if you identify with yourself. How rich that young man felt himself, how identified he was with all his virtues and talents and excellences. He was told to go and sell all he had before he could awaken. He was very sorrowful. Think what it would mean to cease to ascribe to yourself everything you do and think you are—that is, to *sell* all your possessions. Who can imagine what this really means? Have you caught even a single glimpse yet of its meaning in regard to yourself? If so, you will begin to realize where your force goes every moment, how it is used and why people are asleep without knowing it.

A FURTHER NOTE ON THE
STUDY OF LOSS OF FORCE

Let us continue to-night with a further commentary on losing force. Last time we spoke about the necessity of observing how we lose force and noticing what is the cause of it. Amongst other things it was said that internal considering is part of the great subject of identifying and identifying is the greatest evil for mankind. Many people think that worrying about other people will help them. They even imagine that it is right to be in a worried, anxious state about anybody else, but what we have to understand is that it does not help anyone. If you are very worried and anxious about someone who is ill, it does not help either you or the other person. Being identified never helps. It is just in this way that we take force from other people by identifying with them and we keep them, as it were, in prison, and ourselves also. You have probably noticed how easy it is for two people to put themselves in prison and create their own useless suffering.

Now you can lose force by thinking of someone with whom you are identified. We do not treat one another well inside ourselves. We have to release one another. If we could get a right attitude to one another, we should be free from one another. I mean, we should not be in a kind of bondage. To find a right attitude really means to find a point of equilibrium where one is not in either of the opposites. But identifying with the other person is the reverse of this. As you know, being identified is almost the only emotion that we experience. Even if we for a moment experience a trace of real emotion it almost at once becomes mixed up with some form of identifying. For example, we ascribe, say, a momentary feeling of love to ourselves and instantly the whole situation within is changed. Of course, if we believe that there is nothing higher than ourselves it is really impossible not to identify always in one way or another. And this always means loss of force. We do not become more conscious of one another through identifying but less conscious. To become more conscious we require more force. The object of this Work is to increase consciousness. If we were more conscious this war would stop at once. If we became more conscious of other people our whole relationship towards them would change. External Considering is a development of consciousness. Consciousness can grow only in certain directions. Self-knowledge is one direction: external considering is another direction. If you could put yourself in the place of all the people whom you were about to kill with a bomb you would be unable to do anything. It would come to you as a terrific shock to realize what you were about to do. This would be an increase of consciousness. Force would increase in you but you might go to sleep a moment later by identifying with feelings of revenge or personal insult, etc. and then you would lose force and at once the area of your consciousness would diminish and instead of seeing many things together you would once more see only one thing. You would look once more through one narrow window. We can notice the states in which we feel much more awake towards people, much less identified, and in which we begin actually to take in new impressions of others. This means that we are more conscious, that we have more force of consciousness. Then suddenly we become identified as when someone says something that we do not expect, and so on, and we tumble down as it were to our ordinary state which has such a stale smell about it.

One cause of losing force is through not being in the right centre for what you are doing. This is comparatively easy to study in yourself provided you know something of the work of different centres in yourself. For instance, if you are day-dreaming and trying to do some job that you dislike very much you will be losing force all the time. Why? You should discuss this amongst yourselves. If on the contrary you are in the right centre and really engaged in something to which you are giving your attention—in which perhaps even all centres are assisting—then you will not lose force but tend to gain force or to conserve it, because you are acting more consciously. You know what it is to do your daily work mechanically and the difference if you do it more consciously. In the one case, you get no impressions: in the other case, you get some impressions.

You will realize how important it is to seal yourself against states where force can leak out, and how much the Work deals with these and how practically it speaks on these points. Perhaps some of us have not realized it yet. Perhaps we have not made the connection between the teachings of the Work and our own inner experience. In any case you will see that unless a man becomes hermetically sealed he will be like a person putting to sea in a boat that is constantly springing leaks, who will have to keep on putting back to shore. Our situation is really exactly similar. We have got to isolate ourselves from the effects that have been automatically produced in us and this requires a great deal of patient self-study, self-sincerity and understanding of what the Work is about.

Certain ideas of the Work are very important in this respect and I will again call your attention to one or two of them. You have to understand the deeper meaning of the saying that *Man is mechanical* and the saying that *Everything happens in the only way it can happen in life*. You have to realize that *Man cannot do*. You must begin to realize the meaning of these sayings and their truth because otherwise the whole mental outlook will be wrong and of course you will lose force quite uselessly. It will be like having the wrong attitude to a machine that you are trying to run in the best possible way. You do not understand the machine. You keep pulling the wrong levers. You do not see what it really is. It is something like that that I mean when I say that we must understand the meaning of these sayings. For example, if you take everyone as fully conscious you will continually lose force.

We are not conscious. We do not speak and do things consciously. There are not certain people running the affairs of life, some people called "they". Everything is happening in the only way it can happen. Let me quote you something in G.'s words. O. has asked G. what he ought to do:

"What *to do*?" asked G., as though surprised. "It is impossible *to do* anything. A man must first of all *understand* certain things. He has thousands of false ideas and false conceptions, chiefly about himself, and he must get rid of some of them before beginning to acquire anything new. Otherwise the new will be built on a wrong foundation and the result will be worse than before."

"How can one get rid of false ideas?" I asked. " We depend on the forms of our perception. False ideas are produced by the forms of our perception."

G. shook his head. "Again you speak of something different," he said. "You speak of errors arising from perceptions but I am not speaking of these. Within the limits of given perceptions man can be more or less deluded. As I have said before, man's chief delusion is his conviction that he can *do*. All people think that they can do, all people want to do and the first question all people ask is what are they to do. But actually nobody does anything and nobody can do anything. This is the first thing that must be understood. *Everything happens.* All that befalls a man, all that is done by him, all that comes from him—*all this happens.* And it happens in exactly the same way as rain falls as a result of a change in the temperature of the atmosphere; as snow melts under the rays of the sun, as dust rises with the wind.

Man is a machine. All his deeds, actions, words, thoughts, feelings, convictions, opinions and habits are the results of external influences, external impressions. Out of himself a man cannot produce a single thought, a single action. Everything he says, does, thinks, feels—all this happens. Man cannot discover anything, cannot invent anything. It all happens.

To establish this fact for oneself, to understand it, to be convinced of its truth, means getting rid of a thousand illusions about man, about his being creative and consciously organizing his own life, and so on. There is nothing of this kind. Everything happens —popular movements, wars, revolutions, changes of government —all this happens. And it happens in exactly the same way as everything happens in the life of individual man. Man is born, lives, dies, builds houses, writes books, not as he wants to, but as it happens. Everything happens. Man does not hate, love, desire—all this happens.

But no one will ever believe you if you tell him he can do nothing. This is the most offensive and the most unpleasant thing you can tell people. And it is particularly unpleasant and offensive because it is the truth. And nobody wants to know the truth."

THE ENNEAGRAM

I

To-night we will begin to study the diagram called the Enneagram (or nine-diagram). This diagram is peculiar to this teaching. It is found nowhere else. When it was first given by G. he observed that several things in this system could be found in other ancient systems of esoteric teaching, but not the Enneagram. In this connection he said that although several things in this system could be traced in the fragments remaining to us of other systems, there was no proper organization and arrangement of them, and the dependence of one thing on another could not be seen. All the parts of this system are connected together in the right order to form an organic whole—a living organism. Man and the Universe are taken together. The teaching about Man is related to the Universe, whose child he is, and what exists in him is shewn to exist in the Universe. The significance of evolving Man and the significance of the evolving Universe, and the laws in Man and in the Universe are taken together as inseparable.

In speaking of the Enneagram G. said that it formulated the whole of the teaching and that the more a man could read its meanings the more deeply he understood the Work. On one occasion, asked what it was all about, G. said that it represents the union of the Law of Three, or Law of the Trinity, and the Law of Seven, or Law of the Octave. Let us remind ourselves that the Law of Three states that in every manifestation three forces, active, passive and neutralizing, must take part, and that they are the creative forces which create the different orders of the worlds in a descending scale, increasing the number of laws as they duplicate themselves. Let us also remember that a second law exists, the Law of Seven, which relates to the *order of manifestation*. If there be a creative force there must also be *order* in creation, or all will be chaos. The interaction of these two laws in such a way that one does not hinder or stifle the other, and so that all possibilities are attained, is represented in the Enneagram. But at our stage we can only expect a first reading of it.

Its construction is as follows: a circle is divided into nine equal parts. The number 7 is then divided into 1, giving the result *1 4 2 8 5 7* as a recurring period. Lines are drawn connecting these numbers— i.e. 1 to 4, etc.

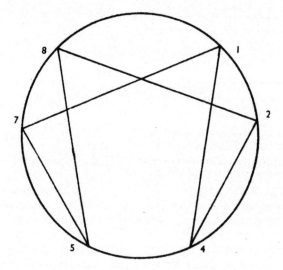

You will notice several things. First, the diagram is *symmetrical*. Second, three numbers are left out: 3, 6 and 9, all multiples of 3. Third, you will notice that the lines cross. One crossing-point is exactly in the mid-line, the other two are lateral and equidistant from it.

Let us next indicate by arrows the directions represented by the lines. The starting-point of the Enneagram is the figure 1, for the Enneagram is a moving diagram and represents movements of things in two ways. I will indicate only two. Starting from 1, there is a movement to 4 along the line 1-4. Then from 4 to 2, across the area where 3 should occur but is missing. Then from 2 a movement goes right across to 8, down to 5, and then across the area where 6 should be to 7. Then the movement returns right across the figure to 1, but in so doing crosses the line 2-8. This is one movement. The second movement is outside on the circumference from 1 to 2 to 4 to 5 to 7 to 8. Let us set alongside the number 1 the note *Re*, and alongside 2 the note *Mi*, and alongside 4 the note *Fa*. This will be sufficient for the moment in order to see the two movements I am indicating. You will see that there is a movement within the Enneagram from 1 to 4, and then to 2—that is, 1, 4, 2. And there is a possible movement by way of the circumference, from 1 to 2 and to 4—that is, 1, 2, 4. Let us put the remainder of the octave notes round the circumference, ending with *Do* at the top point.

The diagram should now be like this:—

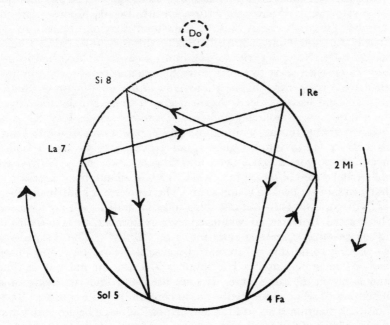

Let us indicate the possible motion on the circumference from point *Re* to point *Mi*, to *Fa*, to *Sol*, etc. by curved arrows, indicating a clockwise movement. The other criss-cross movements taking place within the Enneagram are already indicated by six arrows, one on each of the six lines joining the figures on the circumference in the order of 1 4 2 8 5 7—the number obtained by dividing 7 into 1.

Now let us reflect on this extraordinary diagram, because unless we grasp something of its mystery we will take it as we take everything else. This diagram must fall on higher parts of centres. When you feel something is extraordinary, strange, and so on, it means that it falls on higher divisions of centres. All the Work should fall there. Let us consider one of the great teachings of the Work. The Work does not teach that we live in a dying but in an evolving Universe. Everything is growing in its own time and scale. The Moon, the Earth, the Sun, are all growing in colossal periods of time compared with our little time and scale. Everything created is trying to reach its creator. Let us take an apparently trivial but, I think, a legitimate comparison. The Universe, starting from Unity, is stretched out like a piece of elastic. It seeks to return to its source, to eliminate the tension. (I could say here many things about the chemical table of elements and their various tendencies to combine with each other in order to reach equilibrium.) Now the Ray of Creation represents the Absolute as 1 and all levels of creation proceeding from it as numbers—namely, 3, 6, 12 and so on. In the

381

esoteric school of Pythagoras it was said that all things are *numbers*. Have you ever thought of the relations of numbers? You can multiply or divide them. What does *division* mean? Let us suppose that the number 3 desires to return into 1. Imagine it striving to pass into 1—that is, Absolute Unity. Mathematically, this is represented as 1 being *divided* by 3. Now, if 3 tries to pass into 1 so as to be absorbed in it—and all creation seeks to return to its Source and be absorbed by it—then what happens? Divide 3 into 1. 3 into 1 goes .3 times (that is, into 10) and leaves 1 over. Again it goes 3 times and leaves 1 over. So 3 into 1 = .3 recurring endlessly. And the whole Ray taken as 7 notes, trying to find solution and peace, passes into Absolute Unity as 7 into 1 (i.e. 7 into 10 goes 1 and 3 over, into 30 goes 4 and 2 over, into 20 goes 2 and 6 over, into 60 goes 8, etc. etc.). So you see that 3 and 7 cannot return to 1, whereas 1 is in all numbers. One is in 3, but 3 cannot get back to 1, and so on. The Universe is built on numbers as Pythagoras taught—but one thing must be added. All creation, all the created Universe, at whatever level or number, seeks to return to its source—that is, seeks to enter into 1 or "Unity". The Trinity—or 3—seeking to do this is "eternal" because it always reproduces itself and so remembers itself. The number 7 is also eternal but in time and so not in the same sense. It loses itself and finds its being in a repetition of what is not itself—i.e. in constant repetition of 1 4 2 8 5 7. Since this diagram is about Man and his possibilities, it begins with 7 and the properties of this number in relation to Unity. Studying the properties of 7 in relation to Unity we find that they are given by the number 1 4 2 8 5 7. This by itself means nothing. But given the framework of the Enneagram, we find it gives rise to an extraordinary relation, extraordinary because of the symmetrical diagram. Nothing appears symmetrical about the number 1 4 2 8 5 7 by itself. The only thing one can say about the number is that it repeats itself endlessly in terms of the decimal system and also contains no 3 or multiple of 3 in it. This is remarkable. The number has also other remarkable properties.

But what it is necessary to grasp is that the created Universe seeks by evolution to return to its source and that all things crave this satisfaction or fulfilment. Everything is deprived, incomplete, as a separate creation, and everything seeks completion—an atom, a man, a planet, a sun, a galaxy. In regard to Absolute Unity, we are not merely halved or quartered but under 48 dividing forces. But I give this reflection for those who have already sought to meditate on the Ray.

Next time we will speak of the Holy Ghost within the Enneagram, whereby it is made living. So far we have begun to speak of the series Re, Mi, etc.—that is, the Law of 7—and of the inner relation of the notes.

THE ENNEAGRAM

II

The points connected by drawing the internal lines between the numbers obtained by dividing 7 into 1—namely, the numbers 1 4 2 8 5 7 —give a symmetrical figure of great beauty. But three positions are not included in this figure. Let us join these three points. A triangle appears, super-added to the previous figure and in a symmetrical relation to it, at the angles where the numbers 3, 6 and 9 should appear. Let us add these numbers.

Figure (3)

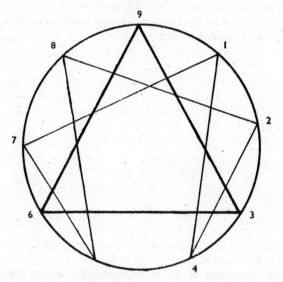

Notice that this second figure, the triangle, now connecting the points 3, 6 and 9, is *not* obtained from the relation of 7 to 1 which gives the first figure only and leaves 3, 6 and 9 out. Here is something strange. Two distinct systems (or figures) are obtained that seem to be independent of one another and yet appear to stand in some symmetrical relation to the diagram as a whole. Let us examine the point of the triangle where the number 3 is. It comes between the points indicated by the numbers 2 and 4 which belong to the seven-figure (I will call the symmetrical figure lying between the points 1 4 2 8 5 7 the seven-figure and the triangle obtained by connecting the points not touched by the seven-figure I will call the three-figure). These two points 2 and 4 are also indicated by the notes of the octave *Mi* and *Fa*. The Law of

Seven is sometimes called the Law of the Shock. If things went in a regular fashion and developed harmoniously without interruption we should live in another world. One origin of evil or of things going all wrong is due to the Law of the Shock—or rather, to its non-fulfilment. We should all reflect on the teaching of this system about *shocks*. It is quite unknown both to science and to older esoteric systems so far as one can know anything about the latter. (Notice here that to reflect is not to dream and that many mistake dreaming for reflecting.) In any series of developments, in every progression, a shock is necessary at a certain point. This point is *represented* by the places of the semi-tone intervals in the major scale—between *Do* and *Si*, and *Fa* and *Mi*. We occupy ourselves at present only with the "place of the missing semi-tone" indicated by *Fa-Mi*, or *Mi-Fa*. If a shock is not given the direction of development or progress of whatever it is will completely change. You start off to do something and end up by doing the opposite. There is no right passage from the state *Mi* to *Fa* without a shock. What follows on *Mi* will not be *Fa* otherwise. Let us draw an upright "octave" leaving out the *Do* at either end.

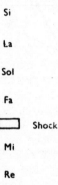

Si

La

Sol

Fa

☐ Shock

Mi

Re

Let us compare this with the Enneagram. You will see that the place of shock in the upright octave, marked by a square, corresponds to that angle of the three-figure that comes between the numbers 2 and 4—or the notes *Mi* and *Fa*—marked on the circumference of the Enneagram. The angle therefore represents in some way a *shock* entering the system at this point.

Since we have an upright octave drawn here I would like you to notice what happens when the seven-figure is applied to it.

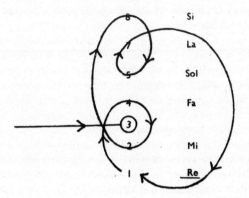

Looking at this curious diagram you may perhaps get the effect of some living thing, some action of circulation going on. But you will notice that when put straight the symmetry of the figure is largely lost. In the Enneagram the octave is put round a circle. The circle is the basis of the diagram.

You must all understand that I am giving you an approach to the Enneagram from different sides. It is useless simply to take it as a diagram. It is a living thing and all life depends on it. All organized living things have the Law of 3 and Law of 7 in them. In the case of animals there is only a part of the Enneagram and only one shock. But of this we will speak later when we come to discuss the two other shocks indicated which can be reached by Man alone on this planet.

Now I will give you another thought that can suggest a great deal if you reflect on it. Let us take anything in time that goes by series and arrange it round the circumference. For example, the days of the week go in succession, in series in time. Let us put Monday opposite the figure 1 at the place called *Re* and Tuesday beside figure 2 or place called *Mi* and Wednesday beside figure 4 and so on. This gives us Sunday at the point indicated by No. 9. Now look at the intercourse indicated by the seven-figure between these days. Something passes from Monday to Wednesday and passes back to Tuesday. Let us try to get rid of the idea of time by means of conceiving the world in higher dimensions—i.e. conceiving that time does not exist and that everything in succession in time is alive and is, so to speak, always *there*, although we seem to pass from one thing to another. Notice where the shock comes in the series of days marked on the circumference and notice also the internal circulation that goes on between the days. My object is to try to make you think about the Enneagram and bring it to some kind of life in your mind and directed imagination. Apparently in some way Monday is connected with Wednesday, with what we call the future, but with what, in the 4th dimension is already there. Then again, Wednesday is connected with Tuesday, and Tuesday is connected with Saturday, which seems very extraordinary. This seems to be a very unusual way of thinking, quite unconnected with our temporal way of thinking of cause and effect, according to which we believe that the present is influenced only by the past. As you will agree, we believe that the cause of a thing is anterior in time to the effect. We have no idea that the future may influence the present. If I were to think that certain things that were to happen on Saturday were in some way connected with what happened on Tuesday, and that as a result what happens to me on Thursday is due to Saturday, which I have not yet reached in time in the series of days, I would certainly be surprised. I would naturally—according to my senses—think that one day follows another, just like that, and that the influences of yesterday acts only on to-day or tomorrow. Yet by deeper reflection I might realize this is not the case and cease to be so surprised. I might even be willing to think that something I do to-day may affect me years hence. Next time we will continue some of these thoughts and reflections about this diagram which is peculiar to this Work.

Birdlip, February 5, 1944

THE ENNEAGRAM

III—SHOCK

Last time we spoke of the Law of Seven as being sometimes referred to as the Law of Shock. For anything to grow, to develop, from one stage to another, stage by stage, in the right order, a *shock* is necessary. The place of this shock is indicated at the point Mi-Fa, or place of the missing semi-tone. What example can we find of such a growth or evolution or development, stage by stage, in the right order? We can find it in the evolution of a microscopical cell into a human being. This is definitely an illustration of evolution by stages of successive transformations, one thing becoming entirely another thing—or one thing belonging to one world, the world of cells, passing into another world, the world of Man (by the double process of differentiation and integration). Realize that your birth stands far away, not merely in time but in vertical scale, in the order of things, in the union of two minute cells, in a world beneath that in which we live—a world that is ordinarily invisible to us. But the Law of 7 applies to all worlds—to starry galaxies, to Man and to cells—just as does the Law of 3, for these two laws are the creative and formative laws behind the Universe and everything it

386

contains, on every level. They are ultimate laws in the sense that they cannot be reduced further—that is, to anything simpler. The Law of Seven demands the existence of a shock. We can therefore be certain that, since the Law of Seven applies everywhere to all things, in every place of creation, whether in the world of atoms or cells or of humanity or of solar systems or star-clusters, *the necessity for a shock* exists, and that if this shock is not given, degeneration or death will take place. In the case of a cell rising by successive stages of the evolution of itself into the world of human beings and becoming a visible person, there is a stage where a complete alteration of its inner arrangements is demanded of it if it is to survive. But you must study this for yourselves if you wish to do so. In this connection you must remember that 9 months of our time is 30,000 times 9 months for the cell. (Work out for yourselves what that period is.) Consider this diagram:

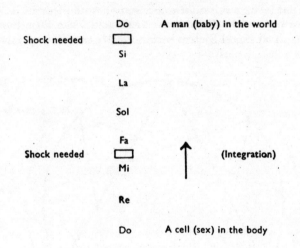

The intermediate stages of transformation lie between *Re* and *Si*. At, let us say, the stage *Sol*, something intermediate exists, something unfinished and useless. Each *Do* (the lower and the higher) is complete in a sense. They represent "cleverer" points than the intervening notes. Or you can think of them as resting points. But you can see how two danger-places exist in this application of the octave to the evolution of a cell into a man. The nature of the upper one is easy to see. The lower requires some special but ordinary knowledge to understand.

When you realize that shocks are necessary throughout the Universe owing to the fact that the Law of Seven is omnipresent in the most minute and in the most gigantic, you become aware that everything must either make *effort* to attain its right growth and development or must receive a shock at the right time.

Let us speak briefly about *mechanical shock*. Man receives a mechanical shock repeated at very short intervals. This shock is *air*. We accept the fact that we breathe, just as we accept everything else, without thought. Air enters the lungs and meets the blood. Here two very remarkable trees exist with a vast number of branches and twigs. The blood-tree intertwines with the air-tree, in the finest branchings, but without penetration, and an interchange takes place, something in the air passing into the blood and vice versa. This is the shock given to the first octave in Man—that is, the Octave of the Transformation of Food. Unless this is given mechanically—if, say, it does not start up quickly enough in the baby—then the physical organism is incapable of working. It cannot work because the shock it needs is not being received. Speaking from this angle, it is obvious that we are simply machines. Everything is done for us and once started up successfully we run a certain time. This shock of air is required by animals and fishes and birds. That is, we see the Law of Seven at work in them.

Let us put up the Enneagram again and write Digestive System, Air System and Blood System beside *Re*, *Mi* and *Fa* respectively.

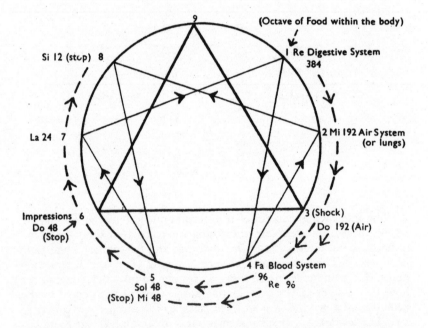

Now the Lungs by themselves cannot give a shock. They can only do so by taking in Air. Nor can the Air give a shock unless there is something to receive it. The Air comes into the Lungs and then the most valuable part of it (oxygen) is selected and drawn into the Blood Stream, the rest being rejected (nitrogen and carbon dioxide).

All created things work by *shocks*. Without these shocks they would begin to die. Now we are given a mechanical shock which makes it possible for the body to live—the shock of air. Why do we breathe? Can we live without breathing? Is breathing something mechanical in us, something arranged for us, something given ready-made? But there is a great deal in Man not ready-made, not given. Man is created a self-developing organism, and if you reflect on what that means you will realize that he is not ready-made. Up to a certain point you are ready-made but beyond that point you are *not* ready-made. At the same time you are capable of some evolution, some development, some growth beyond the ready-made or mechanical level. But since everything is governed by the Law of Seven or the Law of Shock you may be quite certain that any further development depends on shock—that is, you cannot develop beyond the mechanical given level without shocks. Your body is working all the time as a machine transforming physical food into higher and higher substances—substances that make it possible for you to feel, to think, and so on. And it is doing this by means of the mechanical shock of Air entering the octave of the Transformation of Food at a certain point between *Mi* and *Fa*. But the rest of you, by which I mean all that can get beyond the mechanical level, is not working. It is not working because no shock is being given in the right place and in the right way. One lives one's life just anyhow without the slightest idea that one has to give oneself a shock, and certainly one can live one's life in this way owing to the mechanical shock of air. But Man is created for something further. As you know, the Work teaches us that we are capable of giving ourselves two conscious shocks beyond the mechanical shock of air and that unless these shocks are given a man remains asleep and indeed begins to die psychologically. Man's real life lies in the psychological sphere, in the development of understanding, of feeling, of thought, of inner perception. If you think you are simply your body then you make a great mistake. No amount of attention to the body will make it possible for you to give yourselves the two further conscious shocks which belong to the psychological side of you. Man is more than his body, or rather, he is designed to be more than his body. Let us take the first of these additional shocks. This shock belongs to the intake of impressions and the reception of them and the digestion of them. This shock is called the First Conscious Shock. In a fully developed and conscious man three shocks take place—the mechanical shock of air, which is given, and two additional shocks which are not given but must be created. All esoteric psychology is ultimately about the nature of these two additional shocks and the means by which they may be given, and they refer to octaves that potentially exist in Man that can develop by conscious work. To change, to become different, to transform oneself, these two shocks must be understood and continually given to oneself in daily life. But first of all the First Conscious Shock must be given, and a person in this Work must begin to know what it means to give the First Conscious Shock to his ordinary daily life. Unless we know, genuinely, something about the First Conscious Shock which is called the Transformation of Impressions we cannot expect to understand anything about the Second Conscious Shock. Impressions coming into the human machine are a food which constitutes the beginning of an octave. In the Enneagram the left angle of the 3-figure or triangle refers to the First Conscious Shock; the angle on the right refers to the mechanical shock of Air. Now Air comes in on the right side of the Enneagram from outside as a *Do* having the Hydrogen value numerically *192*. It undergoes certain transformations up to the point *Mi*. Let us indicate these stages in the diagram. You will notice that the development of the transformation of Air proceeds to the point *Mi* where the left hand angle of the 3-figure or triangle lies. It then stops because a shock is necessary at this point for it to proceed. But this shock is not ordinarily given. Something must enter here just as Air did in the previous example to give the shock. What enters at this point is Impressions. But Impressions do not give the shock in the same way as Air does unless they are taken in consciously. The nature of these two shocks is therefore different. At the number 3 the shock is passive or mechanical but at the number 6 the shock must be active or conscious. The latter marks the first place of conscious evolution. This is the place where we have to take life, which is incoming Impressions, in a new way. This place marks where we have to transform all daily incidents, all relations with others. This is the place where we have to transcend our senses and the world as we see it by something additional. This is the place where we must digest everything that happens to us, where we must form psychological power that selects and on the other hand eliminates, just as the Lungs select from the Air what is most useful and eliminate what is useless. We will speak more about this subject later on. But you will see that the Enneagram with all its possibilities will not work in a man unless all the conditions inherent in it are fulfilled. When you realize that the Law of Seven or Law of Shock applies to your psychological life you will begin to see why it is necessary to make continual efforts in the psychological sphere. If one does not give these necessary shocks to the psychological octave there will necessarily be a death or degeneration of mind and feeling, just as if the mechanical shock of Air were not given there would be a death of the body.

Now psychological effort, psychological shock, is of many different kinds. The receiving of Impressions in a new way, not taking things always in the same way, taking in new Impressions by directed attention, are some of the aspects that belong to the First Conscious Shock, which can be summed up as work on Being and work on Knowledge. When the Work begins to act on you and is no longer merely a theoretical idea, when you begin to see how it applies to you yourself, when you see for yourself some of the many meanings of giving yourself the First Conscious Shock, which is roughly called Self-Remembering, or being conscious at the place of intake of Impressions from the external world, you will understand how many sides belong to this shock and how very varied it is. At the same time you will realize what it means to live more consciously in the midst of life. And when you have begun to realize something of all this, you will look back on the way you used to live, when you reacted to everything mechanically, with something like horror. You will feel that you would like to have been able to live more consciously in your past life. You will begin to catch a glimpse of how you have lived and how you might have lived. The extraordinary thing is how beautifully it is all formulated in the diagram, how simply it is put when you begin to invest the diagram with meaning, with your own thought and understanding, and no longer take it as something on the board that you stare at. The diagram is all living, all full of meaning, and the words and letters and figures and lines are really sources of meaning once the understanding combines with them. It is like a map which refers to living countries, not the things on the map.

THE INTELLIGENCE OF CENTRES

Diagram (¹)

Four Intelligences

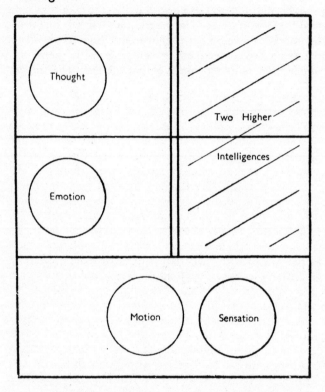

To-night I would like to give some notes on the intelligence of centres. Some of you will remember that it was said long ago that centres in Man do not work rightly. They interfere with each other, hypnotize each other, use the wrong energies, deal with the wrong things, and so on. The first step is to observe centres. This is in fact the first thing taught in self-observation. You must get to know what centre you are in or what centre is interfering, etc. This has got to be done eventually as a necessary task. The inner life has got to be studied and sorted out and put in order.

★   ★   ★

We all connect intelligence with the appreciation of meaning. Intelligence gives a relation to meaning. It conducts meaning. A feeling has meaning. A thought has meaning. A sensation has meaning. A movement has meaning. These meanings are all different. I want you to consider this: are not intelligence and meaning connected? and does not intelligence imply relationship to *something* through meaning? I do not see how you can be intelligent either about *nothing* or about what is meaningless. Each centre relates us differently, through its particular function, to the outer and inner worlds. In regard to what relates us to the outer world, the function of Intellectual Centre as thought, of Emotional Centre as feeling, of Instinctive Centre as sensation, and of Moving Centre as motion, are all quite different. They are four kinds of intelligence or conductors of meaning. You see a snake, you feel a snake, you think a snake, and you run from a snake. This is sensation, emotion, thought and motion. This is four meanings: this is four intelligences at work together.

Can you imagine a centre that has no intelligence being formed in us? It would be a strange notion. It would subserve no purpose. Yet there are centres in us, fully developed, that we do not know of because our level of intelligence is too low to comprehend theirs. You might say that in that case they serve no purpose. This would be right if it were not for the fact that Man is created a self-developing organism and that his growth depends on his getting in contact with influences coming down the Ray from above him and separating himself from forms of thought and feeling that hold him down to his present level. To become conscious in the intelligence of, say, the Higher Mental Centre, would be to be penetrated with forms of insight, knowledge and understanding that are utterly extraordinary and quite contradictory to what we experience ordinarily, and so it would be dangerous. The lower centres must be prepared and developed for a long time first of all. For instance, we must learn to think in *new* ways and to separate from certain kinds of emotion. You know the remark in the New Testament that "the wisdom of this world is foolishness with God," (*I Cor.* III *xix*) and that "the natural man receiveth not the things of the Spirit of God, for they are foolishness to him," (*I Cor.* II *xiv*). A higher intelligence is not comprehensible to a lower one. The higher can understand the lower but not the lower the higher. The Higher Mental Centre is at the level of the Divine Intelligence of the Sun. It works with *Hydrogen 6*. Reflect for a moment on the Table of Hydrogens. Is a higher Hydrogen more "intelligent" than a lower one? or, to put it a little differently, will a function such as *thinking* work better with a lower or higher Hydrogen? It will work better with a higher—if it can stand it. Again, is a raw potato cleverer than a cooked potato? No, it is the other way round, because a cooked potato can be food for Man and stands at the position *768* in the Scale of Hydrogens, which as you will recall is derived from the Ray of Creation. A raw potato stands lower, at the point *1536*. Again, if we take the psychic Hydrogens, the lowest of which is *48*,

393

do you think that a centre which works with this Hydrogen will be as clever as one that works with the far finer, subtler and quicker *Hydrogen 24*? Certainly not. There are intermediate Hydrogens. We do well to try to attract better Hydrogens by not identifying, not losing our direction, and not basing our intelligence only on what the senses shew us. To be intelligent in a big sense is to seek for C influences. To be intelligent is to understand our position on this earth. To be intelligent is to seek to transform the meaning of daily life for ourselves. All this opens on to higher meaning. All this increases the better Hydrogens in us. It is all to do with different sides of Self-Remembering. We all have centres with their intelligences. But when a man possesses Magnetic Centre he has more intelligence than one who has not. He is on a different level of being. He will not be surprised to find that C influences exist and that life as it goes leads nowhere. He will be far more intelligent than scholars or professors. This is what intelligence means in the Work—the *position* of a thing in the Scale of Being, and the influences to which it is open in the Ray.

*   *   *

Now let us come to the question that was asked recently. The question was: *It is said in the Work that each Centre has its own intelligence. What does this mean?*

When it is said in this system that each centre has its own intelligence, it does not mean that each centre has the same kind of intelligence. The Work teaches that the 3 centres are 3 different minds and in this connection it says that these 3 different minds should co-operate and assist one another. They should be like 3 brothers who live in harmony, each one good at something, and each one capable of helping the others to a small extent. We will begin by taking each centre as a whole: the Intellectual, the Emotional, the Instinctive and the Moving Centres. It is necessary first of all to establish for oneself that these centres have quite different minds. The mind of the Intellectual Centre is very different from the mind of the Instinctive Centre, for example. The Instinctive Centre is extraordinarily clever. It attends to the inner working of the organism in all its million and one details, digesting food, healing wounds, looking after the temperature, regulating the respiration and the heart-beat, making and causing the internal secretions of the glands to work in harmony, supplying this, taking away that, modifying this, increasing that. All this regulation is far beyond the mind of the Intellectual Centre. To be able to think of everything altogether is not characteristic of the Intellectual Centre. The mind of the Intellectual Centre thinks of one thing at a time and at the most of two things, but it is almost impossible for it to think of three things at a time.

Then again the mind of the Intellectual Centre is quite different from the mind of the Emotional Centre. People say that the emotions

394

are not logical. However the emotions have their own logic and it would be a mistake to think that the logic of the Intellectual Centre is the only possible logic. To feel a situation is quite different from thinking about it. The Emotional Centre can feel, for example, the inner state of other people, which is hidden from the mind of the Intellectual Centre. The emotions can give you knowledge of others. The mind of the Emotional Centre can even be clairvoyant.

Then again the Moving Centre has a different mind from any of the others. It is constantly making judgments of the most complicated kind which are quite impossible for the Intellectual mind to make. It can judge exactly and in what way and with what strength you must throw a stone to hit a distant object. This is intelligent calculation. One can feel such calculation going on as it were in one's muscles. Intellectual calculation is of quite a different kind and uses the elements of intellectual thought, such as words and numbers. The intelligence of the Moving Centre, however, uses no words or numbers but yet can calculate with the most exquisite precision some complicated series of movements that will give a definite result.

Now let us consider the centres in connection with the way they receive things. You know that you can look at a beautiful picture or scene in quite different ways. You can look at a mountain as a beautiful object in which case you have an emotional relationship to it. Or you can look at it from the standpoint of a geologist noticing what kind of rocks, etc. it is composed of, in which case you have an intellectual relationship to it. Or you can look at it from the standpoint of a climber planning the line of your ascent and the amount of effort necessary, in which case you will have mainly a Moving Centre relationship to it. But I fancy it would be difficult to get a relationship to it through the Instinctive Centre unless there were some famous restaurant at the summit. Now if you will observe yourselves you will find that you look at everything and everyone in these different ways. Let us say that you know all about the technical side of films, then you will tend to look at a film from this angle and not from the emotional value of the story, and so on. The point is that everyone sees things differently and that each person can see the same thing differently at different moments so that its meaning changes. A person's intelligence, in short, is made up of many different intelligences that connect with quite different meanings of the same thing.

Let us take the parts of centres—the moving, emotional and intellectual divisions. Each of these divisions has a different intelligence that gives us a different relationship of meaning to the same thing. Mr. Ouspensky was once talking about attention and how attention lay only in the more conscious parts of centres and not the moving or mechanical parts. The more conscious parts are the emotional and intellectual divisions. He said that ordinary attention, which goes here and there, was not attention. Only attention either attracted or directed for a long time was attention. We gave too much attention to small things connected with moving parts of centres. He said they could perform their functions almost by themselves—with zero attention. If we wasted our attention on such small things we had no attention for big things and so it would be a long time before we could increase our attention. He then put up the diagram of the centres and said that moving parts of centres were simply filled with small things such as conversations we had heard, papers we had read, etc. These things did not belong to us at all, but when things fell on emotional and intellectual parts they then belonged to us and might even create something. He observed that people who live simply in moving parts of centres and so in small things can never understand this Work. In this connection he went on to say that the same idea or the same phrase received in moving parts of centres, in emotional parts of centres, and in intellectual parts of centres became quite different. The centres saw things differently. He said we were to take some simple idea and try to look at it from the different centres. It would become quite different in each. If the ideas of this Work were only received by moving parts of centres they could not be understood—they were too big. Ideas of the Moon eating us and of our Sleep, of Man awakening, etc. were too big. If we allowed ourselves to·be always in moving parts of centres we could not understand this Work—we would take everything in the ordinary way and so on the wrong level. Mr. Ouspensky also said that Magnetic Centre could not be formed in the moving parts of centres. Moving parts of centres could only take A influences. B influences fell on Emotional Centre and C influences on Intellectual Centre. By treating the matter in this way one saw how things inevitably fall into their place. He added that if people talked too much about this Work it put it into moving parts of centres where there is "Zero" attention. It would be better for people in the Work to talk about other things rather than do this.

★　　★　　★

The intelligences of Moving parts of centres, however, are adapted to their own small daily uses, but to employ them for understanding what is beyond them, or what demands the intelligence of the whole centre, will give no results, or entirely wrong results, or contradictory results. The intelligence of a centre as a whole is made up of all the intelligences that .compose its separate parts. The intelligence of the Intellectual Centre as a whole is of a very high order. When the centre is working as a whole—that is, when every part is directed towards a common goal—each subdivision shares in the effort and plays its own part. For instance, the moving parts remember and register in words or figures the thoughts reached by the intellectual part, and so on. But ordinarily, only the moving parts of the Intellectual Centre are used by us and these, working with *Hydrogen 48*, and thinking only in terms of opposites, that is, lacking any consciousness

396

in Third Force, produce very poor and slow results. We can say, then, that under ordinary conditions the intelligence of the Intellectual Centre is that of its mechanical division only—namely, the formatory part. But we are not to suppose that this covers the entire range of the Intellectual Centre, parts of which work with *Hydrogen 24* and *Hydrogen 12*.

We can represent the passage from the Intellectual Centre to the Higher Mental Centre by figures in this way:

Diagram (2)　　　　　Diagram (3)

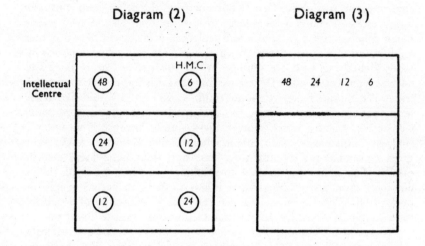

To become conscious in *Hydrogen 6* in the Higher Mental Centre would be to possess an Intelligence far beyond, in fact, incommensurable with, the Intelligence of the formatory part. All contradictions would disappear, for one thing. There would not be any "Yes" or "No" in our thought. All sides of a question would be seen together, and not one by one, and so a state would be made beyond our experience.

ADDITIONAL NOTES

The work of Instinctive Centre is interesting to study in the animal world. When, let us say, a bird builds a complicated nest, it is doing it with Moving Centre but Instinctive Centre is directing the movement. It is noticeable that this sort of intelligence is not very adaptable. The same mistakes tend to be made and if, as in the case of a spider making its webs, something goes wrong, usually the whole thing has to be done over again from the beginning—that is, there is no power of adaptation.

Each centre opens on to a different level of the Universe. The Instinctive Centre opens on to Organic Life. The Higher Mental Centre opens on to the level of the Sun.

The centre that is most important to the *body* is the Instinctive Centre which controls the whole work of the organism. If its intelligence were interfered with the body would be under no direction. The Instinctive Centre tends to borrow force from other Centres when illness takes place. It must keep itself going and its duty is to fight with illness and conquer it. For this purpose it controls vast armies and many weapons. It usually begins as you can all notice for yourselves by borrowing force from Moving Centre. We notice that we feel muscularly tired often before we are aware that we are ill. Then if the illness continues the Instinctive Centre borrows from the other centres usually in succession. When it takes force from Emotional Centre we become much quieter inside as a rule and feel that it is impossible to bother about things—i.e. to identify with things—for our usual emotion in life is identifying with everything. When Instinctive Centre begins to borrow from Intellectual Centre we find that it is impossible to concentrate. We cannot read, we cannot think, and so on. I would like to say here that, in marked illness, the real intelligence of the Emotional Centre can become much more evident simply because identifying is stopped. This is why often people who are very ill and in danger have great emotional insight into their lives and their behaviour towards others. This is nothing to do with thinking—as when we think things out, or reason about things—but it has to do with actual insight or perception. The Emotional Centre can "see" the quality of a person, for example, whereas the Intellectual Centre has to think about it.

You must understand that these are very brief notes on the different intelligences of the centres. The subject is inexhaustible. But the study of it only becomes practical when the personal observation of centres is undertaken not just for a few minutes but for a life-time.

Birdlip, February 19, 1944

WHAT THIS WORK IS ABOUT

In reply to a question asked by new people: " *WHAT IS THIS WORK ABOUT* ? " the answer is that it is for those who are looking for something, who are not satisfied with what they have found in life, and who feel that there must be something else beside success or failure in life, and beside what they have been taught at school and college and by their upbringing in general.

When a person feels that this life cannot be explained in terms of itself, when he or she sees that life taken by itself without any added explanation is largely meaningless, "a tale told by an idiot", a history of crime and bloodshed and frustration, when such a person begins to see that it is very doubtful whether there is any such thing as progress and that everything begins and ends almost before it has begun, then he or she is in a position to search for other meaning and new knowledge, convinced that it must exist. And when people begin this research with any sincerity and any real depth of feeling, they will be astonished to find what a great number of memorials exist in the literature of the past which point unmistakably towards another kind of knowledge and meaning. In all this literature the theme is the same. The theme is always that a man can undergo a definite and pre-arranged transformation in himself, that he can undergo a distinct and certain development, a real evolution or re-birth, if he knows and understands gradually what he has to do. That is to say, all this literature, which constitutes a part of what are called "B" influences in this Work, has the same object. A man has to die in some specific and definite way to himself, to certain sides of himself. And if he dies in the right way, he is born again as a new man, another kind of man, called in this Work a *Conscious Man* as distinct from a mechanical man. He will then know the meaning of his life on this earth—namely, that it is not *an end in itself* but *a means to another end*—for it is by means of a certain kind of struggle against what life has laid down in us that the end or purpose of Man's existence is achieved. If everything were easy, there would be no re-birth, but, as this Work teaches, Man cannot be re-born rightly nor can he die rightly—that is, he cannot see the right things to die to in himself—unless he first *awakens*.

In many esoteric fragments of the past, you will find references to *re-birth* and to *dying*. In the Gospels, for instance, you will find such references, and also references to *awakening*. You will find the word *'watch'* often used: this should be translated as *'awaken'*. But you will not find these ideas, which are the central theme of Esoteric Psychology, arranged in the right order. A man must awaken first, before he can die aright. And if he awakens first, and dies in the right way to himself, he *may* be re-born if there is anything worth while and sufficiently strong and real in him. It will depend upon the quality of the person in the deepest sense. Nothing 'pseudo', nothing false, will be of any use here. But we have not said enough about this process because, although it is necessary that a man should awaken first of all, he must be taught what he must work on in himself and observe *in order to awaken*. And for this he must find a Teacher and a Teaching—that is, a Teaching that is not arbitrary, invented by ordinary people, but one that comes from those who have awakened and left behind them instructions to those in prison in the sleep of life, who wish to get out, to awaken. Therefore he will have to *search*, to *seek* and even if he *does find* something it will not be at all easy for him to establish contact with it. He may be tested from the very first moment or it may be that he is tested years later. In some schools of awakening, in the past, a person had to keep silence for two or three or even five years, or do the most menial tasks, or perform labours that were always being frustrated, and so on, before he was taught anything, or he would perhaps be treated in some rough way so that his pride and vanity were touched and he might become offended. You know how in the Gospels it is said that people were continually being offended and how Christ was always attacking vanity, pride, self-esteem, self-complacency, and the idea that one knows what is right and wrong already.

A person must search, seek. I will try to explain to you what seeking means. There is a phrase: "Seek and ye shall find." The meaning of this is that unless you yourself seek, you yourself will *not* find. Someone may bring you, let us say, to this Work. You may not ever have thought seriously about the *meaning* of your existence or of life or of anything of that kind, or you may have searched a little and thought that it was too confusing, or you may have been quite unable to distinguish between Truth and Falsity in what you found. Now supposing that you hear something of this teaching and it falls a little on your understanding and not simply on your two ears, then your search for this Work will begin and you *may* be able to find it, but you may be in the Work for many many years and never have searched for it and so never have found it. Your search means two things. You may have had to spend a long time in trying to find a real teaching in the world and you may have passed through many stages of thought and endeavour and danger before you have made any contact with the object of your search. Or you may have made contact perhaps even accidentally, straightaway, and imagine that your search is at an end instead of realizing that it has only just begun.

Reflect for yourselves now on this point: if it is said: "Seek and ye shall find," you will have to *lose* first. How can you possibly *seek*, unless you feel you have lost? So we have to go to a still earlier stage, to the feeling that you have lost something, that you have missed something, that something is lacking, or perhaps to the feeling that you, yourself, are lost and that you would like to seek and to find yourself. And this takes us back to the opening of this short paper, to the feeling that this life is inexplicable in terms of itself, and that there must be some other meaning, some other interpretation.

* * *

The movement of this Work is psychologically inwards, at first. Later it is both inwards and outwards. Everyone has an external and a more internal side. But the more internal side is usually governed by the external side. The external side is acquired by the action of life. This is called "Personality" in this system. The deeper, inner side is called "Essence". In the development we have spoken about above—this possible, pre-arranged, individual evolution or re-birth—it is the Essence that must grow. Unfortunately the Personality and the Essence are under opposite signs. Personality is active and Essence is passive. At least this is our ordinary state in ordinary life. The change that has to take place eventually is a reversal of this customary state so that

400

Personality and Essence change signs. This obviously implies a considerable upset of *oneself*. However, it takes place gradually, up to a certain period, and during this time a person very slowly gets to know'himself or herself and realizes that he or she is utterly different from what they imagined. This weakens the Personality or acquired side. As I said, all this means that the movement of the Work is, psychologically, inwards at first, for no one can get to know his level of being unless he goes inwards, through self-observation. One begins to pass into this complex thing called oneself, about which one has so many illusions. But for this purpose several conditions are necessary, one of which is a form of knowledge that will guide one and which must be applied to oneself with sincerity. Some form of "truth", in other words, is necessary, in relation to which one can study oneself. This can be got and lost again quite easily. If you have never really sought for it, you will scarcely be able to say you have lost it. But if you have created a vacuum for it in yourself, if you have felt that you are lost or that you have lost something valuable, then if you eventually find something you will know when you lose it again. As this Work begins to mean something important, something genuine and real, it opens something in the more internal part of a person. This cannot take place if the attitude to the Work is wrong or one's conduct towards it is wrong. The internal side of a person can only grow through what is true. It cannot grow through what is false. The external side, however, can quite easily grow through what is unreal and false.

It is therefore of great importance to notice one's attitude to the Work and those connected with it and also to notice what one is using the work for. For example, to use the Work to increase the Personality and its ambitions is to have a wrong attitude. That should be clear enough to anyone who has any power of sincerity and does not justify everything. When the Work forms an emotional *point* in a person—it actually opens a part of a centre—then that person begins to touch new influences. It is quite easy to know when this has happened. But to keep this point, he must follow and keep to the "truth" of the Work. He must apply it to himself: and if he loses this point, for a time, he must seek for it again. The Work lies in us at first like a piece of silver. In the ancient and lost language of parables, silver represents truth. A person feeling himself asleep, feeling he has lost this point in himself, feeling an emptiness and blankness where he had felt something light, must search for what he has lost all through himself—in every room in every centre, on every floor of the three-storey house called himself. What is he too identified with? What is he internally considering? What is he lying about? What is he expending on pretence? Where is he justifying himself? When did he last remember himself? When has he last made any effort? What has happened to his aim? How many things has he put in front of the Work? When did he last observe himself attentively and go over his mind? When did he last view himself over the past few days? When did he last think clearly about this teaching and search for new meanings? When did he block some important staircase or corridor in his house by leaving a litter of stuff that he should have sorted out and put in place, or slam some door by haste or irritation and forget to go back and open it again? You can all see what a mess of one's house one can make by behaving in sleep for a short time and how easily one can lose something.

Now you will understand some of the meaning contained in the parable of the Lost Piece of Silver:

"What woman having ten pieces of silver, if she lose one piece, doth not light a lamp, and sweep the house, and seek diligently until she find it? And when she hath found it, she calleth together her friends and neighbours, saying, Rejoice with me, for I have found the piece which I had lost . . ." (*Luke* XV, 8, 9)

Birdlip, February 27, 1944

THE ENNEAGRAM

IV

We have already spoken of the idea of a shock being necessary for the progressive development and continuance of a thing and we have seen how the Law of Seven can from one point of view be called the Law of Shock. In the development of a thing, whether it be the growth of a living creature, or the development of an idea, or the learning of a difficult subject, or the carrying out of some enterprise, or the transformation of one thing into another, the successive stages can be represented by the notes of an ascending octave: *Do, Re, Mi, Fa, Sol,* etc. Now a shock must come between the stage *Mi* and the stage *Fa* for that thing to proceed in its right order of development. Otherwise it will deviate from its course and become something else. The stage *Fa* will not be reached. We are familiar with the fact that civilization does not proceed beyond a point, and that also we do not, personally. This is because a shock is necessary and is not given, or not received, or not created.

Let us study the shocks in Man. In the case of Man, the first shock necessary for his life does not have to be created. It is given at the point 3 in the Enneagram and received as air that we breathe in. If a man refused to breathe—which is not possible—he would die. Or if he breathed in something not air, such as carbon monoxide, the shock would still be *given* but not *received*—that is, he would breathe but not take in air and so would die. You must reflect on these two sides of a shock and also upon the fact that the shock of air has to take place at not too long intervals. The giving and receiving of this shock is essential to life. If it is not given, the physical organism ceases to work. Remember here that everything breathes, including the earth. It is very interesting to realize that everything breathes and that this shock is necessary in all things. But since the Law of Seven or Law of the Shock is in all things (together with the Law of Three) it is not so surprising.

In the case of Man two other shocks are *possible*, but not essential. They are not given him or received but must be created. The position of the three shocks is shewn at the angles of the triangle at the points 3, 6 and 9. A man who only has the first shock, at 3, at work in him, is a man of a particular kind. A man who has the first and second shocks working in him is a man of a different kind. A man who has all these three shocks at work in him is a man utterly different from the first or second man.

The creation of these three kinds of men is described in progressive order in the first two chapters of Genesis in connection with the 7 days of creation, which divides Man into 7 different categories and does not take him as one and the same or as equal. The first broad distinction is made between Mechanical Man and Conscious Man. The first description of Man in Genesis is of mechanical or dead Man— in verse 2. In the Work mechanical humanity is said to be *asleep* and sometimes to be *dead*, as when it is said that many people walking about are long ago dead. Likewise in the New Testament, Christ refers to "the dead burying their dead." Mechanical Man has no shock at work in him save the mechanical shock of breathing. However, the term breath or breathing is something also applied to the second shock, as we shall see. The point here is that in Genesis, and in this Work, and in the New Testament, the idea of *dead* Man appears, the dead, living Man. To awaken from the state of being a dead person, a man or a woman must give himself or herself the second shock, at point 6. This person is described in Genesis as following on the "dead" man. Let us consider the "dead" man first. It is impossible to describe him briefly. He is the man of the senses, without an inner life, the man who ascribes his powers to himself, the man of self-esteem, for whom everything real lies in the outer world, the man who has not begun to think or feel beyond himself. This man is called in Genesis "waste and void". This is the man of darkness in whom there is no light. Shall we each suppose that we are not in this state ourselves? This state of darkness of a man is referred to both in the Old Testament and the New Testament. It is said in Isaiah: "The people that walked in darkness have seen a great light." (IX 2) and in John: "The light shineth in the darkness; and the darkness apprehended it not." (I 5) which means that esoteric teaching represented in Christ came as light to those in darkness of mind and understanding. To take one example—this dead man or man of darkness of mind is the *Hasnamus* man mentioned in the Work— namely, the man whose well-being depends on the ill-being of thousands and millions of others. Napoleon is a good example. Such a man cannot think in terms beyond himself and what he wants. There is no "love of neighbour"—that is, no emotional development beyond self-love and self-interest. Or, in Work terms, there is no power of sincere external considering, no ability to put oneself genuinely in the position of another person and to think and feel as he or she thinks and feels, unless it belongs to one's own self-interest and the personal sphere of one's own merit. This is the general state of Man. In the Work it is necessary to get beyond this state and it is very difficult to do so for everyone, without exception. However, it is necessary to do so eventually for the step that has to be taken is *beyond what one is* at present. The first requisite is a *shock* administered to one's present state of mind and feeling. One must begin to think differently and then to feel in a new way. But unless one meets with something that makes this possible, it will remain a step not taken. So one will continue to sound the same *note* all one's life—as most people do.

Now let us consider the man who begins to give himself the second shock, at the point 6. He is described in Genesis. He is no longer a *dead* man, waste and void. Look for a moment at the Enneagram at the point 6. Here is the point where esoteric teaching can enter a man and start a new octave in him. Look at the first octave, made possible by the mechanically given and mechanically received shock of physical air, and note where it goes. Now look at the point 6 where the entry of something new is *possible*. I say that it is *possible*. It is not *necessary* for living in ordinary life. But it is a point where something is *possible*. Here this Work enters into the plan of Man, regarded in the light of a self-developing organism by creation. In Genesis the idea that Man is a self-developing organism is contained in the very first line: "In the beginning God created the heaven and the earth"—that is, two levels, a higher and a lower. This refers to the dead Man for it then says: "And the earth was waste and void; and darkness was on the face of the deep." The man is dead in himself--yet he has been created by God having a heaven as well as an earth in him. That is, although dead, he has the possibility of development, first in relation to "earth" and then to "heaven". The outer side of a man is his "earth" and the inner is his "heaven". For a "dead" man to change, his earth must be developed and planted, but first he must be given *light*. So it goes on to say: "And God said, Let there be light." This is the first stage of the dead beginning to become alive. This awakening man, this man rising from the dead, this man seeking to come into his own heaven through light that is not darkness—and understand here that the life of the senses and of the intelligence based on them is darkness—I say, this awakening man eventually reaches the state of being an image of God. On the sixth day "God created Man in his own image, in the image of God created he him." All that precedes this refers to Man rising from the "dead" and to the stages leading to his becoming an "image of God". Let me repeat. Man at his lowest, darkest level is referred to thus: "And the earth was waste and void; and darkness was upon the face of the deep: and the spirit of God moved upon the face of the waters." This is the beginning of awakening. Then day by day—that is, stage by stage, in the ancient language of parables—the "earth" of Man is planted, and finally Man is created in the "image of God" on the sixth day. "And God created Man in his own image, in the image of God created he him." Now on the seventh day another man is apparently created. (cf. Ch. II). Of this man it is said that "God breathed into his nostrils the breath of life and Man became a living soul". Here we have a man in contact with God. He is not merely an imitation or image of God but actually a living soul in contact with the breath or spirit of God.

Let us understand simply that 3 kinds of men are spoken of in these two opening chapters of Genesis—dead Man, Man in the image of God and Man who has actually become a living soul. By way of *commentary* I wish to connect these 3 men with the 3 shocks shewn in the triangle of the Enneagram. I have already spoken of dead Man—that is, Man in whom only the first shock works. (Let me repeat here that I am making commentaries on the Enneagram.) It is clear that a second Man can exist, one in whom both the first and second shocks are at work. I will compare this Man with the Man who is an image of God, and later I will compare the Man in whom all 3 shocks work with the Man created on the seventh day who is a "living soul"—that is, not an image of God, but one who is in some way directly connected with the highest level of understanding possible for Man, phrased here as the in-breathing of the spirit or the air of God. This Man in the Work is called No. 7 Man—I mean that the highest category of Man in this system is called No. 7 Man. He is said to be a man whose knowledge and being are both at their highest level and so equal, so that all his resultant understanding is practical. This means, for one thing, that there is nothing that he *knows* that he cannot *do*. This unity of knowledge, being and understanding belongs only to No. 7 Man and in consequence it is said that all that class of Man belonging to category No. 7 understand one another and speak a common language. By severe contrast we should reflect on the state of things belonging to our level, and to the world in general, where no one understands anyone else and there is no common language even among those who speak the same language in a literal sense. Even from this sole reflection, which is *understandable*, we can grasp something of the level of No. 7 Man as contrasted with our own level. We see at once that such men must belong to another world, psychologically. Our world lives in the Circle of Babel, in confusion of tongues—not merely literal language but the confusion of our misunderstandings at our level. Here, in this Work, we are attempting to learn a *common language* as a first step, so that we can understand each other a little better and be able to talk in some sort of real way to one another. You will not agree, however, that this step has been attained but you may agree that it is a possible and *understandable* step. Now if all were in touch with the same thing and felt it in the same way, we should have a common understanding. No. 7 Man is in touch with higher centres. In Genesis, this last created Man who has a "living soul" is in touch with God.

As regards ourselves, we have to *imitate* a higher state. We have to be images of God. This may seem fantastic but I do not mean it to be so. I refer to a man who begins to give himself the second shock. He is comparable with the Man "created in the image of God". He is an image: he is not in direct contact. He is not dead, nor is he a "living soul", but in-between. I am not going to try to explain this any further.

Let us return to the second shock—that is, the first of the shocks that are *unnecessary for life*. It is unnecessary for life but it is essential for awakening from sleep. Remember that in the beginning Man is created with an earth and a heaven and that otherwise there would not and could not be any esoteric teaching, which is based on Man reaching another or higher state of himself, called "heaven". If this higher state ruled his lower state, or earth, then what we pray for in the Lord's Prayer concerning the will of heaven being done on earth would be fulfilled. Now first the spirit of God moves on the deep and then light is made. To begin to awaken, a man must meet esotericism and its force and its ideas and its viewpoints. This is light. Then the man must learn to observe himself in such a way as to separate himself from himself (as in my case I from Nicoll) and also to separate himself from useless moods, thoughts, feelings, from all kinds of identifying, states of sleep and negativeness, etc., This is the meaning of these words:

"And God said, Let there be light: and there was light. And God saw the light, that it was good: and God divided the light from the darkness. And God called the light Day, and the darkness he called Night. And there was evening and there was morning, one day."

This is called one day—that is, the first stage of awakening, the first stage of becoming more conscious, one day in the creation of an Awake Man. And this can be said to be our stage in general. Some feel something moving, some see a little light, etc. In so far as we practise the Work and apply it to ourselves, we are giving ourselves the second shock. I speak in a general sense. I mean—and I have said this before —that the action of the Work on a man as a whole begins with the second shock. To observe oneself, to notice what is going on in oneself, to separate oneself from useless states and begin to see one's pictures, to remember one's aims, to struggle against being identified with every mood and thought—and so on—all this belongs to the second shock, whose object is to increase the light of consciousness so that we become conscious of ourselves to start with.

Let us try to reformulate what has been said above in the way of commentary on the Enneagram. A man is born capable of an inner development. This is what the Work teaches. For this reason he has earth and heaven in him. If he were only earth he would be incapable of any inner development. To be created a self-developing organism you must learn that you have in you by creation a higher possible state of yourself. For example an egg is born with a possibility of becoming a bird. It therefore has an earth and a heaven contained in its beginning. A seed, an acorn, etc. is in the same position. Man can remain earth, in which case he serves nature. But to repeat the language of the first verse of Genesis: "In the beginning God created the heaven and the earth." If you imagine that Genesis is about the creation of the world, the solar system, you are making a great mistake. Esoteric literature invariably deals with Man himself and his possibilities. Esoteric science deals with the Man himself and the Man in himself and with what he can become, and with what his meaning is. Ordinary science deals with the external world and the nature of its structure and so on. Genesis is an esoteric book, not a scientific book, and, since esotericism deals with Man and his possibilities, when it says that "in the beginning God created the heaven and the earth," it refers to Man, it refers to this egg, this acorn, this seed, which is created with the possibility of reaching a higher level of development. The lower level is called earth, the higher level is called heaven. An acorn taken by itself is at the level of earth, but when by successive stages it dies to itself and eventually becomes an oak, it attains heaven—i.e. the higher development of itself. But in the beginning the acorn was created with its earth and its heaven, its lower level and its higher level. Now you know that the earth of a man must be filled with thoughts, ideas, emotions, affections, conceptions, before a man can reach a higher level of himself. All these are represented by physical objects—e.g. Man can reach in the stage of his inner development to what is said in verse 11, that the earth brings forth the tender herb and the fruit-tree bears fruit. This refers to different stages of understanding, different stages of knowledge, and finally a man is created in the image of God. From the standpoint of esotericism a man is not simply his physical body, his strength, his violence, his primitive instincts: *a man is his understanding*, from the esoteric point of view, and there are very few men from this point of view. All esotericism is about overcoming violence, about increasing consciousness, first of oneself and then of others. Superman is not a gigantic replica of an ordinary man: superman is an utterly different kind of man. An ordinary mechanical man—i.e. a man more or less as we all are still—is given the first shock, but the beginning of a new kind of man starts from the point where—to quote Genesis—"the spirit of God moves on the face of the waters." As you know, water refers to truth, in the language of parables. When a man has magnetic centre in him, although his earth may be "waste and void" and in thick darkness, he will feel that there must be something other than the external world of the senses in which he finds himself. And so something may move in his mind, which is the seat of his understanding of truth, and his next state may be that he begins to see light. But if there is no movement in him in this sense, if he feels that reality is only in the world of the senses in this ever-turning kaleidoscope of confusion, then no spirit of esotericism will move in him, and God—i.e. esotericism—will be unable

407

to create light. Let us terminate this commentary by saying that esoteric knowledge is light. It is light to those who have been moved already. And the shock of esotericism comes at the point 6 in the Enneagram.

*　　*　　*

NOTE

The triangle of which we will speak more has three points in it marked by the numbers 3, 6, 9. We have touched only on the points 3 and 6. In the Work these points are called the "Points of Shock". Point 3 is a mechanical shock given by air drawn into the lungs and received by the blood. Point 6 is sometimes called the point of the First Conscious Shock because mechanically it is not given. For this reason point 6 is sometimes called the First Conscious Shock and point 9 the Second Conscious Shock. This nomenclature is based on the conception of mechanical and conscious. But one can also speak of the shocks as first, second and third. Next time we have to speak about the triangle in the light that it is the Holy Spirit or Holy Ghost, to use the esoteric language of the Gospels, and also about how the breathing in and out at point 3 corresponds to something similar at point 6.

Birdlip, March 4, 1944

THE ENNEAGRAM

V

As we have seen, Mechanical Man is given and made to receive the first shock at point 3. This enables him to live a physical existence. But he does not give himself the shock at point 6 or the shock at point 9. (We speak again of the triangle within the Enneagram). When he begins to study 'the nature of the shock at point 6 and to try to give himself this shock, he makes a step in the direction of consciousness and inner evolution. One reason why things go as they do in the world is that Man is not properly conscious but assumes that he is. As was said previously, from one side the object of this Work is to increase consciousness. First one must become more conscious of oneself. Paradoxically, one has to become conscious of the fact that one is not conscious. By direct self-study one has to realize that one passes most of one's existence in a state of sleep. However, in this state the shock at point 3 is given and received regularly. If our breathing depended on our conscious attention we would not remain alive very long.

From one angle, then, the study of the shock at point 6 is the study of how to increase consciousness. It is called by the general term Self-Remembering but, as was said, the whole application of the Work comes in at this point also. The Work must be brought up to the place of incoming impressions. This cannot be done unless one is in an unusual state of consciousness, one that is different from one's ordinary state. Between the second state of consciousness and the third there are many degrees. Let us look at the diagram of the 4 states of consciousness. We can mark degrees between the so-called waking state and the state of Self-Remembering.

Suppose you have an aim such as not to be negative with a certain person. You will have to keep awake to your aim and to the inner state of yourself at every moment. This will be a kind of Self-Remembering. When one is remembering oneself one should remember one's aims. The trouble is that we cannot live for long in this state of increased consciousness because we exhaust the available energy for it. Consciousness, like everything else, is weighed and measured. There is only so much consciousness. After a time we increase consciousness gradually, and then, instead of falling very deeply asleep after a period of trying to be more conscious, as so often happens, we retain a certain awareness or memory of ourselves, some continuity in our inner life. But our desire for sleep is very great, so that the attempt to give ourselves the shock at point 6 often exhausts us for the time being. We feel we have done enough. Now sleep is easy because the Work is not necessary for life. If you knew that if you stopped remembering yourself for a minute you would die, then it would indeed be difficult to fall asleep. But fortunately, or unfortunately, a person can begin to identify from the moment he gets up in the morning, even through his inner talking, and remain fast asleep all day. When you catch yourself asleep in this way and realize that you have been completely identified with inner talking and making accounts against others and so on, you are in a position to understand what giving oneself the shock at point 6 consists in. I mean, that you will be able to see the difference between being in a mechanical state of sleep and being more conscious. Self-Remembering cannot be explained in so many words because it is an experience, of greater or lesser intensity. One cannot explain an *experience*. But there is one fundamental description of what the shock of Self-Remembering is to which I will now refer and which I will compare with the shock of breathing.

The shock of breathing consists in a movement out and a movement in, or, if you prefer, a movement in and a movement out. There is inspiration and expiration, and the complete act of breathing or cycle of breathing includes both. But there is no contradiction in the opposite movements because they form together a complete cycle. We make about 20 such cycles per minute. You will remember that in the Table of Time in different Cosmoses, where it is said that "Time is Breath", Man's time of breath is taken as 3 seconds. It is upon the two directions —in and out—that I want you to reflect. How does this correspond with the psychic act of Self-Remembering? You remember the diagram of the two arrows pointing in different ways?

←————————————

————————————→

This is, so to speak, the diagram of Self-Remembering, and you see, apparently, a double or contradictory direction.

Now let us represent the first shock of breathing by two arrows:

←———————————— (inspiration)
————————————→ (expiration)

These directions represent breathing in and breathing out. Now the triangle within the heart of the Enneagram has three points, numerically termed 3, 6 and 9, and each point represents a place of shock. The shock at 3 is that of breathing. I wonder if any of you have thought that the second shock at 6 is in some way corresponding— namely, in some way "in and out" and "out and in"? You will see at once from the diagram of Self-Remembering that it goes one way and then the other way, in and out, out and in, just as does breathing. Do you imagine that the first given shock of breathing can have no relation to the second shock and no correspondence? For those who wish to think of this teaching and confirm it in their minds, I would call your attention first of all to this extraordinary triangle standing in the midst of the Enneagram and then to the nature of the first given shock of Air—that is, the inward and the outward movement of breathing. Then I will ask you: "Do you think that the second shock at point 6 (the first consciously given shock) may not have relationship in character to the first mechanically given shock at point 3?" The diagram of Self-Remembering shews that it has.

It is these two psychic directions or movements connected with Self-Remembering, as distinct from the two physical directions or movements of breathing, that I want you to think about. In Self-Remembering a man must look in and look out at the same time. When a person is doing this you will have no doubt about it as it gives a certain expression to the eyes. To remember oneself it is necessary to look in and look out. One must see the outer and see oneself in relation to the outer. But actually no one can see in and see out at the same time any more than a person can breathe in and breathe out at the same time. A person's attention must go in and then out alternately and if we compare this with breathing we can say that an act of Self-Remembering is an inward and outward movement, not *either* an inward, *or* an outward, movement. An act of Self-Remembering is a double movement as is an act of breathing. And so Self-Remembering can be thought of as consisting in some to and fro motion, psychological in nature, that has to be carried out consciously—that is, with a certain pressure of the attention that is given by aim or by the feeling of the Work. For example, I look at the person, and then at my reaction in the light of my aim, then outward again at the person, then inward at my reaction, and so on. Identifying then becomes impossible.

We will return later to the study of the shock at point 6, but I will add this. Unless you have got to the point of understanding that this Work, and all esoteric psychology, is about your inner states and deals with your *reactions* to others who act on you, it will all seem vague, fantastic and unnecessary. Self-Observation, the starting-point of this Work, is to make one realize one's inner states. Evolution is an evolution of inner states. Self-development is a development of inner states. Only *you* can know your inner states: only *you* can separate from useless, negative or evil states. I repeat that it is impossible to become more conscious, impossible to give the shock at point 6, unless you have begun to be aware of what kinds of things are in you and go on in you, and for this to occur it is necessary to turn the attention inwards first of all and notice your reactions to the outer. But you must also notice the outer. One must find out what external and internal mean and what this out and in movement means, for to be *only* in internals or *only* in externals is wrong. There is *you* and there is the *external world*, transmitted to *you* by the senses. There is the world and there are your reactions to it. If you cannot distinguish between yourself and the external world, you cannot apply the First Conscious Shock. As I said, I will return to this later. At present, notice an external person and notice your reaction to that person and distinguish between them.

Birdlip, March 11, 1944

THE ENNEAGRAM

VI

We will continue to speak about the shock given at point 6 in the Enneagram. I will remind you briefly that this is the First Conscious Shock, called in general the shock of Self-Remembering, and that it does not take place mechanically in Man. I repeat these matters because it is so important for people to grasp them. The whole idea of Esoteric Psychology and its great distinction from Western Psychology lies in the fact that it does not regard a man as being conscious. Esoteric Psychology regards Man as being in a state of sleep in which everything happens to him, a state in which he imagines that he is conscious, a state in which he imagines he has Will, in which he imagines he has a permanent Ego and in which he imagines he can do. Esoteric Psychology teaches us that all this is illusion and that Man attributes to himself what he does not possess. The first stage of his beginning to possess such attributes belongs to this shock at point 6 that we talk about from different angles. Some people think that a shock means only a sudden unpleasant experience. Certainly some shocks are of this kind and are often very useful. But a far larger conception of the shock at point 6 is necessary.

It is here that a whole change of outlook, a whole change of mind, comes in. We have really to understand what it means that things are not as they seem. We have really to understand that we and others are asleep and that we cannot do and that we have no real Will, nor any real permanent Ego, and so on. The realization of all this is a shock, both a slow one and, at times, a sudden one. You have heard in an earlier stage of the teaching one definition of Self-Remembering as the realization of our mechanicalness. When we begin to realize that it is not we who do but *It* that does, then we have a taste of a certain kind of Self-Remembering. But you will understand that if you cannot in any way separate yourselves from yourselves you will never grasp what it means to realize one's mechanicalness. You will call everything 'I' and this is just one of the greatest sins that we can commit against ourselves and against others. We are really Legion and we take ourselves as one and we behave towards other people as if each of them were one. When you observe yourself uncritically and sincerely over some period of time you will begin to notice how much you are mechanical, you will begin to notice that you can scarcely say "It is I who do this" but "It is It which does this". And you will notice that you consent to It and, as it were, call it 'I', although this is not a conscious process, but a kind of self-justifying that goes on in the background and makes everything seem to be all right so that you believe that everything going on is 'I'. For example, there is inner talking going on in you and you go along with it just as if it were you doing it, and really these 'I's which are talking and saying things to you are doing it all in your name or rather you are believing that they are you. Then, quite suddenly, a more conscious 'I', a Work 'I', may say to you : "Why, aren't you in the Work?" And then everything changes completely, the talking stops completely, and the 'I's that were doing it all run away and hide themselves.

Now you cannot give yourselves the shock at point 6 if you always go your own way or always try to go your own way. Always to go your own way is to remain asleep, to remain mechanical, to remain a machine. When you have your own way, when things go smoothly, you are not going against yourself, and you are not conscious. When two things cross, we get a slight moment of consciousness. We wake up a little, for a moment. If you never put the Work in opposition to life you will have no cross, in a big sense, because the Work and life go in different directions, and this cross is not comparable with the little crosses that life produces that come and go and that we deal with in our own life way, but it is a quite different kind of cross. Once it begins to be formed in you it remains and is felt all the time. You know that you cannot have your own way, sometimes more distinctly and sometimes less distinctly, but you know it all the time, and you know that, if things seem easier, you cannot delude yourself into imagining that this is what you want. The reality of the Work becomes a greater reality than the realities of life. When things are easier in life, when one begins to make friends with life for a time, it does not shut out the presence of the Work behind one. Life can give us ease and the Work can give us ease, but they are different in taste. All this refers to what I spoke about in connection with the First Conscious Shock, to the effect that we have to know the difference between being asleep and being awake by inner taste before we even begin to know how to give this shock.

You understand that if you are identified with life you are in life. You respond only to A influences. You are in all the feelings that life gives. You are in all its anxieties. Then you will be far away from the Work. The Work will seem like a dream. You will be far away from any giving to yourself of the shock at point 6. You all understand that you must *re-interpret life* and see it in the light of the Work. But as long as you are completely in life 'I's and completely absorbed in the cares, anxieties, frictions and ambitions of life how can you expect to interpret life differently? Only Work 'I's can do this. Life 'I's know only one language, that of life, but Work 'I's know two languages, that of life and that of the Work. Were not this the case what hope would there be for us save to serve the machinery of Organic Life? How could we separate ourselves from ourselves if there were nothing in us that was different from ourselves? How, if you think you are one, can you separate yourself from yourself? Here there comes in another aspect of the shock at point 6. It consists in always trying to give the chief valuation to Work 'I's at difficult periods. Try to obey what the Work says in any particular situation. Think out how it would be to act in a Work way and try to obey what you perceive and visualize yourself doing it. Of course, you will have to remember about the Work and what it teaches, to do this. This is why it is so important to get to know about this Work, really to study it, really to make an effort to understand its teaching, to keep it alive in one's mind, to see new connections.

Now I wish to return to the early definition of Self-Remembering as the realization of one's own mechanicalness. When we find ourselves talking in some typical way we realize that we are talking from some attitude connected with which are one or two gramophone records. You know that it is not so difficult to see gramophone records in other people once the idea of them has been pointed out to you. It is much more difficult to see gramophone records in yourself and to catch them working. You can recognize them later on by a certain taste and also by an inner feeling of loss of force. Whenever we think mechanically or feel mechanically we tend to lose force. When you become aware of some typical gramophone records, both of the kind that you express in outwardly spoken words and the kind that run inside you internally, you begin to understand something of what mechanicalness is in yourself. Of course you will not if you justify—i.e. if you find some reasons that are sufficient for you to account for speaking outwardly or inwardly as you are speaking. Whenever you find yourself saying things again and again, this is mechanical. When you become aware of mechanicalness of this kind the illusion of yourself begins to be destroyed. A very interesting struggle takes place which I will not attempt to describe as it is an experience that everyone must go through and which everyone will inevitably meet at a certain stage if he works on himself. Now this illusion of oneself must be broken into before the shock at point 6 can really be given. If you try to give this shock when you are filled with the illusion of yourself that you have always had, you will not be able to become more conscious but on the contrary you will tend to go more asleep. We have to realize our position. You remember the story of the rope and the precipice? A man is quite unaware of either. Then he sees the precipice, and then he realizes his true position, and then he sees the rope above his head. Do you understand what this means? A man does not want the rope until he sees the danger, and does not see the danger as long as he is in the illusion that everything is all right. In the same way, a person in the illusion of himself or herself, a person in something not as yet broken open, will make no right effort of Self-Remembering, because, since the precipice is not seen, the rope is not seen.

Now the rope is the Work. The rope is Esotericism that lies just above us but at a higher level. The healing influences of Esotericism can reach us in the 3rd State of Consciousness but not in the 2nd State. The First Conscious Shock is to raise us to that Consciousness, the forms of Awareness, that kind of Light, that belong to the 3rd State.

Now you will understand why it is said that the realization of one's mechanicalness is a form of Self-Remembering. It means that we begin to become aware of the danger we are in, because what we have taken for granted in ourselves we begin to see is illusion and we begin to see that we do not exist. And once this illusion of yourself begins to be broken it begins to be possible to feel the influences of the Work not only reaching but teaching you. If, however, you are convinced that the present pattern of yourself is right, it is naturally difficult to work on yourself because there is no private reason why you should. If you feel no lack, how can you work? If you feel that you have lost nothing, how can you seek? If you feel you know already, how can you be taught? If you are fundamentally satisfied with yourself, how can you change yourself?

THE ENNEAGRAM

VII

We will continue to talk about the First Conscious Shock. You all understand that the reason why I do this is because the whole Work comes in at this point. Each of these papers speaks about the shock at point 6 in the Enneagram from a different side. I am not arranging them in any particular order at present. Last time we spoke about the realization of mechanicalness as one form of this shock.

We take ourselves for granted. We take the fact that we can speak or think or move or see or hear all for granted. We do not realize that we can explain nothing of all this, and that we simply *do not know*. To become aware of this gives a sense of wonder, of helplessness, which has a close connection with one aspect of realizing our mechanicalness. Certainly no one, however much he denies, can say that he created himself and knows exactly how he works and what thought is and what feeling is, etc. Think for a moment and you will see that we really do not know. We are given very complicated machines called bodies and live in another very complicated machine called the world. When you realize all this emotionally you lift yourself off the ordinary level on which you take everything, and this is a degree of the First Conscious Shock. By meditating on the inexplicability of everything, including yourself, you can reach a state of understanding quite different from your ordinary everyday understanding.

Last time the subject of the realization of our mechanicalness was looked at mainly in the light of personal observation and seeing how *It* does, not you. I will remind you here of the importance of Self-Observation in regard to the observation of Personality. Every morning the same thoughts come to you, the same ways of taking things, the same feelings, the same troubles. This machine of Personality to which each person is attached works mechanically. You put a penny in the slot and everything goes by routine. You all know that it is not "yourself" that you have to observe but your Personality. Mr. Smith has to observe Mr. Smith, not "himself". I do not think it can be said often enough that Self-Observation as taught by the Work is utterly different from what we ordinarily conceive as observing oneself. This is one of the places where we fall asleep very easily to the meaning of the Work and where we constantly have to be roused. Mr. Smith comes to see me and talks about his difficulties in the Work and tells me that he tries to observe himself but does not know what it means. He is then asked: "Have you tried to observe Mr. Smith?" He is very surprised. Perhaps you will see what I mean. Of course it is useless to observe yourself as if everything were *you*. You are attached to a complicated machine that creates the larger part of your history. However, *you* are not this machine, because there is something in you that can free *you* from it. If this were not the case, Self-Observation would be so much waste of time. You view your connection with this machine, say, over a day. What has it been up to? What has it been saying? Where has it been? What did it want? Do you like it? Will you justify it? Are you more free from it if you do something with attention? Observe yourself in this way at this very moment. When we realize that this machine of Personality moves us to and fro and takes charge of us at every moment we begin to get glimpses of what it means to realize our mechanicalness. We begin to understand that this is why such a realization is defined as a form of Self-Remembering. You see that you cannot get beyond yourself if you take all yourself as "yourself". How will you cross the stream with all your belongings? How will you get out of prison if you insist on taking everything with you? You have to avoid yourself. You have to be patient with yourself until all the noise that Personality is making has quietened down and you can at last be with "yourself".

There is a phrase that is often used in this Work, and also in other ancient esoteric writings, to the effect that Man is in prison. G. used to say that no one realizes his own situation. "All of you," he said, "are in prison, and all you can wish for, if you are sensible people, is to escape. No one, however, can escape from prison without the help of those who have escaped before. Only they can teach you in what way escape is possible." At one time his favourite statement was that if a man in prison is to have at any time the chance of escape he must realize first of all that *he is in prison*. So long as he fails to realize this, so long as he thinks he is free, he has no chance whatever. If we do not realize our mechanicalness we imagine we are free. We imagine that we do everything from ourselves, by our free will. This prison that G. so often spoke about is first of all your Personality. In the case of Mr. Smith, his prison is Mr. Smith whom he does not observe at all and whom he takes as himself. What does he have to do? *He has to divide himself into 'I' and Mr. Smith.* He is with Mr. Smith all day and so he has plenty of opportunity for observing him and no excuse for saying that he can never get Mr. Smith on the telephone, but because he is with Mr. Smith so much he does not see him and he does not know that Mr. Smith makes him do everything. You will see that really one should say, on meeting Mr. Smith, not merely: "How are you?" but one should add: "But how is Mr. Smith?" And Mr. Smith should reply: "Oh, Mr. Smith is very fit, but *I* am in rather poor health."

Now it is impossible to help this man to separate from Mr. Smith by trying to persuade him. He may say that he does not believe that there is such a person as Mr. Smith and that it is merely a name and he will argue with you and demand that it should be proved. Of course, this is impossible, for it is only he who can liberate himself. He has got to see for himself what is meant by realizing one's mechanicalness. He has got to see that although he may imagine that he always has his own way it is really Mr. Smith who has his own way, and he has got to feel his own helplessness in the presence of Mr. Smith. Of course, this can only be a gradual, intermittent process extending over years of self-study. But once it has begun, once he does perceive for a moment the presence of Mr. Smith, then his eventual liberation begins to be a possibility. Instead of opposing the idea of observation he begins to use it intelligently and then his life will become divided into two streams: one will be the life of Mr. Smith and the other will be the history and reflections of the 'I' observing Mr. Smith. Then for a long time he will lead this twin life which very often is painful. But if he does not allow himself to get negative he will notice gradually that new meanings enter his understanding. Something begins to happen to him. And this change, however slight, is due to the shock being given at the point 6 through which new influences begin to reach a man.

There is a form of Yoga which is based on meditation about oneself and who one is and to what one can say 'I'. In this Work we have to ask ourselves when we say 'I': "Which 'I'?" The realization that one uses the term 'I' quite wrongly begins one's practical work on oneself. It belongs to the shock at point 6 because it can increase consciousness —it increases one's awareness of oneself. It begins to give you a quite new relationship to yourself. Say, sometimes, to yourself in a moment of action: "Which 'I'?".

Now let me give you an example in regard to a person who has begun to realize mechanicalness.' Mechanicalness means *reacting*— reacting as you always do to everything. I think you should reflect on this personal observation of what it means to be mechanical.

"I shall always remember the great and joyful sense of freedom that I experienced when I suddenly, at a meeting, realized what the Work saying 'You must not react' might mean to me and to my life.

Life could be transformed. I was no longer at the mercy of life. I had found a way to deal with life. I need not react. No one and nothing could hurt me or even touch me if I could find the strength not to react. The solution of the difficulty lay with *me*. I had the power, if I could learn to use it, to make life harmless to me. Life was *not* the master. I could overcome the difficulties and the unhappinesses of life by becoming passive to them, not reacting to them."

THE ENNEAGRAM

VIII

There was some conversation on Saturday here about Time and Recurrence. As this subject concerns the First Conscious Shock I will give you a résumé of what was said.

All the ideas of the Work can act as shocks. Ideas are very powerful —much more powerful than anything visible and material. Ideas can dominate whole nations. We cannot see an idea but we can feel its effect. Mr. Ouspensky compared ideas with very powerful machines which if handled wrongly can be dangerous. To feel all the ideas of the Work is to transform our understanding. For instance, the idea that we are not one but many different 'I's can transform one's understanding of oneself and of all other people. In the same way, ideas about Time can change our outlook.

Let us take the idea of Recurrence. It is impossible to understand this idea unless the idea of the 4th Dimension of Time is grasped. What is the 4th Dimension? We are in the three Dimensions of Space: length, breadth and thickness. Let us consider these dimensions for a moment. The movement of a point which has no dimensions generates a line: a line is one-dimensional. Living on that line it would be impossible to conceive how any movement at right angles to it would be possible. The movement of a line generates a plane surface: this is 2-dimensional. The movement of a plane generates a solid: this is 3-dimensional.

Now we cannot conceive what movement a solid must make to generate a higher-dimensional figure of itself. Let us take our own lives as lines, in the 4th Dimension. According to the idea of Recurrence the moment of death is the moment of birth. You will see that it is necessary to bend the line to form a circle so that the two points, birth and death, practically meet. Here a triangle is usually drawn to indicate that something happens between death and birth. A person is born in the same part of Time again and again. It is impossible to understand this unless one can conceive the reality of the 4th (and 5th) Dimensions. *Time lives.* We live in living Time, and each of our lives is fixed in some part of living Time, and this part is our time. If we do not change anything in ourselves everything will be the same again. If Essence remains unchanged it is born again into the same part of Time and once more attracts to itself the same life and surrounds itself with the same Personality. Essence is the indestructible part of us. We know that inner growth means a new growth of Essence, and we know that Essence cannot grow unless Personality is made passive—particularly certain parts of Personality, certain pictures. Esotericism can change the relations of Personality and Essence. Life keeps Personality active. The gradual effect of Esotericism is to make Personality passive. This is why a man should work on himself. If he will sacrifice certain sides of his Personality, if he will withdraw force from them, it may be that Essence can begin to grow.

If Essence grows, when it is re-born it will not attract the same life. Change of Being necessarily means a change in the life because one's Being attracts one's life. If there is a development of Essence there will not only be a change in the life but also there will be memory. A person may remember what to do at some difficult moment: he may remember that he made some mistake.

Since our Being is composed of different parts, some of which are more awake and others more asleep, we can realize that we can represent our lives as a number of parallel lines like telegraph wires. Supposing we are negative, we are on a lower wire. By Self-Remembering we may get on to a wire higher up. By taking everything as heavily as possible we travel along the lowest (the worst) wire, so to speak. By non-identifying and remembering ourselves we get on to a higher (a better) wire. And although all these wires lie, as it were, near together, there are differences between them. One may encounter something on one of them which does not exist on another. For instance, one may encounter *this Work* on one of these lines, and miss it on a lower one. All our 'I's are not on the same level and we cannot meet some of them, say, on the lowest level, because they do not live there.

We have many different kinds of memory, and each 'I' has its own memory. Memory is our relation to the 4th Dimension which extends both into the future and into the past. A man may remember the future. This is not so extraordinary if we realize that we have lived before. This Work stresses very much the importance of remembering. We must remember the moments of understanding that we have had. We must remember that we are in the Work. We must remember our aim. And we must remember ourselves. We must remember to isolate ourselves internally from life and not let its events crush us—that is, we must remember to practise non-identifying, when we find we are identified. There is a chance that some change may take place if one does not identify so much and so continually. By remembering to observe identifying in oneself and to practise non-identifying, one comes under new influences. The object is to reach these influences, which can heal us and give new life. If there were no other influences, if visible life on Earth were all that exists, if there were no Ray of Creation, there would be no Work, and no Esoteric Teaching, and everything would be without hope. Everything would be fixed and mechanical. No one could change himself.

NOTE

Dr. Nicoll in this and the following paper refers to the ideas of Time and Recurrence which are discussed by Mr. Ouspensky in "A New Model of the Universe", Chapter XI.

THE ENNEAGRAM

IX—FURTHER NOTES ON THE IDEA OF RECURRENCE

It seems that many people have great difficulty in understanding what the shock at point 6, is and although it has been explained in every paper that this shock is of different kinds and that in a general sense the *ideas* of the Work and the practice of it give this shock, questions are still asked about what it is. For instance, in the discussion last week it was asked: *"Can one connect this shock of Time at point 6 in the same way as one connects the shock of realizing one's mechanicalness?"* The idea that we recur is a shock when it is emotionally perceived. It changes our relationship to the present and to the past. It makes us see our lives in a new way. Now if you can see your life in a *new* way this is a shock. What is it a shock against? It is a shock against the way that you were taking life before. If you take your life in the same way always you become fixed. To loosen you a shock is necessary. You know how difficult it is to change people's ideas and that it is a sign of intelligence to be able to grasp new ideas. This Work is to make us *think*. All the ideas of this Work can act as shocks if we *think* about them *for ourselves*. The ideas will lift us up to a different level. They will shake us out of the dullness and stupidity of small 'I's that direct our lives all the time. You understand that a *vision* can be thought of as a shock. A man has new vision. He sees light where he did not see it before. He sees everything in a new perspective. Through his vision he has a shock. It is a shock to the old way of seeing things. He is shaken out of himself, and if you are shaken out of yourself you are being given shock. A shock has to awaken us from the deep sleep in which we live our lives. We go to sleep instantly we get up and sleep more deeply than in bed. Not only do the ideas of the Work give us a shock when they are understood and assimilated into the mind, but they can *transform* us. The shock of being awakened is accompanied by the transformation of oneself: the shock of spring on a seed awakens it to a new life which at the same time transforms it. The seed is shaken out of itself. Have you ever been shaken out of yourself, off the basis on which you rest? If so, you understand what a shock is. But a shock is not necessarily a sudden thing: it may operate over a long, long period like a ferment which slowly changes the grape into wine. The answer then to the question as to whether the idea of Time can be connected with the shock at point 6 is *"Yes"*. It was expressly said so in the paper. But it will only be a shock if one tries to understand what it means, and often thinks about Recurrence and how one will always turn in the wheel of one's own life unless one changes oneself. What, then, do we have to do to change ourselves? This Work is teaching us what we have to do every day and every minute.

★　　★　　★

420

In regard to the questions about the different kinds of memory —each centre and part of a centre has its own memory. Memory is not one and the same thing. What was said was that memory is our relationship to the 4th Dimension. It is our relationship to *our* Time. We can move in memory into the past without moving from our seats. Certainly this relationship to the past is very faulty. Underlying our personal memory there is a deeper memory to which we very rarely have access, if at all. In this deeper memory everything is present— everything we said or did or saw or experienced. This is the Book of our Life which is opened at death. We have memory in Essence. Personality is destroyed at death but Essence returns. We have therefore a chance of remembering when we recur only if Essence records anything. Whatever we do *genuinely* touches Essence and Essence will remember it on its return. This is one reason why genius sometimes shews itself very early. In Recurrence everything comes earlier, that is anything in any way genuinely done. Some musicians and other men of genius have begun to remember very early.

Real memory is not connected up in the same way as personal memory. For example, all moments of genuine understanding in the Work will be connected together. They will not lie mixed up with other memories in sequence or mixed up with dates. Memories of the same emotional quality tend to connect themselves. This memory of past time, of day by day, is different from emotional memory. In other words, our relationship to the 4th Dimension is very different. A person may have a very poor time-sequence memory and have a good emotional memory, and vice versa.

The question has been asked: *How can we be re-born in the same part of Time, as our parents will not be there?* There is a misconception here. Our parents are in our time. Everything is there in Time and everything is recurring in Time. The difficulty is to conceive with our sense-based minds what higher dimensions are like. In fact, it is impossible. We can only think of Time as a line, but there are really 3 dimensions of Time so that the line becomes a plane and the plane becomes a solid. In this solid of Time everything exists and everything is turning on wheels, big and small. At the same time there is some general change taking place in the whole Time-Solid. To put it in our ordinary language, some things are ascending, some things are descending, and some things are remaining stationary. In taking the idea of Recurrence, we have to pick it out. We might pick out one wheel from a machine for our understanding, and we must conceive in some way that this wheel is made of some elastic substance that is capable of stretching a little or of being compressed.

With regard to the question as to *whether we can choose* different parents, naturally we cannot if we are under the Laws of Recurrence. We are born into the same part of Time as before and our parents are there. It is only when we come to speak of Reincarnation that this question can arise. Reincarnation is quite different from Recurrence.

In Recurrence one is born into the same part of Time through the same parents; in Reincarnation one is not born into the same part of Time. But Reincarnation it out of the question for us. A very high development is necessary. A man must have reached the end of his life and he must be joined together in a certain way internally by fusion before he can pass into another part of Time.

If we come under the influences of the idea of Recurrence the whole of our conception of the past changes. It is said that a great struggle is going to take place in the world between the religious people who believe in an after-life and scientists who believe only in this life. You will see how the idea of Recurrence satisfies both these sides. When you see that *your past lies in front of you*, then your thoughts about your past become useful.

Birdlip, Easter, April 9, 1944

THE ENNEAGRAM

X—The Beginning of Shock at point 6

Observation of and Separation from "Oneself"

After an interval of some time we will return to the fundamental idea of the Work that in order to change it is necessary to observe oneself and notice what one is like at present. In what part of you is what you are at present? It is in all the rolls in centres, laid down by the particular action of life on you. What does this mean? It means that since childhood you have had laid down in you particular associations that are represented in your centres and that act mechanically. Everyone here has had laid down in his or her centres particular views and ways of taking things, from the mother, from the father, from nurses, from people who surrounded them. You all take this built-up thing as *yourself*. Yet it is merely one pattern of all possible "oneselves". But this is very difficult to grasp. All this associative stuff laid down in centres from earliest life makes you a certain kind or pattern of person. And here I would say, is it not very remarkable that no one thinks that he or she is in any sense a fixed, a particular kind of person—a person who always behaves in this way or that way and so on? It is interesting because everyone has the idea that he or she is quite free and can behave, speak, act, understand and so on just as they wish to. This is illusion. The Personality, built up from Mama. Papa, Nurse, School, etc. is very powerful. It is always acting for you. Yet we have the vision, the feeling, the idea, that we are free and are in no way prejudiced, in no way fixed, in no way machines. I said that this was illusion. Yet at the same time it is not illusion, in the sense that it is possible to dissolve the machine of personality and become free. For this it is necessary to pay and pay for a long time. The Work is to make this payment right. It begins with Self-Observation. What does Self-Observation mean? It means to observe what you are like, how you react, what makes you negative, and so on. This Work teaches you specifically to observe certain sides of yourself uncritically—that is, without justifying yourself one way or the other. To *see* what you take as yourself, to see the machine of responses, the machine of behaviour, the machine of thoughts, of prejudices, of feelings—this is the idea behind self-observation. You will agree with me that a person cannot change unless he or she sees themselves. But people make the most fantastic and ineffectual attempts to see themselves. They usually think they should smoke or eat less or get up earlier or work harder at their money-making jobs and so on. Now this Work does not start with anything of that kind. It starts with one's psychological side. One must observe this side first. This is where what you take as *you* is. First the change in mind must come, the change in your regard for yourself, the change in your very feeling of yourself. As you know, everyone is identified with himself, with herself. And they expect to start from themselves as they are. The Work is about making this "yourself"—this "oneself"—more passive. Who are you? What are you? You are a built-up thing of no use or of little use to *you*. But you are a slave to this thing you take for granted—this "yourself", this "oneself". The Work is to change this —this basis you rest on, this blind acceptance, this thing in you that you have never questioned and so never seen. Life lays down in us, chiefly by our imitating, thousands of attitudes, buffers, pictures, gramophone records—in fact, thousands of associative patterns. We feel uncomfortable if we do not follow them. It is one edition of oneself. The Work is about ceasing to identify with this oneself formed by the action of life and lying in the laid-down personality. Certainly this is a very difficult matter and not for fools. To become orientated in a new way is not an easy matter. One must get under this "oneself". The Work can do nothing for you if you start from this "oneself"— or "yourself"—that is, from personality. And here so many go wrong and cannot see the meaning of the Work. Everyone has a consecrated feeling about themselves, just as they are. But it is in the wrong place —in personality. The personality is not the sacred thing in oneself. The deeper feelings of oneself always have the miraculous quality of sacredness which gives bliss. But we take this thing, "oneself", as sacred —and so we have the feeling in the wrong place—that is, in the self-esteem, in the feeling we are right, in the precious past, in upbringing. It is necessary to shift this feeling, to go behind oneself, to renew it. To ascribe to oneself the idea of anything so deep, anything so full of meaning as the word "sacred" implies, is a crime against oneself.

You remember perhaps, some of you, how in the Holy Grail legends, the young knight riding out to find the mystical school or castle must not obey his mother. This is capable of the crudest interpretations. But what does it mean? The "mother" is the source of your actions and feelings and thoughts. One must disobey the personality. In this Work, what is it that we have to observe? This thing we take for granted and to which all day we say 'I'. But it is not 'I'. It is not Real 'I'. It is many acquired 'I's. It is a machine, a machine of acquired 'I's. One goes about fastened tight to it. One obeys it at every point. It says this—and you think you say it. It does that—and you think you do it. It feels this—and you think you feel it. It thinks that—and you believe you think it. It is a pattern found in the vast associative or silent areas of the brain. It is your pattern, your registrations, your attempts to form yourself. It is a small set of electrical connections, out of billions, owing to which you must always ring up the same places and get the same numbers. It is a machine *in you*. "How," said G. once, "is it possible to make impressions fall on new places in centres? This is my task." He began by making people make new movements. And he also began by making people do things that they were not accustomed to do. "The truth," he said, "is that everything becomes mechanical after a time. How to make things new. Everything becomes mechanical . . ." What do you think yourselves? Have you taken this day quite mechanically? Have you taken your domestic problems just as always? Have you tried to *transform* anything by taking it in a new way? It is difficult, but it is possible. This is the supreme object of the Work—to get rid of one's acquired mechanical way of taking everything according to one pattern, one set of associations, one idea of what is right or wrong.

The subject of this Work is oneself. You and yourself are not the same but you take them as the same. People identify with themselves. You identify with yourself and so yourself becomes you. You, however, are far older than yourself. But since we do not know ourselves, we do not know that there is anything different in us from ourselves and the outer yourself becomes fused to the inner *you* and there is no separation. To observe yourself begins to make a separation. It begins to divide yourself from you. But at first this "you" is merely Observing 'I'. Yet from Observing 'I' arises Deputy-Steward, which leads to Steward, which in turn opens on to Real 'I'. This is *you*. And this *you* is unattainable if you take yourself as you. To leave behind oneself is not quite what people think. Often when they think they are leaving themselves behind they are really more identified. The Work gives some interesting teaching on what it is that we have to observe and leave behind. However, people tend to think they know already and make a problem of, say, eating, or, say, of smoking, or they deny themselves decent clothes or a bus-fare when it is not necessary to do so. Such 'I's need to be observed and separated from. They can form a very powerful system of tyranny in a person. They arise from early associations. A person can remain a slave to them throughout life. It is a dreary slavery leading to nothing. Now in self-observation you begin to notice where you are bound and to what you are bound. This will be in accordance with the feeling of the Work, for the Work shews up life and its action on you. The Work is against life. Life has created 'I's that trade on us and even eat us. These are of every kind. Suppose one could let the influences of the Work make a scourge and drive out these 'I's, we should probably be very surprised at what was driven out—I mean, at what the Work selected as useless.

The first step in the Work is to begin to free oneself from oneself. This Work is not adding something to oneself but taking away from oneself and it is only what is useless to one's development that the Work seeks to take away.

Birdlip, April 15, 1944

THE ENNEAGRAM

XI—The Study of the Shock at Point 6

The Idea of Time, Recurrence and Events

Let us speak again about Time and Recurrence. As the modern scientists tell us, Time is circular and is composed of events. However, this was said long ago, not merely by poets and philosophers, but by esoteric teachers. What is your day composed of? It is composed of events, some, in fact most of them, on a very small scale, such as the event of losing your bag, or the event of the electric stove fusing, or the event of your receiving a letter or a post-card as, for instance, one that I received this morning from a medical firm saying that if I have any skeletons, skulls, or half-skeletons, not in actual use, good prices will be offered for them. This is an event—an odd one. Also my fire would not light: this is an event—a common one. Sometimes events are rather similar: we call this coincidence. But I can see no connection yet between having skeletons and my fire not lighting. What events are you going to ignore and what are you going to identify with? This is what is important, once you can see that life is *events*. Events cluster round the line of the day —the line of extension in Time that we call a day. What are you going to pay attention to and what are you going to separate from, in regard to this cluster of events? Shall I be negative all day because my fire would not light? You lose your bag: are you going to make this event stretch out over the whole of the day with all its quarrels, repercussions and suspicions (such as "Who stole it?") One single unpleasing event can easily be expanded into the whole day. This is what people like to do who select negative things—they sometimes expand an unpleasant event even into their whole lives. This means that, Time being a series of events, you can make one of the events take *all your time*. Your life is *your* time. It is not other

425

people's in the same way. You may share some things. But you are in *your own time*. Time is a series of events and you have your *own* events and share some events. The three higher Dimensions form Time and Recurrence and Eternity. Taking only the 4th Dimension as a line called Time going in a direction at right angles to all the three Dimensions of Space, it passes through each person as a series of events. We lose our bags, which is personal, or we pass into war, which is a shared event. You understand it is not the clock, but events. You say—taking Time as the artificial clock—it is ten-thirty, or, it is 1944. No, that is not *Time*. What events are you identified with at this point in Time called (artificially) ten-thirty, or 1944? Do you imagine that to the ancient Greeks there was anything called ten-thirty or 1944? Time is not dates in clock-time, but *events*. "All the time" you are in some event. You are negative owing to some event. Well, you are in that state and in that event. The event, coming along, seeking what it can take out of you, has got you. You say: "This situation is intolerable". The event has got you. You are incapable either of observing yourself in relation to the particular event, or of remembering yourself in its presence— that is, not identifying with it. Time understood psychologically is a pattern of events, a chequer-board of black and white. It is necessary to expand the better and contract the worse events. You see now that Time is elastic—not clock-time. Do you recollect that once a scientist compared Time with a mollusc? This is where Ouspensky agrees with Einstein. A mollusc is a soft-bodied animal having no internal skeleton and so a creature that can contract or expand different portions of its body at will. A vertebrate cannot do this because it has a framework of bones. We have to become like molluscs in our relation to the day and its events. The idea that we can dwell on things too much is, of course, familiar. One can become halted in one event that happened long ago. But it is not understood and its significance is not realized. You have the power of contacting or not contacting the series of events that make up your day. You can expand yourself into an event or contract yourself out of it. You have observed snails and noticed how their horns sense a thing and expand or contract. It is something like that. Everything physical, everything see-able, visible, is a pattern of something psychological in oneself. One has only to go to the Zoo to realize it. Every animal, every created form of hatred and defence, is represented psychologically in oneself. Man in fact can be far more horrible and cruel than any animal representation. The outer world is in us. The Cosmos is in Man. Man is a Micro-Cosmos. All he sees outwardly is in some way in him—wasp, rat, snake, fly, swine, fox, tiger, chameleon, grasshopper, mole, bird, beetle, fish, stork, and so on. Have you noticed the waspish 'I's in you, or the foxy 'I's? Or have you noticed the chameleon 'I's that change colour according to the situation and like politicians blow hot or cold according to circumstances? Do you know the snake, or especially the fishes in you? What lies in your sea, beyond your present shores? They are all there—the laborious and blind mole, the nervous, superficial bird, the unpleasant-smelling and hard-shelled beetle, the everlastingly reiterating grasshopper, the buzzing, brainless fly, dashing into everything haphazard, the savage, mindless tiger, the secret rat, the upright, solemn, imbecile stork. All these are in Man, as well as the good, stupid animals. Which will you connect yourself with in regard to events?

When you begin to see that there is, psychologically, no clock-time, and indeed no time, even according to the big clock due to the rotation of the Earth that gives night and day, or the bigger clock due to the revolution of the rotating Earth in its orbit round the Sun which makes the seasons, which makes the Earth green and then brown and then white and then green again—when you begin to understand that Time is events and your attitude to them and so finally your inner states, then you begin to be able to think about Recurrence. You begin to think that your past is in front of you. What states have you chiefly lived in? In the states belonging to a mole, or a bird, or what? How have you taken the events you have passed through? According to how you take an event, so is your state. As said, you can contract an event or expand it. This is according to how you take it. Can you separate from yourself—from an event? And, as said, a person can become halted in some event of long ago and, as it were, go into mourning and walk about like some black, dead creature, no doubt thinking it meritorious. Now, since Time is expansible or contractible as regards our taking of events, we can obviously select one event to-day and expand it. Do you notice that the general tendency is to expand an unpleasing event, an event unpleasing to oneself, and contract everything else? You cannot forget, can you, how somebody treated you in a cavalier way, just as if you were of no importance? This is an event. It is an event that can happen to everyone. It is a definite event called: "No one treats me rightly."

When Man was created finally after many experiments, all possible events that could happen to him were also created. It would be useless to create a living thing without the necessary events so that it can have a life of experience. If Time were not the contractible and expansible "mollusc", the soft-bodied, muscular thing, everything would be rigid, like a foot-rule. But "Time"—that is, events—is not of this kind. It can and should be accompanied by a method of selection, of choosing and discarding, of giving attention to and withdrawing attention from the incidents or events or situations that inevitably attend its apparent passage through our limited consciousness. "Time" is all there—like a countryside. But we come on it bit by bit and we pass through it according to our state. If we add conscious state to mechanical state or blind reaction to events, then we are at a higher level of being, and then we can begin to realize that some events should be contracted—even squeezed up and thrown away—and some should be left as they are and some expanded with all one's powers of inner work and Self-Remembering.

427

THE ENNEAGRAM

XII—THE HYDROGENS AND THE ENNEAGRAM

On the periphery of the Enneagram there can be inscribed various Hydrogens in series, beginning with *Hydrogen 384*. Why does *Hydrogen 384* begin the series marked on the circumference? Because human Food, *Hydrogen 768*, is not in Man. You take the general substance called "Food for Man"—*768*—into your stomach. But unless it is digested it is not yet in you. The first action of digestion is to make food into something that passes into you—that is, in the form *Hydrogen 384*. Food regarded as *768* is external to us. It could be removed by a stomach-pump after we have eaten it. But once it becomes transformed into *Hydrogen 384*, called "water", it cannot be removed, because it is part of the physical organism, in your blood and lymph. So one can see why *Hydrogen 384* begins the series of transformations in the Enneagram. If you swallow a metal button, it passes, let us hope, right through you. A button is not food for Man. It is not *768*, nor even the lower *Hydrogen 1536*, which is food for cattle—grass, raw things, fibrous things, etc. which Man cannot eat. Man cannot eat grass which belongs to that class of stuffs called *1536*. He needs an external transformer. This can be a cow, for example. She eats grass and Man eats and drinks her. This is the external transformation of *Hydrogen 1536* into *768*. But Man has inner transformations also, which begin with *768* passing into *384*. You begin with grass, let us say. It is transformed (or cooked) by cows. Then Man eats cow and milk. Both are cooked in Man and so transformed into something else and so on. All life is continual transformation of one thing into another. Digestion is transformation into something *higher*. When a beef-steak is digested by the action of *carbons* already present in the body—that is, the enzymes or ferments such as exist in the acid gastric-juices in the stomach, and the alkaline secretions of the liver and pancreas in the small intestine (for digestion of food is double, first acid and then alkaline, and so under two triads)—then the beef-steak ceases to be a beef-steak and is not only dissolved but transformed into finer matters, in the scale of the Universe, which pass into the blood. In the first stage *768* becomes *384*. Then the beef-steak is in you and circulates round your body *via* the lymph and blood-systems, not as a beef-steak, but as a finer collection of matters called *384*. Then *384* is transformed into *192*, and so on. All this is done for us by the art and chemistry of the Instinctive Centre which governs the inner working of the organism. Everything to do with the lower, denser Hydrogens is done for us. But it is left to us whether we make anything of the higher Hydrogens. Man, the Work says, is created a self-developing organism. But first he is created ready-made—that is, with an incalculable amount of inner factories, of inner chemistry, of inner transformations, and inner machinery. Notice the transformations. Food as *768* passes to the higher level, *384*; *384* passes to *192*; *192* passes to *96*; *96* passes to *48* (*48* is the energy used in thinking—the beef-steak has now become thought); *48* passes to *24*; *24* passes to *12*. All these transformations are done for us by chemical factories. This is the Octave of Food, that takes place mechanically and makes it possible for us to exist. For it is necessary to create a being capable of existing first of all, before there is any question of this being developing into something different. So we all start with the given—the materials given by the Octave of Transformation called the Food Octave.

But the Work is about *what is not given*. It is about manufacturing more materials, more Hydrogens, than the Food Octave gives us. This only begins when the First Conscious Shock is given—that is, the shock at point 6 in the Enneagram. At this point the Work begins—that is, if we value the ideas, ponder them, and apply them to our lives. This requires a certain inner thinking. If we begin to live them, a new octave begins, starting from *Hydrogen 48*. This begins to penetrate us from the top to the lowest storey. That is, the effect of it will be gradually felt in every part of the human machine.

Diagram of the New Octave begun by the First Conscious Shock

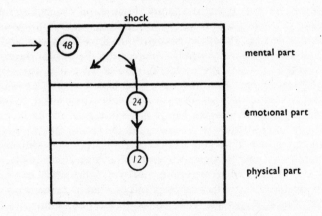

Understand that this beginning of a new octave is not given by nature. It must be created. It is extra. It can only be created by giving oneself a shock in the mental part of oneself. Since this shock is not given by nature but must be given by Man to himself, it is called a *conscious shock*. It has many sides, many forms. In this respect it is different from the mechanical shock of breathing which nature gives to the Food Octave. It is very important to understand all this as clearly as possible. The above diagram is one shewing a man working on himself, remembering himself, creating a new *Hydrogen 24* and a new *Hydrogen 12* as a result. This begins to change his Being.

All the ideas of the Work when they are received, assimilated and given a place, and when an attempt is made to live by them, assist in giving the shock in the upper or mental compartment. This place corresponds in the Enneagram to point 6. The mind must change before the rest of the man can change. This is the same teaching as in the Gospels where it is said a man must first *repent* which really means in the Greek, *change his mind*. To change one's mind means to think in a new way. But, to think in a new way, one requires to have new ideas and new knowledge. For example, if you acknowledge the idea of Time and Recurrence, you begin to realize that your past lies before you, so you will begin to have new thoughts about life—that is, change your mind. I do not mean instantly, but gradually, forming over many years. These thoughts open up a new part of your mind that otherwise would remain unused. This is an example of a "slow shock" in the mental part. It is a gradual transformation of the mind in regard to Time. This affects the emotional part, and in turn affects the physical part. All the ideas of this Work, when perceived in the mind and acknowledged, act like ferments, like leaven, and begin gradually to change the mind, the whole way of thinking, *and especially the feeling of 'I'*. This has all to do with the shock in the mental part, or First Conscious Shock, which is shewn in the Enneagram as the shock at point 6, and in the diagram of Man as a 3-storey Factory in the upper compartment, acting on *48*.

If you begin to live this Work and think about everything from the ideas that it teaches, and struggle to separate yourself from negative emotion and useless ideas that simply drain force from you, and so on, and if you will try to feel yourself walking carefully amidst the events of life as if you had something protecting you on your feet, then you will begin to give yourself the First Conscious Shock and create the extra *Hydrogens 24* and *12* in you. But you must also know what it is to have a long inner struggle between Yes and No in regard to the Work for it is only your inner attitude that counts. As you create this extra *Hydrogen 24* you will notice that your thinking changes. You will begin to understand emotionally, to see the truth of a thing emotionally, and at once you will see endless meaning and you will understand how the Work is inexhaustible in its meanings and in what it can shew you. For, to think from *Hydrogen 48*, with which we have to begin, is a barren thing compared with thinking from *Hydrogen 24*. You all know by now that a higher Hydrogen is more intelligent than a lower. You remember the expression, the saying, that a cooked potato is more intelligent than a raw potato because *768* is higher in scale than *1536*? So you will understand that thinking from the intelligence belonging to *Hydrogen 24* is far more full of inner connections and meaning than thinking from the intelligence of *Hydrogen 48*. By means of *Hydrogen 24* you can see yourself walking about on this earth, you can stand outside yourself, because you are lifted out of yourself.

430

THE ENNEAGRAM

XIII—The Inner Circulation of the Enneagram

At every moment a person on this Earth is under one or other of the *48* orders of laws or influences that play upon this planet owing to its position in the Ray of Creation. The influences come from higher, middle and lower parts of the descending octave of the Ray in which our Earth appears. These *48* orders of laws from different levels in the scale of things govern the Earth and all the Earths in the myriads of Solar Systems in the Milky Way, to which our Solar System belongs. Recollect also that there are myriads of Milky Ways or Galaxies in the Universe. We are therefore very small, practically insignificant. If our Earth were shattered, by a comet, it would be of no importance to the total sway of all the vastness of created things in the Universe. Shattered planets in our minute Solar System exist which revolve round the Sun as small bodies—planets only a few miles in diameter, hundreds of them. This is looking at the visible, physical side of things known to science concerning the external Universe and is either marvellous or is weakening to self-feelings. But when we look at the whole matter according to esoteric psychology, the picture becomes transformed. The Work teaches that a human being is not merely a function of the world he is born in or a slave to it. The apparatus of the Universe is, so far as our Ray of Creation is concerned, for the purpose of Evolution. It is a vast distilling machine, to extract the finer from the coarser. This is an old image wonderfully described, for example, in the teachings of Mani. What is individual evolution, in the esoteric sense? Seeing by long, inner work, and then choosing the *finer*, and eventually willing and ultimately living the *finer*. Do you recall the ancient Smagdarine Tablet of Hermes which begins with saying that you must "separate the finer from the coarser?" This begins personal work. It takes a long time before it begins. What is meant by finer? If you have a moment of fuller understanding, of insight or of outer perception by means of *Hydrogen 24*, it will be *finer* than anything that can be achieved by the intelligence due to *Hydrogen 48*. You see hundreds of connections that you never saw before. In exactly the same sense, a cooked potato is *finer* than a raw one. It is a higher Hydrogen and becomes food for Man and can enter into him. Instead of being eaten by cattle it can be eaten by Man. But cattle cannot cook potatoes. The intelligence of Man is necessary to make fire, to make a vessel holding water, and so on. A raw potato is classed in the Table of Hydrogens as belonging to the order of Hydrogens designated by the number *1536*. This Hydrogen comes low down in the Scale of Being derived from the Ray of Creation. A cooked potato is capable of another destiny just as we ourselves are if we shift our level of being even a fraction. The being of a cooked potato attracts a different life from the being of a raw potato. How does it ascend in the

431

Scale of Being? By means of something acting on it—something higher. The whole business of cooking things is the action of something higher on something lower. But notice that the result does not reach the level of what is acting on it. The intelligence of Man applied in the form of heat and water and vessels and so on to the raw potato does not mean that the result—the cooked potato—knows how to cook other potatoes. A higher force acting on a lower force, or a higher matter acting on a lower matter, brings the lower up to a stage beyond what it was but not up to the level of the acting force. This idea is represented in the Work in terms of the three forces. An active force acting upon a passive force produces an intermediate force. When food is taken into the body it enters, according to the teaching of the Work, as material conducting a passive force. It is then acted upon by an active force present in the body and the result is an intermediate force. Thus *768* is acted on by *192* and the result is *384*, which is intermediate. Any matter conducting passive force is transformed into a higher state by means of a matter conducting active force, provided there is an intermediate possibility. But the higher matter into which it is transformed is neither one nor the other but a third thing, intermediate between them, conducting neutralizing force, as long as it remains within the sphere of influence of the forces that gave it origin.

Thus:

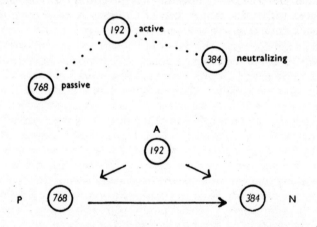

Or, if we arrange these figures in ascending order of fineness:

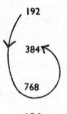

If *192* is not present, *768* cannot reach its next stage of evolution into *384*. Nor can *192* by acting on *768* expect to get anything equal to itself. It can only create something in between itself and what it is acting on. So the higher acting on the lower can only transform the lower to a stage beyond what it was, but not up to the level of the higher. And the lower cannot reach its next stage save by the influence of something higher than both. This idea is very deep and explains not only many things in life, but also many special things, as in the chemistry of the body. It also explains, in one sense only, what Esotericism is. Esoteric ideas, and the fire and light behind them which a man can feel when he gives them real valuation, can be regarded in this connection, and only in this connection, as active force. Acting on Man, taking Man as a Hydrogen whose centre of gravity lies in *48*, these influences coming from a higher point in the Sun-Octave can transform or "cook" him up to the level *24*. But actually esoteric ideas are first to be taken as *12*—that is, higher than the product or result. For when Carbon *12* acts on incoming life taken as *48*, it can only give origin to *24*.

Let us now take the right-hand area of the Enneagram which is marked with the numbers *384*, *192* and *96*, in progressive series on the periphery. Many other things can be arranged round the circumference, apart from the Hydrogens, but it will be easiest to discuss the reverse movement in terms of Hydrogens. Notice that in the inner lines *384* is connected with *96* and then with *192*. Something goes forward and then back, in a reverse movement.

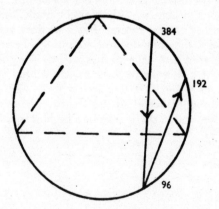

The inner line between *384* and *96* indicates some action, some connection, between these two points as a first movement. Another line then goes to the station *192* as a second direction. The order of these inner connections is different from the order of the outer series on the circumference, namely, *384*, *192* and *96*. That is, the inner circulation in the Enneagram takes a different form from the outer. We think, naturally, that *384* should become *192* and then *96* in a regular manner. But internally, behind outer appearances, another system is at work, which is very strange if you reflect on it. You are probably looking at the mystery of life in the inner circulation of the Enneagram, whereas, looking at the outer series of numbers, you are perhaps looking at what corresponds to that powerful but erroneous form of thinking called thinking from appearances, from the senses. You notice that the higher must exist before the lower can undergo transformation. This is not difficult to grasp, once the Ray of Creation in its naked meaning is emotionally perceived and privately acknowledged, for in it the higher forms the lower so that, if the lower seeks transformation, the higher is there awaiting it. This is one reason why it is a good thing to ponder the Ray often in one's inner thoughts. The Ray is a series of transformations of the finer into the coarser from the highest to the lowest.

What is the Enneagram about? The Enneagram depicts a series of transformations from lower to higher, from coarser to finer. Now in order that a lower may become transformed into a higher, it must be *passive*. That is, it must allow itself to be acted upon by a higher influence. How else could lower become higher? How else could the food we eat become cooked and re-cooked, transformed and re-transformed into higher and higher substances, unless it submitted to the six stages of digestion? Digestion is transformation. Work is transformation. And if the higher influences of the Work are to act on a man, he must *in one sense* become passive to them and permit them to act. He can realize he cannot do, but he must realize also that Greater Mind exists, otherwise he will be in confusion. If he does not admit that anything bigger than he is exists, or if in some way he thinks he made himself, he cannot be acted upon and so cannot evolve. But if he does become passive— that is, capable of *hearing* and then of accepting—he must not expect to get beyond his own *next* stage to begin with. He cannot equal the Work. It would be a mistake to think so. He cannot equal the forces that are transforming him. If you reflect, you will see there must always be something higher than any man, whatever his stage, if evolution is possible, and so there must be a highest that is unattainable.

THE ENNEAGRAM

XIV—Further Note on Hydrogens

Many questions are asked about the position of Hydrogens in the Octaves. There is, for example, *Hydrogen 48* which is created out of the food that we eat by successive transformations within the body. This is the Hydrogen that we use for our ordinary thinking and which works the relatively mechanical part of the Intellectual Centre or mind. With this Hydrogen we can only think in terms of Yes or No and so we see everything divided into irreconcilable opposites. When we think with *Hydrogen 24*, however, we have a different picture of things for by means of this psychic energy we see everything in a much finer way, in a much more subtle interconnection, so that the stark opposites disappear and everything appears blended together in a marvellous harmony.

Now these *Hydrogens 48* and *24* are connected with the Notes *Sol* and *La*. *Sol 48* arises out of the transformation of *Do 768* into *Re 384*, into *Mi 192*, into *Fa 96*, into *Sol 48*, and then into *La 24* and finally into *Si 12*. Now let us suppose that the Impressions Octave is set to work by means of a man's living as consciously as he can for a short time. Here there is *Do 48*: here is a Hydrogen again of the value of *48* but on the note *Do*. This Hydrogen by transformation within the awakened mind passes to *Re 24*. There are now two *48's* and two *24's*—*Do 48* and *Sol 48*, and *La 24* and *Re 24*. What difference can there be in these cases? Let us think of the matter in this way. Suppose that you have a hundred golden sovereigns and you divide them into two lots. You decide to pay half of these golden sovereigns into your Bank and to use the other half in payment of your debts. Now the golden sovereigns are just the same in regard to their matter but they have quite different destinations and potentialities. That gold which you pay into the Bank can accumulate whereas that gold which you pay out has gone as far as it can, and I am sure your thoughts about the two sums will be quite different. And I think you will agree that the 50 sovereigns that you are going to pay into the Bank have a fresher feeling about them than those that you are going to pay out. And in somewhat the same way emotions that you feel through *Re 24* are far fresher than those of *La 24*. You know how anything that is capable of many transformations has a certain quality of newness and vitality, like small buds, whereas a thing that is nearly over, that has nearly completed its course, is quite different. *Re 24* is in an earlier position in the Octave than is *La 24*. A full Octave lies between *Do* and *Do*. Actually the new *Do* starts a new Octave. We develop from a cell which passes to the state *Si*. We are then born as babies and begin a new *Do*. The Octave that we left, which began with the fertilized cell as *Do*, we know nothing about now. We became old and then became young again. So you understand that *Mi 12* is younger than *Si 12* and that *Re 24* is younger than *La 24*. And in general you must understand that the same matter may be under many different potentialities and destinations according to its relation with the things that surround it. "In the country of the Blind the one-eyed man is King."

If you find it so difficult to understand about Hydrogens and their relationship, look at the outer world and see how things are of quite different materiality, and how their destinations are different, and how you can classify things by their uses, and how nothing is independent but everything is connected together, how one thing depends on another and how its significance changes in accordance with circumstances, and how a thing at one moment may be the most important thing and at the next moment quite unimportant. In seeing outer life like this you are looking at different substances which are constantly being controlled by forces acting on them. You are really studying substances and the Law of 3 and the Law of 7. You all know better and worse in the outer world, finer and coarser, more rare and more common. You all know what things of high quality and things of commoner quality are. You all know what refining means, what separating means. You can distinguish between great literature and common literature. How then should it be so difficult to understand what the Hydrogens are that work your psychic apparatus, that work your mind and cells, that work your centres, either in a poor way or in a better way? I fancy that the real trouble that most of you have is that you do not try to get hold of these very simple diagrams and so you always remain in a state of confusion simply because you will not give yourselves the easy shock of trying to grasp the general meaning of the diagrams. You have got to use *Hydrogen 48* first of all—that is, you have got to try to concentrate on these diagrams with your formatory centre so that you can write them down yourselves. Then when this has been laid down and you begin to think about the meaning and you begin to hear some of these commentaries, you will have moments of seeing more deeply their significance and this means that you will begin to use *Hydrogen 24* in your understanding. Sometimes this happens as if there were a sudden flash, and in this connection I will quote you an example that I came across the other day:

The mathematician Hamilton, who had thought for years about how to multiply two-dimensional quantities, suddenly while walking along a country road saw the solution, which he said came to him "as though a circuit had been suddenly completed in my mind and a blaze of light resulted." He was so amazed that he took out his pocket-knife and cut the formulae which he had just seen on the stones of a bridge near by.

This is seeing a problem through a high Hydrogen in the Intellectual Centre. This is definite proof amongst hundreds of other known examples that the mind can work on different levels. If you can see this, then you are beginning to see what different Hydrogens mean, and if you have never felt anything of this in regard to your own states and the quality of your own feelings or the understanding of your minds, then it is because you do not give yourself even in the slightest degree this First Conscious Shock that makes it possible for a man to touch new influences.

*　　*　　*

Questions have been asked as to why the highest Hydrogen appears in the lowest part of the 3-storey factory. You must all understand that these different storeys do not mean, for Man as he is, lower or higher. Man as he is uses only *Hydrogen 48* in the top storey whereas his Moving and Instinctive Centres work with *Hydrogen 24*. This simply means that the work going on in the first storey is infinitely more intelligent than the work going on in the 3rd storey. That *Hydrogen 12* is at the note *Si* means that it can only do one thing. What is this *Hydrogen 12* at this point in the Octave? It is the Hydrogen connected with the possibility of a destiny that is capable of uniting with its corresponding opposite and so starting a new octave. This very high living Hydrogen contains the possibility of producing a new *Do*—that is, of starting something quite new—a new Octave. The shock between *Si* and *Do* is looked after very carefully by the cosmic influences that wish to keep life on earth constantly multiplying. It may be asked therefore what *Mi 12* means and what children it can produce. Let us remember that *Mi 12* is not made mechanically, naturally, ordinarily. If a person begins to give himself the First Conscious Shock, the shock of Self-Remembering, the shock of the whole Work, if he begins to transform his daily contact with life and not take things as always in the ordinary way in which he always takes them, if he feels deeply that he is always doing something else and that he is related to something else which gradually becomes more important, then he may make *Hydrogen 12* at the point *Mi* in the Octave—that is, *Mi 12*. This *Mi 12* will create as it were a child that he has to look at very closely if he wishes to remain in the Work. What is this child created by *Mi 12*? It is something quite new in him. He must pay attention to this new-born thing in him which is the beginning of his own re-birth. This new thing, this child, can easily die if he goes to sleep. When this child exists in a man or woman it must be given the right food and they must be very careful of it. Of course you cannot see this child externally, and you must remember that this child born in yourself, this child that is your relationship to the Work, this child that both men and women can have, appears at the note *Mi*. It is not at *Si* where it has to become something else instantly. This invisible child is at the note *Mi* and therefore it is at a place where there is a missing semi-tone, in a way similar to the child born out of *Si 12*. Now the shock that has to be given to the child born at *Si 12* is obvious. But what is the shock that is required to carry the child born at *Mi 12* beyond the place of the missing semi-tone? How often people give rise to a small child which they murder because they have not the strength

437

nor the depth of feeling and aim necessary to bring this child up beyond their ordinary level. How many spermatic seeds the Work sows. How often people have for a moment a child in the Work—please understand that I am speaking of these invisible children born in your own understanding—and how often these children, like their counterparts in life, suffer from scurvy, typhoid-fever, etc. as when you become negative in the Work.

The power of conception of Man in the spiritual sphere—that is, in his thinking and his feeling—is very weak, especially when a man or woman is left without help for a time, without praise or without special attention. In this Work you have to keep something invisible going in spite of all external difficulties. In the Gospels it is called Faith: in this Work it is work on yourself in connection with your aim. You remember that it was said you have to fight for this Work. All the time there are negative 'I's based on sensual life, on the visible scene, that attack you. If you have no capacity in yourself of inner conception and inner thinking and inner feeling, the Work will fall by the wayside or on stony ground, and when the heat of the sun is too strong this little thing born in you from the spermatic seed of the Work will fade—i.e. the children born of *Mi 12* will continually die. You will have a period of enthusiasm and then when you are offended, having no real power of inner conception, your children will die. It is a very strange thing to reflect on what it means to keep this Work alive and young in yourselves. Certainly this is not possible if you look to the evidence of the senses for proof. What did that unknown writer, supposed to be a woman, say in Hebrews (XI 1): "Faith . . . is the evidence of things not seen." Now when you understand something and see the truth of it in your own mind, do you wish to be supported by the evidence of things seen? Do you wish to have people to agree with you or are you strong enough to do without the proof of external and visible things? If you are not strong enough to conceive a child in your own mind and keep this child alive, this new-born thing in you, then you can only expect that it will die through sheer starvation. Every time you connect thoughts, see new meaning, apply the Work to yourself, notice what you are saying, see your own mechanicalness, separate from negative emotions, not allow yourself to go with weak, silly 'I's or dangerous 'I's—in short, every time you give yourself the First Conscious Shock, the Shock of this Work—you give nourishment to this child that is your new self.

SELF-OBSERVATION

Let me ask you all this question: How do you touch life? Well, how do you? It is necessary to realize that each one of you touches life in your own way. Suppose that you have some old-fashioned attitude, then you touch this so-called modern life partly through it and therefore will judge it as if you knew better. But do you see yet that each one of you touches life according to implanted attitudes? Recently someone asked me why he disliked a certain person. That I could not answer. How could I know why he disliked this person? Later on he said that he now liked the person. One of the most interesting things in self-observation is to begin to realize that you are always touching life in a certain ingrained way—through attitudes and buffers, etc. It is an extraordinary experience to become even a little freer from this acquired way of taking life and taking others. Everyone, tightly wrapped up in his or her acquired Personality, takes things just as he or she does every day. However, with insight into oneself it is possible to take things in a new way. This is one of the ideas of the Work. Must you always take things and people in the same way? Can you change? What does this involve? It always involves a change in oneself. But, of course, there is nothing wrong with oneself. How difficult it is to realize what the Work teaches about this. Are you not all convinced that your views, your judgments, the way you take things, and the ways you touch life, are right? Yes, of course you are. To realize that you *yourself* must change is an awkward business. It ceases to be a joke. Yes, the Work is serious. It requires an inner self-glance—not once, but twice, and not twice, but a thousand times—to see what this acquired person called yourself is really like, to see that one is often a very narrow, biassed, or even unpleasant person. Here, however, we are all sure that we know that we are not unpleasant people. The Work is to dissolve this really terrible self-complacency based on pictures, attitudes and buffers. The Work is to break up this maddening pseudo-creation called *yourself*—this no doubt proud and charming picture, so deeply-rooted, to which one is a prisoner, a slave—this acquired machinery that one takes as oneself.

I have often thought of what G. taught—namely, that many moments of self-observation lead at length to whole *photographs*. This means that the practice of the Work leads us to catching real time-photographs of what we are really like and have been like over years and years. This can indeed be shattering. Yes, it is an awkward business to begin to see this. But it is dangerous unless you know how not to become identified, not to be negative; otherwise I say it is a very awkward business indeed. This can happen only when you insist on taking yourself as *one person* and when, therefore, you attribute everything you observe in yourself to yourself, to something that you call 'I'. The Work teaches that this is Imaginary 'I'. Of course, if you take everything you observe as 'I', then you will be in very great difficulties. But, as you know, the Work begins by teaching you very earnestly that there are many 'I's in yourself. Unless you can bear to realize this, you cannot do this Work beyond a certain point. You cannot *separate* from yourself and if this is the case you cannot really grasp the Work. Everything will remain personal. You will be offended. Suppose, for instance, you always identify with the 'I's that are against this Work. Then you will suffer in a manner that is quite useless. Have you ever really observed and got to know the negative 'I's that say all sorts of things and often blaspheme this Work? Are you going to say 'I' to them? All sorts and kinds of small ignorant 'I's try to eat us all day long. Do you know what inner separation means? If not, then these small, negative, ignorant, narrow, stupid 'I's will eat your Work force like a lot of beetles and mice and rats every day. It is a pity to give them the authority of 'I'—of yourself. You will then be dragged down from the moment you get up in the morning. It is really a tragedy to see a person in the Work, who really feels and wants the Work, quite incapable of realizing different 'I's in himself or herself. I say that it is a tragedy for a person not to understand what the Work first of all insists on—namely, that we are not *one* but *many*. If you cannot begin to see this, all your work will be in a mess. Every one of you has many 'I's which are useless and worse than useless. Everyone has 'I's that hate this Work because they know they will have to starve and even die, so they fight for their own lives and try to persuade you that they are *you*. If you say 'I' to them, what can you expect? On the other hand, if you can see them as 'I's in you that you do not care for and deliberately decide by experience not to consent to or believe in what they say, then you begin to enter the way of this Work, even if they overpower you often for the time being. There is a phrase in the Work: "*This is not 'I'* ". Can you understand what it means? It is interesting to notice how much vanity and pride enter at this point so that a person insists he is fully conscious and knows himself and always acts consciously from a real 'I'. Of course we don't. It is foolish to imagine we do. But it is intelligent to notice that we don't. And this begins work on yourself. It is a very extraordinary experience to begin to undergo this losing of one's Imaginary 'I'. It means a loss of vanity. But it cannot possibly be begun—indeed it is not permitted—unless your valuation of the Work is strong enough to hold you up during this loss, this de-personalization. The Work can only help you if you have caught hold of its teaching in one point of you genuinely—that is, so that it can touch and hold you when you have to begin to lose hold of False Personality.

Let us take persons who regard themselves as solid, consistent men and women. To such people the idea that they are not one person, but many different persons, often contradictory, will be something abhorrent. They will insist that they know themselves, that they are always one and the same person, and so on. And if any rather too transparent contradiction occurs, they will justify themselves. Why?

To keep this imaginary idea of themselves intact and inviolate. What a business it is to get a person to realize in this Work the existence of many different 'I's and to feel their existence in him or her. You recall, some of you, how some questions were answered in the earlier days of the Work. A person, let us say, asks a question like this: "I always think that . . ." The answer was: "Which 'I' thinks like this?" You will agree that it is rather baffling to receive an answer like that. But is it not a real reply? Is it not based on the teaching of the Work which begins by telling us that we must realize we are not one 'I' but many 'I's. An answer like that is a real answer. If the above person asked the question in this form: "There is a certain 'I' uppermost in me at this moment that appears to think like this . . ." well, then, the answer would be different. It means he is not identified at the moment. But who of us yet can reach this step of seeing clearly that he or she has different 'I's uppermost at different times? Who of us can see yet the turning round of different 'I's in ourselves and from that insight not identify with any one of them and not always take them as 'I'—as you —as yourself, solid and permanent. Thinking, imagining we and others are always the same, does violence to us and to others. But if you have got as far as not quite taking every psychic event, every viewpoint and thought, state and feeling as 'I'—as *you*—then you begin to understand what the Work says about inner separation and selection. Some 'I's are your friends: other 'I's are your enemies. Some 'I's give you force: other 'I's rob you of force: and some actually eat you. How then can a person in the Work live in a self-complacent sleep saying 'I' to everything in him or her? Is not all development through a process of rejection and selection. How can you either reject or select if all is one and the same to you—if all is 'I'? If you keep a garden, do you not throw out weeds and cultivate and nourish and tend useful plants? Is it not impossible to do this in your inner life if you take everything as *you*? You have bad thoughts or bad feelings. Will you not see that if you take them as 'I'—as you—you strengthen them? Suppose you begin to understand this great teaching of many 'I's and of non-identifying with yourself: Well, if you identify with these negative thoughts and feelings coming from these 'I's and regard them as 'I myself' thinking and feeling, where will you get to? Perhaps you will say: "Yes, but these bad thoughts and feelings are in me so what can I do?" What can you do? You can agree with them, consent to them, identify with them and give them the authority of 'I'. But supposing that you do not agree with them, consent to them or identify with them and do not say 'I' to them? Will they get stronger or weaker? Well, think for yourself. Do you think that all these people on the pavement are you?

The object of this Work is to make us conscious in ourselves and to ourselves, to what is going on in us, to the vast inner traffic of thoughts and feelings that lies within, in the psychic invisible realm as distinct from the vast outer physical world of things and people that the senses reveal to us. Here, in this inner world, and in what we select and reject in it, lies the key to the Work, and so to evolution. You all know how to reject and select things in the outer world. You discard useless things from your business and cling to useful things. It is the same idea. Suppose, by long observation, you notice that 'I's create moods, thoughts and feelings, that depress you, that eat you, that make you despondent, or negative, or suspicious, or evil-minded. Then what are you going to do? Are you going to give such moods, such states, full approval? Are you going to regard them as *you*? Why should you? If it is pouring with rain, do you remain in it or separate from it? Are you going to practise non-identifying with these bad inner states, not going with them, not listening to them? But if you cannot see you are *many* and insist on regarding yourself as *one*, then you can do nothing with regard to your inner life.

What is this Work about? It is to open us to new and better influences coming down from the Ray of Creation. What is life? It is a machine under certain influences that nourish the Moon. You see it at work now. Notice it. Think what it is like. It is not an exceptional state of things that prevails now. It is the ordinary state of things, of life. But the Side-Octave from the Sun comes down to us carrying the possibility of new influences. In that brief spiritual period of Ancient Egypt, under Amen-Hotep, I think, the Sun was represented by long rays ending in hands. It did not mean the literal, visible sun, of course, but a higher level of understanding and life such as that belonging to Conscious Humanity—not to this violent, greedy, asleep and chaotic humanity covering the surface of the Earth and used almost entirely for cosmic purposes. This is quite understandable. We are already quite familiar with the esoteric teaching, with the Work, in that respect. We can easily understand why Amen-Hotep represented the Sun with hands at the end of its rays reaching towards the Earth. But they were never shewn, however, as quite reaching the Earth. You remember that rope, of which the Work speaks, to which it is necessary to jump up in order to catch hold of it? Now if you estimate this Work by your practical business 'I's, or your ordinary pleasure and worldly 'I's, you will not be able to realize you are not one but many. It requires a trace of Magnetic Centre. It requires a little emotional understanding and not merely formatory proof. How can I prove to you that a strawberry tastes different from an apple? Not by any formatory arguments, I assure you. You must taste and see for yourselves. How can I prove to you that to begin to feel the many influences of the Work is different from being soaked in life? Of course I cannot, by any formatory argument. Nor can I prove to you that this Work is true. If you are wholly in life, best not to attempt it. In fact, the Work will not seek to touch you. You are then just in life with its horizons. If that satisfies you, then why attempt a new interpretation, a new meaning for existence on this imperfect and violent planet? This Work is for those who feel some conviction that life cannot be understood in terms of itself. If you are satisfied with all your experiences, if you feel life is all you need, if you are thoroughly satisfied with yourself, if you are content with everything, as yet experienced, then, I repeat, why seek this Work? But if not, then you must be intelligent enough to connect your dissatisfaction with this Work. You must begin to be able to realize that your many discontents are not exceptional and catch a glimpse of what the Work says about life—how everything happens, how your being attracts what happens to you, and so on. Otherwise how can the Work help you? I would like you to consider what is meant here. It is a very deep idea. It is far too easy to become negative and blame others or circumstances. This occurs on all sides. It is the usual life-opera. But Magnetic Centre makes a person feel there must be something else. He has an idea there is another opera—not all negative emotion and tragedy. The problem is an inner one. Its solution begins with self-observation according to definite instructions. So unless you can observe yourself, the Work remains dead. In order to observe yourself, it is necessary to realize that you are not *one* but *many*. Unless you can see eventually different 'I's in yourself, you cannot reject or select. And without the Work and the understanding of what it is about, you will not be able—eventually— to reject and select rightly. But if this is done, new influences begin to enter your inner life. You begin to feel the beginning of new life, and very gracious it is. If you listen to it, something begins to grow. If you know when you are out of touch with it and feel a deprivation and seek it again, then it will return again. For a long time—and inevitably— one swings between the old and the new. It is a question of inner valuation, of that strange thing called *Will*, which is like turning without violence in one direction in spite of upsets—like a magnetic needle. But all this—all the beginning of this octave we spoke of that creates new energies—I say, all this remains almost impossible if you say 'I' to everything in yourself. Then one is in total darkness as in the opening verses of Genesis. Light is not yet divided from darkness.

Now I would like some of you especially to notice 'I's that eat your force. Recently I had a plague of them and for a time did not notice them. I took these thoughts and words and feelings as 'I'. That is, I was asleep. You are, each of you, surrounded inside with negative, weak, carping, poor, suspicious, narrow, stupid 'I's. Some of them have gained great strength by long habitual consent to them. You observe a person—he or she suddenly loses force—becomes weak, negative, lost and so on. What has happened? Some 'I' is eating that person. Our inner life is far more dangerous than our outer life and its dangers.

Now you must understand, all of you, that this doctrine of 'I's does not relieve you of all responsibility. Only a fool can imagine that. To reject 'I's or to select 'I's is a very real thing. To go with wrong 'I's must give you real pain, real suffering. This is useful suffering. You must learn to hate 'I's in yourself. Otherwise you will make the Work trivial, an excuse for doing just what you want. There are periods when the Work comes down very hard on you. Then it passes for a time. But if it never comes down hard on you, you may be sure it is not yet willing to touch you.

443

Last year I was told a dream by someone not here now. This person dreamt that all his uncles and aunts, his mother, his father, sisters, brothers were standing round him. He was lying in bed, dying and almost dead. All these people were in deep black. I entered the room looking very thin and ill and pale and then left in a hurry without looking directly at him. Well, here you see an emotional parable-picture of this person's inner state. All the acquired life-'I's surround him. He is dying. The Work enters, but in a very poor way, and leaves hurriedly. Perhaps this will shew you why this person died as far as the Work is concerned. He had in himself no free power of choice. In a way he saw the Work, but his 'I's were too strong. Remember the Work is exactly as strong in you as you allow it to be. It is a question of valuation.

Birdlip, May 20, 1944

THE MEANING OF EVOLUTION IN THE WORK

The doctrine of 'I's is the most important part of the psychological teaching of this Work. Unless a person begins to see that he is not one he can never be otherwise than completely identified with himself. Just think what this means. I repeat that unless a person begins to see that he is not one but many different 'I's he cannot be otherwise than completely identified with himself in everything that he does and thinks and feels. Now such a man cannot evolve. Being fixed to himself as he is, he cannot separate himself from himself. When you speak to a man like this he is very surprised when he is told to observe himself and he is quite incapable of understanding what it means.

Now all evolution in the Work-sense depends on a certain number of 'I's moving into new positions and gradually gaining an increasing control over the remaining 'I's. If a man were just one and the same 'I' it would be impossible of course for this to happen. The new position into which these 'I's, upon which a person's evolution depends, have to move, is towards a more central position in the person and at the same time, if it is possible to explain it, they must have a special place, they cannot be on the same level as the other 'I's, they must be given a certain rank, a certain distinction, or, as the Work puts it, a certain valuation—otherwise immediately a man gets immersed in the affairs of life, making money, etc. these 'I's will all get scattered and in a short time a man will not know what on earth this Work is about, even if he caught some glimpse of it before. Of course this depends on the kind of man he is. If a man has Magnetic Centre, if he has always felt that there is more in things than appears on the surface, if he has noticed that certain kinds of teaching very similar in nature have always existed which are quite different from those referring to the affairs of life, then it will be possible for him to understand what it means to keep certain 'I's in him away from the street, from the level of the ordinary traffic. For a man who is purely material, to whom everything real is merely what hè can see and touch, this will be impossible, And so for the same reason individual evolution will be impossible. For a long time we can observe the struggle going on in ourselves with regard to the above situation.

Sometimes individual evolution is defined in the Work as a new growth of Essence. Taking Essence simply as something more internal than Personality, it means that Essence is a growth of something internal, rather than external in Personality. Personality surrounds Essence and so is external. As we know, Personality—that is, the acquired side of us —may so surround Essence that a person becomes dead. He is completely cut off from Essence. He may appear to be a very highly organized being or have a strong Personality and so on, and yet he is dead. Now when a man is held by Personality there is no real man inside him. I would ask you to pay attention to what is going to be said. If a man is held by Personality and by nothing deeper he is not a man at all and there can be no individual evolution of him. When, however, a man is held by something internal to Personality he begins to be a man and is capable of an individual evolution into a conscious being. We are, of course, mere outlines, experiments. We are experiments in the creation of a self-developing being. At the same time we have to be able to live in ordinary life. For this reason Personality is acquired, which enables us to make contact with outer life and to do our work and so on. But this is only an external development. You can talk, if you like, about the evolution of the Personality, but this is not what the Work means by individual evolution. Certainly this is a preliminary step, and the richer the Personality, the more material, the more inscribed rolls in centres, the more experiences, the more knowledge, the better. But this does not make Essence grow. Essence can only grow through the weakening of the Personality. From the ordinary state of an adult person where the Personality is active and the Essence is passive a new state must be eventually reached in which the Essence is active and the Personality passive. You can understand that this is a very long journey and you can also understand that you cannot understand it right away. But it is very useful to remember it very often, especially in moments of struggle.

Now for the Essence, or inner, part of us to grow and become gradually active, a màn must be able to be utterly sincere with himself when the occasion arises. Essence cannot grow from anything false. I said just now that as long as a man was held by the Personality he was not really a man nor could he evolve individually. When a man is held only by the Personality everything he does is insincere, relatively speaking. It is pseudo. For instance, he gives something to the poor because he wishes to appear charitable, or he may do it in secret and yet in a false way in order to keep a picture of himself alive or in order to be found out later. Let us take a man who keeps the law only from the external side of himself. He will be afraid of loss of reputation, of being arrested, and so on. He will not do many things which he would do at once if these external restraints were removed. So you see that he is not really a man.

Now when a person is in this state—and a great many people are —they are really governed by fear of consequences. They will pretend and ever-pretend to themselves that they would not steal, for example, but as soon as they feel they can do so without being discovered they will proceed to steal in all the thousands of ways that it is possible to do so nowadays. And if all external restraints were removed, law, police, government, social opinion, etc. they would simply do exactly what they wanted. Now when a man is bound by no inner restraints, if he has any conception of God, it will be of a god of fear and violence. It is quite possible to see what is meant here. To a man bound by nothing internal, God is fear and violence. Now when the internal or essential part of a man begins to develop, his conception of God, however vague it may be, changes. It changes from the negative sign of fear and violence to the positive sign of affection or interest or valuation. The internal, essential part of a man cannot grow through fear because, when a man does a thing because he is afraid of the consequences if he does not do it, he is doing it under the compulsion of fear. The case will be quite different when he does a thing from himself.

Now what does it mean to be bound by something internal? In the first place it means that such a person will always maintain a certain integrity quite apart from outer circumstances. He will have a centre of gravity in himself. He will not completely alter his conduct when external circumstances change or when there are no legal restraints or fear of police and so on. When a man has seen the truth of something for himself and feels it emotionally, it is no longer a question of the external personality but of a deeper inner side evolving. Many people take their impression of life from what happens in life. Such people lose their hope or become cynical very easily. The Work teaches that everything simply happens in life and that life is a big factory used for cosmic reasons.

Now when a person begins to see that there is something else and begins to see for himself the meaning of it, he begins to grow internally. A person may not manifest negative emotions because of external reasons. Socially we are taught not to express negative emotions, at least in public; but once the external restraint is removed, once the fear of social criticism is temporarily absent, a man or woman will express his or her negative emotions to the full. But if we have ever thought and seen deeply enough we will realize what the Work teaches about negative emotions, we will realize the truth of this knowledge we have been taught and realize it for ourselves. It is then possible to begin to work in a quite different way. The more essential part of a person will then begin to grow.

*   *   *

Let us look briefly at the idea of evolution as taught by the Work and compare it with the modern idea of evolution. This Work, just as science, teaches that evolution exists. The difference is that the Work says that mechanical evolution does not exist save within already created types. In the case of some particular species of animals, those who are hardier will naturally or mechanically be selected and so tend to survive rather than their more weakly brethren. Also, the Work says that a particular species of animal, such as the horse, can be bred by selection by Man and so be improved. But it teaches there is no gradual mechanical turning of one species into another. A monkey does not, little by little, turn into a man any more than a sow's ear gradually, little by little, turns into a silk purse. This Earth, so low down in the scheme of creation, is subject to many influences apart from those already known such as solar radiations or cosmic radiations. All living things on this Earth, in the thin film of organic life covering its surface, were created by that level that corresponds to the Sun physically in the Ray of Creation at that point in the Octave of the Ray between *Fa* and *Mi* where a shock is necessary in order to transmit influences to the Moon. But in creating this sensitive film, this pain factory, the primary object of the Sun was to create a self-developing being. First of all, all sorts of experiments were necessary, all sorts of plans. For this reason the Work speaks of the solar laboratory. Finally, after many experiments, Man himself was created as a being capable of an inner evolution. For this reason, in esoteric psychology, Man is called a seed. As a machine he springs from a seed in the womb. All this is given to him. This is his first evolution, the result of millions of experiments. But he is capable of a further evolution, an individual evolution, through his own understanding and efforts. In every age, every epoch, every period of history, there is sown into the world esoteric teaching which gives the outlines of his further self-development.

Man is born with a great part of his brain unused, a fact which no mechanical theory of evolution by selection and immediate advantage can explain. These unused parts of the brain represent his further possibilities of individual evolution. What is he going to build up in these unused parts? What ideas? In our epoch we have had given the esoteric teaching in the Gospels indicating the direction in which individual evolution should take place at this stage. However, these teachings have been perverted and turned into something almost useless. Yet it is obvious that if people really were Christian, in the sense that Christ taught, all wars and many other evils would cease. But what Christ taught and what Christianity teaches are two quite different things.

DEEPER SELF-OBSERVATION

When the last paper was read here it was suggested by Mrs. Nicoll that people should observe their inner angry conversations and their own particular forms of self-justifying which repeat themselves continually in these deeply negative states that were spoken of in the paper. I am speaking now to those people who wish to work seriously. Mrs. Nicoll called the attention of the Group to the necessity of often writing things down—things which are the result of self-observation. I remember a long time ago that Mr. Ouspensky told us to write down the things that we observed in ourselves over a short period. He advised us however to lock the door in case anyone should come in and see what we had written. If things are written down they become clearer, for so much of our self-observation is inadequate. Incomplete self-observation is certainly inevitable at first. By writing down what we observe in ourselves we make the observation fuller. We remember more. I have advised you sometimes to keep some kind of private book in which you write down things about yourself, about the Work, about your observations.

Supposing a person writes down in such a book his or her observations of inner complaints against others as they arise day by day over a period. It is of course necessary to be sincere with oneself when one does it. That is to say, it is necessary to write down everything. If you do this you will be very much surprised when you turn the pages over and see that exactly the same things were taking place in you a year ago or a year before that, while probably all the time you have been thinking that your complaints were quite new and fresh, quite exceptional, that you may have made inner complaints once or twice in your life before but certainly nothing like every day and every year. It is observations of this kind that give us relationship to our lives lying in living time— in the fourth dimension. Now supposing that you find (I am quoting an example given here) supposing that you find that you have always complained of the same thing in everyone, however different from each other the other people may have been—i.e. you have the *same* complaint against quite *different* people—what conclusion can you draw from this observation of yourself? (I remind you again here that I am speaking only to those who wish seriously to observe themselves and work on themselves.) What conclusion can you come to? The only conclusion that you can reach is that there is something in yourself that is working all the time of which you only notice the effects or results. The fault does not lie in the other people against whom you have these continual complaints but in something in yourself that you have not observed. Now the other people may know what it is, or something of what it is, but you cannot see it yourself. But once you have realized that this reaction of yours is quite typical, and you have always had complaints in exactly the same way, it will give you a shock. It will startle you. You will see that it is this complaining itself that you have to notice in yourself and not what you imagine causes it. Next time that these complaining 'I's begin to resume their customary activity the shock that you had may just be able to give you the emotional force to observe them before they start using your mouth in your name. You will have the shock of remembering yourself. You will have a moment of being separated from these 'I's—that is, you will no longer identify with them. You will see them as something in yourself to which you have been giving full sanction and full belief all this time and which you have been justifying and so nourishing.

The Work teaches that we should struggle against self-justifying. Self-justifying means always putting oneself in the right. If a man always puts himself in the right in all circumstances he will of course never know what real suffering means. He will become negative, he will pity himself, he will seek comfort and pity from others and he will use a great deal of force in justifying all that he does. Such a man has of course no Real Conscience. When Real Conscience awakens in a man he knows what real suffering is. This only begins to happen to a man when he can bear it. The Work teaches that Real Conscience · exists in everyone and is exactly the same in everyone but that it is deeply buried. So we have to find it outside in the form of Esoteric Teaching which, when it is accepted by the understanding and lived by the Will, will begin to connect us with this Inner and Real Conscience by means of which we can know and see what everything is and its quality and use. Now if we continually justify ourselves—and who can stop it—we will always be in the right and the more our blame is pressed home on us the more, so to speak, will our pride and vanity make us, as it were, kick and scream and shut our ears and refuse to listen. I mean that, when better and more conscious 'I's in us try to speak to us in the midst of our self-justifying, we simply will not listen to them and may be very violent. They will get their chance at a later stage when our attack of sleep is beginning to pass away. Then we seem to be in quite another atmosphere, another light, which illumin- ates the mind in a quite different way. The state we were in, the 'I's under whose power we were, are at a distance now and can no longer hypnotize us. It is a very good thing in self-observation to try to remember what happened in this state, how things looked, what 'I's said what, what voices spoke, what arguments were used and so on, only you must be careful that you do not identify and re-enter the state. This can easily happen especially at first with rather chronic negative states. Indeed, it is sometimes a very interesting experiment to make with oneself to deliberately revive some sore place in the memory and observe what power it still has. As long as you are in conscious attention you are in no danger, but if for a moment your attention is distracted, as by someone coming into the room, a little later you will find all those 'I's that you revived actually in charge of you once again. That is, you have identified with the 'I's. But when you observe yourself in a

449

state of attention—and all real conscious self-observation demands inner attention—you will be in no danger of becoming identified by calling up older scenes. It is like being surrounded by a magic circle when a magician calls up spirits, but once the attention breaks you may fall into the old state once more. Different states have immense power over us when we are in them. Everyone should notice this with regard to every side of life. When we are out of them they lose their power. Usually we go round a circle of recurring states which exert power over us one by one in turn. Negative states attract other negative states to themselves and you will all have observed by now that when you are in a negative state your memory is different—the unpleasant things move up into the foreground and the pleasant things become faint and indistinct. Or again, say, the argument for a thing becomes emphasized and the argument against it becomes weak. You cannot be identified with unpleasant things and with pleasant things at the same time. In the case of 'I's, you are identified with one 'I' although you may see and hear another 'I'. Sometimes by completely relaxing, knowing that one is in a wrong state, and trying to stop all thought and movement and tension both in the muscles and in the brain, the situation is quite suddenly reversed and a better state takes its place. You suddenly feel a change of sign in yourself. Everything becomes lighter. Or it is as if you had been wearing a lot of oppressive garments and they suddenly fall away from you and you feel free again.

This stopping of thoughts and relaxing, which it is so important to practise every day, is a form of Self-Remembering. Self-observation without Self-Remembering is simply not good practice. The two things are quite distinct by inner taste and I would be glad if none of you asks questions now as to what is the difference. You can think of Self-Remembering from one standpoint as a kind of lifting oneself up from the uproar of things in oneself, or of opening a door and going into another room and shutting the door and sitting down quite quietly. Remember that when we are identified with all our thoughts and feelings, our emotions and sensations, our grievances, our inner monologues, our self-justifying, our account-making, etc. we cannot possibly remember ourselves. We are right in the thick of things, right in the noise of the traffic, right in the crowd—which is not oneself. It is a very marvellous thing to experience a moment of not being identified with oneself, with all this uproar, with all this ever-returning and useless turmoil. It is then possible to realize how we always identify ordinarily and how nothing can ever be real, nothing can ever be right when we are in this state. And we realize how true it is that help cannot reach us while we are in this ordinary state called the 2nd state of consciousness in this teaching. It is only when this quietness begins that help can reach us from the higher parts of our own centres, from higher centres themselves, which are fully developed and always working in us, but which can only reach us when we are in the 3rd state of consciousness —i.e. in some degree of Self-Remembering.

she has dominating pictures that are served all day. They are too close, too much ourselves.

The side of what we actually are, and the side of what we pretend and imagine we are, are two contradictory sides. These two contradictory sides, however, exist in everyone without exception. The action of the Work, once it is beginning to be wished for, makes us become gradually aware of this contradiction—over many years. Then we begin to have traces of real suffering—interspersed with all sorts of attempts at self-justifying and excuses and reactions—until we become, by inner taste, sick of self-justifying and excuses and so on. This marks a stage in the Work, a definite point in self-development. Here pictures weaken. For a long time the Work is something outside. One makes notes about it and draws diagrams and asks questions about words. Then it either begins to penetrate into the understanding or not. If it does, and you wish it, the Work enters oneself. Then it begins, as it were, to judge you, to point out this or that, very mildly at first, more distinctly afterwards. One tries to avoid it, of course. But, once it has penetrated oneself, by trying to avoid it one only increases one's inner difficulties, realizing that one cannot do without it and that to be deprived of its mild current of new meaning is worse than death. One realizes then what it means to be dead in the sense of the Work. This stage is easily imitated and often is. Then one talks a lot of one's difficulties, etc. Later one becomes more silent. To talk about one's difficulties is a sign that one has not understood much. But it is a necessary stage for everyone to pass. The Work is a series of stages in the understanding of it. If it does not penetrate it remains words—on the surface. Then you argue about everything. But its ideas are spermatic—that is, capable of penetrating and fertilizing the mind and feeling—otherwise it would not be Work—real teaching. It corresponds to something we have forgotten, something waiting in us, something to which we have gone to sleep long ago, something covered over by continual life. That is why this ancient teaching can awaken us. All awakening is unpleasant. One can always avoid unpleasantness by means of all the apparatus of the False Personality—by ingenious or even stupid arguing, by insincerity, by buffers, by self-justifying, by negative attitudes, by lying, by not trying to think, by resorting to pictures, by resorting to all kinds of things to keep one's sleep intact. But if the Work penetrates, this becomes more and more difficult. One begins to become aware that the Work is really saying something hard to catch and that perhaps it is quite true. This is painful. It is sometimes scarcely endurable and at the same time a very marvellous experience. It is painful to one side of us, marvellous to another side.

Of course all this will sound very strange to those who come to meetings expecting that the Work will cure their rheumatism or improve their business or help them to have a jollier time or tell them exactly what to eat and drink. I do not see how such a level of regarding the Work can lead anywhere. The whole conception is too small, too extraordinary. We are easily satisfied in this respect. We move about on the surface of things and like and dislike or love and hate, and so on, and it is all, as far as we are concerned, taken for granted. There is no sense of the strangeness of the whole business. If this is so, then certainly we are asleep and it will take a good deal of pain and unpleasantness, a good deal of startling experience, many heavy shocks, to awaken us to the beginning of our real thinking.

Life contains many natural shocks of which one is death. Being confronted with death can sometimes make us begin to think in a real way. But the torrent of the senses, and the screaming note of modern life, dulls and deafens this thinking-point, so that it rarely emerges and becomes felt. Certainly we are upset if we do not have our own way in matters that closely concern us, but this does not make us think about what and where we are, but, on the contrary, usually puts us more to sleep than ever. We again plunge into life expecting to have our desires ultimately fulfilled and regard all temporary or continual failure in this respect as very exceptional. However, all this is necessary—*until* we begin to think. Then a new situation is begun in us. *We have begun to think.* This Work is to make us think—not to think how we can get the better of someone who we feel has let us down or how to attract someone who ignores us or how to get more personal power, more attraction or more pleasure, more comfort, better position, or how to say more unpleasant things of others—no, this Work is to make us think exactly of all that side of us, through self-observation, so that we begin to see what and where we are ourselves. However, this takes a long time, and nothing is worse than to *pretend* we know already. A person who pretends to have or to know what he or she does not have or know —such a person has a picture of himself or herself. This stops everything real in every direction of development. Of all the casting out of devils mentioned in the Gospels, the casting out of pictures of oneself must surely come first, for pictures hinder every new experience and every line of inner development. We all have pictures of ourselves. Wherever they lie, there they stop development in a more real sense than a ton of concrete will prevent anything from growing beneath it. We think of the imagination as a light airy nothingness. But the imagination is very powerful—very real—like concrete. Pictures are formed out of imagination, controlled by vanity. They are fixed forms of imagination, woven by vanity. Vanity is a terrific force in us and imagination is the powerful builder and bricklayer of vanity. It builds pictures of ourselves. Then we cannot move into a new stage of ourselves, into new ideas and feelings, and experiences and meaning. Of course we do not see either our vanity or our pictures of ourselves. They are too close to us. We are them. We may see the *results* of vanity, but not it. We see the results of it when we are insulted or taken for granted. We take ourselves for granted, but do not like others to do so—a paradox at first sight, but not really so. In short, where we are vain, there we are blind to ourselves. None of us thinks he or she is vain, none of us really thinks he or form of self-remembering is the realization of one's mechanicalness. This is direct realization that one has no Will, but many wills, and no real Consciousness, but many intermittent small consciousnesses.

Now people say that they observe themselves and get to a certain point and then they cannot bear to go on and turn away from what they see. If this is genuine, they will find they will be brought again to the same point by some other route. On the other hand, if this is not genuine, if it is merely a bit of self-dramatization, they will go to sleep at this point. It seems to me that the general teaching of the influences of the Work acting on you, once you have sincerely begun to work, will always guide you if you do not interfere too much and think that you know best.

Now I will say something that is of considerable importance, I speak again to those who wish to work sincerely. Every morning, or at least every day, you must put yourself deliberately under the influence of the Work. There are Work-states and life-states in us. Now if you are in a Work-state you are, as it were, protected from a number of unpleasant states that otherwise you might very easily fall into. Sometimes when you are in a Work-state you reach momentarily this central position that I spoke about, where you have the marvellous experience of a moment of not being identified. You must put yourself, I said, into a Work-state every day. To do so you must find the best way in your own case. There is, for example, the remembering of your aim and the attempt to remember yourself at the same time. There is going over in your mind something that you have heard and read in connection with the Work. There is going over in your mind the previous day or remembering something that you have to be more conscious about in connection with another person, and above all, there is the feeling of standing in the presence of the Work and seeing things in the light of the Work. This helps very much—in fact, to an incalculable degree. But it will depend upon the quality of the effort. If you give nothing you cannot expect to get anything.

Birdlip, June 10, 1944

STAGES OF AWAKENING IN THE WORK

We are accustomed to our own smells. Now as long as we live comfortably in the thick and nauseating atmosphere of ourselves, taking everything for granted, including ourselves, we cannot awaken. Why is this so? It is because we have never begun to ask ourselves any questions as to what we are or what anything means. We simply eat and sleep, fight and quarrel, talk and hear, see and touch, move and feel. We take it all for granted, not having the slightest idea that it is distinguish his inner surroundings, for, as I have often said, we live in two environments, one revealed to us through our external senses which contains a great many people, some good and some bad, and the second an inner environment which again contains a great many people, both good and bad. This second environment we live in and when we live in the darkness we really know nothing about it. So we take it as ourselves. But through self-observation light enters and it is this light that begins to separate us. Esoteric teaching is light, but only when it is understood, valued and applied. You will get no light without this valuation. You cannot use esoteric teaching simply for personal reasons or to improve your memory or something like that. This light also begins to make many of the ideas of the Work much clearer. We cannot understand the ideas of the Work unless we work on ourselves. This is because understanding is the result of a development of knowledge and a development of being. Now your being will not change if you are completely identified with yourself. There is then no light. You are in a state of darkness. You cannot see that you have a single 'I' in you. You think that everything is "I myself". There is no light because you are identified with yourself. Then there can be no change of being. And if there is no change of being then there can be no change in your understanding of this Work. You may receive this Work as knowledge but you will not understand it. You will be unable to see anything in it at all. And this is because there is no light. When you begin to observe yourself, to catch glimpses of yourself, to notice what is going on in you, you begin to separate yourself from yourself. This lets in light. Self-observation lets in a ray of light. This light is called in the Work *Consciousness*.

The object of this Work is to increase Consciousness. We do what we do because we are not properly conscious. We are the people mentioned in the Gospels who live in darkness. One of the fundamental ideas of this teaching is that all mankind is asleep and this is why all these horrible things happen on the Earth. What is the real reason? The real reason is *absence of Consciousness*. If Man would wake up, if he would become more conscious, everything would change. First, however, he must wake up to himself; his self-consciousness, his self-awareness must enormously increase. Now if he takes himself as one this is impossible. He will remain as blind to the many different things in him as ever. In speaking about identifying, Mr. G. said that it was one of the greatest evils, one of the most terrible diseases, and that first of all a man must struggle with identifying with himself. Man, he said, possesses all sorts of illusions, all sorts of pictures about himself and with these illusions and pictures he is identified. He thinks himself one person who has Will and full Consciousness. This is identifying with oneself. It is one form of it. Now you may know all this but the point is that you still go on acting and behaving as if you had Will and full Consciousness. This is because it has not yet penetrated but lies simply in the mind as knowledge. You know it is said that the first from nothing that you observe in yourself. "Yourself" is not one thing, but composed of many, many selves. Self-observation is to observe these selves that we take so easily as "I myself". Now self-observation must not be done with identifying. You must not identify with the idea of observing yourself. It is very different from identifying with what you observe in yourself. People sometimes get very identified with some word in the Work such as 'self-remembering,' 'self-observation', 'negative emotion', 'internal considering', and so on. This prevents them from understanding what such terms might mean. If you practise self-observation in a very identified way with a kind of anxiety or exaggerated tension, straining as it were to do it, then there will be no results. You cannot do anything in this way. You cannot do anything in an over-anxious state because you are at once in wrong parts of centres. You are really working in a negative state and so failure depresses you. The practice of self-observation is done without shewing it to others and without shewing it to yourself in a certain way. I sometimes think that it is looking sideways at something—that is, going on as if one were not paying much attention to it. A great many processes taking place in the mind stop when you try to look at them too directly. This is of course specially true of the imagination. Self-observation requires a very delicate touch because the machinery that it is touching is very sensitive and delicate. Then again, you must not expect that because you have observed yourself for a comparatively short time, you will get results right away. There is a saying in the Work that we should not work for results. One reason for this is that if you work for results you get too easily disappointed and the second reason is that very often results do come but not the results that you expect. Self-observation gradually increases light. Sometimes in this Work a man's inner state is compared with darkness. Self-observation lets in a little ray of light. Now many things cease to be able to take place in the presence of light. It is merely this letting in of light that may begin to change in a person quite different things from what he or she is expecting to be changed. Sometimes we have heard it said, and it was said to me: "The light can cure you." Now I begin to understand what it means. The practice of self-observation gradually lets in more and more light, so much so that when one turns one's inner sight backwards on to one's life it is as though one saw it lit up, though still faintly, by all these moments of self-observation that lie in the past.

Now Man as a machine works better when he has some light in him. Mr. Ouspensky used to compare the centres in Man with very complicated machines of extraordinary delicacy that Man is trying to work in the dark. When he lets a little light into himself, when he begins to become more aware of himself along certain definite lines, he sees his machines better. He begins to know how to use them better and he also begins to see where they are wrongly connected and how many mistakes he made when he was working them in the dark. Now this light that a man lets in through self-observation enables him to

NON-IDENTIFYING

In reply to some questions asked on the last paper, you will remember that it was said that it was a very marvellous thing to experience a moment of not being identified. When you are in such a state you seem to live in a quiet central place in yourself although you are aware that on all sides things are trying to advance on you and seize hold of you. It is like a crowd being kept at bay by some invisible policemen. In such a state you can see what one of the main objects of self-observation is. It is to separate oneself from so much that is continually going on inside the heart and mind and laying hold of oneself continually and in fact often dragging oneself down. All this is, from another angle the "house in disorder" in us. Now we can establish in this house a certain amount of order. For this reason I wish once more to speak about what non-identifying means because I think that many of you get so far and then stick completely in understanding what it is necessary to do. So once more I will say to you that when you are trying to observe yourself you must not put the feeling of 'I' into what you observe. You are observing *It*, a machinery of emotions and thoughts, which is self-running and never still, and, if you look, you will observe an 'I' in you, a person in you. But this person is not you, although he lives with you, and feeds on you, and takes your name—i.e. your force. You will only get into a state of complete confusion if you think that you are one 'I' and think in some way that this 'I' can observe this one 'I'. People have the illusion that only one thing acts in them and feels and thinks. Having this illusion, they can form no idea what self-mastery may mean. If we suppose that there is only one thing that acts in a man then it will be impossible for one thing to command, another to obey. When the Work says that Man is compared with a "house in disorder", a house that is full of servants who are under no proper control, it means what it says. It means that there are a great many people in Man, a great many persons, all quite different, whose master is absent, who speak through the master's telephone as if in his name and just act as they please in the house that does not really belong to them but to the master. Now if one observes any part of this house in disorder and keeps on taking it as oneself, one is making a fundamental error in self-observation. One has to observe that one is many and not one. I have very often told you that this is a very difficult thing to do. I mean, it is difficult to realize it and to practise what results from the realization. At the moment it is one of the most wonderful discoveries that one can make in this Work. Now if you identify with everything you observe you will not be able to stop it, you will be continually standing in your own way, you will be continually holding on to what you should separate from.

Now listen once more: if you take yourself as one, you can separate selfish, too self-centred. A deeper sense of life is necessary—one that can eventually grasp the three lines of Work—work for and on oneself, work with and for others, and work in and for the Work itself. There is a saying in this Work that it is to transmute "lead" into "gold". This is speaking in the terms of ancient alchemical language. The subject of *real* Alchemy was Man and his inner transformation. But the Work adds that a person must already have gold to make more gold. A person must have some special understanding to start with. This is called the possession of *Magnetic Centre* which is the first sign of *different Being*. You would do well to reflect on this point and discuss it. Speaking from another side, the Work aims at the development of mechanical Man, 1, 2 and 3, into No. 4 Man—that is, Balanced Man. In this respect certain kinds of efforts are expected apart from working on oneself in the line of non-identifying, Self-Remembering, inner separation, and so on.

· I must say here once more that *Self-Remembering* is the most important thing of all and has many degrees and stages. Everyone can, to a limited degree, begin to practise and understand Self-Remembering. Full Self-Remembering is one thing, but many degrees exist in the approach to it. Obeying the Work at a critical moment is one form of Self-Remembering. But, to continue, since the goal of No. 4 Man refers to a man whose centres all have some development, so that a person is not one-sided, merely a good golfer, or merely a good scientist, or merely an artist, and so on, it is necessary to *educate* oneself. "How," said Mr. Ouspensky, on one occasion, "How can you expect to come into the possession of Great Knowledge when you have made no effort to get to know any of the ordinary knowledge that is accessible to everyone?"

Now if we divide a man's work into work on the line of his Knowledge and work on the line of his Being, it is possible to realize that work on the line of Knowledge may include not only the special Knowledge of this Work but also the ordinary knowledge in which he finds himself too much lacking—that is, knowledge of all kinds. This demands normal effort, but efforts of this kind are necessary. Sometimes people enter this Work with really hardly any ordinary knowledge. They then have no means of comparing the special knowledge of this Work with ordinary knowledge. They have no power of judgment and so take what they are taught as if it were just ordinary knowledge. They have nothing ready to receive. This is a great difficulty because, having no power of contrasting, they take this Work as ordinary knowledge, which means that it falls on ordinary parts of centres, just as the arithmetic table might or a talk on ways to cook eggs, or make hydrogen from water, or find a square root. The more you study ordinary knowledge the more you will see how all that the Work teaches is *extra*ordinary knowledge and how it rises over the ideas of ordinary knowledge which are all disconnected. But by filling rolls in centres through the effort of getting to know what can be known, the whole machine is made stronger and the breadth of the mind is increased. I repeat that you cannot do this Work from a too narrow basis, emotional or intellectual. Again, ordinary knowledge sometimes nourishes the Work directly, as when one can see connections and illustrations, and sometimes indirectly, by shewing us how it is wrongly understood. In the Work, *everything* can become useful—once the Work has begun to penetrate into one's mind and will and being, and no longer merely lies in the memory. Then "all life becomes your teacher," as G. once said.

Birdlip, June 24, 1944

PICTURES AND IMAGINATION

I

We spoke last time of imagination and pictures of oneself. It was said that as long as pictures of oneself are dominant no change of oneself is possible in that direction. The reason is simple enough and need scarcely be explained. If you have a picture of yourself as being a person who never tells a lie, then naturally you will never notice that you lie. Your picture of yourself as being the kind of person who never lies will satisfy you however much you actually lie. Now here is something that has to become a personal experience as regards the practical psychology taught in this Work. You have to experience yourself in a new way. Nevertheless this teaching about pictures is little understood, even in theory. One reason is that people do not realize that they have pictures of themselves and that they live by their means a great part of their lives. Pictures are formed out of the powerful force of imagination and govern us all and can replace the actual by the imagined. As you know, imagination can easily satisfy the centres. We should all know something of this by now. It is not merely that we have imaginary pictures of ourselves, but we have them of others as well. And this is why it seems to us often that the Work is brutal. Some older philosophers have asked whether everything is not imagination. The Work says that the human family is hypnotized and asleep through the power of imagination, but that there are things in us that are not imagination. The curious thing is that much that the world thinks is imagination is not, and vice versa, from the standpoint of the Work. For example, many think that this Work and all esoteric ideas are imagination and that the aims and affairs of life certainly are real. So people live in this century of abnormal war and wonder why it is all as it is. Can we see that all is as it is because the human family is asleep and all the horrors are done by people who are asleep?

I remember Mr. Ouspensky once saying in connection with this idea of the Work that several writers have tried to express it, dimly realizing the situation, and he mentioned the early work of Wells, called "In the Days of the Comet". This phantasy, as the critics called it, speaks of a cloud that passed over the earth and made everyone awaken so that people all suddenly asked themselves what on earth they were all doing—they were at war at the time. It was regarded as an amusing idea.

Pictures of ourselves are formed from imagination and keep us asleep. Everyone has a certain number of pictures that take charge of him or her, blinding people to themselves, making them believe that they are what they are not. This is the action of a picture. All of us live mostly in pictures of ourselves. Now in studying any one thing in oneself from the Work angle, we should connect it with the main teachings of this Work. Suppose that you think the idea that Mankind is asleep is all nonsense, then you will never be able to see the pictures of yourself that dominate you. You will never be able to accept the idea that you are largely imagination, largely imaginary, and that the modicum of what is real in you is very small. In order to understand better, more deeply, we must continually realize and re-realize our position on this earth, where so much that is obviously evil and certainly unnecessary continually takes place and will continuously take place unless we awaken. The Work says we are *kept asleep* because we are part of a substance called Organic Life which covers the earth as a living smear or sensitive film and whose function is to transmit force from the higher part of the Ray of Creation to the lower part—like a wireless receiver. We come at a place where a *shock* is necessary in the cosmic creation. Yet we are actually created to get free from our bondage on earth. So we have a double function, and a double view of everything is possible. Man is kept asleep—but can awaken. In order to keep Mankind asleep so that it serves nature something must be done. A parable exists in the Work in which it is said that Man was deliberately hypnotized—that is, acted upon through his imagination—to keep him in bondage. Otherwise he would have escaped long ago from bondage —before other factors were fulfilled—that is, before a general evolution of the lower parts of the Ray had taken place. I often think this explains very much in our inner feelings. We are between two fires, as it were. The explanation of everything is double.

I will remind you again of this Work-Parable, as it were, related by Mr. Ouspensky, on the basis of what G. said. It describes our situation on Earth. We are the sheep in what follows:

"There is an Eastern tale which speaks of a very rich magician who had a great many sheep. But at the same time this magician was very mean. He did not want to hire shepherds, nor did he want to erect a fence about the pasture where his sheep were grazing. The sheep consequently often wandered into the forest, fell into ravines, and so on, and above all they ran away, for they knew that the magician wanted their flesh and skins, and this they did not like. At last the magician found a remedy. He *hypnotized* his sheep

459

and suggested to them first of all that they were immortal, and that no harm was being done to them when they were skinned, that, on the contrary, it would be very good for them and even pleasant; secondly he suggested that the magician was a *good master* who loved his flock so much that he was ready to do anything in the world for them; and in the third place he suggested to them that if anything at all were going to happen to them, it was not going to happen just then, at any rate not that day, and therefore they had no need to think about it. Further the magician suggested to his sheep that they were not sheep at all; to some he suggested that they were *lions*, to others that they were *eagles*, to others that they were *men*, to others that they were *magicians*. And after this, all cares and worries about the sheep came to an end. They never ran away again, but quietly waited the time when the magician would require their flesh and skins."

Starting from this big scale we can begin to study this hypnotism in ourselves as particular examples. You will agree that, starting from this big scale, we cannot expect to be able to see quite easily how imagination works upon us. Something very powerful, in other words, is behind our small personal forms of imagination and our pictures of ourselves—something very powerful indeed and not to be treated lightly. A terrific fight is necessary before this power of imagination can be loosened, and a great deal of thought and trial and experiment and failure and quietness and patience.

Now let us try to get some superficial idea of what 'pictures of oneself' mean. You see a person walking along looking rather important, smiling a little, nodding, suddenly bending down to smell a flower, gazing round to see if anyone is watching, and so on. This person is in the power of a picture. Or again, you see a person striding along, looking serious, frowning, ignoring others, sombre, as if supporting the Universe. This person is in the power of a picture. Or you see a person doing as it were his best not to be a gentleman, a hail-fellow-well-met person, who laughs at everyone who has some gentlemanly picture. This person is equally in the power of a picture. Pictures of every kind exist. You can have a picture of yourself as a good democrat, or a Tory, or a gentleman, or a revolutionary Republican, or a tough guy, or an aristocrat, and so on. They are all pictures: they are all imagination. Behind all these pictures the real person stands, but the real person never stands in his or her pictures. A question was once asked: "Are pictures of oneself not sometimes real, true?" The answer was: "*No—never.*" If you have a picture of yourself as a tough guy you are not one, and vice versa. I have often thought about this and I advise you to do so. What is genuine and what is imaginary can never meet. They are two different orders of experience on different planes —and how long we take even to begin to see what depth of meaning lies here. The imaginary man and the real man are as different as the imaginary woman and the real woman. We live, however, chiefly in imagination, and meet *via* imagination, and a very exhausting nuisance it is, for everyone concerned. However, it all happens in the only way it can, because we do not see these pictures that govern us and interfere with everything. Only being conscious can alter mechanicalness. The destruction of pictures is not possible unless something else has begun to form itself behind them that we can hold on to. This comes from long and conscious self-observation which on one side is debunking oneself or 'seeing through' oneself into something rather odd and strange lying behind. I fancy pictures may change a little according to one's age, but their power remains. Now people often say, and sometimes emphatically, "Well, granted I have pictures of myself, what ought I to be?" This is certainly a question that shews a wrong approach. *If* you can begin to see a picture, *if* you become conscious of it, *if* you begin to dislike it, *if* you try to get away from it, to separate from its hypnotic power, *if* you begin to see you are not at all like that picture but invented, then the change that results will be exactly what you need. You will fit into what has always been waiting for you, and what you went out of long ago as a child. Let me remind you that so much of the Work consists in getting rid of things, of stopping things, of *not-doing*. For instance, if you have some well-developed systems of negative emotion or depression in you, it is useless to say: "Well, what should I *do* instead?" It is necessary to see and continually separate from the hypnotic power of these well-developed systems of negative emotion. You may be sure that something else will gradually take their place, if you clear away the dirt. You may feel *new feelings* that you could not have imagined. But the task is that the dirt must be cleared away to expose the new. That is where practical work on oneself lies. It is not a question of " What should I do?" but "What should I not do?" It is the other way round—at least, in the main. One exception, and the greatest of all, is that one must try to remember oneself—at least once a day, and deliberately. To give ourselves this shock, the First Conscious Shock, is a thing we can try to *do*. It is possible. But we have no time. There is always the roar of things, the torrent of thoughts and worries. There is always something to worry about. Yet Self-Remembering is not going against the flood-stream of inner and outer things. It is raising oneself—not contending. Contending is another kind of effort. Self-Remembering is a non-identifying with oneself—for an instant—as if one were merely acting and had forgotten. When one remembers oneself one forgets oneself. One is no longer in a picture. However it is possible to form a picture of oneself remembering oneself. Just notice here how you work and what is the quality of your effort.

To return to pictures: occasionally pictures are in abeyance and something odd and strange emerges. I remember it was said of someone "she is very nice when she forgets herself". It is often said that a person is nice when "you get her alone." Men sometimes relax. They are no longer in uniform. These uniforms, these dresses that we wear, belong to the side of pictures. "I am at least married," or, say, "I am

461

at least respectable": these phrases belong to the picture of oneself as being a particular sort of person, having a label. "I am an educated man," "I am an educated woman," and so on, or say, "I am of ancient family," or "I am a self-made man": all these phrases belong to this picture of oneself just as do the phrases "I am a wronged person," or "I am a genius."

Owing to the multiplicity of one's being it is very difficult to know, to feel, what one is. This is because (1) we have lost touch with Essence and (2) because Essence is not developed. It is a great labour to feel or know even the beginning of oneself. It takes a long time—this discovery of oneself. But it is always different from what one imagined. People lead all sorts of invented lives owing to pictures. We dress ourselves in pictures which often to others are laughable—but not to ourselves. It is sometimes extraordinary to notice a person active in some picture. One wonders why the person cannot see the picture. This is very simple. What is not simple is to see that you yourself are a picture. Pictures are formed from what you have read at an impressionable age. Novels of a period often form the pictures of a generation, either in one way or in the opposite way by reaction. One identifies with the hero or heroine or one tries to be different. The stage also contributes to pictures. I remember behaving like Lewis Waller for a week until it was forcibly pointed out to me. Films give rise to obvious pictures often in quite nice people. They begin to look, speak, in another way. All this is hypnotism. However, it is more deeply due to the lack of any real centre of gravity in ourselves which renders us easily hypnotized.

Now we forget the source of origin of our pictures and after a time are unaware we have pictures of ourselves. We no longer see imitations. We have no gold—nothing real. *Gold is something not acted on.* This happens perhaps more often to-day than formerly. Modern science renders hypnotism more easy by means of films and the radio, etc. People imitate others and form pictures of themselves being like what they are not. But actually this has always happened in all ages—but I fancy the means of hypnotism are more numerous to-day. Quite simple uninvented people are hard to find in modern life. Everyone must needs be something he is not. Yet you must remember that all this goes back to the "hypnotizing force acting on Mankind" which made Mankind imagine they were eagles, lions, magicians, etc. and so it has probably always been much the same. G. used to say that things were always much the same in all ages—that is, the general balance of things.

I have often been interested in the remark "I am a man who respects himself." This has given me many thoughts, even before I met this Work. However, it is a picture. Which self? I can understand a man respecting his Work "I"s but not himself. If we possessed real self-knowledge and if we began to come into the feeling of "Real I", I suppose we would never make any statement about the kind of people we are. Real Being makes no statements about itself. It *is*. To *be* is not to imagine. It is what it *is*. However, having no Real I we have to make shift first and to keep up some pictures—such as that we are ideally happy and so on. Unfortunately we never see these pictures. They make us behave as we do. They act us. We do not act them. This is not a misfortune as long as we are not dissatisfied with ourselves and begin to desire some definite knowledge that can make our existence more real. People are satisfied by their pictures of themselves. A thick dark dull atmosphere is produced as a result but a very ordinary one. It is possible to dislike it and wish to come into a greater sincerity and more light. But this is not necessary for life—for cosmic purposes. We strut about satisfied. Really we can expect nothing but what happens to us, under such circumstances, and there is nothing further to be said. There is your food, there is your money, there is your position, there is your job, there is your motor-car, and there are your pictures. It is all quite simple. But it has nothing to do with age-old esoteric psychology. It has nothing to do with the Work and the efforts it demands. You are encased in jelly. But this "jelly" of life is hypnotism. One is transfixed in self-illusion. It is really a tragedy. Why is it a tragedy? Because all the time we are not doing anything actually belonging to us, we are not being anything we can be, we are not in the right place in our sense of ourselves—and so we are eventually discarded as useless experiments in self-evolution. Is this too harsh a statement? I think not, for first we must fulfil the function of a *Good Householder*. That is a definite and real possibility. Why? Because a self-satisfied person will say: "Why on earth should I alter my viewpoints, my thoughts, my outlook, my standards, once I have become a reasonably "Good Householder", a reasonably responsible and educated person?" Certainly. I often wonder why anyone should. Why leave Egypt and go out into the wilderness? If pictures of oneself are very strong, very profound, and so very much identified with, the idea is sheer nonsense. "Do you not know who I am?" This is a summation of all pictures of oneself. Yes, we all say this after a certain degree of insult. All the same, it is a tragedy. We crystallize out long before it is necessary. We keep on driving about in the carriage of our picture. We never discover ourselves. Is not this a tragedy? Instead we cling to and fasten on to our pictures of ourselves. I am quite certain that it is a tragedy. It is hypnotism. Do you think that when the Work says we are deliberately hypnotized on this Earth it means nothing? Why, if you begin to see pictures in yourself and to see how you have been identified with them all your life then you will know that *you yourself* have been actually hypnotized and shared in the general hypnotism. But to see how you yourself have suffered is exceptionally difficult. It is of course obvious that everyone else is suffering from hypnotism— and that therefore everyone else is rather a fool or silly. But not oneself. No one thinks he is a fool. What you really think is this: "I am a lion, a genius, or an eagle, a remarkable, a fine person, an exceptional person, not in this particular and common way but in that subtle, unnoticed way, a violet not yet disclosed, a person not yet grasped and, in fact, a person who should never have been born into this soulless world". Yes, we all have such delicate false pictures without exception, but do not notice them. They furnish us with a great deal of satisfaction until there arise in us, when we begin to awaken, very powerful contrary forces that for a long time we cannot understand—that is, because we still cling to those ideas of ourselves, or that sense of ourselves, that are derived from our not realized pictures. Let the forces of growth and evolution act on you and if you have not yet seen at all what stands in their way, you naturally suffer unnecessarily. You do not see what they are at in you, as long as you are accepting your pictures and not seeing them. But if you have begun the laborious task of removing your sense and meaning of yourself from these rather cheap pictures of yourself, these forces become infinitely full of meaning. Naturally, one cannot change if one clings to what one is. However this is what we do for many years—until at last we know that a turning-point has been reached.

Birdlip, July 1, 1944

THE PARABLE OF THE HORSE, CARRIAGE AND DRIVER

One of the many ways in which the Work illustrates the position of Man is found in the Parable of the Horse, Carriage and Driver. In this parable or correspondence, Man in his ordinary state is compared with a horse, carriage and driver in the following way. As Man is, according to this parable, the driver who should be on the box and control the horse and carriage is drinking in a "public house" and spending nearly all his money there. The driver is not on the box because he is drunk and as a result the horse gets little or no food and is in a bad condition and the carriage is in a bad state and needs repairs. The first thing that is necessary is that the driver should wake up from his sleep and begin to think of his situation. Have you ever thought what the public house is and what the drink is and what the drunkenness is?

Now supposing he does awaken to a certain extent and leaves his pictures and his illusions about himself a little and begins to think of his situation. He must leave the public house and then he will begin to see the condition of the horse and carriage. The horse is starving, the carriage in very bad condition. He notices that the horse is not properly harnessed to the carriage and that there are no reins between the horse and the box—that is, nothing to communicate between the driver and the horse.

Let us take only this part of the parable—viz. that there are no reins. Obviously it would be useless for the driver to get on the box unless the reins were present. Perhaps you know by now that you have no reins between the Intellectual Centre and the Emotional Centre. In this parable the horse represents the Emotional Centre and the driver represents the mind. There is no proper connection between the thoughts and the emotions. We may mentally think and decide to behave in a certain way for instance, not to lose our temper, but when the actual situation arises we find our thoughts have no control of our feelings—that is, no control of the horse. In the parable this means we have no reins between the driver and the horse—I am assuming the driver is on the box. Is it not true that we decide mentally that we will not allow ourselves to behave in a certain way and fail? For what usually happens? We cannot control the horse. The horse behaves independently of what the mind has decided upon. You may, for instance, decide to be very brave in the presence of danger. A bomb bursts and you find yourself unable to control the horse. You begin to shake all over and so on. This is because there are no reins connecting the driver with the horse. *The trouble is that the driver and the horse speak different languages.* The horse —that is, the Emotional Centre—does not understand the words of the driver—that is, Intellectual Centre. I remember how often G. used to speak of the reins—that is, the way of connecting the driver with the horse. What language does the Emotional Centre use? It uses the language of visual imagery. The Emotional Centre does not know any intellectual words or theories, but it understands visual images. For instance, if you are in danger and feel nervous, and you meet a man who is visibly quiet, it helps the horse—that is, the Emotional Centre. The calm man is a visual image and this affects the horse and calms him. From one side, then, the Emotional Centre is governed through the language of visual imagery. How can the driver connect with Emotional Centre? You understand, it is not enough to have thoughts alone because the Emotional Centre or horse does not understand those thoughts which usually take the form of words. I mean that ordinary thinking takes the form of language, words, such as "I will be brave" or "I will not mind what he or she says." So you begin to see that these reins that connect the driver with the horse are interesting things, and the reason why G. used often to talk of them. Now suppose you are up against some situation that can easily make you negative. You say to yourself "I will not be negative" or "I will not react to this situation", and you may use many phrases like that in the mind—that is, the driver —and yet when the situation arises the horse gets out of control. I remember G. saying on one occasion in France: "Yes, driver he know, horse he not know. Horse he not understand. He not understand what driver says." That is to say, there are no reins passing from the driver to the horse. The driver does not know how to control the horse. He thinks he can control it himself by arranging his thoughts in a certain way. The horse does not know this language. It does not receive the

465

messages. *In fact, the horse does not know the decisions of the driver.* And if the driver knows nothing about the horse and how to approach the horse and tell it things, then he is exactly as if he is in the position of a person on the box who has no reins to control the horse. How can the horse understand the language of the driver? Whether the driver speaks and thinks in English or in French or in German or Hindustani, the horse does not know any such verbal language or thought. I suppose all of you have noticed this—that you have no reins between your thoughts and your feelings. I was talking to someone the other day who has been in the Work a long time, and this person said it was so interesting to think of these reins that connect the driver and horse, and how obvious it was from self-observation that there was no connection. And this remark reminded me of many things said in the past. It also reminded me how easily we accept some parable of the Work, some teaching, and never think deeply of what it means. I would like to remind you what has been said many times in the past that the Work is seeing more and more deeply what has already been heard. People understand the Work superficially, for instance, that you must observe your negative emotions, but what a long time it takes to do this. All development, all inner evolution, depends on the seeing more deeply what we at present see on the surface. So people hear about this horse, carriage and driver and also hear there are no reins between the driver and the horse, and just take it as a statement. People may say, for example: "Why, don't you know the parable of the horse, carriage and driver already? Don't you know there are no reins?" Yes, but have you ever thought what it means?

Now you must understand that we are not talking about the *waking up of the driver* in this conversation. I am talking about the driver who has wakened up a little and is no longer in the public house. I am speaking of people who have got a little beyond sleep, vanity and pictures of themselves, people who have seen through a little of their False Personality, people who have begun to see that they are not in the least like what they thought they were. What does this mean, this first stage of waking up from drunkenness? After a time in this Work it is possible to see the people who are faster asleep than you are, people who are more drunk than you are—drunk with their own importance, their own negative states, drunk with the idea that they can do everything, etc. As I said, I am not talking of such people, for it is quite obvious that as long as a man or a woman thinks that there is nothing wrong with himself or herself and that they are going to take this Work as something added to themselves as they are, they will remain drunk in the public house. Of course, they will never think they are in a public house in a drunken condition. On the contrary they will have wonderful ideas of themselves, namely, that they have Will, that they can do, that they are efficient, that they know best, that they have a real permanent 'I' and all the rest of it. Unless they have wakened up from these profound illusions and have begun to feel their own helplessness and nothingness, they will never be able to climb on the box. We are speaking of people who have wakened up a little and are trying to sit on the box and control the horse, and are not still completely drunk in the public house.

Now let us reflect for a moment on one meaning of the connecting reins between the driver and the horse. I suppose each one of us who has gone far enough in the Work begins to know a little of this connection. But I must assure you all that it is no good for me to try to tell you *exactly* what this connection is. You all know this type of question: "Will you tell me *exactly* what the reins are?" It is often said that we have to pay for Great Knowledge by long work. When I meet a person who understands this and does not ask me: "What exactly does Self-Remembering mean? What exactly is self-observation? What exactly is this Work about?" I know he has begun to wake up from his drunken sleep in life—that is, in the public house. Then I know that this person is waking up from this terrible hypnotism that plays on mankind. Here then we have somebody who is emerging from the public house, perhaps not very steady on his feet, but possibly capable of looking at his horse and carriage. He may climb up to the box and fall off (as we all do) and yet there is some understanding that this is what we have to do. And I can assure you that if you have reached this point you are in the Work. Of course, you often go back to the public house. Often you get so far on the box and fall off again, but you have already got an idea of what this Work is about. And I would add, do not mind if you fall off the box very often, so long as you have something more in you that knows you are off the box and a real wish to get back. It is here that you have to work against negative emotions of a certain kind. The reins are not made between the driver and the horse—or rather only wrong reins are made mechanically. They are not made in the first and second states of consciousness. The first state is actual sleep, the second state is the so-called waking state. To establish a right connection between the Intellectual Centre and the Emotional Centre—that is, between the driver and the horse—you must be able, to however limited an extent, to remember yourself and be in attention.

Now why does a parable exist? Why is the teaching in the Gospels in the form of parables? It is visual imagery. The horse understands visual language, the driver words, and the parable connects the two. Visual imagery is a universal language. It is the language of signs. The horse only understands a universal language of visual images. That is why, if you wish to control the horse from the mind, you must visualize and not merely think. One of the things we are taught in this Work is visualization. You must visualize what you have thought of in regard to your behaviour to any particular person. That is, you must take that person into your visualization. To visualize a person is a form of external considering, in the deepest sense. (I would say visualizing another as yourself, visualizing his or her individual troubles as if you yourself were that person, is the beginning of making reins between the

467

driver and the horse, and this really means visualizing the other person eventually). You cannot visualize a person in the right way if you are negative towards the person. You have heard that the Emotional Centre is clairvoyant when it is purified of negative emotions. Now you cannot visualize another person if you are doing it from duty. I would advise you very strongly not to attempt it. Visualization is a very quiet activity, a very quiet process. As a rule you only get a quarter of the way and give it up. You can only visualize another person rightly when you know something about yourself. We become human to one another when we know ourselves. An exercise was given to us to visualize one another and to say to the person visualized: " What is your trouble?" and if rightly done it was said that the person would tell you. That is, the image would speak to you. I can only say that I know this is possible but very difficult. The purification of the Emotional Centre is one of the tasks in the Work. We have to handle one another far more gently internally than externally. Many things, some illnesses, headaches, sudden loss of force, begin to happen to us at a certain stage of the Work if we treat *one another* wrongly. The Work is a very pure thing and depends on inner purity. You all understand what it means to be pure by now. What is meant by purity? Purity is sincerity. I was much amused the other day to hear someone had talked very badly about the Work about which I was told and then I was told that this person was furious with the person who told me about it. Is this purity? So when you try to visualize someone else, and it takes time to do so and is certainly not worth doing if you are not pure in this sense, you must remember that the whole of the Work comes in at this point. You can help one another, but not without the Work behind you. This visualization is the connection between the Intellectual Centre and the Emotional Centre and if you have an aim to behave rightly towards somebody, you must visualize yourself behaving rightly, and not merely think it. It is remarkable that a little pure visualization helps everyone and yourself. Merely thinking does not help enough, but is necessary. Mere talking is worse than anything, because by talking you are so often justifying yourself. You know how often you say: "Well, I am going to do my best to help him and I promise you I won't say anything unpleasant." And then what happens? Well, observe it in yourself. You have merely fed your imagination and your vanity and done nothing to help the situation. You know when a cat rubs himself against your leg he is caressing not you but himself. Visualization is *directed imagination*, not a self-pleasurable imagination.

FURTHER NOTES ON MEANING

Reflect for a moment on the *world of meaning* in which you live—in which all people really live. What is meaning for you? You want food, say, or you wish to get some appointment or to see someone. All this is meaning—different meanings in the world of meaning. Now is this meaning tangible or visible? I do not see how you can say that meaning can be touched with the organs of sense or seen by the eye or heard or smelt or tasted. For example, money has meaning to everyone. But is the meaning of money touchable or seeable? It is surely not an object of any of the senses. As an object of the senses it can take any form— paper, silver, gold, scrip, or just credit—but the meaning *remains* the same quite apart from the visible form. It is necessary to point this out as people often take an object and its meaning as identical. *Meaning* is not the same as the seen object or the object of the senses, as this particular external world of things which we are wired into by our present sense-machines, this particular variety show with its ever-repeating programme.

Now you notice how meaning waxes and wanes. The object does not alter but its meaning alters. You get sick of a thing and then later think it is not so bad and return to it. All this happens in the *world of meaning*, not in the external world of the senses. You see that when it is said that we live really in a psychical world, in an invisible world, and we are really invisible to one another, it is not an exaggeration. If you observe in yourself the changes of meaning, you may come to the conclusion that the visible object and its meaning are different things.

Now once a person can separate, in himself or herself, what might be termed "meaning" from "object", that person begins to understand this Work. This Work is not about external objects, but about meaning and what gives you *meaning* in regard to them. We all live in a world of meaning, and we are all *deeply* ill in this world of meaning. How are we all deeply ill in this private *world of meaning*? Do you catch what is meant here? How much "illness" is due to wrong connections of meaning and has nothing to do with the external object, the person. Well, I could write about this for a long time. But unless you begin to understand that every external object is a question of the meaning you project into it, unless you see what is meant, I think it is a vain task. The object and the meaning of it to you are two different things. This is the first separation, I would say. The revival of former meaning, or the deliberate bringing into a present event other meaning apart from the meaning the event has for you mechanically, constitutes one of the fundamental ideas of the Work on its practical side. This is *effort* about meaning, not about the external event. Efforts are not external things, like taking long walks or giving up smoking, etc. Work-efforts are inner efforts in regard to oneself, and the way one takes life and its ever-

apparently nothing can fill at the moment. When you feel you have been betrayed by a friend you feel undermined. But to feel you have been betrayed by yourself is worse.

The self-love shuts out certain things and opens the door to others. It includes the circle of one's ordinary life, of people who on the whole do not disagree with or criticize one, the family, the pride in house, children and friends, the daily personal interests, business interests, one's possessions, and so on. Now we are told that there is a development of the Emotional Centre possible which is called the "Emotional Centre awakening". The development is one that goes beyond self-love and has to do with the feeling of our nothingness. Ask yourself this question: What different kinds of love have you observed in yourself? Are they all the same? You love food, you love comfort, possessions, children, you love being praised, you love money, you love power, you love going to the theatre, you love dress, you love smoking, you love hearing scandal, you love getting the better of someone else, you love scheming, you love your dog, you love being a success, you love chocolate, you love—well, what? These loves, however moderate, are varieties of self-love. They all lead to oneself as the spokes of the wheel to the centrepiece. One can feel very startled when one realizes that it is always this thing called *oneself* that is being comforted, exalted, titivated, soothed, flattered, satisfied, and that when it is not, it begins to whimper, like a baby. And it is always this odd restless thing that is being offended, upset, negative, indignant, downcast. Cast down from what? From its centrepoint of self-love. How often have you perhaps by now come near to hating this "oneself" and all its tiresome intrigues and insincerities and lying complications and crude ambitions and rivalries and account-making, and all the ways in which it ruins every thing and turns all good situations into dust. Yes, one can hate its falsities. But what do we find? We find it seems impossible to get rid of it. We seem fastened to it. We react to its influences continually. It has so many tricks, so many pretences and deceptions, that we simply cannot deal with it. We are just too late. But new emotions can catch it in time. You remember that the speed of emotions is greater than that of thoughts. In short, we cannot deal with it without the help of something else. Let us glance at some things said in the Scriptures. A great deal is said about hating. Let us begin with what is said in one place about "living in malice and envy, hateful, and hating one another." (*Tit.* III 3.) This is the usual state of self-love. It is inevitable, for at bottom the self-love is against everything that does not feed it. A person may include others within the area of the self-love so that it looks like disinterested love of others. But it is not so. Or a person may delude himself in a thousand ways, for the self-love is very clever and hides its true form. The point is that the self-love can only feel against others, fundamentally because it cannot love anything beyond itself. It is pointing in one way only—to oneself. Whatever devious paths it traces, it leads to the same central place. It is *self* love; it is *self* liking;

it is *self* interest; it is *self* everything. It sits down in its centre and gathers everything round it and whispers to everything. Have you ever noticed it doing this? When you do then you may *begin* to "hate yourself." Now some things said in Scripture refer to "hating oneself". This is going against self-love. Sometimes people say they hate themselves. You may be sure this is a pretence—a subtle picture—that they imagine is real. But imagination is never real and the False Personality, based on self-love, is composed of the powerful substance called imagination. We are told somewhere in Scripture that unless a man hates himself he cannot understand the teaching of Christ. We are also told, in a strange manner, that a man must hate father, and brethren. Christ said : "If any man cometh unto me, and hateth not his own father, and mother, and wife and children and brethren, and sisters, yea, and his own life also, he cannot be my disciple." In the Greek, the word translated "one's own life" means "soul" or "psyche". For example, the phrase "to lay down one's life for one's friends" should be translated "to go against one's own soul for the sake of one's friends." We can understand that going against one's soul is equivalent to going against one's self-love and that to hate one's life is to hate this oneself that is formed and controlled by the self-love. We can conceive the soul at our level as a point of intense self-love through which we are made to identify most powerfully. When it is interfered with, we hate. It is curious to notice that hate is the opposite to self-love and that we do not understand love as a positive emotion—that is, as one to which there is no opposite and so no inner contradictions. It would be another matter if the opposite to self-love were self-hate. Again, we might conceive that the opposite to love is self-hate. But love, as was just said, as a positive emotion has no opposite and attracts no contrary to it, having everything in itself as one. It is a union of opposites, a third thing that we do not know because we swing from one side to the other on the pendulum.

When, through the practice of uncritical self-observation over long periods, photographs begin to be taken of typical aspects of yourself —and they come suddenly, like a plate being developed, being suddenly formed by a great many separate observations running together into connection to form one photograph—then uneasiness or dislike of oneself can begin. Now there is danger here unless the Work is followed. It is a mistake to think there are no instructions in the Work or that in any case they have no significance. You will learn otherwise and learn by experience how and why you must follow instructions and think them out alone. For instance, if this dislike of yourself is genuine and not another fashion and it becomes negative through self-pity, it is dangerous. It has slipped into the wrong place and got mixed up. And again, if you still take yourself as *one*, it is dangerous. We have got to realize that we are not one. It is essential for the eventual action of the Work. We must realize it daily. Otherwise we stand in the way of everything. We stand in the way of ourselves. The Work cannot act on you, if that is the case. It cannot alter or take away anything from your room, so to speak, because you shout: "Hi, that's mine." Also you cannot get to certain emotions that come from beyond the zone of self-love, if you take yourself as one. One of the first of the many subtle strokes against the self-love that the Work gives is the idea that we are not *one* but *many*—and, in fact, that there is no Real 'I'. This is not flattering to the self-love. Of course, the further idea that one is mechanical is such a stroke against the self-love that it can scarcely be agreed to by anyone. And to say we are all asleep and not yet conscious is intolerable to the self-love. You may be sure it will defend itself and tell you the whole thing is nonsense. That is, it will, like Pharaoh, continue its rule and will not let you go free. Something else in you, apart from the self-love, has to see the truth of such ideas. And if there were no emotions possible beyond those belonging to the self-love this would not be possible and so no development would be possible. It is upon the appearance of these other and new emotions and their gradual strengthening, that development depends, and this is when *being* changes.

Birdlip, July 15, 1944

COMMENTARIES ON SELF-LOVE

II

Let us form some image of the self-love. It has a broad base and a narrow apex. It can be diagrammatically thought of as a triangle:

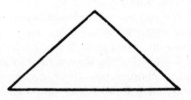

The base of this triangle is the extent of the self-love. As it grows from its base into life and others it narrows until it is a point. In these commentaries on "Self-Love" I suggest that this triangle can represent the rapidly narrowing interests that extend from the broad self-interests of the self-love. In matters a little further away from us we are less and less interested. We care nothing for anything far away—for other people, other countries. Nor do we care about any ideas about this world we are in, or the cosmos, or anything so remote. "What," we say, "What on earth has it got to do with me?"

474

Let us draw a similar triangle but the other way up and superimpose them:

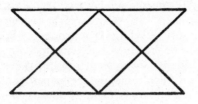

This symbol is very ancient. Like any symbol it contains many meanings. G. once said that "symbolism should act as a shock to our knowledge" and spoke of four kinds—Hebrew, Egyptian, Persian and Hindoo. The symbol with which we are dealing here belongs to the Hebrew symbolism and is called the Seal of Solomon. It represents the interpenetration of two things or two media or principles of levels. Notice that one triangle ends as a mere point in the other where apex and base meet and that there is a lozenge-shaped intermediate area where both mingle, and four corner areas where there is no mingling of the two. If one triangle were cut out of blue glass and the other out of yellow then there would be two blue and two yellow areas and a middle green area where the colours mingled.

Now let us suppose that the triangle with its breadth above and its apical point below represents some principle which runs counter to that of the triangle of self-love whose breadth is below and apical point above. And let us understand that the symbol represents a universal interpenetration of a lower by a higher principle in everything (save at the cosmic level of the Moon). The recognition that there are two orders, or principles, or forces, or influences, acting on life is the characteristic feature of *magnetic centre*. You remember that magnetic centre is that discerning power in us of distinguishing between A and B influences. We need not here explain all this again. A influences are created by life and they obviously have connection with the self-love—love of power, possessions, and so on. But there also exist unusual and really inexplicable influences, and also curious sides of history and strange examples of things that have no connection with business interests, and so on. The quite marvellous things that survive in our culture, that have clearly no connection with small self-interests, are a visible expression of some other kinds of influences that have been felt and expressed by those having magnetic centre and more, and translated into architecture, painting, poetry, literature, sculpture, sainthood, teaching, chivalry, and so on, which are unconnected with immediate personal greed or private advantage. Unless this wonderful wave of force, this extraordinary light, had been transmitted in a thousand ways, we would be nothing but barbarians—that is, we would have no idea of anything beyond the self-love and its greed and narrowness.

It is true to say that a person may recognize all this theoretically without seeing his or her own condition in this respect. One object of self-observation is to become aware of one's motives. This is not a nice and easy process. Ask yourself sometimes: "Why am I doing this?" or "Why am I saying this?" or "Why am I behaving in this way?" or "Why am I writing this?" Whatever imaginary robes of self-righteousness we clothe ourselves in, these questions tend to undress us again. In this respect we should understand that the Work is rather terrible and cannot be denied. People imagine they can pretend. It is impossible. Only what is real can remain. When we have gone more deeply into self-observation and self-knowledge, we simply have to give up a lot of the manifestations of the self-love, disguised as something genuine. Do you remember what was said of the Work in Revelation: "All the churches shall know that I am he that searcheth the reins and hearts: and I will give unto each one of you according to your works." (*Rev.* II 23).

The object of this Work is to separate us from what is false. I once told you that when my wife and I went to the French Institute we were warned that "Personality here has almost no right to exist." But the more the self-love, the less can it happen. What a long journey it is. Yet it is a quite real one. It exists. It is not invention. Esoteric teaching is not an imaginary thing. It is the most real thing in the world—more real than a cheque, more real than a house, more real than another person. So we are speaking at present about a deeper honesty to oneself, a deeper sincerity, that has nothing to do with the requirements of life.

Now we must return to this upper triangle which is upside down to the triangle of self-love—that is, life. If you are certain that this life is all, and if you take your meanings from it, and think only in terms of it, then there is no upper triangle at work in you. We spoke recently of meaning and how a visible thing is one thing and its meaning is another and how, if you could not see this, there could be no inner work of separation and transformation. We can transform life by new meaning. We cannot transform people and things whose existence is revealed to us by our senses. But we have inner senses. The mind is the first transformer. Thinking in a new way, our attitudes change and so the meaning of the world changes. But to think in a new way, we must receive and acknowledge new knowledge, new ideas. It is really quite simple, but the enormous difficulties that arise in us before we can do so do not make it quite as simple as all that. We are so fixed, so identified with our opinions, and so on, that it is really a very great labour. Do you remember the allegory or parable about the labours of Hercules? One of his tasks was to cleanse the Augean stables which were full of dung. What is dung in the meaning of parables? All your negative emotions, all your petty view-points, your personal values, your self-love, and so on. Hercules diverted a *river* to cleanse the stables and cleanse the horses of the mind. Water means truth, as you know. The Work teaches truth. Truth about what? Truth about what ways, what ideas, what efforts, are necessary to this change of being, that we, I think, all of us, secretly long for, in the background of ourselves. This means that esoteric truth, esoteric knowledge, can cleanse us from this continual, inadequate, uneasy and half-guilty feeling that probably all normal people possess. And a normal person in the Work means a person with magnetic centre. *Normal* being means that. If you are content with yourself, then it is far better to remain so. The work will only upset you and do harm to you. This is one of the difficulties that has to be thought of, in connection with other people. A good householder in the ordinary sense is a person who does his job properly and decently. But in the strict Work sense he is a person who does his job without believing it leads anywhere and yet sees his responsibilities, and fulfils them. He has not yet got magnetic centre but is close to it. He does his job and sees that he must but realizes vaguely that it leads nowhere and does not yet realize there is something else. I do not mean that he denies there is anything else.

This way, the Way of Good Householder, is a definite line of ascending Being by Recurrence, only, we are told, it is a very long way. There is no sense of an upper triangle, only a dissatisfaction with the lower triangle. However this is at least genuine. It is infinitely better than pretending, from hearsay, from pseudo-attitudes, that you know about the upper triangle when actually you are dressed up in the clothes and ribbons of the lower triangle. The most terrible crime in this Work is pretending—because it means lack of sincerity and the Work is based on sincerity and if you have not a very deep and sincere relation to the Work itself, from yourself, great dangers may result if you pretend. This is why it is important to think of people whom you wish to touch this Work. It is a live-wire, a million-volt circuit. I speak of what it is ultimately—not in its introductory stages. I remember G. saying once to us all in France: "Why are you here?" This made us all think. Why were we there? Could I say to myself deeply I was there in order not to lose touch with the Work, or was all vanity—the lower triangle—or what? It was certainly not financial advantage, but I found then many things in myself that were spurious. This is an example of a shock, given at a certain moment rightly.

Now let us speak of the upper triangle, which is reverse to the lower in principle, in motive, direction, feeling and thought, attitude and aim. The upper triangle is the Work. It is the influences that come from the level of the Sun psychologically, that is, the level of the Conscious Circle of Humanity. This seems vague. Well, try and see for yourself. Does it change people? The upper triangle is *esotericism*. It is thinking in an utterly different way. It is new meaning, new ways of taking everything that happens on this Earth with all its recurring events as we see them through the senses. It is a sky, fitted over the Earth of ourselves. It demands a love quite different from self-love. In fact, it is against this thing "oneself" and it demands a struggle with this thing "oneself". It seeks to start up this struggle in each of us. Every idea of this Work, of the esoteric teaching of the Old and New Testaments, and a vast number of other sources and fragments, is about this. It always goes against the self-love. It does not make you feel more comfortable. Not at all. It makes you first uneasy and then definitely uncomfortable inwardly—but with direction. All this goes against the complacency of the self-love—of this person you dream you are and which you are not, of this brittle life-mask of yourself. If you never apply the Work, if you never observe yourself through the teaching of the Work, if you never judge yourself from the Work, you remain as you are. A spark is necessary. It is necessary to catch fire. It is necessary to see we are in the presence of something real—yes, real, but finely made, and very gentle, very delicate, and beautiful. When new emotions begin, they catch and transmit the Work. They are caused by the thoughts and private ponderings on this Work. If you do not really need this Work, nothing really will or can happen. How could it? And how many people really need the Work? I repeat the question: "Why are you here?" Do you remember what is said in Hebrews:

"For the word of God is living, and active, and sharper than any two-edged sword, and piercing even to the dividing of soul and spirit, of both joints and marrow, and quick to discern the thoughts and intents of the heart. And there is no creature that is not manifest in his sight: but all things are naked and laid open before the eyes of him with whom we have to do."   (*Heb.* IV 12, 13).

As was said, these two triangles in reverse, this Hebrew symbol called the Seal of Solomon, belonging of course to the esoteric and not the literal side of Hebraism, transmits to us the teaching that there is always an upper level acting on the lower level. But this does not mean that the lower level receives it. The same idea is contained in the Work when it says that higher centres are fully developed and constantly working and lower centres cannot catch their meaning. If we could at any moment cease to identify with ourselves, cease to follow the influences of the lower triangle, we might receive influences from the upper triangle, but for a long time we would not understand them. The entirely new thoughts, the entirely new feelings, would not be recognized, or they would seem mere nonsense. When a man has magnetic centre, when his level of being is characterized by this fact, he already has some sense of this triangle. But if he is entirely immersed, entirely identified with the lower triangle—i.e. with everything belonging to his self-love, his self-interest, everything of his senses, everything literal—he is entirely insensitive to the upper triangle and seeks to interpret life in terms of itself. For him there is nothing.

INTRODUCTORY NOTE TO PAPER ON WILL

To-night I wish to talk to you about Will and what Will means. In order to talk about Will rightly it is necessary to talk first about influences coming down the Ray of Creation. You have heard already that one of the objects of this Work is to put us under new influences by means of certain work on ourselves, certain efforts. If there were no new influences to connect with there would be no point in this Work. As you know, the Ray of Creation shews different influences which come down from the top of the Ray. Let us study these influences for a moment. (I have often given people the task of drawing these influences in the form of a diagram.)

As you know, the Will of the Absolute does not reach the earth. The Will of the Absolute in passing down the Ray of Creation reaches us indirectly through an increasing number of mechanical laws or forces, which is one reason why it is said in the Lord's Prayer: "May Thy Will be done on Earth." This means simply that the Word of God is not done on Earth. However, the object of all real esotericism is to connect Man with the Will of God and to break him from his own self-will. If one does this Work from a good spirit, if one tries to work on oneself as regards non-identifying, non-internal considering, etc., if one tries to remember oneself in the sense of the Work, knowing from its diagrams that there is something higher that one can touch, then it is possible to speak of what Will means. Will consists in feeling finer influences and finer influences reaching us from a higher level as forces coming down the Ray of Creation. If you feel your self-love and self-interests you will not feel the presence of any other kind of influences.

You will perhaps see that this paper tonight about Will is connected with the two previous papers, one of which is about new meaning and one about self-love. From self-love, of course, we only have self-will with all its interesting forms of imagination. We dream, for example, of having power, of everyone being our slaves, for instance, and so on. This kind of cruelty cannot possibly give any relationship to higher influences coming down the Ray of Creation.

As you know, in this Fourth Way people must be in life and must begin to know what life is like by experience. A person in this Work who has not been through the influences and experience that life offers on this Earth is not necessarily ready for it. Here a double thing comes in. On the one side there is feeling that there is something else—that is, if a person has Magnetic Centre. On the other side there is a feeling of lack of life-experience. That is why it is so difficult in this Work to see whether a person should be more in life or more in the Work. I think that most of us by now understand this. But the point is that, unless we put ourselves under the influences that we know, and learn from these influences, we cannot get to new influences. Unless you have been to the primary school you cannot possibly enter the secondary school. The idea of the Work is to be able to connect with new influences, and the Ray of Creation shews how these influences exist. These different levels of forces, these different levels of influences, are like further schools of meaning and thought and feeling and ultimately of action. When the Work-influences begin to act on you you will find what was full of meaning becomes either more full of meaning or less full. The highest school that we can belong to on this Earth is the Solar School, the school that sounds the note *Sol*. The intermediary school is the Planetary School, the note that sounds in the Side Octave the note *Si*. The school on Earth tells of the Side Octave from the Sun and sounds the three notes *La, Sol, Fa*: that means that we are all on this Earth meeting one another in the schools *La, Sol or Fa*. Unless there were this Side Octave there would be no chance of development of any kind—by "development" we all imagine something that is quite impossible, quite contrary to what development means. Look at what the Work teaches about negative emotions, non identifying and False Personality: going against these influences means rising in the Ray of Creation. All esotericism teaches that in order to go up you have to go down, and no one understands what this means: to get more you must go down and to get less you go in the same way as you always go—your Being transmits your life. If you have nothing that at present satisfies you completely, it is because of the state of your Being, and you will never get what you want as long as your Being is tuned in to that wave-length. You have to change yourself to get new influences, and changing yourself is always "getting rid of yourself". If you want to have Will you must always have Will about, as it were, what you are not, not from what you are. If you try to increase yourself as you are you will only become worse than you are at present. The development of Real Will consists of feeling new influences.

Birdlip, July 22, 1944

COMMENTARY ON WILL

I

Let us speak tonight of what the Work teaches about Will. It says that such will as we have is the resultant of all our desires, and also that each 'I' has its own will. In order to keep one's aim Will is required. Let us suppose a person makes a small aim such as not to walk in a hurry or something of that order. For a short time he manages to keep his aim. But next moment he hurries as before and for weeks forgets what he decided. Or say, a person makes a small aim to keep a pleasant expression on his or her face and does so for a time. Then dinner is served and the face assumes its ordinary expressions.

How can we increase Will? Let us take the example of a person who makes a bigger aim than those mentioned. He or she wishes not to identify with a particular recurring negative emotion. One way is to think about what external considering means here and then to try to practise it in reference to the source of the negative state. The self-love, however, does not wish to externally consider. It does not bother about people in far worse situations than we are in ourselves and so feels a right to be negative when it chooses. Nothing is easier than to bear the misfortunes of others. One of the vows in the original Buddhist Schools was to have compassion for all others. But it is curious to reflect on the connection between external considering and increase of Will. I mean, it is curious to begin to see on what Real Will depends, for obviously Real Will is not *self*-will. One may imagine Will means having one's own way. Yet this is not the case. But I will not speak more on this aspect of the development of Will, because the Work itself will shew you where the connection lies. It is useless to hear and not to experience, to be told and not to practise. In fact, being told prevents experience. If a man is told something about himself that he is not within miles of yet experiencing for himself, it only hinders him. He says: "I am told I am negative" or "I am told I am greedy." The Work acts on Being according to our understanding of it—our level. Nothing can take the place of understanding. Being told is not the same as seeing. We are told all day long by kind friends. Now when people agree with us we feel reinforced in our ordinary will, and vice versa. If we decide to do something and people approve or praise us, we feel as if we had more force, but if they disagree, we feel deprived of energy. Here lies a turning-point. Of course, all sorts of complicated personal reactions take place under such circumstances. But we very rarely make aims or decisions that do not depend to some extent on the support of someone or other or possibly the public, or the press, and so on. This is aim made in public. A decision, an aim, made in solitariness seems unreal, thin, without colour, uninteresting. This means that we do things usually with some admixture of "being seen of men". We do not do our alms in secret. In making an aim and in thinking about Real Will and its quality and taste it is always worth while reading the 6th chapter of Matthew in its opening verses. Here are some very deep formulations about wrong aim and will. Will made from False Personality, however, is interesting to study. It fails, of course, but that does not mean it is necessarily wholly wrong. But it has no soil, no depth. As an aim descends in depth it changes. It becomes more essential. It becomes an aim without words—a wordless thing—a direction one seeks to go in, rather than a phrase. Yet it must start with some kind of phrase, some sort of word-command, some formulation.

On one occasion I had a conversation with Mr. O. about Will in the Work-sense. I said that it was possible to see how from one moment to another what we call our Will changes and this was due to the separate wills of different 'I's so that whatever we did finally was the resultant of the desires of all these different 'I's. "Yes," he said, "But people must see this first. People do not realize it. They feel they have Will." I asked him: "Is it possible to describe what Real Will is like?" He said: "It is like suddenly seeing the solution to a mathematical problem." This reply eventually gave me insight into some things that I had not understood. Usually we associate the concept of Will with a set jaw, a dogged resolve, etc. This is a negative view of Will. The idea that Real Will is something positive is eventually of great value in personal work. Ordinarily we think of Will as something negative because we conceive it only as being exerted against something. We say often, for example, that we will resist this or we will not do that. We tend to associate Will with resistance to something, like brakes to stop something. This is a negative idea of Will and it has its place. But you will see that Mr. O. refers to a different idea of Will. It is something that finds right solutions. It unites separate things, it arranges in right order, and so creates something new. It contains the idea of new *possibilities*. It is not mere denial, mere negation, mere stopping of everything, but the reaching to a new combination, or a new attainment. It has to do with the certainty that a solution *is possible*, and with a certain kind of active patience towards the at-present unsolved situation, where one does not as yet see the next connection. I say a certain kind of active patience because it has nothing to do with resignation. Very often Mr. O. used to say to us in our difficulties: "The Work will find a way." This is the patience required. Often enough we feel confused, especially after a shock. It seems that everything is scattered, in little bits, without relation, particularly when we have been asleep for a long time and working only in imagination. Now if we lose our orientation to the Work, things can indeed break up. What does Will mean in such a case? A mathematician who has culled a lot of facts and cannot see how they are connected to get as certain a solution as possible is in the same situation. Suppose, however, he is actively patient. G. once said that "patience is the Mother of Will". There *is* some solution. There *is* some possibility. The confidence of a mathematician is based on his feeling that relations between physical things are expressible in terms of mathematical formulae and that some sort of solution for a mass of scattered observations can be found eventually. It is the same with the Work. It has meaning, or rather, out of every situation it is possible to get meaning. Things apparently diverse can be brought into some unity of meaning. It is like asking and waiting.

Now change of meaning must mean change from former ruling meaning. So we can connect the positive idea of Will with the attaining of new meaning and not merely with negation and deprivation. When a mathematician suddenly sees a solution he sees new meaning. It was to this that Mr. O. compared Will. When we begin to realize that Will is delight rather than privation we begin to realize what aim might mean—as something worth attaining. First we all have to make aim that is negative. We understand no aim otherwise at first. It has often been said in the teaching of the Work that negative things breed only negative things. We are very fond of this negative garden and collect and re-sow its seeds and bulbs with care. Its atmosphere is bad and we catch a lot of illness while walking about in it.

The centre of gravity of the Will is in the Emotional Centre—this centre that it is the object of the Work to awaken and which works so badly in us as we are at present. Let us put up the Three-Storey House of Man once more and write in each storey the function chiefly connected with it:

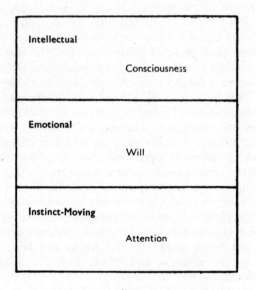

| Intellectual |
| Consciousness |
| Emotional |
| Will |
| Instinct-Moving |
| Attention |

We have been speaking recently on new meaning and new emotions. Will is connected mainly with the Emotional Centre. It is from the development of this centre that Will begins. To return to what I said earlier, our ordinary concept of Will is a set jaw, a stern resolve, and so on. Actually, it is a new emotion, a new insight, very quiet and without violence. To have, speaking in a relative way, a new Will in any familiar situation is to have a new emotion entering this familiar situation. I mean that it is one way in which one can begin to think of Will. It has many sides. Again, as was said, it is a unity of things rather than a splitting-up, a synthesis rather than an analysis.

The next idea about Real Will, already touched on, is that it is infinitely flexible. If you live on the causal plane of life, the level of cause in the past and effect in the future, you will have that kind of will derived from the past. Why? Because in Time a cause always seems to be in the past. Yet causes can be in the future. This is an odd and strange idea. Everything you build up in yourself by work becomes a transforming cause *in the future*. To live mechanically on the level of cause and effect is one thing that we have to notice to know about. Here nothing can happen save that the past gives rise to a mechanical effect in the future. One must know a great deal about this aspect of life—this possible viewpoint. If there were no Mercy of God it would work out as inevitable. Yet even Science, which was based on the study of cause and effect, has reached that point at which it says that things are not determined, but *casual*. (Casual is not causal). To regard one's life as nothing but *causal* is not to grasp the idea that everyone can come into *new* casual influences, by Self-Remembering. Otherwise, there would be only "Truth" and no "Mercy". This idea is expressed in religious literature as "forgiveness of sins". But if you feel there is nothing else than literal cause and effect, it is really impossible to transform life. All transformation depends on the idea that you can be under one set or another set of influences. And the Ray of Creation teaches that there are many orders of influences. Now *Will* is a question of new emotions, new thoughts, new feelings, and its quality depends on transmitting them, hearing them. On one scale of influences things look like this—by the cause and effect of that level of influences. But it is possible to see everything in a new light. Then the whole series of cause and effect in your life takes on a new meaning. But if you believe that life is just as you see it, then new orientation does not visit you. That is one of the central teachings in the Gospels, in the fragments of Christ's teaching. Is there not a great deal said about the forgiveness of sins, the forgiveness of your neighbour and so on? And why? One has to see that on one plane, one level of living, there can be only mechanical cause and effect—the level of cause and effect belonging to it. But the Gospels and this Work teach that—*if you do this Work*—there is a totally different line of cause and effect, and a transforming force enters your existence.

I will continue later to speak of what *Will* in the Work-sense means. You will realize that it is a very great subject. But it depends on getting under influences higher than oneself. Will is not self-will. Read the Gospels and read what Christ says in his temptation. Whose Will was he following? *To will the Work* is an easy phrase. To see what it means is another question. I remember once that Mr. O. said that before you can have Will in a real sense you must feel your own nothingness—that is, the nothingness of your own personal and vanity-aims. He was asked: "How can you feel your own nothingness?" He said: "Apart from many other things, there is one way: *"Like what you dislike."* Is it not strange that Real Will depends on going in a direction that has nothing to do with one's own wishes?

COMMENTARY ON WILL

II

Let us continue the commentaries on what Will is from the Work point of view. It is necessary to recapitulate a little. We have at present, the Work teaches, only the diverse wills of many different 'I's. We have no real, no permanent and steady Will. First of all, each 'I' uses us at the moment and so each 'I' speaks through the telephone—that is, through our mouth—and says all sorts of things and calls itself 'I'. If there is any doubt, any hesitation, what speaks is the resultant of the several wills of these different 'I's. This resultant decides. It is called Will but it is not Real Will. It is a compromise between many different voices, like a Parliament (which means a Speaking-House). The final vote is the resultant of many different parties. It is the resultant of many different wills and desires. This is the state of what we call our will. It is the resultant of many wills, many different desires. But Real Will cannot be a *resultant*, for Will in a real sense is *Master* and is above the desires of life and all life-'I's.

On one occasion G. was speaking of aim. He asked people round him what was their aim. People said different things—such as that they wished always to be happy or to do good to others and so on. Someone said: "I wish for self-mastery." G. said at once that this was a real aim. "This", he said in so many words, "is something the Work is about. This I can teach you if you are willing to go through all the difficulties that must be overcome to attain it. Real Will is possible because it exists in Man. It is Master. But Man is cut off from it."

Master —Real 'I'—Real Will
|
Steward
|
Deputy-Steward
|
The many 'I's of Personality

Now you have heard that Master will not come until the Horse, Carriage and Driver are in a proper state and relation. The Driver must emerge from the inn and eventually get on the box. This is the first step. Let us think once more of this first step. The Work teaches that it is impossible for the Master—that is, Real 'I'—to come unless certain conditions are fulfilled. The first condition is that the Driver, wasting his money in the public-house—that is, in dreams and illusions and pictures of himself, and especially in imagining he is master of himself—wakes up and begins to see what he (or she) is really like. This shock requires a special force. I mean, people can even enter this Work and yet remain for years in the public-house *dreaming* and pretending they are working. They merely add this Work, like an extra cockade, to their dreams of themselves. However, no one can use the Work in that way for long. In the full swell of Personality, one may imagine one can strut about with an extra adornment or use the Work in some other way. The Work, however, is rather ancient and well-versed, and no one can possibly deceive it. But to understand this, it is necessary to realize there is something higher than oneself. This Work comes from what is higher. If a person has no inner relation to the Work and cannot see it, or sense or feel it, in himself or herself, as the beginning of Real Conscience—that is, Work Conscience—then, naturally enough, there may be a wrong contact. This is always dangerous if the force of the Work is withdrawn. Things may suddenly collapse, being founded on the sands of False Personality. I say this tonight because of the subject on which these commentaries are being made. Real Will—that is, *Master*—comes from *above*, not from life and its level of interests. If you have no above in you, in your thought and outlook, there is no chance of touching either Real Conscience or Real 'I'. That is, one merely fails in the real purpose of having been created on this Earth. One is no good—useless—so much chaff to be burned, as the Gospels say.

Let us examine once more the ideas taught by the Work on this question of *Master*, which is Real Will—that is, Real 'I'. You understand why G. was interested at once in the remark: "I wish to have self-mastery." Self-mastery, from the Work-teaching, means having *Master* in you, and this is only possible if Driver, Horse and Carriage have been put in some right condition. Then—as the Work says—then the Driver, sitting on the box, with the reins in his hands, with the right harness and so on, may, on looking round, find the Master sitting in the carriage. But he must, so I once heard, start driving himself in the way he thinks best. He must *start* driving before he can expect any directions from the Master. Let us see where Master comes from—that is, Real 'I'—which we all lack, and keep on inventing in so many unsatisfactory ways. If one really knew, if one really felt, if one really saw where to go—would it not be wonderful? Real 'I' comes *down from above*, as the diagram shews. That is why it was mentioned that if you have no idea of anything above yourself, you cannot reach your reality and meaning —that is, Real 'I'. You will always be an invented figure, now trying on this suit or dress and now trying on that one. Inside you will be uneasy. If you have a well-trained façade, you will spend a lot of money painting it and re-stuccoing it and, so to speak, sailing out into life each day as fresh as possible and quite empty inside. This Work is not about that kind of thing. It is about finding where and what you are. It is about opening connections which have been lost. You can say, if you like, that it is about finding oneself, but not exactly in money or position

486

or in successful affairs and so on. I wonder if some of you see what is meant? The inventions, the pseudo-yourselves, etc. are many. It takes a long time to get underneath them and separate from them. It is not really a "long time". Why? Because it is really not a question of time but a question of sincerity with oneself. One may profess the Work and talk very badly of it. Is this sincerity with oneself? This branch of the Work suffers severely from this kind of lip-service. It is just as well that I stress it at this moment because, as was said, if you touch this Work up to a point and are really insincere to it in yourself, it can become very dangerous. It may kill you, as G. once said. I must confess I am still astonished by the inner insincerity of people who profess this Work.

Now what does inner sincerity mean in connection with reaching Real 'I'—that is, Real Will? Can you see any connection yourself? Suppose you are not sincere with yourself and are always pretending and imitating sincerity and have none in yourself. Can you possibly reach anything? Suppose you take the Work as a temporary convenience. Can it lead anywhere? Of course not. Yes, but why? Have you reflected on this yet? Have you seen for yourselves that you can get nowhere in this Work save through inner observation and inner sincerity? It is strange that this has to be said. It is still strange to me, after many years, that people think they can belong to this Work without working, or think that they can belong to the Work by pretending to work, which is worse. I still cannot quite take it in, and certainly I do not understand people of that sort and cannot grasp what they mean. However, this is a useless thing to speak of. Either it is so, or it is not so. A certain purity of feeling is necessary and if it is not there, then it is not, and if it is, then it is. Otherwise everything becomes argument. One sees, or one does not see. One feels, or one does not feel. One understands something, or one does not understand anything. Something is planted, or it is not planted. Something grows, or it does not grow. There is no argument possible. It either is, or it is not. It is either worth while, or it is not worth while. One either wants it, or does not want it. One either values it, or does not value it. There is no argument. Persuasion is useless. A *persuaded* person is worse than useless, to himself or to herself or to the Work. It is possible to "buy" a person for a time, but not necessarily a good thing. One cannot ransom another, if there is no Magnetic Centre; if there is not, then there is no Magnetic Centre. If it is all really nonsense to the person inwardly, it is all nonsense, and it is no good—and actually evil—to pretend it is not nonsense, when your inner side sincerely thinks it is. That is the situation. I mean, as has been said from the beginning of this teaching, that inner sincerity towards it is the only thing that counts, no matter how you fail, however badly you do. To pretend, to imagine you can act as if you believed, is of all dangerous things the worst. The Work says that to pretend is the worst thing possible to do, the most deadly thing in its ultimate effects. Pretending is lying. Lying in this sense destroys Essence. Essence can only grow through truth, through what is sincere. If essence is destroyed everything is destroyed except nervous excitement.

The Driver must awaken before the Master—that is, Real Will—is felt as a guiding force. This Work is a guide. The phantasies of oneself, the pictures, the ideas, the valuations, the various senses of superiority and all the stuffing we stuff ourselves up with, all must begin to weaken under this guidance. By what means? By uncritical and remembered self-observation. Something then awakens and emerges. It eventually climbs on the box. A tiny thing. Yes, a very tiny thing, a very little man, a very small woman. But it emerges from the uproar of the public-house—that is, life and one's ideas of life and of oneself in life—and this tiny thing begins to move in the direction of the box and tries to sit on it. No doubt it cannot for long, but it really wishes to. This is the point. If it really wishes to, then this tiny thing, this grain of mustard-seed, can attract a trace of Real 'I'. Now Real 'I', as said, comes down *from above*, but only when there is something to come down to. Let us speak of Real Will again in connection with the feeling that there is something above, something higher than oneself—something beyond the level of one's inordinate and usually undetected self-love, self-will, self-liking, self-admiration, and self-exertions, beyond one's vanity and self-prejudices, beyond one's selfishness, beyond one's self. All Work leads in this direction. All esoteric teaching leads in this strange direction. It is called a desert.

What does it mean—this direction, this journey *through oneself* and all the false 'I's in oneself? After a time in this Work it is necessary to look every day at the whole matter of the Work and at what it is saying. For such a long time we lie prone on the ground beneath Jacob's Ladder. What does it mean to get up? It is to get out of the public-house. Jacob lies asleep at the bottom of the ladder. Yes, but what does it mean to get up? There is a very curious series of inner mental actions that lead us to get up. Have you ever had real private thoughts—thoughts that have nothing to do with outside matters, with passing examinations, with putting up your daily show? Have you ever really thought—quite deep down—thought what it is all about and who you are and so on? It is here, at this level, that the Work begins and that Real Will begins. It is very difficult to describe. Such thoughts are not about duty or about other people or about keeping up your idea of yourself or power or money or anything like that. This kind of thought is very strange. One of the remarkable things about this indefinable kind of thought is that it easily understands the ideas of the Work. It seems, in fact, to be the Work itself. When you get away from yourself, you can reach this level of thought. But, of course, for the time being, you do not really exist. You are nothing. It is not strange that here, at this level, you can find and see what Real Will might mean—and that you can realize that ordinary will, as it is called, is by comparison a lie and simply nonsense. In this state of thought and inner perception you can even detect what it is you really need to do—which is always surprising, always something you could never have thought of yourself. And you then can know for certain that it is not self-will. But if there is no sense of the Work, no affirmation of anything higher, no belief in influences coming down from the Ray of Creation—well, how can you expect to get even one single taste of what Real Will is? How, if you deny an unknown, can you ever expect to feel what you have as yet never known? Do you not know everything already? One is a small opera, a short play, always repeating. There are other larger operas, other longer plays. Yes, but who really feels this and acts on it? Who really feels deeply that he or she does not know? Who realizes his or her ignorance? One *knows* surely? Is that not so with every one of you here? Well, then, there is no room for anything else to enter in. One knows—already. One knows—everything. How do you think and move? Do you know? Just look and observe yourselves. You all act and think and judge as if you *know* already. The more you *know*, the less you know. Is this right? Of course—but have you seen both sides like that? When you feel you *do not know*, you feel deprived of Personality. That is why we have to learn what it means not to be negative in the face of a possible new stage of understanding. You will never get to a new level if you are going to feel negative when your present level is attacked and diminished in self-importance. *Will*, in the Work-sense, comes from a level above the level one is at, and so is above all self-will and self-importance. Will is a higher influence acting on you and responded to by you if you can sense it. But how, if you are sure you *know* already, can you give room for anything new? It is our *knowing* like that that stops the first entry of new Will. Change *knowing* and you may feel something entering that is new and often strange—provided you do not get negative. That is letting go. People often say that they do not know, and that they are ignorant. But do you think they mean it? Do you really think you do not know? Don't you see that all your judgements and inner ways of taking your problems in life are based on the idea that *you do know*? And so, as a consequence, from this mess of wrong acquired knowledge, we live and condemn and quarrel and kill and argue and speak. All that is your *machine* and have you noticed that most machines seem created for unhappiness? We are told to study our machines. Have you yet begun to separate from yourself, from your machine? How, if not, can you expect any taste of Real Will, of Master? Why, there is no room for him. You *know* already, don't you? You chatter away and criticize all day—as if you *knew*. You do not yet notice that you do not know—that you really have not yet the faintest idea and that you are talking nonsense and lying all day. No—but why? Because there is no self-noticing, no inner sincerity, no pain with oneself, about this thing to which one is bound as to a huge machine of turning wheels of thought and feeling. How then can Real *Will* visit one, when one is so identified with all this machinery and keeps on saying that it is 'I' and that it knows, and keeps on feeling one knows and keeps on acting as if one knew? Catch yourself at the moment of saying something. Is a dissolving of Personality necessary? Yes, certainly—a dissolving of False Personality and all its imagination and illusion. This the Work teaches. A realization of one's mechanicalness is necessary. This the Work teaches. This is already a form of Self-Remembering. Will, Real Will, can find this level, the Third Level of Consciousness. Then one feels a new taste, something very extraordinary, something delicate, vitalizing, full of meaning—not something harsh and negative and denying—as we think Will is. How can we expect to reach such Will if we do not take hold of the Work and work? If we identify with everything in ourselves, if we think we are already conscious and have Real Will already, if we think we know and can do, if we believe we are one, if we live contentedly in negative emotions, if we always make accounts, if we ascribe to ourselves a hundred and one qualities that are purely imaginary, if we justify ourselves all day long, if we never observe ourselves, if we never remember ourselves—and so on and on—then what can we expect? Have you noticed what the Work is about and is always saying?

Real will comes from above, from a higher level. What does higher mean? Where we see one thing at our level, at a higher level a million things exist. We imagine Will as inflexible but we have to conceive that Real Will is infinitely flexible and discerning and ultimately contains all things and so has direction towards fullness. This was called in the Gospels πλήρωμα—fullness of all meaning. However, I will try to explain it in this way: Real Will is full of new meaning. It is not the absence of things, the negation and denial of doing things. Its real nature does not consists in the words: "I will not". "I will understand more" is a better formulation. You know the sterility of people who always *will not*. They seem to die in themselves early owing to this negative idea of will that conducts no new meaning. Negative things can only conduct negative things.

In connection with the idea that Real Will is increasingly fuller meaning and so is positive and not negative in quality, we can bring into the thought-associations of tonight another idea of the Work. The Work-ideas are to establish new associations and so new ways of seeing and feeling life. The idea that can be brought in here is that of *inner octaves*. Let us take two notes *Do* and *Re*. Between them a whole octave exists, namely,

$$\text{Do} — — — — — — — — —\text{Re}$$
do re mi fa sol la si do

And again, between each of the notes of the small octave a whole octave exists. Now how is it possible to understand what is meant by this? What is meant is increasingly finer and finer perceptions, increasingly finer seeing of differences. Where one saw simply *Do—Re*, one now sees a whole octave of finer differences and so on. And this means seeing finer and finer meanings. We imagine we know ourselves, or others.

490

This is, as it were, *Do—Re* on a coarse scale. But in order to develop these finer perceptions and so to lose the violence of *Do—Re* on a coarser scale, a willingness to accept the Work and its ideas is required as a starting-point. Then by this first real willing, the Work—that is, your own higher centres—can begin to teach you. So Real Will must first be made possible by accepting the way to it. If you do not will the Work, you begin wrongly. There are many meanings to every single thing. To see a thing only and always in one light is like seeing *Do—Re* on the coarse scale—as we do in terms of buffers and prejudices. A thing is either right or wrong. There is no real thought. But things are more complicated than that. Differentiation—that is, seeing many differences where one saw none, or where one saw only opposites, is the beginning of the growth of *Will*. We can handle ourselves very roughly, as well as one another, by lack of inner perception. Mr. O. once, when speaking of aim and Will, said that at first it is as if we looked across a valley at night, and saw a distant light which we wished to reach. And off we went, thinking it all quite simple. But between this distant light and ourselves lies the whole valley and many other smaller lights and many winding roads. When you think of what good-will means, say, to the Work or to another person, you realize perhaps that it can easily be self-will. Realizing this, you begin to see that Real Will means great meaning and great understanding and great flexibility and a great amount of going against *what you thought best*. This requires that active patience that the Work demands and which becomes so easy to understand once you cease to have illusions about your self and your knowledge and your right judgments and all the rest of the lies that we try to live by. Patience of this sort is called in the Work the *Mother of Will*.

Now let us try to gather together some of the things said in this paper. People are often fond of "doing things" as they say. This they call will. They like arranging things and so on—doing things "on purpose", as they say. This may certainly be right on that scale. But it so often happens that they miss what is being done for them or do not see what is lying to hand, before their very eyes. They go along one straight line and think it is manifesting Will. On a small scale it is, no doubt. But can you all see that it is possible to miss so much by sticking to one narrow line of self-will and mistaking it for Real Will. It is, of course, self-will—having your own way, being efficient, being first, and so on. But Real Will is different. It is, in taste, very gentle. When you reflect that external considering is realizing the existence of other people and seeing their difficulties, from the realization of your own, and acting accordingly (if you can), then you will understand why I said in the previous paper that Real Will and external considering are closely connected. To see another apart from what *you* want to see and do, is to take in new impressions. To take in new impressions is to have an increase of meaning—actually, a new octave of force. To solve a problem apart from self-will, apart from having your own way, to see a solution from a new intake of meaning—this is one of the ideas of Will in the Work. To repeat: "What," I asked Mr. O. "is Real Will like?" He answered: "It is like seeing the solution to a difficult mathematical problem." That means, it is a force that draws things together into an enlargement of meaning. Recollect that in higher centres there are no opposites, no contradictions. Try to imagine what it would be like to feel the influences of higher centres—in which there are no opposites, no contradictions. Then think of the level of will that we think is Will—that is, self-will. Does it produce opposites on every side? The whole of the Work, the whole pondering and feeling of esoteric teaching, leads to Real Will—that is, *Master*. So you will perhaps see in a practical way that unless you will this Work from good-will nothing can happen in the attainment of Master. This is why I have emphasized so much the question of inner sincerity to the Work. This is why the Work-octave begins with evaluation of the ideas of the Work and why it starts from the level of Being of a man who has Magnetic Centre. This is the first sign of special Being.

Birdlip, August 5, 1944

INTRODUCTORY NOTE
TO COMMENTARY ON WILL (III)

Before the paper is read, I would like to remind you that ideas have a real existence. What are the most powerful forces acting, say, at present? Ideas—and the clash of ideas. Now the ideas of the Work are such that if you have something in you that can receive them, they begin to act on you. Modern psychology does not teach the difference between certain ideas, nor does it understand the reality of ideas. Ancient and mediaeval psychology, as Mr. Ouspensky said, understood better. But certain ideas require long preparation for right contact—including the *idea* of Master, or Real 'I', or Real Will. First, a definite teaching, a definite knowledge, is required and must be studied. Every idea is a delicate machine liable to act wrongly if it is wrongly handled, as, say, by False Personality. Unskilled handling of an idea may result in an explosion. Also wrong reasoning, formatory understanding, the literal, logical level, can destroy ideas or turn them into something dangerous. Some ideas can reach to the depth of the soul and leave a trace, even in early life. But a *wrong* trace may be left. The whole Work is to prepare people for the reception of higher and subtler influences—that is, ideas. Its knowledge must become your knowledge —that is, if you really want the Work. For a very long time, one has to study the Work, make efforts, think of and nourish it with the most genuine parts of oneself. Then one may become aware of being in contact *internally* with its ideas.

492

COMMENTARY ON WILL

III

Every day it is necessary to think about identifying and what it is, and in what forms it is at work in oneself at this minute. It is not a word. It is a psychic activity, very wasteful, continually taking place, something that the Work says must be continually struggled with. We lose force by it. If we knew for certain that there was another and better world and had seen it, we would not be drowned so much by the events of this very imperfect one. If we knew we were in a strange and dangerous country, we would be careful how we acted. Would it not be wonderful to know for certain, like that? By our knowledge and certainty we would be protected from identifying in the way we do with everything and everyone.

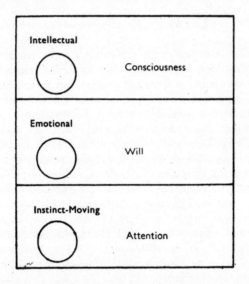

Since the Emotional Centre has in it the centre of gravity of Will (see diagram) we can realize that identifying is not likely to lead to any contact with Real Will or Master. We are told we really only know the emotional feeling of being identified with everything and everyone. The Emotional Centre is swamped with identifying. It is not that we identify merely with our negative emotions, but with all such emotions as we have. By this identifying, which sometimes takes the form of a continual sense of worry and anxiety, the right working of the Emotional Centre is prevented, force is continually lost, wrong inner chemistry is set up and wrong connections are made between centres. Whatever we identify with, we are under the power of. But if we had Real Will, if this Master the Work speaks of were sitting in the Carriage and the Driver *heard* his voice and obeyed him, we would no longer be under the power of what we identify with, but under another power, having nothing to do with being identified. I say, nothing to do with being identified, because when we are identified we are, so to speak, deaf. One cannot, for instance, *hear* the Work when one is identified. To obey the Master would be to obey the Work. To obey the Work would be to have Will. The Work tells us not to identify—first, with ourselves. Suppose we try, after seeing a little what this command means. A small part of oneself awakens to the influences of the Work. Of course, this is not yet Real 'I': this is a few 'I's comparable to the stage called Deputy-Steward.

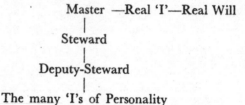

Master —Real 'I'—Real Will
|
Steward
|
Deputy-Steward
|
The many 'I's of Personality

Now suppose one begins to see more deeply what is meant by struggling against identifying with oneself and the reason for it. Then the matter is no longer a question of obeying something you heard from outside, some commandment, a truth entering by the external senses, but becomes something better understood from within. One begins to perceive the excellence of the Work. It makes an inside connection. Then one is under deeper influences of the Work—that is, higher in the Ray and so more internally perceived. The Ray is internal. This is the direction of Master and Steward. First, Steward: he is deeper insight. He is not external—a command. He understands for himself. He knows. His state is like that which I mentioned at the beginning. He knows there is a better level. He knows it is necessary to walk carefully. The stage called Deputy-Steward does not. For Deputy-Steward the Work still comes from outside, as something taught, something in note-books, something you are told to do without seeing internally its excellence.

If we believe there is nothing else—no higher state, no other meanings, no other levels, no other insights and understandings, no new ways of taking our lives, no other kind of people, no levels in the Universe save this Earth—how can we stop identifying with everything we see? How and why should we seek to draw the force of identifying into Self-Remembering? It has been said that to remember oneself one must have a sense of something superior to oneself. Self-Remembering is a lifting up of oneself to another set of influences. However, this is rarely understood, because people are interested only in life. Still, look at life and think about it for yourselves. The Work starts with the mind, not with the Will. It says certain things. These things refer to the mind at first—to thinking. Have you ever tried to look at life from the ideas of the Work? Everyone at their present age must have noticed that life is not what they expected. Yes—but have you begun to see life from the Work-ideas? The Work is not exactly encouraging about life and one's imagination of it and of oneself but it suggests another direction as possible. This is an important thing to begin to understand. If this Work were about being a greater and vainer success in life I do not see how it could be the Work, which is about coming under new influences—a new neutralizing force, different from the neutralizing force of life. Shall we have talks on how to be more popular, how to attract more money, how to gain more power? I cannot see that the Work has this direction. Is the Work about that? Some understand the strange direction of the Work from the first, some gradually see it, and some never understand what on earth the whole thing is about but hang on from some insincere personal advantage. The idea of new influences and of coming in contact with them is the centre of the Work. If there were none, the Work would be about nothing. It would be mere nonsense. However, the Work is actually about something real, because higher influences exist and contact with them depends on *inner* change—not imitated change, not pretended change. This smells. But it is impossible to deceive the Work. When one eventually becomes sensitive to psychological bad smells, they are not a thing of which one particularly likes to become aware.

In the function of Will a great deal depends on realizing oneself and seeing from what any momentary will comes. Say that you want to have Will, in some real sense—and suppose you know nothing yet of yourself. It will be "own-will" or "self-will"—some form of having your own way towards life or other people. You cannot possibly begin to have Real Will as long as it goes in this direction—having more power, more possessions, more this, more that. This is not the direction of Real Will. It cannot work in this direction for Real Will knows nothing of the external world. This is the secret. It comes from the upper triangle which is merely a point in the lower.

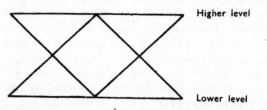

Real Will is from the upper part of the diagram of Master, Steward, Deputy-Steward and the many 'I's. It is about Master and Steward. It is about *something else*. It is not about smoking or sleeping or exercise, or even about another person, however dearly loved. Real Will is about the Work and not about things down here, things and people visible *via* the senses.

So you see that when the ideas of the Work and all its significance, historically speaking, enter into a man and begin to touch his emotional understanding, he is more likely to begin to feel traces of Real 'I' than a person who takes the Work externally, as a thing to listen to and to try to do because one is told to. In the latter case there cannot be Real Will because Real Will lies deeply and not on the surface. When we think deeply, we move inwards—towards emotional and intellectual divisions of centres. Whenever we move inwards meaning increases. As said, it is moving upwards in the sense of the Ray. As you know, the density of vibrations increases in passing up the Ray. Where there was one, there are a million. Now Real Will cannot impinge on such crude meanings as we ordinarily live by nor can it be negative in the sense of merely not doing something. Where we saw one thing before, we begin, by self-observation, by inner sincerity, and by much thought, to see a hundred meanings. Again, where we thought we knew, we see that we did not. What is experience? Is it not realizing one does not know, not negatively, but because one sees so much more than formerly? This seems a loss. But it is not a loss. Internally one feels loosened. But nothing could be better. How else can anything new enter—and how indeed can Real 'I' enter when one is tightly shut up in one's own narrow ideas which so soon form a grave for so many?

Birdlip, August 12, 1944

LEVELS OF CONSCIOUSNESS

Let us study the Law of Seven or the Law of Octaves to-night. As you know, the supreme example is the Ray of Creation which shews how there are different levels or notes: *Do, Si, La*, etc. descending to *Re*, which represents in our case the smallest most undeveloped part —i.e. the Moon. According to the Law of Octaves the notes of the descending octave involve more and more laws, and vice versa. A part is under more laws than the whole. The Moon is under 96 laws or orders of laws, the Earth under 48 laws, and the summit *Do*, the Absolute, is under no laws save the laws of its own unity. From this it is seen that the lower down anything stands in the Octave the more laws it is under—i.e. the Will of the Absolute does not reach us directly but in the form of 48 orders of laws which produce for us in their varying combinations the conditions of our life.

Now any organization or organism is built according to the Law of Three and Law of Seven in the same way as the whole Universe which is a vast organism. Let us take Organic Life which is an organism spread like a thin film over the Earth to receive and transmit influences from the Sun and Galaxies. Man is an organism within Organic Life.

He is a minute part, a minute cell, in the body of Organic Life, comparable to a brain-cell in his own body. Let us construct an octave between Organic Life and Man. Once Mr. Ouspensky asked us to think about this and at the same time he himself constructed the octave as follows:

Do	Organic Life
Si	Humanity
La	The White Race
Sol	Our Civilization
Fa	Europe
Mi	A Nation
Re	A Family
Do	Man

Mr. Ouspensky said that we should think in terms of the Law of Octaves about the present situation of Man on Earth. This was some time before the present war started. He said that if we would study the Octave as he had constructed it we would see that at the place of shock between the notes *Mi* and *Fa* something was necessary to make ascending force pass from a national Consciousness to a European Consciousness. Man as *Do* had reached the patriarchal or Family System *Re* and later he had reached the Consciousness of the Note *Mi* —i.e. National Consciousness. An Englishman, for example, feels himself as an individual, he feels himself as family, and he feels himself as nation. He sounds, as it were, three notes, *Do*, *Re*, *Mi*, but he does not feel Europe—i.e. he does not sound the note *Fa*. He is not conscious at this level. In this respect it is as if people came up against an obstacle, against something that requires a shock for them to get past. Everyone will agree that at the level of Consciousness belonging to the note *Re*, the organism which we can call roughly the Family, it would be absurd for them to lock themselves up in their houses and try to throw bombs at each other. Everyone would know it was ridiculous. In the same way all European war is equally ridiculous and equally criminal. The Franco-Prussian War in the seventies of the last century was a criminal war quite different from earlier wars when there were few means of communication. Europe is like a house full of flats. For one flat to make war on another flat is criminal and is really liable to destroy the whole block of flats, for just as Man himself is an organism, and a Family or Class is an organism, and a Nation is an organism, so should Europe now become an organism, especially with the development of methods of communication, that has taken place within the last hundred years. These have increased the power of governments, as is quite obvious, and if government is bad then the situation is very bad, far worse than it used to be before Europe had the possibility of becoming an organism. There is no nation in Europe that can live without another nation just as there is no organ in a man's body that can exist without the other organs.

Now all evolution is an ascent of an octave. Psychological evolution is an increase of Consciousness, a bringing together of more things into a unity—because Consciousness means a knowing together. In the same way an evolution of the emotions is a bringing together of many different feelings and this makes Conscience. And the two—this knowing together and this feeling together—are the lines of psychological evolution, both for Man himself and for Humanity. So you see that one explanation of the present situation in this century, which should have seen a definite step forward, is due to a lack of development in Consciousness beyond the national level—beyond the note *Mi* in the constructed Octave between Organic Life and Man.

Now notice that a man, a single individual, must first of all belong to a group of some kind, which in turn is connected with a larger organisation. The more one studies the Law of Seven the more one sees that it is a uniting framework, a skeleton, as it were, for all forms of life, psychological or physical. Everything is united, everything is connected together, nothing can exist independently, yet each thing has its own individual existence although it is connected with what is below it and what is above it. You remember that Mr. Ouspensky used often to dwell on this point, that everything is connected and that nothing is separate. He used to say that people's consciousness was so poorly developed in this respect that they did not even realize that all our food came from the Sun. Sometimes he used to say that the object of this Work is to increase Consciousness. It is not, he said, based on faith, or hope, or love, although all these are included. What is emphasized is Consciousness.

He said that G. was constantly speaking about this necessity for the development of Consciousness, and that he used to compare the inner working of Man's being with complex machines working practically in the dark. The first development of Consciousness is to become conscious of Personality and of the many different 'I's that compose it, some useful and some useless. This is a definite development of Consciousness and from this step it is possible to develop Consciousness still further by becoming conscious of another person. But without being far more conscious of oneself one cannot become conscious of another person, save in an illusory way, in imagination. We have first of all to be able to bear ourselves before we can bear others.

Now these developments of Consciousness are exactly comparable to the developments shewn in the Octave between Organic Life and Man. Each step seems an increase of Consciousness. In the case of an individual, self-study carried out on the right lines leads to a new note being sounded in him. We need not discuss which note. But with the beginning of the sounding of this note he will experience quite new sensations of himself and quite new feelings. He will become unfamiliar to himself and if he does not know what is happening he may think that something is going in a wrong direction. But if you begin to leave the room in which you have always sat, you will necessarily find yourself in new situations.

Now just imagine what would happen if there were a development of European Consciousness and the whole of Europe were drawn together into a new organism. We would, of course, experience quite new sensations and feelings. We would no longer pride ourselves in the same ways or be connected as we were before. So there would appear to be a loss of something which we apparently regard as very important. But it is precisely this loss of something that will enable a new note to sound in one's individual psychological evolution. There must be a loss of something for a new note to sound, as all the forms of vanity and most forms of pride must change, must cease to give us their various secret satisfactions as they have hitherto done. At the same time the conditions under which a new note sounds in the octave of one's own development will necessitate an increase of Consciousness in regard to knowing and feeling more together. If we could know everything our present feeling of ourselves would completely change. Fortunately we cannot do this, because, as you know, we would go mad, because we would become aware of all the contradictions in our lives. In order that we should not see these contradictions an appliance called "buffers" is introduced at an early age with the inevitable result of narrowing of Consciousness. So you see that an increase of Consciousness implies ultimately a weakening of buffers and I think the same parallel can be drawn in connection with an increase of Consciousness in the other octave. For each nation to be at the level of Europe many national buffers would have to disappear.

I will add a few words in this connection about Will of which we have been speaking recently. You will remember that Real Will is not exactly making decisions or negations but consists in finding solutions. For this reason with our limited Consciousness we can scarcely expect to have Real Will. In order to do so we must be able to be conscious of a number of things together and not merely one at a time. With our narrow Consciousness we see one thing and then another and then a third and we cannot see any connection between them and they seem to us to be opposites and so mutually irreconcilable. You remember the Eastern story of the sages who had to examine an elephant in the dark: one felt the tail and another felt the trunk and another the ear and so on, and at the end each gave an entirely different description to the Caliph. Our situation is somewhat like that. If we could see the whole elephant we could give it orders and we would understand what all its different parts were. But as it is, we see little bits at a time and we try to make aim and have Will about these little bits without seeing their connection with the whole. But even as we are we can have small aim and believe we have Will to keep it. But the supreme Aim, without which we can never reach Master or Real 'I', is the Work and all that it means. This, as you know, is phrased in the Gospels: "Seek ye first the

Kingdom of Heaven and its righteousness and all these things shall be added unto you." How can we really expect, save for purposes of experiment and observation, to get any result from making aims based on self-will and how can we expect that in this way our Consciousness will be able to increase beyond its present level? The whole idea of Will must become intelligent. You may have to sail North and South and even East at times in order to cross the Atlantic. But if you have got some real self-observation, and if you have sounded the *Do* of the Work strongly enough, and if above all you feel that you cannot lose hold of this Work, then although you may find that you have often to go in apparently contradictory ways, which are often very confusing, yet something will give you a kind of feeling when you are really going in the wrong way, but it will never tell you when you are going in the right way. As you know, in the Parable of the Horse, Carriage and Driver, when the Driver is on the box and has the reins, he must start as best he can and then the Master may be found sitting in the Carriage and may say something. Remember that Real Will or Master comes down from a higher level and cannot reach the ordinary so-called waking state of consciousness. Something must be awake in one to have any contact and that means that there must be some state of Self-Remembering present. After a time one can begin to tell when one is asleep inside—i.e. when there is no kind of Self-Remembering taking place.

It is said sometimes when you are in difficulties that the Work will find a way for you. Yes, this is so, but only when you feel the Work and value it. It must be in you, not merely something outside you. When you have affection for something, when you value something, it is in you. The Master can speak through the Work, and the Work can speak to us, but the Master cannot speak to us directly.

Birdlip, August 20, 1944

VANITY

Let me say a few things about *Vanity*. First I will quote the derivation and meanings given in the Dictionary:

Vanity—from Latin *Vanitas*—emptiness, worthlessness—Latin *vanus*—empty. (1) Quality of being vain, empty or worthless; futility, unsubstantialness, worthlessness, emptiness; "the vanity of human wishes," "of earthly greatness." (2) That which is vain, worthless; an unprofitable, futile thing, act, etc. "All is vanity," "the pomps and vanity of this wicked world." (3) Quality of being personally vain; exaggeratedly high opinion, pride in one's own appearance, physical or mental capacities; conceit. "An injury to vanity will never be forgiven."

Before I speak of this subject, there is one thing that everyone who has been in this Work for some time must realize—i.e. that everything you have done genuinely remains for you and will help you at difficult moments, and everything you have done from vanity is lost to you. As you have often heard, G. always hit hard at vanity and pretence. Recently I have found that many conversations that I had with O. return to me—conversations that I had forgotten. This is one of the interesting things about *memory*. Memory is not one thing, but many things. There are many kinds of memory. Things are laid down on different rolls in different parts of centres, according to their emotional reception. Under certain circumstances rolls turn, and, lo and behold, forgotten things enter consciousness. Small 'I's remember only small things. Bigger 'I's remember other things. Memory is in scale. A person is not all at the same level. First he is a three-storey house and then each centre in each storey is again a three-storey house and then again. G. took vanity and self-conceit as the worst possible evil in regard to right relation to centres. What is the reason? The reason is that False Personality is composed of vanity and all its unreal imaginations and that these invented 'I's cannot ever connect with Real 'I'. Vanity is the contrary of inner sincerity and only inner sincerity can lead to Real Will or Real 'I'. However, in all of us vanity is difficult to notice and separate from. I recalled, recently, a former conversation with O. He had spent two or three meetings of the older group in asking what was the most important thing to work upon and make passive. Some people said negative emotions, others sleep, others internal considering and so on. Someone said False Personality. O. still shook his head. At last someone, who, let us say, was called Mr. Robinson, said that the most important thing to notice and work upon and separate from was Mr. Robinson. O. nodded. I thought the answer good but had no realization of what it meant. Afterwards I was speaking to him privately and he said: "People can be divided in a very rough way into those who are living the life of False Personality, with all its intrigues, illusions, pretences, and ambitions, and those who wish for something different and are tired of themselves." He added: "However, this is a useless definition save for those who can catch some glimpse of what is meant. It is useless to argue about it and if you mention it everyone will argue."

You will remember that it was previously said that *arguing* is useless. One either sees the truth of something or does not see it. The point has been emphasized so many times in the Work that *arguing* is useless. To argue is not to understand. It is necessary to avoid a person who wants always to argue about the ideas. He does not *see* their meaning. He will never be convinced. He is not ready. He does not wish to cook a dish of the Work but to smash up everything in the kitchen. Literally, to argue means to turn things into *argentum*, which is the Latin for silver. Silver in parable represents truth. But mechanical arguing turns things into lead, into dirt. If you have no inner *perception* of the truth of any idea of the Work, if you do not see *it is so*, then it is in the wrong part of a centre and has become sown in the wrong place—

by the wayside. On the other hand, to argue in order to make things clearer, more silver, and more shining, is different, but this is not the ordinary mode of arguing. The ordinary mode is not positive but negative—to negate what you hear, to pick holes, to use words and not meaning as a weapon—in fact, to *argue*. Now, if you know by experience that China exists, you will not argue. It is so.

On one occasion years ago I was sitting with O. in a small old-fashioned inn in which were many old coloured prints of former bucks and generals and grand ladies, all dressed in the most extraordinary costumes, wigs, hair-fashions and so on, belonging to the period. I pointed them out to him. He said: "Yes, you can see how everyone represented there has a mental disease—namely, vanity." And then he turned to me with a smile and said: "You are a psychological doctor, whatever it is called. Why do you not write a book about real mental diseases?" I said, as carefully as I could: "Whom should I begin with?" His eyes twinkled—and I knew of course that he meant with myself— and then he said: "Well, with Hasnamous men. Start with Lentromuss." This term G. invented and formed out of Lenin, Trotsky and Mussolini. Hasnamous men are people like Napoleon who derive their well-being from the ill-being of others. He went on to say: "Actually, no one is sane. To the Circle of Conscious Humanity we on this Earth are all insane—much more insane than the vain monkeys appear to us. In the East it was once the custom to regard lunatics as sacred and visited by God. I have often thought of this. Are you sure that our ordinary ideas of what a lunatic is and what a sane man is are not wrong? Are not we perhaps the lunatics and the lunatics sane? To really see what we are like ourselves . . ." He shrugged his shoulders, and became silent.

Having begun to notice my own forms of vanity, after being certain for a long time that I had none, I often used to try to get him to speak more about vanity and its forms and power over people. He said once: "Vanity is an unnatural, outward manifestation of yourself." He used to remind me of the Magician-Farmers who hypnotised the sheep and told them they were eagles, etc., and finally that they were *men*.

On another occasion I was telling him of a patient I had had, an extremely rich woman, who dressed expensively always in new dresses every day. He said: "Yes, now, that is a disease, you know. She is really insane, from vanity. You will find nothing in her save this illness of vanity. But no doubt she thinks she is charming and imagines she is a woman." I agreed that this was so. He nodded and said—well, something (but not to repeat) which referred to the Egyptian custom of embalming dead corpses expensively. He said that men had vanity as much as women and that in different ages it might take rather similar forms but usually different forms. He said: "People always dress up owing to vanity. But a few may dress apart from vanity. Vanity separates us from everything real in ourselves because it is unreal. So it prevents all real inner connections. A person may have the moment's reward that vanity gives but, feeling nothing real, must continue to produce an effect. Nothing can grow from False Personality save increasing inventions of oneself, increasing falseness." He said—and this reminded me of something G. had said—that vanity by causing continual, unnatural, outward manifestations of oneself produced a certain formation or psychic substance that surrounded a person's inner life and shut him or her in, as in a prison of their own daily manufacture. A person becomes enclosed in his or her vanity-pictures and then cannot make contact with anything real, after a time, even though he or she wishes to. Their own creations, their own posturing and pretence and self-absorption, that they have nourished with so much force, render them impotent to understand anything or be anything. O. said once, about serious people, people who do not appear vain but take themselves very seriously, all day long, that it was just the same thing —they enclose themselves in their own seriousness of which they are vain.

As you have heard, G. said he had found that his task, in trying to teach Western people the Work—to quote his actual words—lay in "quarrelling ruthlessly with all manifestations dictated in people by the evil factor of vanity present in their being." G. said also: "We should be really god-like creatures capable of entering into and understanding the position of others—of understanding the *psyche* of our neighbour." But, he added, in so many words, this is impossible because of the factor of vanity which, admiring only itself, feels itself better than others and so produces not only wrong impressions and wrong results outwardly but causes wrong connections internally, preventing any deepening of man or woman. The Work also teaches that through the terrible power of vanity, of pretending, of affectation, we ascribe to ourselves all sorts of qualities, capacities and values that we do not possess. The Work must undo this in a person. We believe we can help others when we cannot help ourselves. We believe we have some extraordinary merit or value which is not the case. We imagine we know ourselves and can do. We believe we are capable of devotion, and so on. To gain an insight into vanity in oneself—that is, into this imaginary pseudo-side —is to begin to become more free. It is half-pleasant and half-painful. One part is glad. One part suffers. Consider the endless enslavements that vanity compels you to be under, both in yourself and in relation to others, inventing yourself and inventing your relation to another. When you think of the meaning of freedom you must ask: "Freedom from what?" What do you ask to be free from?

* * *

Vanity, conceit and so on, all lead to manifestations that are not only unnatural but, by making wrong inner and outer connections, prevent any further development of understanding and so prevent any evolution of Man on Earth. We should already be tired of the manifestations of "Man on Earth" and our own. Suppose we were to ask ourselves the meaning of the *Eucharist* and then consider how such a feast would be impossible if everyone present were occupied with vanity, with being first, with intrigue, and sly unpleasant things, with getting power over another and with inner hatreds and negative states and so on. The meaning of the word Eu-charist is good-grace, or good charity—εὐ meaning in Greek good or well, and χάρις grace, mercy, a sort of *inner* beauty. You know that the word Evangel (in the Greek εὐαγγέλιον) means "good news". Suppose that no real inner and outer connections can take place without *good-will*. *Will* originally in our language had the meaning of *"choice"*, to will was to *choose*, and *good* meant *"rightly put together"*. It would seem therefore that goodwill has always had the meaning of something conscious. The feast of the Eucharist, which is the commemoration of the Last Supper, was originally only possible among people who had in some sense good-will to each other. Now think how this can ever be with vanity, conceit, and False Personality.

⋆　　⋆　　⋆

Continuation of Commentary on Real Will

Let us return again to the question of Will and what it might mean to have Real Will. As you have seen, Real Will, or Real 'I', which alone has Real Will, or Master, comes down from a higher level. As we are, with many conflicting 'I's in our Personality, we have only that quality of Will that is the result of their different small personal wills. It seems necessary to say again that Real Will or Real 'I' or Master comes down from above. Let me ask you this question: Have you formed any idea of what this means or have you had any trace of experience of it? When we make up our minds it is really the different 'I's in us that do this. Now when you "make up your mind", as it is called, you follow the ideas of little 'I's. Real Will, however, is above them and operates through quite different ideas. What does "above" mean? *Above* is the same as *inner*. What is inner in you? To-day I want to speak of what is *inner*—that is, above—or higher. What is higher is inner. The higher influences coming from the Ray of Creation are *inner* in you. The outer part, the Personality, this Mrs. So and So, or Miss So and So, or Mr. So and So, are under outer influences—relatively the lowest in the Ray. To climb the Ray—and now I speak of the Side-Octave coming down from the "Sun"—to climb it is to become more *internal* in everything you think and feel and do and say. What does this mean, to become more *internal*? From what do you act and feel and think? Yes, I think this is a very good thing for everyone to reflect upon. Let us take a person who wishes to get attention, who is vain and from vanity wishes to get on in the Work, and behaves in certain ways with this aim in view. From what is this person acting? Is this person acting from Personality or not? Well, what do you think? Now can this *give* anything in the Work? Of course not. Yes, but why not? Here we come up against the very Work itself and its real meaning. The

Work is to weaken Personality and to make what is real in us—that is, Essence—grow. Do you think that if you act in the Work in such a way as to get some advantage, some place and so on, your efforts will be any good in the Work-sense? I do not see how, in view of all the Work teaches, this can be expected. However, one may ignore the teaching of the ideas of the Work and make an aim that is entirely from Personality and so useless for any growth of Essence.

Now I wish to talk rather seriously to all of you. First, everything pseudo, everything pretended, everything false, is of no use in the Work. To reach anywhere, to get anything, you must be sincere with yourself. You must have *inner sincerity* and that means that at least you must be able to detect by self-observation when you are not genuine, as far as you can at your level. When you try to make "Will" from an insincere basis—that is, insincere for oneself at one's present level—you will not touch Essence, and so not Real 'I', which is close to Essence.

I often think now how remarkable it is to ponder alone with oneself the meaning of the Work and all esotericism, and notice what in one's being wishes it genuinely. Everyone enters the Work with his or her Personality at full blast. For a long time everything is mixed up. I know this very well myself. Later, one begins to think those more *inner* thoughts about the whole matter. And here is where a person is close to sounding *Do* or not. To sound *Do* is to value the Work with inner sincerity. Yes, but what does this mean—to value the Work? It means *you* do—all that you can call *you*. Yes, but that sounds vague. This is right. How many years does it take to sound *Do* strongly, more deeply? You may catch a glimpse and sound a weak *Do*, partly through another force. That is a good thing. But this weak *Do* is easily caught away elsewhere, as it were, by trials, so the *Do* is not yet a real starting-point. The Work begins *in you* when you have to struggle for it yourself and keep it alive for and by yourself—because all that is best in you really wants it and feels a loss if it is not present. People can think they have sounded a genuine *Do* and have as yet done nothing of that kind. When you are in False Personality, everything you do is outer, superficial, for the sake of attention, self-interest, or praise, or merit. This is *outer* and so *lower*. What then does *inner* or *higher* mean? It means something very interesting once you begin to see. It means a continual struggle in yourself to get to what is real and to discard the pretended and invented side. Here one enters a sort of desert in which one is tempted a great deal in regard to the Work itself.

*　　*　　*

Now I wish to speak about the place Will comes from, ordinarily speaking. Can you will what you know? As you know, lying destroys Essence. This is only another way of saying that Essence can only grow through what is sincere in you. We take a long time to connect the Work with life and what happens every day to us in life and our reactions to what happens. For a long time there is a gap between the practice of the Work and one's actual life and behaviour. One sees people taking what happens to them in life as if it has nothing to do with the Work and one sees people obviously entranced by their imagination of what life should be like and their reactions to their imagination. In both cases, the important thing is non-identifying. Certainly it is difficult and long work. It is difficult to wake up. We have to connect the Work with our daily lives. One cannot dream of the Work or dream one is a conscious person. However, the imagination can satisfy every centre and part of a centre, and continue to do so for a long time. We were once told to try to use imagination actively, as, for instance, to imagine what it would be like to be conscious—to visualize it—and then to will it. There is a certain kind of necessary *inner persuading* of oneself that has to do with the directed imagination— and so with deliberate visualization it tends to create something definite. However, this cannot be spoken of at present. You remember something was said of this in connection with the *reins* between *Driver* and *Horse*.

Now as regards the place of origin and the quality of Will. Will originating from outer 'I's in False Personality is of no value. Again, so-called Will from daily, momentary, small 'I's, which have short memories and go to sleep, will soon vanish. We must found *Will* on something better and deeper. Now that is a quite wrong phrase. Did you notice it is? You cannot *found* Real Will—you must attract it because it comes from above—that is, from within, from deeper thoughts and feelings. But since to pray is very difficult and requires a very great intensity and sincerity, we must find out some other preliminary way of gaining access to Real 'I' or Will. It was said last time that the Master cannot speak to us directly but only through the ideas of the Work, and unless the Work is already represented in our understanding we cannot hear Real 'I'. The first thing is to try to understand the Work and what it is about and what its background is and why it is necessary and has always existed, why B influences exist, and so on. This is the *first step* to attract Real Will. No one can do anything like this from vanity, from False Personality, which is the most outer, most turned-to-life side. Since Real Will or Master is internal to us as we are now psychologically, internal to all the things we say and feelings we have, internal to all jealousies and troubles and identifications and account-making—since Real 'I' lies deep to all this tossing sea of oneself, it is necessary to observe oneself as the starting-point, for self-observation means that you begin to move inwards, behind yourself, deep to the surface upon which you have tried to find the full meaning of your life.

COMMENTARY ON CHIEF FEATURE

Sometimes it is necessary to start more small octaves in one's life. All octaves must begin with a *Do* and this means that in order to start something one must *begin* actually. One's life, as it passes, easily contracts, if one simply turns around in the interests one has already which may become mechanical habits. On one occasion O. said it was necessary to have "many irons in the fire". He was speaking of the difficulty of getting beyond some present stage of oneself or of getting on further with one's aim. He said: "Octaves can give shocks to one another. You may stop at *mi-fa* in one octave but another octave may give the right shock to the first. By going on with something else you may be able to get on with what you started first of all." The difference is like playing the same tune on a few well-worn strings and feeling the need of a larger instrument with more strings. However, it is not easy to get one. We become creatures of mechanical habits, long before we realize it. Then what one calls new experiences are really the same as before—the same tune. They fall on the same place. All this is held together by the *Chief Feature*, which governs the Personality. What one believes is new is really the same, because it leads as before to Chief Feature, which must be satisfied and will not release us without very much trouble and indeed humiliation on our part. However, it is possible to begin to free oneself from this Ruler of "Earth"—that is, of one's Personality, which is one's earth—and to begin to experience another voice, another sense of one's life, another feeling of oneself, another idea, another view of what it is all about.

The ordinary circle of things in our lives in turning continually, daily, weekly, yearly, brings us to the same points in sequence. As the special memory, the consciousness of oneself, grows through uncritical self-observation, the taste of this always returning to the same points, this taste of recurrence in life, becomes stronger until it is stronger than the attraction of the points one revisits, which have in the interim grown fresh graces. All this is very confusing for a long time unless one realizes that in this constant *returning* and the consciousness of it one can have a new attitude and a new way of reacting to the old. The effect on oneself may then change. The things, the events, may not change very much. But to change anything in oneself, there is always this obscure problem of the *Chief Feature* which governs us, as we are, and holds us to the same circle. One may sense after a time that something always seems to keep us where we are long before we can see what it is. "Why," one may ask, "am I always here at the same place?" This is no handicap for many: many prefer the same. Now ordinary memory is very short. In the Work, Work-memory—this returning of familiar experiences— may begin to awaken one to oneself, because it becomes a source of an inner flatness or even misery. One may become aware of where one is **in** this turning circle and remember how one was there before—and before—and before—away back into the past. This is an expansion of consciousness already. One says to oneself: "I have been here before." Even so, the power of the point of the event one is at is too strong with this slight insight. "Why", one says, "should I *not* be here again?" This will not of course occur if one has no sense of the turning circle of oneself—one's life. The illusion of being free and able to do what one wants, the illusion of Time going straight on as if to new things, instead of seeing that *Time is repetition* and so a circle—this illusion we hold, in spite of the self-evident circle of day and night, summer and winter, that the mere *passage of Time* will bring us what we dream of—all this makes it difficult to understand *oneself* and *one's life* and *what has happened and is happening to one*.

Now the approach to beginning to see Chief Feature depends on one's power of enduring it. We forget how sensitive we are to the slightest discouragement or criticism and how very difficult it is to endure any loss of esteem, even if we imagine we are either hardened or have full self-knowledge. In no case can anyone be *told* his or her *Chief Feature* because no one would believe it and then no one could stand it. The action of the Work gradually brings an individual to the point of catching glimpses of it. It is like being undermined: it is incredible: it is like being accused of theft or murder or criminal lying. Not only is it very painful but at first impossible. However it is true. What does *true* mean? All *truth* is relative to one's power of comprehending it. To be told that something is true, when one cannot see it and is a thousand miles away from the power of seeing it, does not make it *true* for us. Truth is a development: that is why all truth must be relative to the power of being able to see it. Take for example a phrase like this from some ancient book of Indian Esotericism: "By the delusion of the pairs of opposites that spring from desire and from hate all born beings fall into bewilderment." Who can see for himself the truth of this truth? No one is ready yet to see it, so it has no power over anyone, for one must have the power to see the truth of a truth in order that it may have power over one. Just to hear it is nothing. Anyone can hear anything with his ears. To hear with the mind is another and a very long matter. And finally to hear with the understanding is a still longer matter. But, in that case, the truth can begin to exert power over one's life. And that again is a long matter. How much stands in between. Can we believe that the Chief Feature in each of us is going to let us understand truths that are utterly opposed to its hidden power over us? Can you, in ordinary life, turn out people who hold supreme official posts and have done so for years as easily as that? It is the same thing. The Chief Feature is not to be turned out of office easily. He is established where he is, and he is not going to let go his hold upon you, and you are entirely in his power, and he knows very well how to conceal himself and how to argue with you reasonably and make out that he only wishes to help you. He will make it difficult for you to start new octaves, new interests; he will always explain why it is silly or unnecessary and so on, especially if you try to start something that might weaken his power directly. As long as he is satisfied, you will feel satisfied. You will feel at peace with the world of yourself. However, this Work is not to make us feel at peace with ourselves as we are. There is another peace described as "passing all understanding"—but we do not possess that peace as yet and certainly cannot as we are. The kind of small, mean peace we feel is very different. When we awaken a little, we feel less of this somewhat smug, small peace.

I said above that our power of seeing Chief Feature depends upon our power of enduring it. The Work does not allow us to go beyond ourselves, if you can understand the expression. Since Chief Feature belongs to our Being, and since work on Being is only possible by self-observation, we cannot expect to catch a glimpse of Chief Feature unless we have begun to see our level of Being. What does it mean to begin to see our level of Being which has attracted our life? Certainly, mere isolated observations of oneself will not make it possible for us to catch a glimpse of our level of Being, and you must also remember that it would be impossible to catch a glimpse of one's level of Being unless one could endure it. Now the only way that you can endure it is by having something else that you can hold on to. If you have something else that you value and that you can hold on to and trust, you can then endure a certain amount of devaluation of yourself. In other words, you may be able to endure catching a glimpse from time to time of your level of Being. These glimpses run very far back. They do not begin until the stage of taking mental photographs has been reached. Isolated momentary self-observation is like turning a small flash-lamp on to a small part of the room that one lives in. But a mental photograph is like seeing a number of things together in the room in a certain relation to each other just for a moment. Suppose that you have observed yourself for some considerable time and you begin to see yourself over the period of time acting in a certain way. You see how something starts, leads to something else, and so on. In fact, you see yourself in action, in movement, so to speak, inner and outer, in some typical way of behaviour. This is a photograph. You can say that it is a photograph of an 'I' or that it is a photograph of a group of 'I's, of some sub-division of the Personality, of a personality in your "Personality".

G. once said that it was necessary to collect a large number of photographs of oneself and keep them in an album, so that one could see them together. Now seeing one's level of Being means of course an increase of consciousness, an increase of self-consciousness. As consciousness grows, the result is always a greater power of seeing together. What you saw as separate and apparently without relation becomes connected to form a larger design and from this larger design you see another meaning, just as in fitting together the bits of a jig-saw puzzle you suddenly begin to see the picture emerging and see what it means.

Now for all this to take place it is necessary to make continual contributions to one's consciousness, even although one does not apparently get results. The Work teaches us the method whereby results can be obtained if we apply the method. But how and when the results will come belongs to the inner action of the Work itself which always remains an incomprehensible secret to us. The method tells us to observe ourselves and become more conscious.

Now when these photographs begin to form themselves the next stage is that one notices flashes of insight into one's life that go far back. Then one begins to become more conscious of one's level of Being, of the kind of person one has been all this time and has never seen owing to the action of buffers. Now is the time when it begins to be possible to gain some idea of what one's Chief Feature is. When this stage is reached you will be uncertain whether it is one out of three things as a starting-point. Now at this stage you will notice a great decline in confidence both in yourself and in things in general. You will feel an inner weakness and will have to be careful about certain new forms of negative emotion. Another thing that you will begin to notice is that the necessity of the Work becomes far stronger: you notice that it is all quite true and that you cannot ignore it. If you have not prepared yourself for this stage, if you have not done the work that you ought to have done, and you meet this stage, you will inevitably collapse, simply because you have got to a place which you should never have got into. You will begin to try to swim before you have learnt how to swim.

Now as regards the kinds of things that form Chief Feature—in the first place, they are never nice things. I mean that they are, when you begin to see them, all of such a nature that they are unpleasant. I do not mean horrible. You may feel moments of horror when you realize that such unpleasant things have been woven through your life, but no doubt you could get quite accustomed to them again and not notice that they are unpleasant, provided you have not really awakened to them, because it is impossible to die to them unless one has awakened to them. To gradually wake up to Chief Feature is a preliminary to dying to it or causing it to die. And you will remember that the right order of these things was talked about once by G. when he spoke of the idea of re-birth in the Gospels; he said that there were many references to dying, re-birth and awakening in the Gospels, but that they were not in the right order. "First," he said, "a man must awaken before he can die to himself, and then by dying to himself he can be re-born." Now since the Chief Feature is the axle round which everything in us turns, it is clear that if one wishes really to change, this central axle must be taken out, as it were. In that case, something else must hold the person together. But we have to consider the whole process as gradual and not sudden. There must be something to hold on to so that you can let go. If your life in life is very important to you, you will find it difficult to let go. If you do let go, your friends may not recognize you. Here it is necessary to act, if it is possible to do so. If by means of work over a long period a man begins to awaken to himself, he is going in the direction of awakening to his Chief Feature. He is on that journey. It would be foolish for him to attempt to die to himself without having worked. Some people have attempted this by terrible forms of asceticism. They have attempted to die to themselves without having awakened, and although they may have made "Second Body" they have simply become "things"—what G. called "immortal things". All the work that we do at present is connected with awakening to ourselves, with becoming more aware of ourselves, with letting light in to ourselves. Consciousness is light. If you begin to observe yourself uncritically you let in light. Eventually this light will shew up Chief Feature but not until you have caught hold of the rope, of something to hold you. If you are going to shift yourself from one place, you must prepare another place to stand on. I would advise you all not to identify with the words *Chief Feature*. Try simply to understand that everything, all your reactions, your attitudes, your behaviour, your thoughts and feelings, revolve round a central axle, which keeps them fixed. If one can see one of these spokes, it is like taking a photograph. Then one sees another spoke, and so on. They all lead to the same thing in the centre. Remember finally that no one can see his or her Chief Feature unless he or she is ready for it.

Birdlip, September 16, 1944

A NOTE ON PERSONAL WORK

It is always necessary to speak of personal work and what it means. We have continually to remind ourselves in our private thinking, and to remind others in the way we refer to the Work and speak of it, what it means to do this Work. We easily forget. It is not that we willingly forget but that we have not the force to remember. "A man," said G., "is not a man unless he remembers himself. But, when he realizes he does not remember himself he soon finds that he cannot remember to remember himself. His habits of forgetting himself and being asleep in life are too strong." He is then a man asleep realizing at intervals that he is asleep, and this is our situation, so we have to notice what puts us to sleep. By observation we can see how the events of life put us to sleep, and some especially, and how the habits of imagination and day-reveries, inner talking and accounting, being hurt, having negative thoughts and all their forms of contriving, self-justifying and so on, do the same. There is enough to work on. But we can reach that stage that is comparable with half-waking from ordinary sleep in bed—as when we know we are asleep and yet cannot open our eyes or move our bodies, or as in some cases where we cannot get into our waking consciousness and are still amongst moving dream-shadows which we know are dreams. It is as if we can get nothing into focus. There is not enough force. We cannot concentrate enough to awaken. Now in the Work we are often like that, going about all day feeling we are asleep and being unable to give ourselves shock—that is, the First Conscious Shock of Self-Remembering—which requires an effort of concentration, of inner attention and so enough force. Concentration needs force. When force is running into negative states or day-dreams or anxious cares, you cannot concentrate. Nothing is more easy to observe in yourself. For example, you are reading a book that requires directed attention to follow. A sound outside reminds you of something that made you negative yesterday. Instantly, rolls in centres begin to turn on which are recorded the incidents of yesterday. Your attention leaves the book, being now *drawn* effortlessly into this negative state and no longer directed by effort. You may still sit in the same position and even continue to read with the moving centre. But you are taking in nothing. You cannot concentrate. This shews how we lose force so easily for any particular thing we are aiming at. We become distracted and sit biting our nails metaphorically or actually while all sorts of mists, fogs, whirlwinds, thunders, lightnings, inundations, eruptions of steam and torrents of rain take place within our delicate psychic life, all of which we contemplate with satisfaction. It follows that if our force passes into such "natural" phenomena, our psychic country does not produce very much in the way of crops.

When G. said, in connection with his different definitions of what he meant by Man, that a man must remember himself, he referred of course to a state of consciousness which in this Work is called the Third State of Consciousness. And in saying this we can easily understand that he meant that no one was a Man unless by raising himself up internally he made it possible for new influences to reach him. As we all know, this Work teaches with the greatest emphasis that in our two ordinary states of consciousness, physical sleep and the so-called waking state, influences coming from higher levels in the Ray of Creation cannot penetrate to us. Our ordinary so-called waking state, with all its cares and anxieties, with all its innumerable forms of identifying, with all its negative states, and with all its totally erroneous outlooks and wrong ways of taking the ever-recurring series of typical events to which we are all exposed every moment, cuts us off completely from the influences coming from higher centres. It has often seemed to me that the idea that we have higher centres, that have a far greater knowledge and understanding than we have, is not enough reflected upon. The Work teaches that there are in us, fully developed, two higher centres that are sending their influences down on us continuously, only we cannot hear them. The centres communicate with influences coming from higher levels. The object of the Work is to cleanse our *lower* centres, to clear them out, to open their windows, so that they can begin to transmit these ideas and directions coming from higher centres. Now at our ordinary level of development, at our level of being, which is such that we cannot hear, cannot even receive these higher influences, it is necessary to practise Self-Remembering as far as we can and when we can, because it is only at this level of consciousness, called the Level of Self-Remembering or Self-Consciousness or Self-Awareness, that we can receive them. We begin by hearing them dimly and usually as new kinds of feelings, new kinds of emotions and thoughts and insights. It would be a great mistake to think that our emotional centre as it is now is developed. Our emotional centre as it is now is a very poor and inadequate and, in fact, dangerous instrument. It is largely governed by negative emotions and the tragedy is that with this poor inadequate emotional centre that we possess, we imagine we can love. So we blunder along in life with this wretched instrument, not realizing that our apparatus is in a hopeless condition for any fulfilment of what we really want, and the result is that we become engulfed in a continual mass of perplexed half-thoughts, half-feelings, half-imaginations and disappointments, and so on, that make up our own inner psychic life.

Now the Work says that we must lift ourselves out of this dark state by acts of Self-Remembering and this, as was said above, requires force. It requires some power of concentration, of attention, and you will never have this power if you let your force run into this inner chaos, this continual procession of mechanical associations, this stream of images, this formless vagueness, that is really our inner state. The Work says that we must at intervals gather ourselves up inside and as it were stand on all this shifting mass and feel our individual existence and remember what we are aiming at and why we exist. This requires *force* and if you will allow your force to be deflected and distracted at every moment by automatic associations, by random thoughts, by the shifting scene of external life, you will never have the force to remember yourself. The stream of things will carry you along. In all Self-Remembering the person must remember the *Work* and *what it is about*. He must remember, for example, that by the act of stopping all these mechanical streams in himself he may lift himself up to other influences far higher than he is. Unless you feel that the existence of higher centres is a possibility, you will not be able to do this—that is, unless you feel there is something beyond yourself and your poor little muddles in life, you will not be able to lift yourself up and as it were surrender yourself to something above you. Of course, if you really think that you yourself make your own thoughts, your own consciousness, your own physical life—if you ascribe everything to yourself—this act will be impossible. The reason is that you will not be able to concentrate force sufficiently or to have sufficient power of internal attention because you do not believe in what the Work teaches and its possible help. If you do not believe in a thing, you have no force for it. If you do not believe in a thing, it is not important to you. You may give it lip-service and that is all. But if you believe it worth while then the emotional evaluation will concentrate the force for it. In the illustration that I gave about reading a book and being distracted by a negative train of thought, the point is that if I value this book and the knowledge it contains I will retain enough force not to identify with the train of negative emotion automatically set going by association. It will become unimportant to me in view of the importance of something else. I remember O. once saying to some of us: "If you will make unimportant things important, how can you do this Work?" One of his meanings was that if you identify with unimportant things, and so put a great deal of force into them, you will have no force for concentration and attention. Your force will continually be drawn into 1,001 activities. Everyone should make a real effort to remember himself or herself once a day at least—and this cannot be done in the running stream of things. No one can remember himself in the running stream of inner and outer events—there has to be a distinct action, a distinct stopping of everything and a raising of oneself up to the whole idea of the Work, to the idea of higher centres that are speaking the whole time, to the whole idea of esoteric teaching throughout the ages, which has always spoken and is always speaking of the existence of these higher influences with which Man can come in contact. Man has been created to come in contact with these higher influences and in regard to them he has hitherto missed the mark, and so, in the literal meaning of the term he has "sinned"—because the word "sin" in the Gospels means to miss the mark, and the Gospels contain wonderful fragments bearing on esoteric teaching, and in this connection remember that this Work was defined by G. as the esoteric side of the Gospels.

Now please all remember that you have to do this Work fresh every day. Every day it is necessary to make yourself conscious of the Work internally, to be aware of it, to think of it, to try to remember any small aim you have and to try to get what the day will teach. You will remember that the Children of Israel were fed by manna from heaven and were told not to keep it to the next day, so do not think that because you understood something yesterday you will always remember it. Everything is changing but the Work remains the same. Once you have a point in the Work—and that means roughly a small centre of gravity—you will then know it presents itself differently every day like a wheel of turning meaning. Do not think that because you understood something last week it will remain always the same. On the contrary, all understanding grows because the Work is life and life must grow. So you will find that your understanding keeps on changing as the life of the Work grows in you, and yet it is always the same thing. When you begin to get force from the Work through your evaluation of it you must remember that it requires care. You may for days be unable to make proper effort, yet, as it was said, you know you are in some intermediary state. If you notice—if you have gone far enough—you are being tempted. Negative 'I's, violent 'I's, rude 'I's, contemptuous 'I's, that do not wish to work, are trying to beat down your feeling of the Work. These periods are in fact very interesting if you will observe them and if you have a certain power of noticing by inner taste negative

'I's. If you will keep a certain integrity in yourself and make an effort at the right moment or at least not let yourself be overcome, you will find that after a time this intermediate state passes and you will feel the Work again, but in a new form. Some people always stick here, but you must remember that in passing from one state to another even in the smallest degree there is an interval or gap between each state or level, and here you are bound to have doubts and inner distress. I advise here one thing only: if your doubts and distress are connected with anyone external you will never pass this interval. You have to see in some way that the trouble is really in yourself and is due to buffers, attitudes, habits of mind, etc. The Work is about change of being. Change of being is change of yourself. It is you yourself that has to be pulled through the sieve so that certain things are left behind. When one comes even on the smallest scale to this sieve the trouble always seems to be outside. Then you lose your force in negative states—self-justifying, self-pity. Now suppose you have no real experience in self-observation and have not done any preliminary sincere work in this respect, what will happen? The interesting state that you are in which might lead to a new state or level will lead back again because you have not given your own authority to yourself in overcoming this state of temptation, so to speak. I mean, you have forgotten that you are working on yourself. You may be dreaming you are working, just as you dream you are jumping over hurdles, but when you come to a real hurdle you do not see what it means and are merely offended. You instantly identify with everything in yourself, with all your negative 'I's; you forget to give any authority to your Work 'I's; you do not see you are up against a real situation, a real hurdle, that can only be passed over by actual work on oneself, against 'I's that are trying to keep you back. You are, so to speak, taking the situation from a life point of view, and not a Work point of view, in which case life is not your teacher but your destroyer. Life only becomes your teacher when you take it from a Work point of view.

Birdlip, September 23, 1944

A FURTHER NOTE ON PERSONAL WORK

ON SEEING SECOND FORCE IN ONESELF

We spoke recently of how long it takes to see that difficulties can be taken in a Work way and how we can be what I called tempted without seeing it simply because we take difficulties as if they should not exist. Now difficulty—that is, the force of resistance—is everywhere present and runs through the whole texture of life and also is present in ourselves. Mr. Ouspensky once said: "In trying to study Second Force it is best to begin to try to observe it in oneself." Everyone has inner difficulties but does not recognize them as being due to Second Force and takes them merely as handicaps from which they feel perhaps that they suffer unfairly. People say: "If only this . . . etc." The idea of Second Force is expressed in one of the laws of motion in Newtonian Physics where it is said that to every force there is an equal and opposite force. The laws that this Work formulates as being fundamental— i.e. the Law of Three and the Law of Octaves—exist both in nature and in ourselves. It is the Law of Three that concerns us now, which does not say that to every force there is an equal and opposite force but that in every *manifestation* three forces are at work: Active Force or the initiating force, Passive Force or the force of resistance, and Neutralizing Force which connects the two otherwise antagonistic opposite forces so that something happens—i.e. a manifestation takes place. But for the Third Force the other two forces, being equal and opposite, would produce a stationary state of affairs by being interlocked, like the horns of two equally powerful stags. It is the Third Force that by making a fulcrum makes things possible, that brings opposing things into harmony, that makes use of the otherwise irreconcilable opposites. The Work teaches that if we begin to see Second Force in ourselves we may catch a glimpse of Third Force but that first we must see First Force. We spoke recently about Will being defined in the Work as finding a *solution* and not as the negation of something. When you see some form of Second Force operating in your life, something that prevents you from attaining some object, which can be regarded as First or Active Force, something that keeps standing in your way, the situation demands a *solution* and not a denying merely; and it is here that an act of Will begins—in the reconciling of the situation. You cannot do away with Second Force by violence because it will only become stronger, but you may be able to be a *peace-maker* and in some way make it co-operate with Active Force through some new attitude to the situation, as Third Force. One of the most marvellous experiences is to realize how much useless Second Force we create in ourselves owing to our attitudes and imagination, and how endless forms of Second Force arise simply because we do not realize that we possess a number of attitudes and forms of expectancy which we do not observe and which act in such a way as to complicate every single thing in our lives by creating unnecessary and blind Second Force. To separate oneself a little from some of one's attitudes, from some ingrained prejudices and finally even from the power of some buffers, if this is possible, is to experience a degree of freedom that is very difficult to describe. One realizes that one has been in the power of something that one has never suspected and notices that one no longer has the same kind of artificial difficulties as formerly. Such an experience makes it possible for one to see one's life in the past more consciously because when there is a shift of the psychological state through an increase of consciousness—that is, say, of awareness of what one is like—one can see one's life in the past more distinctly from this freed and so more conscious point. One cannot see one's life, which is what has been made by one's level of being, from the *same* level of being. We are quite unable, for example, to see how extraordinarily foolish we have been in a thousand and one things or how unnecessarily complicated we have made some things, unless a new point of consciousness is born in us, from which to see it. You will not be able to see because you have nothing to see with—that is, no new standpoint. But if something has changed in you and you have thus so far been freed, say, from some attitude towards yourself or towards others or towards life, then you will be able to see how this attitude has worked in you throughout your life and you will know one meaning of the sentence: "Your level of being attracts your life." It is an interesting experience.

Now, to get back to what we were speaking of—that change of attitude or the freeing of oneself from some attitude will change the nature of Second Force in one's life—Full Will is defined technically in the Work as being connected with a power of being conscious in all three forces together. On one occasion it was said: "We are not even conscious in one force, still less in two, and never in three." This is partly to do with the fact that we can usually think of only one thing at a time. We find it very difficult to think in terms of two things and impossible to think in terms of three things. But this is not quite the same as Full Will, because being conscious in a force is not the same as *thinking* about it, just as being conscious of the truth of something is not the same as having a conviction about it, or being conscious in the state of Self-Remembering is not the same as thinking about Self-Remembering. To be conscious in First Force is to know what one wants; to be conscious in Second Force is to know what difficulties stand in the way; and to be conscious in Third Force at the same time is to be conscious of how what one wants and what opposes it can eventually reach some solution. Each Force modifies the other and indeed so much so that in the final solution the result is never like what you set out to attain—i.e. it is never like the Active Force with which you started. Nor, on the other hand, are the difficulties the same as you first were able to see them before the necessary Third Force or Neutralizing Force entered into the conscious sphere of experience and adjusted the relations of the First and Second Forces so as to make some manifestation possible.

Now I know all this may sound theoretical but it is not theoretical: it is quite practical and can be experienced up to a point even now if one knows what to look for and if one has the patience to do it. We must, first of all, be conscious as far as we can in what corresponds to First Force. That is, taking the forces as they act within us, psychologically, one must be conscious in what one wants, what one wishes, or what one expects. By making this force conscious, instead of thinking about it, which one can often do by a process of inner dialogue, as well as self-observation over a considerable period, one becomes aware of the Second Force that is inevitably called up by the particular quality of the First Force that one has—i.e. what one wants. Each Active Force calls up its own Second Force. If you are in a hurry, everyone will seem to you to be moving very slowly: if you want to move slowly, everyone else will seem to you to be in a hurry. When you live for a time in the consciousness of what you want, you will at the same time see more and more the Second Force that it gives rise to, so the more will you become conscious in two forces simultaneously. You will see that you cannot do this or that because of that or this. Yes, but you will see why. By not identifying with either—and this we practically always do, which spoils the whole experience—you may catch a glimpse of the Third Force entering by magic that makes the First and Second Force come into a possible relationship, so that they are no longer felt as opposing forces, as a conflict of opposites. This is finding a solution and you will notice that it has to do with *Will*, Will having three aspects in itself, or three forces, and Conscious Will being therefore consciousness in all three forces, which leads to an act of Full Will. While this is beyond us at present it is possible on a small scale. However, we take a one-sided view of "Will" and conceive it always as something that cuts away, that divides, that prohibits, that is harsh, intolerant, unyielding and negating and sticking to one unvarying course. You must see that Will from the Work point of view refers to something responding, something flexible and intelligent that it is not one-sided but three-sided. Will is of course from Master or Real 'I' in us and this we cannot expect to know directly. But as long as we are one-sided in every sense nothing can come from this upper level from which the influences of Real 'I' come that give us our real meaning and inner peace. We must at least learn to have double thinking first of all, to see things from different sides and to externally consider—not only to see the difficulties of other people by putting ourselves in their place, which is a definite conscious act, but to see the difficulties in ourselves without identifying, and as objectively as possible, because in this way we get a new feeling of ourselves and a new and more flexible sense of what we are, which has a very strange effect on us and is due to an increase of consciousness or light and is really the beginning of the action of the Work upon us.

★   ★   ★

We so often feel we are up against things. People often live in this state all their lives. It is then necessary, as by inner dialogue with oneself, such as: "What is it I am up against?" etc. to find out what it is you are up against, because what you feel you are up against is due to what you want. Then perhaps you are full of impossible and vague wishes that create useless Second Force and so produce in you the equally vague feelings of resistance, of being up against things. Then you have to begin to become more conscious in First Force, in what you want. This sharpens the mind and makes you practical. But do not think it is easy. At the same time it is not right or good to live always in a vague sense of being lost, of disappointment, of looking back. This eats your force. Where are you? What do you want? What is the matter with you? Such harsh questioning of oneself becomes increasingly necessary in the Work.

Birdlip, September 30, 1944

WHAT THE WORK TEACHES ABOUT WAR

This is an important paper. Many questions are asked about how the Work regards War and particularly this war. People say: "What is War? Why should War be?" Or they say: "Does God will War?" and "If God wills War, can he be a God?" In fact, many people who have some Magnetic Centre, some power of seeing differences in the quality of things, some power of spiritual thinking rather than physical thinking, become overwhelmed by the increasing horrors of War.

Some people asked O. at the beginning of this war why it happened, what was the reason for it, and so on. He said: "All of you in this Work must try to *understand* why War exists." He constantly taught that the most powerful force that we can create in ourselves is understanding. He said: "This Work gives us knowledge about our situation on this Earth; and understanding means to understand the knowledge that we are given about our situation on Earth. However, most people think that understanding can be gained simply from their ordinary knowledge and do not realize that, in order to *understand*, new knowledge is necessary, and that this new knowledge must combine with our being in order to create new understanding."

Now the first thing that is said in this connection is that the Will of the Absolute does not reach this Earth directly. If you like, you can call the Absolute God in the supreme sense, only the work does not use this term. The Ray of Creation explains how the Will of the Absolute, or the Supreme God, passes downwards in successive stages of creation through the action of the Law of 3, the Law of Three Forces, continually reduplicating itself. As you know, on this Earth, in terms of the particular Ray of Creation to which we belong, we are under 48 orders of laws. The Will of the Absolute, according to this teaching, can only reach us in the form of 48 orders of laws—i.e. the Will of the Absolute cannot reach us directly. It was said once at a very early meeting that if the Will of the Absolute intervened, the direct result would be that the whole of Creation would be smashed and destroyed. O. once talking about this said: "It is like a card-game. If you alter the rules of the card-game, then there is no game." This is the central idea that we must start from in thinking about why War and all its horrors exist on this planet very low down in the scheme of Creation. And here you

519

must remember that the Work teaches that we must try to put ourselves under the laws that operate from higher levels in the Ray of Creation. This is the first point.

The second point is that the Work teaches that all War is caused by extra-terrestrial forces coming most immediately from the movements of the planets. On one occasion O. asked G. what was the cause of War and G. said: "It is something like this. Two planets approach each other rather closely and produce a tension which reflects itself on the Earth and may go on for many years in regard to human Time." From this remark of G.'s O. understood that Time was different on different scales—i.e. planetary Time may be momentary to the planets, but a long time to Humanity on this Earth. O. then asked G. how Man could prevent these extra-terrestrial tensions from acting on him in the way they did. G. said that these tensions affected Man because he was not yet properly developed, not yet fully conscious, and that if Man were conscious these tensions would produce quite different results and instead of producing a destructive course of events would produce a quite different course. What would be the result of an increased tension between planets if it were more consciously taken? This inner tension, whether it be due to planets or things happening on the level of the Sun, would act on Man working more consciously by increasing his consciousness and would make him more awake instead of making him more asleep, more violent, more destructive. As you know, the object of this Work is to make it possible for our ordinary centres to receive higher centres in the right way. As we are now, if we receive force directly from higher centres, which would be comparable to receiving millions of volts suddenly, we should either go mad or get very violent or have epileptic fits, or become 1,000 times more negative, more full of hatred and desire to kill. Because Man is asleep the Work teaches that he cannot receive force for his awakening unless he works on himself for a long time, and so prevents any increase of force that comes to him from turning into more negative states and violence. All esoteric teaching is about this preparation of lower centres and working on them for the reception of higher centres from higher up in the *Ray of Creation*.

The third point is that although Man is part of Organic Life on the surface of the Earth, which is created in order to give a transmitting shock between the notes *Fa* and *Mi* in the Ray of Creation so as to pass influences down from the higher parts of the Ray to the terminal buds which are the Moons, it is no longer necessary for him at this stage to serve under this slavery. G. said that just at this period it was possible for mankind no longer to be slaves to this *pain-factory* on the Earth called Organic Life through whose sufferings the lower parts of the Ray are nourished, including our Moon which is gradually developing in terms of planetary Time. He said that if Man would only become more conscious his slavery might end, but that owing to habits formed through centuries, habits of feeling, habits of thinking, attitudes, etc.

it looked as though Man would continue to serve a purpose that was no longer necessary. "The problem is," he said in so many words, "that Man has reached a stage in which he can become more conscious, and if he did so everything would change. But because of traditions, prejudices, because, in short, of his mechanicalness, he cannot reach this point, and so is going downhill just at the moment in which he might give a shock to himself and pass into a new world-order." Asked whether this development of totalitarianism were a step in the right direction, he said: "No—quite the contrary. Man is simply putting himself under more slavery by these collective movements. The development of consciousness is an individual development. And, as I have said frequently, when War comes Man throws away even the small amount of consciousness that he normally· possesses. In fact, he becomes quite insane and does not see his insanity. Consciousness is weighed and measured and there is only a certain quantity of it. But there is enough of this force of consciousness to change everything on the Earth if people would only use it." Asked what he thought about the future G. said that people were going in the direction of decreased consciousness and would form either colónies of bees or colonies of ants. He said on another occasion: "Well, you have your choice. Would you be bees or would you be ants?"

The fourth point is that Man is at a certain place in the Octave of his own development between the notes *Mi* and *Fa*. O. suggested that we might think of this in the following terms. Starting in the ascending Octave from *Do*, he said: "We might regard a single individual as *Do*, a family group as *Re* and a nation as the note *Mi*. As you know, between *Mi* and *Fa* it is necessary for a shock to be given. All our ordinary life consists of broken octaves of the order of *Do*, *Re*, *Mi*, over and over again." O. continued: "To get to the note *Fa*, with regard to mankind, while Man must retain his individual feeling at the note *Do*, his family and responsible feeling at the note *Re*, his national feeling at the note *Mi*, he must pass to a new feeling at the note *Fa* in which he can feel the existence of other nations." He said: "Right creation of international feeling—i.e. the note *Fa*—must always depend upon the 3 previous notes being sounded—i.e. *Do*, *Re*, *Mi*—and finally *Fa*. The artificial attempts to sound the note *Fa*, which we might call international consciousness, are being made at the expense of the notes, *Do*, *Re*, *Mi*. That is to say, people are being asked to be entirely collective and to sacrifice their individuality for collective organizations." People throw away even the consciousness to which they have a right when they unite in enormous masses as in revolutions, wars, etc. This is collectivism. A man must isolate himself from these collective forces inwardly before he can even hope to feel the magic touch of the individuality awaiting him at a higher level. Although he has to isolate, himself inwardly he has to play a collective part as a Good Householder without identifying with it. Let me remind you again of the definition of a Good Householder as a person who, whether man or woman, does his or her duty and feels responsibility in regard to life but does not believe in life. This does not mean that a Good Householder believes in anything else. The integrity of the world at present and in the future depends on the number of Good Householders that exist in every nation. As you know, there are certain theories arising at present to the effect that Man is made for the Sabbath. The present war is really between those who think that Man is made for the Sabbath, and those who think that the Sabbath is made for Man. This is the real formulation of the present conflict. Ants and bees think that Man is made for the Sabbath —i.e. for the state—and you can see what has happened to them. All this present situation was formulated 2,000 years ago in that form of esotericism which is transmitted in the Gospels in the teaching of a Conscious Man who said, when he healed a man with a withered hand on the Sabbath and was accused for so doing: "The Sabbath was made for Man and not Man for the Sabbath." The hand means power of doing and to have a withered hand was to have no power of individual action. Do you not think there is some very deep connection here? Do you not think that if the view that Man was made for the Sabbath gains ground every man's hand will become withered? If you sound the note *Fa* wrongly you will have a situation produced in which individuals have to sacrifice everything for the sake of a world of inter-nationalism. All development of consciousness must take place through definite stages *each of which must remain as a note sounding in the individual development*. The attempt to increase consciousness by such forms of international groups will only make Man more and more collective and less and less individual. It is quite true to say: "Patriotism is not enough." But if internationalism does away entirely with patriotism you will get the wrong octave. The consciousness will not develop in the right way and we will go in the direction of the bees or the ants who have given up all sense of individuality and have become simply state-insects lacking consciousness, and hating other ant-heaps or hives.

Let us represent the Octave that O. suggested in the following terms:

Do	Organic Life
Si	Humanity
La	The White Race
Sol	Our Civilization
Fa	Europe
Mi	A Nation
Re	A Family
Do	Man

You will see that each note must depend on the strength of the sounding of the lower note—i.e. unless *Do*, which is the individual person, sounds strongly enough, Man will lose all individuality in the sounding of the note *Mi* which is the state. What we are fighting for really is not in my opinion expressed by the word democracy but in the sounding of these different notes *Do, Re, Mi,* in their right harmony, as it were, with the possibility of sounding the note *Fa*—i.e. international consciousness and feeling—without loss of the other three notes.

The fifth idea of this Work is that Man is created a self-developing organism and can reach a higher level of being by right knowledge and work. This, perhaps, is the most central idea of all. Man is *inferior* to himself as he is, asleep in the world and serving nature—i.e. the necessities of the Great Ray which uses Man as part of Organic Life for its own purposes. Here people must study the origin of Organic Life, as a Side-Octave from the level of the Sun. Man asleep, Man mechanical, is *used*. But he is created not to be so used—if he makes an *individual* effort to awaken and separate from Personality. But he must be helped by esoteric teaching. All this part requires long and deep thinking over many years.

★　　★　　★

Now I will add one thing more. *If Essence could remember, War would cease.* When Essence is re-born in Recurrence it chooses the same situation, the same part of Time, and everything will be the same, *if it has not grown.* All development in the Work-sense is the development of Essence, and this always remembers. Of course collective War can scarcely make people remember because collective War is a manifestation of Personality. State War is obviously a manifestation of a collective Personality. However, some people in their war experiences may remember. All people who are killed in this war are being born again in the past and some may remember next time. This means that in Recurrence people may remember and so change the future that when they come to 1938, say, they will remember. But if they have fought spuriously, if they have never deeply thought about what they are doing and understood it, they will do it all over again. All progress in Humanity depends on those who remember, those who, recurring again in the past, remember what happened before—"in the future".

VALUATION OF THE WORK

On one occasion G. spoke about the importance of being good merchants. He said in so many words: "Many things are said about merchants in ancient sacred writings. For example, several things are said about merchants in the Gospels. You have to learn what it means to be 'good merchants'." On another occasion, speaking of the Work he was teaching, G. said: "I have good leather to sell for those who wish to make shoes."

★   ★   ★

Practical common sense must enter into the Work. For instance, if I do not value the Work, practical common sense will tell me that I will begin to lose it. One easily loses what one does not value. A practical relation to the Work is necessary, as G. indicated in the above words—not a sentimental one. When I do not work, I find the Work at an increasing distance from me. It is not surprising that this should be so. It is a practical question. When I work, I get something from the Work sooner or later, and when I do not work I do not get anything from the Work. This is a practical relation of things, and as a good merchant I should be capable of seeing how the matter stands and what to expect. If I put nothing into the Bank I will soon be overdrawn. But remember that in the case of the Work as a Bank it pays good interest—it gives back considerably more than you put in. This idea is often spoken of in the New Testament and elsewhere—for example, in the Sermon on the Mount, the words occur: "Give, and it shall be given unto you; good measure, pressed down, shaken together, running over . . ." (*Luke* VI 38).

Let us take the saying of G. that he has leather to sell for those who wish to make shoes. Two stages are shewn: first, one must buy the leather, and second, one must make it into shoes for oneself. What does this buying of leather mean? No one will buy leather if he does not value it. Later on the question continually arises as to how one values the Work. What one started with becomes useless. What is the quality of one's evaluation of it at this moment? On this depends the capacity of eventually making shoes. However, for a long time one's valuation of the Work is inevitably mixed up with all sorts of other ordinary valuations in life and has to lie side by side with them. Afterwards a separation begins. The inner taste is developed to the point of discriminating internally between one's different kinds of valuing. Valuing has really to do with what one loves. Now, for a long time, we love through ourselves as reflected in others. Love is a difficult word, used in many senses, on many scales, and usually absurdly. The central idea of the Work is that there is another order above us. If one disbelieves this, then the Work remains as something on the same scale as life and its interests. In life, we do things from a certain side difficult to define.

On this subject Mr. Ouspensky once spoke in private. Someone said: "Self-love." He was not satisfied with this definition. Others said: "Self-admiration," "Self-merit", and so on. Someone suggested "Self-liking". Mr. Ouspensky seemed more inclined to this word and said: "Yes, something like that. One has to see it acting, however, apart from words." If one does this Work only from "self-liking", one's valuation of the Work is mixed up with this factor. The Work is not a higher order yet, not something beyond oneself. It rests actually on one's self-esteem. Naturally, if the self-esteem, the self-liking, is offended, the Work fades, and becomes a remote thing. This difficulty belongs to everyone. A man or a woman, people like ourselves, through self-admiration, or self-liking, really love themselves in preference to others and under the influence of this form of love despise others in comparison with themselves. It is not difficult to observe this point or level in oneself. In that situation or at that level of being, we are liable to dislike or even hate those who do not pay us proper attention, and in some way respect or honour us and our viewpoints and behaviour and do not to some extent praise or approve what we do or say. So we feel a desire for revenge, for retaliation, or even cruelty, if this form of love is not satisfied. We may love very much all those who pay us sufficient homage in one way or another—that is, our love is connected with an expansion of our self-love. It is rarely independent of it. From this basis we usually start in this Work. So we take the Work as an expansion of ourselves, that feeds the self-merit. This, I have already said, is inevitable at first. Its presence can be seen by self-observation and reflection. The Work then is not really something bigger than oneself but something that under favourable circumstances makes one feel bigger. But this is a usual course, an experience that one must have until some feeling makes one face it and see on what basis one values the Work. One asks oneself: "What is the quality of my valuation? Where do I put the Work in myself? Is my valuation of myself far greater than my valuation of the Work?" The first step is to realize that it is, and not pretend.

Now a change in the quality of the love always represents a change in the level of being. One can be taught all things but, unless the level of being is raised; it leads to nothing. This is the greatest problem of esoteric or conscious teaching, whose aim is to raise Man from barbarism. Barbarism increasingly threatens us to-day in this age when knowledge is taken as the goal and not change in the level of being. Knowledge and being must grow together to produce understanding. Now self-liking, self-love, self-admiration, self-merit, vanity and so on, if they take the first place, indicate a level of being from which the Work cannot develop later on. One must love the Work—not oneself only. There is a certain insight possible whereby one sees, in a glimpse, the size of oneself in respect of the size of the Work. However, this insight comes long before anything can be done about it. But it means that some 'I' or some 'I's that wish to work have got free momentarily from the mass of 'I's that live in the atmosphere of life-interests, of self-praise, etc. and begin to feel other influences. It is like the difference between something thick, dark and heavy and something freer and lighter and having more light. One can then only be aware that one has not got the right kind of valuation. It is a feeling, uncritical in itself, comparable to realizing that one is dressed badly or in some vulgar style. It means, of course, the attitude to the Work is wrong. An attitude is what we are mentally dressed in, our mental clothes. One has to find how to dress the mind and feeling. One has to search for clothes of the right kind, and change them on the right occasions.

The Work cannot be a function of life—I mean, we cannot make our feeling of it depend on our daily personal successes or failures. It is certainly different in quality and demands a different quality of love. I say love because I see little difference between love and valuation when taken in a practical way. I say that *valuation is love*; and I say also that if you say you love a person and do not value that person it is not love. You must *love the Work* to feel it and to teach it. Peter is asked if he loves, and answers "Yes", and is told by Christ: "Feed my lambs". But he cannot because his love is mixed with self-love too much. So he is told at last: "Feed my sheep". Peter does not possess the quality of love denoted by the word used when Christ asks him the question the first and second times: he understands love as a violent, jealous, easily-hurt state—a self-love expanded. Then nothing penetrates to the Essence and feeds it. So the third time in asking the question Christ uses another word for love, the word used by Peter all through the passage. Christ has been speaking of Conscious Love that has no opposite. Here is something marvellous for us to think about—the quality, the valuation of our love. Everything starts and everything depends on this groundwork, which must change and so change us —otherwise one crystallizes out at a poor level. There is a valuation that feeds everything young and fresh in us and is capable of infinite varieties of understanding and growth, compared with lambs. That cannot be anything heavy, sheep-like. It cannot be something tedious. Nor can it be connected with any ingrained insincerity of mind. One can take pleasure in the existence of this Work. One can take interest in its teaching and in reflection on what it says about Man and his life on this planet. These are necessary forms of valuation. But they do not conflict with the self-love, so they do not make the Work emotionally strong enough. "You must," said G., "be capable of being turned and twisted in every direction in this Work and keep your direction". This means, of course, that your valuation of the Work, your attitude to it, your love of it, is stronger than all the manifestations of the self-love. Nothing that can happen to you can break you. The Work is then another being in you, another body. But this being, this body, cannot be formed from the self-love. This is the point. For a long time all that can be done is to notice oneself in all these connections of which I have spoken above.

SELF-OBSERVATION AND SELF-REMEMBERING

Part I.—A person's Understanding of the Work is relative to his Level of Being. He may know the ideas of the Work. But Knowledge does not give Understanding: to know is not to understand. The Knowledge of this Work is of a kind that can act on Being and as a result give rise to Understanding. Understanding is not Knowledge and Understanding is not Being. Knowledge and Being together, in conjunction, give Understanding. If my Being is such that it wills what I know, the result will eventually be increasing Understanding. If it does not will what I know, I will have Knowledge only. But if some 'I's wish to follow the Knowledge of this Work, their will to do it will pass into Understanding on a small scale compared with what would happen if the whole Being were to act as one and will as one to apply the Knowledge of the Work and live what it says. That would be Real Will, which is beyond us. So we have to start where we are, with all our separate and conflicting wills, and maintain an inner steadfastness amidst the confusions that take place in our mixed Being. That is, we must value the Work and keep Work 'I's in us alive and protect them from all kinds of crude, rough or cynical or negative 'I's. Of course, unless there were this struggle, there would be no work. To work means to work: and work means effort. Work is the effort to connect one's Knowledge of the Work with one's Being—that is, the effort to bring *what one knows* into relation with *what one is.* For this, self-observation is obviously necessary in order to notice what one is. And again, for this, Knowledge is necessary, to shew what to observe. This is a plain and logical sequence —namely, that to know what one is one must observe oneself and in order to know what to observe one must have Knowledge. But the Work teaches a Knowledge not only of what we have to observe— as, for example—negative states—but what we must do—as, for example, practise non-identifying with ourselves and especially with False Personality. But all this teaching is in view of the supreme idea of the Work and indeed of all esotericism in the past—i.e. that there *is* a higher level of consciousness possible for Man that he can reach if he cleans his machine and gets rid of many useless things that complicate his life and keep him in a state of sleep. And here comes in the most important instruction given: not only must a man *know* and *observe*, but he must *remember himself.* And he must do this because only in that state of consciousness called the state of Self-Remembering can influences reach him that can act on his Being, for without help a man can *do* practically nothing, or will only effect one thing at the expense of another. Now 'I's that wish to work and connect the Knowledge of the Work with their lives and feel unhappy if they do not and ill if they do not keep awake—these 'I's change in their Understanding. They must be fed so that they can see things in a new way. That is, one has to re-think, re-visit, re-interpret the ideas. Merely to know one must observe or self-remember is nothing: the matter must be gone over again and again. One must return to first principles again and again. So the fresh discussion of what has been discussed more than once is something absolutely necessary.

A question was asked at the last meeting held here, as to Self-Observation and Self-Remembering. This is the question:

> As I understand it there is a difference in quality between the State of Self-Remembering and an Act of Self-Remembering and many degrees of, or levels of, quality between Acts of Self-Remembering; yet the least of these is greater than—i.e. on a level above—the fullest Self-Observation. There can be no progress unless and until a man remembers himself. All work on himself below that level is preparatory to progress towards Consciousness. Further—a man can protect himself psychologically only by Self-Remembering. *How can one evaluate and through evaluation increase the power to value, not for what it can give but for what it is, this state of Self-Remembering?*

I will begin by speaking in a general way about Self-Observation and Self-Remembering. The observation of oneself is not the same thing as remembering oneself. On one occasion G., speaking of Self-Remembering, said: "Which self do you wish to remember?" This gives one clue to the meaning of remembering oneself. On another occasion he said that Man is sub-normal because he is not conscious at the place of incoming impressions. "At this point," he said, "where external impressions enter, it is necessary to create something."

* * *

Let us now pass to the idea of Self-Observation and return later to the question of Self-Remembering. I was once asked by someone this question: "I do not understand what the Work means when it says that we do not observe ourselves. I have always observed myself." No doubt, it is true to say that a person to a certain extent observes himself. People look into a mirror and this mirror is constructed from what they have been taught—that is, what they have acquired by their upbringing as to right behaviour, correct manners, the right things to wear, the right things to say, the right people to know. This acquired part of us is the Personality and the formation of the Personality in everybody is a question of the period, the environment in which one is born, school influences, the fashion of the day, the nation to which one belongs and the standards which it sets. Into this mirror everybody gazes—and indeed it is not only psychological but it is also the actual literal mirror. But this mirror is not the same mirror as the Work teaches us to gaze into: the Work-mirror is something quite different. It has, so to speak, nothing to do with whether you eat peas with a knife or put your elbows on the table or wear the right tie or use the right lipstick or know the right people. The Work-mirror refers to a quite different kind of Self-Observation. Through the Work-mirror it is possible to begin to see what one really is apart from what one appears to be and pretends to be. However, at first the Work-mirror may be all wrong. That always arises when we do not see what the Work is about and when Magnetic Centre is weak. We still look at ourselves from the life-mirror and try to connect our acquired virtues, that we appreciate through our self-love, with the Work-mirror.

Some of you have reflected on the Knowledge this Work teaches from which we have to observe ourselves. If so, you will probably have felt that it seems to teach something that is remote from the life we are leading. For example, what connection is there with our ordinary life when we are told to observe the work of centres, to observe three distinct persons in us, and then to observe many different 'I's in us, to observe our state of sleep, to observe internal considering and the making of accounts against others, to observe negative emotions, to observe identifying, to observe our ignorance, to observe the Level of our Being, to observe how we never remember ourselves and so on? It all seems remote, difficult to grasp; yet, from all these ideas the real Work-mirror is formed. No one can look into this Work-mirror unless he or she has acquired Knowledge of what this Work is about, and loves it. The Work teaches us from what points of view we must observe ourselves. It picks out certain things that we have to notice in ourselves. Imagine being told to go into an enormous store and being told merely to observe it. You would not know what to observe. But supposing you are told to go into this store and observe a few special things only: then you will know what you have to take notice of. It is this that the Work teaches. The Work teaches how to approach yourself, through self-observation, what to notice and what to work against. In this respect it gives very definite directions which, however difficult they may be to follow, are yet *very definite*. If you love the Work—that is, if you value it—then you will be able to assimilate the knowledge that it teaches, according to your level. If you assimilate, even to a small extent, the knowledge that it teaches, you will begin to possess a mirror in which to look at yourself. For a long time we have poor mirrors that distort things. After a time, we may realize that we have wrong attitude to the Work. But it is exactly this realization that can give you a new mirror. Then you begin to see yourself better; you begin to see how you have treated the Work so far.

Now I will repeat again that Self-Observation without definite knowledge as to what to observe will lead nowhere in the Work. Ordinary, mechanical self-observation may lead you into social life, but this is not the same thing. The mirror of social life is one thing and into this all people gaze. The Work says nothing against this. But it speaks of another mirror having another quality. The ancient inscription on the Greek temple: "Know thyself," is by itself quite ineffective. How can you know yourself? People all think they know themselves already but the Work teaches that we have to know ourselves in a new way and from certain angles, and the object of this particular kind of knowing of oneself is to make it possible to separate from a number of useless things that go on in us so that we can begin to touch influences coming from a higher level that will give us thoughts and feelings and understanding that we have a right to have, but with which we have lost contact owing to our state of sleep. All esoteric teaching is about awakening to far finer influences—yes, here down on this Earth. Mr. Ouspensky once said: "Here now on this Earth you can be under different laws, different influences and know and understand what they mean, provided you work on yourself." I remember when Mr. Ouspensky said this many people were astonished because they thought that being in a better state meant being in a better world, that no doubt they might reach after death. As you all know, the general idea taught in the Gospels that one must die to be re-born is taken to mean physical death and being born into some other world called heaven. The Work and the Gospels teach, however, that if we can reach higher influences that are already playing on us now we will be in a different state of understanding. For example, the Work says that we will no longer be under the Law of Accident—and negative emotions especially put us under the Law of Accident. However, this belongs to another talk.

To continue: the whole Work is about putting our ordinary centres into a right state so that they can transmit intelligently the influences of higher centres which exist in us fully formed and are continually at work, but to which we cannot respond. "Why," asked someone, "is this so?" "Because," Mr. O. said, "we are continually identified with a thousand and one useless things both in life and in ourselves." Mr. O. always especially emphasized the importance of working on the negative part of Emotional Centre. He said on one occasion in so many words: "We identify with our negative emotions more than with anything else. It seems as if we felt we had a right to be negative whereas I teach you the very reverse—i.e. that we have a right not to be negative." When we are negative it is as if we had a blood-vessel cut, pouring out our blood. As long as the negative part of our Emotional Centre, which we were not born with but have acquired from others, is allowed to exist unchallenged, so long is it impossible for our Emotional Centre to feel the influences of the Higher Emotional Centre. For this reason the observation of our negative states and the separation from them is one of the most important sides of practical work. The transformation of negative emotion belongs to the Second Conscious Shock and here the whole Work comes in and the whole evaluation of it. You may be negative but you must feel that it is not you that is negative but *It*. This is the beginning of inner separation, of not identifying with negative states, of not identifying with oneself.

To resume what we were speaking about—you can understand that to be taught the knowledge that you are taught in this Work about negative emotions is one thing, but as mere knowledge it is useless. It remains theoretical only—in the memory. You have to apply the knowledge to yourself and this is only possible through observing yourself. Unless you connect the knowledge of this Work with Self-Observation, nothing can happen to you. The Work will remain purely theoretical and not practical. The function of Self-Observation, therefore, is something that can be understood quite logically. Its object is clear. However, at first Self-Observation is very crude, very irregular, and mixed up with life-observation of oneself—that is, the Work-mirror is mixed up with the life-mirror, and this is inevitable. In fact, for a long time, the Work-mirror is little else than the life-mirror. It is, as it were, connected with the neutralizing force of life and not the neutralizing force of the Work, which latter force comes from an entirely different source. As the evaluation of the Work deepens the two mirrors become separated and in that case where you may derive a great deal of flattery and self-delight from the one mirror you do not see the same image in the other, and this causes inner trouble. Yet I say the two mirrors are not antagonistic. They reflect different aspects of oneself. In the 4th Way, which is this Work, we have to be both in the Work and in life, and the 4th Way does not make a contradiction between life and Work. Some sides belong to life and others to the Work. It is more like making a right arrangement of the different 'I's and putting them in their right place and having the strength not to see merely opposites. It is the distinction of 'I's by inner taste. We need both the Work and life, and from both we can get force. It is like two rooms, quite distinct, and yet opening into one another, both being part of the same house of oneself. No one is told in this Work to cut himself off from life, to go into a monastery or into the desert. And yet the two are entirely different and their force comes from two different sides altogether. G. once said in so many words: "Everything this Work teaches you will help your life and help you to attain your life-aim." Just imagine a man in the Work who could pass into the affairs of life and through inner work had learned not to identify—you can understand that such a man might attain some aim in life far more easily than a mechanical negative man. But in order to do so he would continually have to feel the Work to such an extent that his evaluation of the Work was far more intense and real to him than anything he valued or attained in life.

Now we identify through the unobserved petty feelings of ourselves which cause us to make endless internal accounts and build up endless negative systems in us. These negative systems, once formed, are very difficult to deal with. On this level we do everything in a pseudo way, from our self-love, our self-liking, to advance ourselves in some way, to merit praise, and so we are very easily hurt and dejected. Remove this stimulus and we scarcely exist, and may seem to have no objective. This is being a machine. All this basis of self-feeling does not lead far in the Work eventually. It is only vanquished by a sense of something greater than ourselves. This brings us to the question of *Self-Remembering* which is so much emphasized in this Work as the constantly necessary accompaniment to self-observation. "A man," said G., "should always remember himself but as he is he has not the force and even cannot remember that he has to remember himself." On another occasion Mr. O. said at the beginning of his teaching in London when people were continually badgering him with questions as to what they should do—whether they should smoke or not, eat or not, and so on—: "The most important thing is to remember yourself. You can do what you like so long as you remember yourself." This sounded very strange to many of us. It seemed to mean that you could do anything you liked —yes, as long as you remembered yourself. Supposing you give way to your appetites and become identified, say, with your food, and then tell yourself that you are allowed to do anything—the Work says so. But does it say it like that? It says you can do anything you like as long as you remember yourself and it is obvious enough that if you are identified with your food you are not remembering yourself. Self-Remembering puts us into a different state of consciousness. In that state of consciousness you cannot do certain things without going to sleep at once and you can see it happening—that is, you can see yourself becoming identified. Or, to put the matter differently, if you do certain things and remember yourself at the same time, you will do them in quite a different way. When you begin to understand the subtlety of this remark: "You can do what you like as long as you remember yourself," you will see that it really means that you cannot do what you like, at least in the ordinary way that you do it. One form of Self-Remembering is feeling the sense of "I doing this" or "I saying this". If when you are angry and speaking internally or externally in a bad way you feel the sense of 'I' saying this, it will completely change the situation. You realize that "*It*" is saying it—your machine.

Now let us once more go through the things said about Self-Remembering. Let us say to ourselves: "I am not me". It will be best if I take my own case—suppose I can say: "I am not Nicoll and Nicoll is not me" or say that Mr. Bush says to himself: "I am not Bush and Bush is not me" or Mr. Taylor says: "I am not Taylor and Taylor is not me". If we can say this to ourselves rightly it will give us a very strange feeling as to who we are. Certainly this feeling is connected with a sense of the dissolving of one's Personality. Yet as you know this is one of the objects of this Work expressed in the great formulation that Personality must be made passive so that the real part of one—the Essence—can grow. But it can only be through a long gradual process of insight. I remember Mr. O. saying to me: "Why don't you say sometimes: 'What is Nicoll up to?'" Now supposing I could always say to myself: "What is Nicoll up to?" and Mr. Bush could say "What is Bush up to?" and Mr. Taylor: "What is Taylor up to?" and all of you could say correspondingly the same thing in some real way occasionally, it would mean then that there was some degree of inner separation, some awareness that one is not the same as one's acquired Personality, with all its acquired prides and buffers—this artificial figure that life has built up, and that one takes as oneself not knowing any better.

Such a feeling, such an inner sense, is the beginning of Self-Remembering. When I try to remember myself I do not remember Nicoll: I do not wish to remember Nicoll, but of course he is always there. But if I have no feeling that I am not Nicoll (although actually I am a slave to Nicoll) when I remember myself I will simply remember Nicoll. Of course, Nicoll will always remember Nicoll mechanically and certainly Nicoll is satisfied with Nicoll and no doubt regards him as a marvellous person. In that case, Self-Remembering would only increase one's self-satisfaction—that is, it would enhance Personality. But this is not Self-Remembering, or, let us say, it is remembering the wrong self. It is not a conscious act but a mechanical act. Do you notice how you always justify yourselves? It is not a reaching up to something else, but an intensifying and justifying of what one is already. So it cannot lead to a change in the level of Being. It has nothing to do with Self-Remembering in the Work-sense. It usually means there is not real self-observation—that is, self-observation done through the mirror of the Work. The Work has not yet begun to break up the Personality. One is simply taking the Work from the Personality as something added to one's own merits, like a medal. Of course this is not the Work. The Work cannot start from the fullness of the Personality. The Work can only start when you realize you are not what you thought, not what you pretend to be. You have only to read the Sermon on the Mount to see what is meant. When the Work really strikes home, this house of cards that one takes as oneself begins to fall to bits. You know the Work speaks about the necessity of coming to the point where one realizes one's own utter *nothingness*. This, however, is·mercifully delayed and it is not something you can artificially realize. You cannot pretend to be nothing. It is very painful to see a person pretending that he or she is nothing.

Now Self-Remembering is connected with all this. To remember yourself simply as you are now is not Self-Remembering. Self-Remembering comes down from above and full Self-Remembering is a state of consciousness in which the Personality and all its pretences almost cease to exist and you are, so to speak, nobody, and yet the fullness of this state, which is really bliss, makes you, for the first time, somebody.

SELF-OBSERVATION AND SELF-REMEMBERING

Part II.—In this second paper we come to answering the question that was quoted in the last paper. I will repeat the first part of this question:

"As I understand it, there is a difference in quality between the state of Self-Remembering and an act of Self-Remembering, and many degrees of, or levels of, quality between acts of Self-Remembering; yet the least of these is greater than—i.e. on a level above—the fullest Self-Observation . . ."

The act of Self-Remembering is a conscious effort made in order to remember oneself. The state of Self-Remembering is the result of the act and the quality of the state of Self-Remembering depends on the quality of the act—i.e. the quality of the effort made to remember oneself. Let us try to illustrate this in an easy way. The act of taking my guitar and striking notes on it is different from the state of being able to play music on it. However, I will have to make an effort to take the guitar and play on it before I can reach the state of being able to play music. Again, if I want to behave better or have better manners the act of trying to is not the same as being in the state of having better behaviour or manners. If I make right effort, I may reach the state that I wish to attain, and the result will be according to the quality of my effort. The act of trying to remember myself is to endeavour by trial and failure to reach some new state of oneself called the State of Self-Remembering. If already I know how to reach this state then the act or effort that I make will put me into this state. But I cannot expect at first by performing the act of Self-Remembering to reach the State. It will only be by long work, by innumerable acts, that I gain any success in reaching the state that I aim at reaching.

Now let us take the second parts of the question in which it is said:

"There can be no progress unless and until a man remembers himself . . ."

I think that it would be best to say here that unless a man can lift himself up by Self-Remembering he does not receive help, and that unless a man receives help he cannot reach a different level of being. But at the same time unless he prepares himself by means of Self-Observation and trying to separate from what the Work teaches are wrong functions, he cannot receive the influences coming from Higher Centres. Man has to prepare his lower centres so that they can hear the voices of Higher Centres which are always speaking to us and always trying to change us but which we cannot hear. I do not mean that the Higher Centres are trying to change us exactly, because they are neutral, not violent or accusatory. You feel the absence of Higher Centres in the general feeling of uncomfortableness as if you had forgotten something you once knew. Unless lower centres can begin to hear Higher Centres there is no possibility of getting help for evolution.

Remember, Man is created a self-developing organism, but he must receive help from esoteric teaching in order to evolve. He is disconnected from Real 'I' which belongs to Higher Centres and can transmit their meaning. Real 'I' understands the language of Higher Centres but false 'I' does not. Real 'I' is what you are and why you exist: or, rather, why you exist is to come into contact with Real 'I'. In one of the esoteric writings of India it is said: "If a man fails to reach God he is continually re-born into existence. And so he goes round and round in the whole cycle of possible births until he understands why he exists." Since everyone has Real 'I' in them but at a higher, that is, a deeper, level than that from which they ordinarily live and think and feel, everyone is created with a possibility of making contact with this Real 'I' of which they are nothing but a foolish reflection or imitation. Everyone has an eternal centre of gravity, but, being swayed by the senses, by the feeling that they are nothing but their bodies and by the impact of impressions coming from external life, they get far away from this centre of gravity. Self-Remembering is the beginning of the attempt to bring us back into ourselves and so into our real centre of gravity. That is why a very external person who is simply governed by the effect he or she makes on other people has a very great difficulty in understanding what Self-Remembering means, and indeed what this Work means.

On one occasion G. said: "Behind Real 'I' lies God." But the beginning of all this way back to our real origin starts with Observing 'I'. This means of course that it starts with the Work itself, for Observing 'I' must know about what to observe and do it from what the Work teaches. If you have a wrong mirror, a wrong Observing 'I', some social 'I', it is not in the Work-sense Observing 'I'. But if you can establish in yourself a point of observation from what you understand of what the Work teaches you to observe, you are on the first rung of the ladder that reaches ultimately to Real 'I'. People think it is easy to establish Observing 'I' in this real Work-sense. I would say it is a very difficult matter and requires a long struggle, a great deal of inner sincerity and a great deal of failure. When this Observing 'I' is established it collects other 'I's round it that wish to work, that wish to understand better, that wish to find the secret of one's existence. Everyone really has this secret feeling about themselves but they do not put it into operation; they do not know what to do and so it simply becomes a source of negative emotion. When Deputy-Steward is formed it may attract Steward and finally Real 'I'. But these are words of very great density of meaning. To understand anything of this ladder of the Work takes a very long time and very deep reflection. For example, it needs a great deal of thinking what the Work is about, and re-thinking about it and seeing the state of one's being and re-seeing it. It requires a great deal of inner realization, it requires continual access of valuation, continual renewing of valuation, a continual re-understanding of what one understands, a seeing of where one is and what one is. And in this connection I might say that all of you who are following the path of the Work, and have long ago understood that it is not something on the blackboard, will find that even the simplest sayings of the Work transform themselves into deeper and deeper meanings. You will find, in short, that this Work and all its brief formulations could only come from a source that knows and understands far more than we do.

Now as regards the passage in the question we are discussing:

"Yet the least of these (acts of Self-Remembering) is greater than—i.e. on a level above—the fullest Self-Observation."

I find some difficulty in answering it. It means to begin with that an act of Self-Remembering is greater than an act of Self-Observation. I would say, to begin with, that speaking of fullest Self-Observation is beside the point. Full Self-Observation could only come with an enormous increase of consciousness and in that sense would be the same as that increased consciousness of the State of Self-Remembering, Self-Awareness, Self-Consciousness. To be fully aware of oneself would correspond to the Third State of Consciousness. An act of Self-Remembering for us, as we are, is a very weak thing. An act of Self-Observation may be more distinct. The two are not on the same level, but a state of full Self-Observation would belong to the level above us. But how could we at our level of consciousness expect to observe everything fully in ourselves? How could we, for example, fully observe the whole of our lives, altogether, or indeed how could we observe at our level of consciousness all that is going on in every part of a centre? You know there are many stories of people who when partially drowned remember the whole of their lives. I think these stories are probably quite true. I believe that at the point of death a man may pass into a different state of consciousness. In the terms of this Work we would call this the Third State of Consciousness—i.e. the State of Self-Remembering, Self-Consciousness, or Self-Awareness. Then, no doubt, a man would have full observation of himself—yes, and full observation of himself in a way he never dreamed of. But, as we are, Self-Observation is a very small thing, but quite essential, like carrying a tiny light through a big dark house and seeing one thing after another. After a time memory—that is, Work-memory—or memory created through conscious effort in Self-Observation—may connect together all these separate small illuminations into something bigger. This means that a man begins to take photographs of himself—that is, he begins to observe himself over a period of time, altogether. From this moment he can begin to catch a glimpse of his Chief Feature; he can begin to see strands running through his life. He begins to see patterns in the carpet of his life. You notice that in the three definitions of the Third State of Consciousness the term Self-Awareness connects with full Self-Observation. I find this part of the question difficult to answer because it assumes that full observation is a possibility at our level of consciousness. If a man at his present level of consciousness had a moment of full observation he would probably go mad, because it would mean that he saw all the inner contradictions in himself. To reach such an insight requires long work and the Work will never allow a person to see more than he can stand. I think we all make a mistake in thinking we can attain a higher degree of consciousness just in a moment. Consider how long it took you to learn to read or write. One hears the Work for a long time, just as a child sees his letters for a long time, but it takes many years before it can speak or write. A curious thing here, if I may add, is that suddenly a child finds it can read and just in the same way in the Work suddenly you find you understand something you have heard time after time. This means you are ready for it, you have earned it.

Now to take the last part of the question:

"All work on himself below that level is preparatory to progress towards Consciousness. Further—a man can protect himself psychologically only by Self-Remembering."

I have no comment to make on this part of the question but it requires to be understood. The phrasing is right. To be protected psychologically from the external scene of life one must remember oneself. This means that one must find something to take the place of identifying with all that goes on in life. If you take life as the whole business, and think you are nothing but your body, you will not be able to remember yourself. If you think your eyes see, and not that something sees through them, you will not be able to remember yourself. If you think that everything you do and feel and think belongs to your body you will not be able to remember yourself. You will then be like religious people who think that heaven is something above and hell something below them, and do not understand that heaven and hell are in them—in themselves. You take as reality the messages coming from the external senses, and no doubt you will think that Real 'I' is something that exists far away in the visible stars. You will not understand that it exists in you at a deeper level of your understanding and that you can only reach it by understanding all that this Work says about separating yourself from wrong activities going on mechanically every day, that keep you glued to the most external, most superficial side of yourself, that side that is governed by everything that happens to you outside, that side that depends for its well-being on how people behave towards you. And this is inevitable as long as you have no inner behaviour that you are following. The Work is about this inner behaviour which gives you a centre of gravity independent of external things, but, I repeat, if you think you are the same as your body and that your eyes see and your ears hear, and if you have no sense that it is you who see through your eyes and you who hear through your ears and that there is something different in you from your physical senses—and, in fact, something higher—then you will not be able to remember yourself. If you are a natural man, a man who believes only in the reality that the senses shew him, who believes that the natural world with all its events is the cause of everything, you will never be able to remember yourself. Nor will you be able to understand the Ray of Creation, nor the Side-Octave from the Sun. You will never be able to understand that influences are acting on this Earth coming from a higher level and acting on yourself as well, and that you receive these influences according to the quality of your being.

Birdlip, October 28, 1944

MAN AS AN EXPERIMENT

I would like to talk to you to-night on one or two of the general explanations that the Work gives concerning our existence on the Earth. As many of you have heard already, this Work teaches that Man is an experiment on this Earth—an experiment in self-evolution. The Work also says that many similar experiments have been made and proved to be failures and that it is quite possible that Man may be found to be a failure, in which case he will be made very small and insignificant like the ants. As you know, the ants obviously began to tamper with themselves and following some kind of scientific logic sacrificed everything that might make them individual, even their wings and their sex, and became subject to a purely state-organization, and apparently organized themselves for a kind of continual military service, for it is obvious that they attack each other mercilessly and are completely ruthless. On one occasion Mr. O., on being asked what were the best conditions of life, said that the best conditions prevailed when esoteric teaching could reach people. "All esoteric teaching," he said, in so many words, "has as a basis the idea that Man can undergo a change that is already possible for him, and that is, as it were, arranged for. Man is a far more complex organism than is necessary for merely living in this world. He has far more in him than is necessary for ordinary life. He can become an individual, which is the real meaning of his existence. But in that respect he is an experiment of the Solar Laboratory and may prove a failure. You must all try to understand what it means that Man is made a self-developing organism. It does not mean, for example, that Man is ready-made but that he must find himself, find the path in himself to follow, and for this reason teaching is always sown into the world and given in various ways and outer forms to shew him what he has to do to re-create himself, to evolve up to himself." In regard to these words of Mr. O., I think you will all agree that the general tendency to-day is to disregard the individual and to bring all human life under vast collective schemes of social security and so on. This turns Man more and more into a state-dependant, a state-controlled person, and indeed makes him less free in the name of liberty. As such, he becomes a being who is told what to do and think, and sees the goal of humanity only in the future of Time lying in some increasing mass-amalgamation and general uniformity spreading over the whole surface of the Earth. Everything will then be the same and no doubt nature "will be conquered" as they say. But this teaching says that it will be the beginning of the end and that another experiment will be made. And we must remember that "Nature" means many things in this teaching. Many influences act upon the Earth coming from six different levels of the Ray of Creation—apart from the Three Forces belonging to the Earth itself which keep their own balance. To conquer nature, then, is not so easy, but unfortunately many lunatics exist to-day in Science and Politics—lunatics in the sense of the Work-definitions concerning Householder, Lunatic, Tramp and Hasnamous. We have already seen many Hasnamous men coming into power in this century —men whose well-being depends on the ill-being of others. This combination of Hasnamous and Lunatic does not augur well.

*   *   *

Part II.— Socrates says somewhere that "Man is glued to his senses," and for this reason loses contact with himself. Man has lost his way. His soul has become immersed in outer things, in possessions and power. The soul must turn round to find its right direction and so restore to Man the realities and meanings he has lost. The soul is an organ that relates Man to influences at a higher level of intensity than the influences of the world. Socrates says: "When the soul returning unto itself reflects, it goes straight to what is pure, everlasting and immortal and like unto itself, and being related to this cleaves unto it when the soul is alone and is not hindered. And then the soul rests from its mistakes and is like unto itself, even as the Eternal is with whom the soul is now in touch. This state of the soul is called wisdom."

Now all this reminds us of the teaching of the Work. We speak little of soul, but the Work says Essence has come down from a very high order in the Ray of Creation and passed down to the level of the Earth, where it must become surrounded by Personality. Then, for those who remember something—that is, for those who have Magnetic Centre— a way back begins, by working against Personality and making it gradually passive, so that Essence can grow. Through the growth of Essence a man reaches individuality, Real 'I', and at the same time becomes conscious at another level of influences.

Let us reflect on the idea that we are experiments. Once grasped a little, it alters a little our relation to ourselves and our lives. Say to yourself: "I am an experiment." If you say this rightly, in the right place in yourself, you will notice the meaning of the sentence strikes against something resistant, something that will not believe it, that perhaps even wants to kick and scream rather than accept this view-point. Perhaps you have already noticed this thing in relation to other ideas of the Work—how it is totally disinterested and hates to listen to

It is not the thing or the event but the force it conducts for you at the moment that matters. Love makes us see a thing in one way: hate makes us see it in another way. It is the same thing, but it conducts different forces at different times. This, you may have noticed, is confusing and a great nuisance as long as we live solely under the law of the pendulum. After a time one may shift oneself in consciousness more towards the centre and not identify with extremes so much. This means becoming conscious in one force. We really do not know what we want—that is, we are not conscious in 1st Force in us. Yet it is acting in us and creating its own 2nd Force all the time, although we do not see what is doing this. As was said, the nature of 2nd Force depends on 1st Force. If we take what we want, desire, wish for, expect, hope for, as 1st Force, then, whatever the nature of our wish, it will arouse a specific and definite 2nd Force that opposes the wish. Sometimes the 2nd Force appears at once, sometimes it appears after an interval. It necessarily appears, but not necessarily in the form that we might forecast—that is, we may see no connection. In fact, 2nd Force may appear without our understanding why it arises. Self-knowledge makes us see better. Since every 1st Force arouses its related 2nd Force, we cannot study 2nd Force in ourselves unless we are more conscious of 1st Force, which, as was said, may be acting all the time without our seeing it. Always expecting to be different is wishing. It is a kind of continual, vague 1st Force. It will summon a continual, vague 2nd Force which will appear as something lying in outer circumstances. But the 2nd Force is not in outer circumstances, but in oneself. You may find this difficult to believe, but when we have no self-knowledge everything seems to be the fault of something outside. Our senses are turned outwards. We do not observe ourselves. These are fundamental ideas and are constantly repeated to people. Recently in a conversation about 2nd Force in ourselves someone asked why outside things always seemed to prevent us from getting what we wanted. The person meant that it was difficult to see that 2nd Force was in oneself preventing one from getting what one wished. Another person said that she had noticed that when outside things went well she still had a feeling of dissatisfaction which shewed that 2nd Force was really in oneself. This is a good observation.

Where is 2nd Force *in myself*? I do not see that I am stupid, ignorant, lazy; selfish, narrow, mean; I do not see my shallowness—that, say, I am slanderous, lying, incapable and difficult. All this is 2nd Force in me. O. once, when speaking about 2nd Force in ourselves, said that ignorance was a very common form of it. People always liked to pretend that they knew things. They answer as if they knew things when they really do not know and this increases ignorance in them. Really to think one is ignorant in respect of something is quite different from pretending to know it and becoming confused if one is asked about it. If one becomes conscious of one's ignorance regarding something, it may create a wish to know about it. The situation is then quite different. Where there was formerly pretence and unawakened ignorance there is now self-acknowledged ignorance and a desire to change it. Now all forms of pretending constitute a 1st Force which inevitably gives rise to certain forms of 2nd Force. The Work says that one of the greatest evils is to pretend. A change in consciousness arises through self-observation, and the feeling of oneself changes, and with this there is less and less pretending and more and more realization of what exists in oneself and what is the state of one's Being. All this changes 1st and 2nd Force in us.

But this change is effected through the orientation of the Work. What is the 2nd Force in us in regard to the wish to self-remember, to awaken? You see at once that the Work tells us what are the forces that resist awakening in us. The whole Work can be understood in this light. If I am very identified with some life-ambition this will be 2nd Force in me in regard to the Work. It will put me to sleep. Now suppose we could do everything from the Work. Nothing would change in what we were doing perhaps, but the inner relationship would change. In this respect it is very interesting to study the nature of 2nd Force in ourselves in relation to the three lines of the Work.

You can often see by self-observation that one 'I' in yourself opposes another 'I', or one group of 'I's opposes another group of 'I's. When the opposing force gets the upper hand it becomes 1st Force. Some 'I's may, for instance, be talking wrongly and other 'I's may see that this wrong talking would stop if you could remember yourself. Which group of 'I's is going to become 1st Force? I said some time ago to you all that you should be very careful on getting up in the morning to work carefully on yourselves and, in fact, before getting up. All sorts of unpleasant 'I's may start talking about their troubles and taking a certain view of the day and if you listen to them you will be absorbing negative impressions and so starting the day well-poisoned. Remember that you need not take things as you do and that this applies to the inner life as well as to your behaviour in outer life. If you let yourselves take in numbers of negative impressions from your own thoughts and memories you will increase 2nd Force in yourselves in connection with the 1st Force of trying to awaken and live in the life of the Work to some extent during the day. There are two lives that you can lead. After a time you begin to know what the other life means that you can lead in yourself which the Work can form in you, and you can distinguish it from the life of the ordinary affairs of the day. Eventually you should be living in both. They gradually should cease to be in opposition to each other.

I repeat: to see 2nd Force in ourselves we must become conscious in 1st Force. I remember many years ago someone telling me of a recurring dream. "I dream," this person said, "that I am sitting on a high throne. It seems as if an immense concourse of people surrounds me with heads bent. Suddenly the throne gives way and I feel I am falling and I wake in fear." Here you can see, as it were, both 1st and 2nd

Force at work in the person. The person had an intractable pride, but was not conscious of it. This seems to me a very bad arrangement of forces in oneself and one that is likely to make life as difficult and disastrous as possible. Since the Three Forces exist in us as in the whole Universe, it is not surprising to find that checks exist in us that, for example, prevent us from realizing the idea contained in such a dream as this one quoted above. In this respect perhaps you will be reminded of a similar type of dream in the Old Testament, where a person of overweening ambition and vanity is described. This is the dream of Nebuchadnezzar which he related to the prophet Daniel. He said: "I saw, and behold a tree in the midst of the earth, and the height thereof reached unto heaven, and the sight thereof to the end of all the earth. The leaves thereof were fair, and the fruit thereof much, and in it was meat for all: the beasts of the field had shadow under it, and the fowls of the heaven dwelt in the branches thereof and all flesh was fed of it." The King goes on to relate how in his dream a "watcher and a holy one" came down from heaven and ordered the tree to be cut down, leaving the stump of the roots in the grass, saying "let it be wet with the dew of heaven, and let his portion be with the beasts in the grass of the earth." This was to be done so that "the living may know that the Most High ruleth in the Kingdom of men." Daniel interpreted the dream as a sign that because of the King's overweening ambition, which was reaching up to heaven and to the end of the earth, he was to be cast down until he recognized that all power on the earth was God's to give to whom he would.

What I wish to point out is simply that with a wrong 1st Force the whole inner state may be rendered ineffective and even dangerous—that is, one has a very bad relationship to oneself. So it is the 1st Force that one has to look at and observe, and gradually become conscious of. What do you want? Consider in this connection the ideas contained in the Sermon on the Mount and the ideas in the Lord's Prayer.

Birdlip, November 18, 1944

INTRODUCTORY NOTE TO
COMMENTARY ON THE MIND

Many things have been said about change of mind—about μετάνοια in the Gospels (so wrongly translated as repentance) which really means change of mind—and so much has been said about the Work making us think in a new way. To those who do not understand how the Work can make us think in a new way, I would say that I advise them to think what the Work says. Do you see what I mean? What does it say? I would advise them to think about themselves and what the Work says about ourselves, and what teaching the Work gives about things with which we have to struggle and with what object. For a long time the Work remains external, as something on the blackboard of the memory. But after a time a person may realize it is quite true that he or she is asleep and has negative emotions, etc. Or they may realize some other thing, some other idea that the Work teaches. The Work asks us to think from itself—to have a Work-mind, a mind formed by the ideas of the Work, to see things from what the Work teaches about ourselves, others and life. When the Work becomes emotional and ceases to be on the blackboard you find yourself confronted by it. You find such questions as: "Have you spoken wrongly? Have you spent the day in internal considering? Have you remembered yourself? Are you identified? Have you made any kind of Work-effort to-day? Have you observed yourself? Have you cancelled debts? Have you remembered your aim?" All these questions and many others begin to stand in front of you—between you and external life. You will then begin to understand what it means to *think* in a new way, to have another mind.

To have another mind means that the ideas of the Work are beginning to stand between you and life. Remember that we think from our ideas. It means that you begin to have a sense of another discipline of ideas. It means that you begin to feel influences acting on you that come from the Work and not from life. All this begins to shew you how you can have a life-mind and a Work-mind as two distinct things. Both are necessary, but they are different kinds of minds. For a long time we have to take some things in one way and others in another. But if you think from the Work about some situation you will find that you are thinking quite differently from what you would if you thought of the same situation in life. Here, at this point, the Work begins.

COMMENTARY ON THE MIND

I

A question was recently asked about *minding*, as to what is the difference between not minding and being indifferent. I will repeat the question:

"If you do not *mind*, things do not hurt you. After a time, perhaps, we learn this great lesson *rightly*. But most people think that not to mind means to be indifferent. A long time ago it was said by O. at a meeting that being indifferent is one of the worst states of sleep that one can be in. What difference can you discern between 'not minding' and 'being indifferent'?"

We are told that one of the worst things is to be indifferent and the point of the question was to draw a distinction between 'not minding' and 'being indifferent'. Now we *mind* according to our minds. The object of this Work is to change our minds. What are our minds? We imagine perhaps that our minds are infinitely flexible. However, such minds as we have are built-up things, acquired things. We are, for example, by education, told that we must think this or that, imitate that, and so on, and all this forms our minds—the minds we go about with. Most of us have very rigid minds in this sense. These acquired minds of ours are parts of our Personality—i.e. of the acquired side of our psychology. Now you must all understand that this Work begins with changing the mind and this means changing the way we think about everything. You may have been taught that you must worry about this or that, and this forms part of your mind, of your acquired mind, and therefore when this or that happens you will *mind* it, because that is your form of mind. You will feel that you *must* mind because your mind has been formed by what you have been taught as regards this or that. So when any impression falls on you from outside life that hits your mind in this way you will mind it. You will think of it according to this mind that has been laid down in you, and so you will not see any other way of taking the incident that has happened to you—that is, another way of *minding* it. In fact, it will never occur to you that you need not *mind* the thing in the way that you do mind it. Let us say, for example, that you have been taught that such and such people are very bad: then you will always *mind* those people because your acquired mind has had laid down in it this way of minding, this way of taking people and thinking about people.

Now one of the first great objects of the Work is to make us think in a new way about everything, including ourselves. Mr. O. used to say continually to us at one time that the object of the Work is to make us *think* in a new way. That means, to have different minds. Now to think in a new way is to have a new mind and this means that if we think in a new way we will not mind all the same things as we formerly did. Change of mind is the basis of all esoteric teaching belonging to the period since Christ. Speaking more deeply, the reason is that Man is now so closed up, so almost dead, so asleep, that the only thing left open for esotericism to touch in him is the route via the *mind*. For this reason Christ taught μετάνοια, or change of mind, as the starting-point of his esoteric teaching, and we can say in general that no one nowadays has any chance of awakening and of inner transformation, or of feeling new influences, except through the pathway of the mind. The mind must change—i.e. the minding of things must change. Therefore it is a very good thing to observe how you mind things because all your minding of things depends on what form your mind has been made to take, by example, by what you have been taught, by acquired prejudice and imitated attitude, and so on. However we take all that has been laid down in our minds as quite real, quite true, and, in fact, as the only *mind* possible. But as long as we do this, our minds do not and cannot change. Everyone has certain mental standpoints, certain mental prejudices, certain ingrained ideas as to what is right and wrong, and as long as all these remain unchallenged by the person himself through attentive self-observation—as long as they are not observed—that person will continue to *mind* always in the same way and will not realize that the ideas of the Work seek to change this fixed mind and make the man think in quite new ways. For if the mind is fixed, no one can think in a new way. We think from our form of mind.

Now supposing that your mind is very fixed and limited, then you will always mind in a fixed and limited way. For example, you will feel it is right to be upset about this and angry about that, or depressed about something else, and so on. You will *mind* all these things. Why do you mind them? You mind them because this is how your mind works. You mind them because you have been taught all these things, all this way of minding. Now the mind is an infinite thing, and this thing that we call our minds which we have acquired is not total mind at all. It is like a little heap of stones on a vast open plain. It is something very small and arbitrary, in the sense that one has acquired it without thinking for oneself. One of these stones may be your own, but the rest are acquired. One has been taught to make this little heap of stone and to take it as if it were the whole of one's mind with all its infinite possibilities of understanding and insight. When something strikes the mind that we cannot entertain we say: "Tut-tut" or we get angry because we can only take in as through a little chink certain things that correspond with these little heaps of stones that we call our minds. So we go about, as it were, with a very small instrument that has been created more or less haphazard in us and receive all life on this little quite inadequate instrument—this heap of stones.

Now how do you *mind*? Have you noticed how you *mind* things? Are you satisfied with the way you mind things or might you mind things differently? If you have noticed this, then you are beginning to reach the point of changing your minding and this means changing your actual minds and having new minds. To change the mind new thoughts are necessary. How difficult it is to change our minds. One reason is that we never observe our minds or how we mind or why we mind things as we do. We take our minds and so our minding of everything for granted. We believe our troubles have nothing to do with our minds and the way they are formed. We can notice that we mind things, but we do not connect that up with what kind of minds we have. In fact, we don't know that we have minds *having a particular form*. We do not attack our minds, *suspect our* minds. All our mental habits are to us not habits, but truths. They are quite right to us. There can be no other point of view. We cannot see them as habits. This is a tragedy. So we cannot see that so many things we keep on *minding* so much are due to invisible mental habits. Of course we have to worry, of course we have to think that this is impossible. Of course we have to say we have never heard of such a thing. Of course we have to say "Tut-tut", "Well, I never", and so on. And why? Because we take our mental habits as ultimate truths, as ultimate standards—not even realizing they are mental habits that we have acquired insensibly over a long period, over, in fact, that long dark period that inevitably intervenes—the Dark Ages—before we start to think for ourselves about ourselves, about life, and about why we do and say the things we do and say, and about who we are.

It is certainly very difficult to realize one's mechanicalness in the 3 centres. We may notice our mechanicalness in the Moving Centre but it takes a long time for most of us to realize our mechanicalness in the Emotional and Intellectual Centres—that is, habits of emotion and thinking. Now the Work starts with the mind or Intellectual Centre and for that reason its approach is called psychological. It does not start from Fakir point of view, with torturing the body, or with Monk point of view, with breaking the emotions. It starts with the mind as do the Gospels. It starts with changing the mind, with seeing things differently, with new teaching, new ideas. Unless this begins to take place, unless we begin to see, mentally, ourselves and life in a new way, we cannot expect to work on the other centres except in a purely unintelligent way. I may sit all day on my haunches; I may refuse food; I may subject myself to the greatest physical torments as a Fakir —but the result will be quite useless because it is not linked up with my understanding, and so will lead to no inner development. But if I start with my mind and observe, let us say, how I mind things, in what way I mind things, and ask myself why I mind things in this way, and think of the Work, I will begin to have some insight into the thing I have always taken for granted as being indisputably myself and always right, which I call my mind. I will begin to see that my mind, such as it is, with this little heap of stones in it, is a funny, limited thing and something that I cannot possibly say is always right. In fact, I will begin to see that my mind is possibly wrong and all my ideas may be wrong and that, in a sense, I have to get rid of this form of my mind, of this small way of thinking about everything and so of this way of minding. Can you imagine someone coming to you at a moment when you are minding something very much and saying: "Do you not see that the reason why you mind this so much is because there is something wrong with your mind, and that you are wrongly minding and you should try to change your mind and think in a quite new way about this thing you are stupidly minding so much?" No doubt you would be very cross. Now try to look more deeply into this question of why you mind things and catch a glimpse that it is because there is something in your minds that makes you mind in this way, something in your thoughts, which only come from your minds, such as they are, for as long as your minds are formed in this way they will always produce the same kinds of thoughts. I mean, try to see that you must mind things, because of the heap of stones that you take as the only mind you can have.

I remember G. once making us all shout at the top of our voices: "I can work." Now when you are minding something very much shout to yourself: "I can work," and see what Work means at such a moment. That is, summon up the Work-mind. All this means that we should observe more deeply what prejudices and ideas we have been taught in the past that make us mind as we do. Supposing you merely say to yourself: "*I need not mind in this way,*" and repeat it, will that be Work? Will that be self-observation? Will that be trying to get down into what one's mind is like? Will that be seeing mental mechanicalness? Why, of course not. We have to struggle with ourselves more than that and see what our stone-heaps are like, formed of all these acquired things, buffers, prejudices, all these little local environmental things that have formed our small minds. Just to say: "I must not mind," and go about with some awful and sacred expression saying: "I must not mind," over and over again is not the Work, and has nothing to do with the Work. But if you say now: "*Why* do I mind?" then perhaps, through sincere observation, you may notice something in you that has reigned undisturbed in you, some acquired idea of life or of others or of yourself that is the cause of your minding so much. You know how often a person begins to bristle and say in so many words: "Do you mean to say I don't know what is right and wrong?" or a remark of that kind. Why, you must all have noticed that reaction in yourselves and how quickly you come up against your level of being. This Work is to teach us a new right and wrong, because the object of this Work is to lift us to a more conscious level where people do not bristle in that way, where people do not *mind* as we ordinarily mind. The Work is to lift us to a level where people's minds are different from our minds, to a level where people *mind* things differently—where people *mind* being negative, through the light of their new minds.

I remember on one occasion Mr. O. was talking about attitude and how marvellous it was if you could find the right attitude to things. I had to take a group for him soon afterwards and made the mistake of allowing people to talk of attitudes as *emotional* things and received a good dressing-down, and quite rightly. *Attitude begins as a mental thing.* He said, in so many words: "You must understand that attitude starts in the Intellectual Centre. It belongs to the mind. Change of attitude is a change in the Intellectual Centre *to begin with.* Our mental attitudes affect our Emotional Centre but their origin lies in the Intellectual Centre—in our minds. People have all sorts of mental attitudes without knowing they have them. Negative attitudes are like dead places in the mind. Nothing grows. Instead of thinking, people have an attitude which has been acquired from their upbringing and imitated from parents. It is only by thinking in quite new ways that these ingrained attitudes are altered and the mind is freed to think for itself." It should be quite clear to most of us that our minding comes from our mental ideas and attitudes which we take for granted, and are therefore unaware that we have them. Negative mental attitudes can be called prejudices and if they increase they become buffers. On another occasion Mr. O. said to us: "What people call education is usually, as regards the mind, nothing more than the acquisition of a number of stereotyped negative attitudes. The mind then becomes almost dead. You must understand," he went on, "that the last thing people will do is *to think*. No one wants to think. Thinking is too difficult for most people. They prefer to go along with the *minds* they have acquired and if a person has no Magnetic Centre the outlook is not good."

★ ★ ★

NOTE

I suppose that none of us understands how we resist thinking in a new way. I was reading recently a history of the Universities in England in mediæval and Renaissance times. A large number of young students settled in Oxford in the early thirteenth century influenced vaguely by the new movement called the Renaissance that was spreading over Europe. The inhabitants of Oxford resisted the presence of these strange clerks, as they were called. They hated them because they were studying something new. In those days there was no University, as we understand it, no college-buildings. There was an uproar owing to some woman and all these students marched out of Oxford and some went to Cambridge and others to Northampton and elsewhere. Here again all the inhabitants resented their presence because they were studying some kind of knowledge. These Town and Gown rows took place for a long time before either Oxford or Cambridge was able to form a definite organized body and build its own colleges. We often see reflected in history what happens in our own minds. We all resist new thinking, we resist change. All history from a mental point of view shews us how anything new is resisted. If we apply history to ourselves we find exactly the same thing. We find it very difficult to change our minds: we notice a very powerful force of resistance. And if we take our ordinary minds as the Town and our new minds as the Gown there is always a fight between Town and Gown.

Have you ever thought what forces influenced all these young men to flock together to form centres for teaching—not for war or revolution, but for learning? Conscious influences can only act on humanity at rare intervals "when things happen to be open", as I was taught. Is not this an example? It is only at times that the influences of the Side-Octave from the Sun—i.e. Esoteric Influences—insert themselves between the terrific forces coming down the Ray of Creation. Things are open for the moment and then closed for a long time.

★ ★ ★

II

Now perhaps you may have noticed that by a change of attitude everything becomes quite different. What does a change of attitude mean? It means not *minding* in the same way—because attitudes are

550

mental—not taking things with our minds in the way we are accustomed to. To realize that we can *mind* differently, that we can transcend our present minds, is a wonderful visitation of consciousness—in fact, a lovely experience. A change of attitude may make some situation which seems unsurmountable become nothing difficult at all. But we do not see our minds with their ingrained attitudes and their ideas from which come our modes of thinking. We do not see the root of so much of our trouble as lying in the kind of mind we have acquired mechanically, unchallenged, taken for granted. It is like having been given a gramophone with a few records, not knowing either that there are other forms of music. Now to that form of mind those are the only gramophone records that can be played by it. The mind is then a gramophone with a few records. Everything else we suffer patiently as it were or we say, as I said above: "Well, I mustn't mind," or "I must try not to mind." But to repeat this is not working on oneself. This is a very short cut to martyrdom with all its unpleasant aroma. You all know people who go about saying: "I must not mind", or "Who am I to mind?" and all that pious nonsense, which is so irritating, and rightly so. I fancy that of all the forms of unpleasant manifestations of other people that we must allow and understand and endure, among the worst are such pathetic manifestations of this brave injured suffering. The Work is a very strong, clean thing, and so demands a great deal of inner cleanness and strength and sincerity with oneself. Who are the unclean in the Gospels? Every form of hypocrisy and pretence, every form of looking down one's nose, every form of sighing slightly, every form of pseudo patience—yes, all this is uncleanness and we come to know it. It is a very good stage to reach, when one knows it.

So let us observe ourselves also from the angle of minding and let us try to register moments when we mind something and observe more deeply our Intellectual Centre, our thoughts, our ideas, our attitudes —if we can—to see why it is that we mind. And here also come in many forms of imagination, many forms of expectancy, many wrong ideas about ourselves—in fact, all the imagination that comes from False Personality. All this is a very long task. It is a very long way, a long journey, in which we make mistake after mistake, but you may be quite certain, if you have a genuine valuation of the Work, you will find the right roads or be brought back to them in an indescribable way. And you may also be quite certain that *if* you are on this journey which is so strange and so *quite unlike* anything you thought with your ordinary minds, you will begin after a time to see what you used to mind so much and now do not mind in the same way, and this means at once that *your* mind *is changing*, that your whole way of thinking is changing, and then you will inevitably be shewn many places in your lives where you minded so foolishly and so wrongly. This is because of an increase of consciousness.

Now this light of consciousness is shed also into the past, into the time-body, and from what we are conscious of *now* we can see as having acted on us in the past, as having misled us, simply because we were accepting ourselves and our minds as we were brought up, without even thinking who we were or where we were going. Remember that every stage of slightly increased consciousness begins to alter us and the past. The past is *living* in us. It is all round us—not a long way off. Whatever you do now alters the past, as well as the future. Whatever you cease rightly to mind now you will change in the past—all those past similar mindings. Whatever new insight you gain now will give you an insight into your past and change it. Consciousness is the force that changes us. This is a good thing to think about because it means that in recurrence you will meet your more conscious self, as it is *now*, much earlier, even perhaps at school, and feel there is someone shewing you something, someone speaking to you. It is yourself. How can this happen if you always mind in the same way as you always did and have never changed your mind at all or seen any reason to do so?

Birdlip, November 25, 1944

ON SEEING LIFE IN A NEW WAY— ## AS A MEANS, NOT AN END

Self-observation cannot increase without the help of the ideas of the Work. Fortunately, the Work-teaching gives many angles from which to observe oneself. You cannot observe yourself if you have no standpoint from which to observe. You must, so to speak, get out of yourself in order to observe yourself—otherwise you are yourself as you are. Is this clear? An increase of consciousness of *oneself*, which is the first aim of the Work, means that one gets further back inside oneself, so that one sees what lies in front of oneself—that is, what one took as oneself. This direction, as you know, leads inwards towards Higher Centres, through higher parts of ordinary centres. This direction, gained from increasing self-observation, leads slowly to an increasing consciousness both of what one is now and what one has been. All this leads to the only possibility of change. Now this process, this becoming more deeply conscious of oneself and seeing oneself continually in a quite new light, in the light of the Work, is called *awakening*. It is like an advance inwards against an enemy with here and there very tough points defended which must be surrounded and which can only be slowly reduced. This entry into oneself is called in the Work *awakening*. Here what the Work teaches is very clear and should be grasped by us. It is expressed also in the Gospels, but obscurely.

The Work says that a man must first of all *awaken*. This takes a long time. When he has awakened enough then he must *die*. When he dies then he can be *re-born*. These are the three steps in re-birth—that is, transformation. There is no other way. To try to die to oneself before one has awakened to oneself is to do something in a quite wrong and foolish order and so leads to no result. To try to die to something before one has awakened to it and seen it, is wrong. One is not yet ready. One does not know yet what to do, what to die to. If you try to die before you are awake you have not the conscious force to die to the thing in question. One may try and fail. Then the danger arises of becoming negative, of feeling some variety of despair or hopelessness. When this happens the whole sense and feeling of the Work may become all distorted owing to the sense of failure. This is a very serious kind of temptation to be exposed to. We may mistake it for being passive. We may mistake it for many other things, but the state is a very dangerous one because we are letting in negative 'I's that hate the Work, by the back door, as it were, and very soon all feeling of the Work becomes dim and even disappears. When this happens we can always know at once that we are in bad company in ourselves—that is, going with wrong 'I's. Sometimes we have to be in bad company and this constitutes a struggle, and one from which only by not identifying is it possible to escape with any success—I say, by not identifying—for reasoning is useless. When one reasons one can come to any conclusion that one likes, but with emotional perception the case is quite different. Good and evil in us can only be seen by emotional perception in the light of the Work. We use our reasoning mainly to justify.

Now to-night I want to talk to you about how in the long stages of awakening the ideas of this Work are necessary, and how if we have not ideas from which to observe ourselves we cannot awaken from the sleep which life has induced in us, long ago, from infancy. The sleep which life has induced in us has been formed by the ideas of life that we were born into, and to awaken we must have ideas from another source. You cannot awaken from opium by taking more opium. You must find some *antidote* to opium to awaken from its powers over you. How can you awaken from life by means of life? How can you awaken from what life has built up in you by example, by suggestion, by imitation, by imagination, unless you have another system of ideas that does not belong to life. As you know, there is a cosmic reason for the sleep of humanity and each fashion, each period of life, acts on Man. A man even believes that because he can laugh at the customs of the last generation, their clothes, manners, and so on, he is therefore more awake. He does not see how clever the hypnotism is and so thinks he is awake by comparison. But actually he is just as much asleep himself. So what can awaken us in a real sense? Only teaching can awaken us, only ideas that come from those in every age, who, overcoming the hypnotism of life have become conscious and have found the way out from the prison we all live in and do not notice—the prison of "cosmic hypnotism"—this prison of oneself as laid down mechanically.

Now to begin to free oneself from this prison that life has built into

553

us by the ideas of everything we have imitated and absorbed, as was said, new ideas are necessary, and so a new out-look. The idea that we are not one, but many contradictory 'I's, is one of the Work-ideas that starts at the exit of this prison in which we are confined without realizing it—and have to be, to begin with. The idea that we are not one is an idea that stands outside the ideas life has planted in you. However, few people will apply this idea even if they hear it many times because it seems to them they are one. Beyond the prison of ourselves in which we are confined without knowing it, there lie a series of ideas that can lead to our own freedom once they are rightly understood. Mr. O. says in his last book that an idea is a very delicate and powerful instrument that can easily be wrongly handled. Surrounding us as we are there are a number of ideas different from the ideas on which we are built. The idea of liberation has always existed and led to all sorts of revolutions. People feel vaguely that there is something else, some kind of freedom that they do not possess. But as a rule they take it in terms of existing conditions, of outside re-arrangements, of murdering some class or other, and so on. These ideas of liberation that surround us outside the prison refer to ourselves and not to material conditions. We are surrounded by liberating ideas, whether we feel them or not. If we have Magnetic Centre, we feel that liberating ideas exist. But we may feel that they lie somewhere in some distant school in Thibet, for example. Certainly, the teaching of the liberating ideas may be in some distant school, but if you were to go to such a school you would find that these liberating ideas are not in a school but that their action lies in the effect that they have on yourself and the response that you yourself make to them. Schools—esoteric schools—transmit ideas that can liberate us. These ideas come from those who have liberated themselves—and this knowledge has always been handed on. But these ideas that are taught are similar to the ideas that the Work teaches. The Work teaches liberating ideas but the action of the ideas will not be effective unless a person begins to think about them, to feel he must apply them to himself. The illusion that there is such a thing as higher education that you only have to be taught in order to reach a new state is quite wrong. There is no redemption possible for any of us by some school of teaching unless we learn and understand and do the teaching that is taught.

In the Gospels it is said: "The Kingdom of God cometh not with observation: neither shall they say, Lo here! or, lo there! for behold the Kingdom of God is within you." It is not something outside that if you would only join you would be liberated. When it is said in the Gospels that the Kingdom of God or the Kingdom of Heaven is within you, by the Kingdom of Heaven is meant a state in which the hypnotism of life no longer acts on us and in which we are invested with the influence of ideas coming from a quite different source.

Now let us take one of the ideas of the Work from which we are taught to observe ourselves and from which we must think and build up within ourselves a new point of view. There is the idea that *Man cannot do*. Have you ever thought about this idea? Remember that an idea is comparable with a very delicate and complicated machine which, if handled wrongly, may do you very great harm. If you were to handle a great dynamo wrongly without understanding its connections you might easily be killed. Now this idea that Man cannot do is like a great dynamo. It can furnish you with light or it can kill you. You can take it wrongly, as I have seen many people take it, as when they say some such thing as this: "Well, if we cannot do, what is the good of trying anything?" This is a quite wrong understanding of the idea that Man cannot do. "Everyone," said G. on one occasion, "is doing the only possible thing that he can do. Everything that is happening at this moment is going the only way it can possibly go." He was talking about mechanicalness. As long as Man is asleep things will go the only way they can possibly go, by an infinite number of lines of cause and effect. But the Work teaches that a man can come under new laws and ultimately that he can reach a higher state of himself in which he can do, in which he has Real Will. Certainly such a state is very far from us at present. But in applying this idea to ourselves that Man cannot do, we have first of all to notice, to observe, over a long period, what it means in this personal application. We have to observe ourselves by means of this idea of the Work.

Perhaps, very gradually, we realize one of the meanings of this tremendous idea. We begin to see that what we call our doing is really not doing but mechanicalness. We realize that "IT" does. Now this is a preliminary stage which can lead to new experiences of oneself. It is a very good thing to have new experiences of oneself and if this occurs, by means of the light of the Work, these experiences will not make us desperate but on the contrary open up quite new aspects of understanding. From this right realization of what it means that we cannot do, we will begin to see what it means that mankind cannot do in general. Our understanding will no longer be theoretical but will begin to be practical. We will then understand the necessary idea that *life for us cannot be an end in itself*. People who are very much in the physical senses believe that life can be so far improved that it will become an end in itself—i.e. that it will lead somewhere. But the Work does not take life as an end in itself because it says that life is under a great number of mechanical laws that always keep it in more or less the same condition. The Work teaches that we must take life as a means to a quite different condition. The object of the Work is that we should awaken. It is solely about something that Man can do to himself. For this reason the Work says that Man is created a self-developing being. As long as a man takes life as an end in itself and hopes sooner or later to reach some kind of success and triumph in life, he does not understand the aim of this Work. He is confusing the issue. If such a man takes up this Work and finds that it does not lead to success in life, for example, he will become disappointed. But the Work is not about such an aim. The Work is about oneself and about a certain development

555

in regard to life and to its accidents that can transform our whole being. If you can keep right in yourself towards the Work, if you understand the direction of the Work, then whatever happens in life will not destroy you. You will not be surprised at what happens in life, because you will know that life is like that—i.e. that Man cannot do. Then success and failure in life will mean less and less to you. You will not expect life to give you what only the Work can give you.

Birdlip, December 2, 1944

FURTHER NOTES ON DEEPER SELF-OBSERVATION

We spoke recently about taking life as an end in itself and about the quite different Work-idea of taking life as a means to a different kind of end. We spoke about how the Work has gradually to come between us and life in such a way that we begin to be able at certain moments to see the difficulties we have in life through the ideas of the Work. This at once changes our relationship to outer events, outer problems, outer difficulties. As was said, this takes a long time because, as we are, we are totally identified with the outer world, with people, with things, with happenings, with situations. In this sense we are machines driven by life. For a long time we cannot see how the Work applies to our situation in life. We have nothing intervening, we have no kind of magic mirror or magic lens through which we look. We are, so to speak, naked in life, naked to life. We have no proper shoes to wear, no proper clothes. It has often been said that it is quite extraordinary what a change takes place in some typical life-situation if we can bring the Work up to the point of incoming impressions. It means that impressions instead of falling directly on us pass through the medium of the Work. When we are awake—i.e. when we are surrounded by the strength of the Work and are conscious of what it teaches—then impressions of life are transformed. They have another meaning. It is not the external situation that we think about and react to, but the ideas of the Work to which we react. Life does not fall directly on us, but passes through this medium of the Work, and then life becomes a teacher to us through this medium of the Work. When we are very much amongst life-people we can see quite plainly that they do not transform anything and also that they take life as an end in itself that is going to lead somewhere in the future of passing time. They really think that it is going to lead somewhere. Such people do not observe their inner states, nor do they see that the most important thing is change of inner state. The object of the Work is to change our inner states so that we do not react mechanically to events. This requires a shifting of the point of consciousness and this begins through self-

556

observation. When this begins to take place we dimly realize that it is not life that is the problem but oneself. Then one no longer expects that in some distant future everything will be much better; one no longer leans on Time expectantly; one becomes aware that as long as these different mechanical reactions, these different manifestations of Chief Feature, these intolerances, these rigid and unquestioned attitudes these forms of grievance, these systems of making inner accounts, these habitual negative states, these unchallenged forms of imagination, govern us, we cannot look towards the future to bring us into a better state. Realizing this, one begins to see what it means that one must not take life as an end in itself but as a means to a quite different kind of end which has to do with one's own level of being and all the states that arise from it.

Have you ever thought that you might in this 4th Way Work be deliberately put into some external situation which is extraordinarily difficult in order to see whether you could pass through it without becoming hopelessly identified? Certainly this would not be possible if you did not bring the Work up to the point of incoming impressions and deal consciously with the situation by means of what you understand of the Work-ideas.

Now to-night I wish to speak to you about self-observation again, because without some practical and tested knowledge of what self-observation means no one can do this Work. We cannot do in life but we can do this Work to a certain extent if we feel it and know about it, and through doing this Work we may indirectly be able to do in life, but only indirectly. Remember that if we change ourselves even a little we make room for others to change even if we only change ourselves temporarily. If at some characteristic moment you to some extent remember yourself and so bring the Work up between you and life, you will, according to your level of being, be doing the Work. This will have results for other people. It is only this indirect doing that is possible, but you must do the Work because you yourself see the necessity of it, because you feel the need of it—you must never do the Work to help other people.

Now we come to the great and inexhaustible subject of *self-observation*. The object of self-observation is to get behind yourself, to become more internal to yourself. Now the external part of you, the mechanical or even automatic part of you, is the lowest side of you in scale. When a person is very much identified with outside things, he is in the lowest part of himself—as it were, in the basement of the house of himself. Lowest corresponds to most external. The moving parts of centres are the lowest and most external parts of ourselves, and here live a great many small 'I's, which only understand in a small limited way. When we live in these 'I's we are fast asleep as regards the Work. We become full of the cares and anxieties of life. But behind these 'I's—that is, more internal to them—are bigger 'I's, and again behind them still bigger 'I's, and so on until the influence of Real 'I' can begin to be felt. Some people always live too far in front of themselves, really outside themselves, and cannot get into themselves because of the hypnotism exerted on them by small, outwardly turned 'I's. If this goes far enough something like hysteria can begin.

Now every act of attention, of concentration of the mind, tends to put us in a more internal position as regards ourselves. This is one aspect of the meaning of self-observation. Self-observation puts us behind ourselves. However, Observing 'I' may be very externally situated and, so to speak, may be one of these external 'I's and nothing deeper. Then self-observation has no strength and cannot penetrate inwardly. When self-observation really begins, the Observing 'I' passes gradually inwards—that is, in the direction of Real 'I'—and as a result of the gradual penetration inwardly of Observing 'I' it sees more and more because it gets behind more and more in ourselves. Now the higher can only observe the lower: the lower cannot observe the higher. Or, put differently, the inner can only observe the outer: the outer can never observe the inner. As we deepen our consciousness through Observing 'I' we can see more and more what lies outside or external to Observing 'I'. Observing 'I' cannot penetrate in this way more internally unless it is aided by emotional feeling—that is, if we do not think it worth while we cannot really observe ourselves except very superficially. Catching a glimpse of oneself, however, may deepen the emotional valuation of work on oneself through self-observation. For example, a person may see that he lies in a certain way when according to his pictures of himself he is quite certain he always speaks the truth. Such a sudden glimpse means temporarily that one has observed oneself from a deeper level—one has got behind oneself a little way. What happens after that depends on the quality of one's own sincerity with oneself and upon the valuation that one gives to the Work. Practically always the tendency is to justify oneself. In that case, having caught a deeper glimpse of oneself one will lose it in the uproar of self-justifying. We are told to observe self-justifying and not to go with it. Certainly you will be unable to stop mechanical self-justifying, when you catch a glimpse of yourself, but that does not mean that you agree with your self-justifying. All self-justifying leads to no result in the Work-sense. To justify yourself means that you make things right to yourself. If you do not go with self-justifying—or, let us say, if you only half go with it, half believe in it—you leave, as it were, a point in you which may grow and lead to another glimpse of yourself. This is like breaking through some crust that one takes as oneself. But if you justify yourself this possible point of growth is at once arrested and turned the wrong way round. Remember, the more you find yourself self-justifying the more certain you may be that you are lying to yourself. The False Personality, however, is very powerful, and will maintain itself at all costs and by every method, one of which is self-justifying. The action then of self-justifying will be to prevent the Observing 'I' from passing inwards. It will prevent you from seeing anything more deeply about yourself. It will keep Observing 'I' on the surface as a sort of toy with which you play occasionally.

You must understand that everything in us fights against real self-observation. Unless Observing 'I' gathers round it other 'I's that wish to work, that can hear something of the meaning of the Work, it is without any strength. For this reason, if the significance of the Work continually grows cold in you, Observing 'I' will remain on the surface. It will remain ineffectual. The relationship between the power of Observing 'I' and the evaluation of the Work is thus made clear and is formulated in the diagram which concerns Observing 'I', Work 'I's, Deputy Steward, Steward, and Real 'I', in vertical scale. To try to observe oneself not from the Work-side is useless. The Observing 'I', so to speak, must be surrounded by the feeling of the Work for it to penetrate through the outer crust of Personality. We are told that we must observe ourselves from what the Work teaches. This is the only way, as far as we are concerned, in which Observing 'I' can follow the path that it is destined to follow—namely, the path inwards. As was said, the effect of this passing inwards of the Observing 'I' is that we gradually become aware of things that we knew nothing about, because we were, so to speak, in front of these things so that they acted as it were from behind us. If the Observing 'I' deepens, these things of which we were unconscious, because they lay behind us, lie in front of us so that we can see them more clearly. You can only see a thing if it lies in front of you: you cannot see it if it lies behind you. How else do you think it would be possible to become more conscious of oneself except through a movement inwards of oneself? To become more conscious of oneself it is necessary that the consciousness of Observing 'I' must increase. The Observing 'I' is a part of consciousness in us not turned outwards via the senses but inwards towards our being. You can call it an organ of sense if you like, provided you say it is an organ of internal sense. This point of consciousness exists in everybody but remains as a rule totally undeveloped. It remains undeveloped because it is not supported by the necessary knowledge, the necessary ideas, the necessary emotions. Life does not increase it. The Work can increase it and is designed to do so. For this reason, Observing 'I' must be supported by Work 'I's, by 'I's that feel the Work and long for it. Simply to observe yourself without any deep feeling for the Work can lead only a very short distance. On the other hand, to feel or to think one feels the Work deeply and not to observe oneself through it is again unlikely to lead to any results. Certainly great faith in the Work may help. But self-observation is the initial method of this Work and so it has to be often thought about and considered and attempted. It may take a long time to begin to observe oneself from what the Work teaches. That is to say, it may take a long time to make this connection between self-observation and the Work. But if there is anything real, this connection will inevitably begin to be made after a time and then self-observation is no longer some theoretical thing that one must try to do because one is told to do it, but it becomes a constant accompaniment to one's life. It becomes something that does not interrupt but accompanies. And when this accompaniment ceases, one knows instantly that one is asleep. Remember that it is said that self-observation must be uncritical. You do not observe yourself in order to criticize yourself. If you do so it will at once stop self-observation and lead to internal considering. When self-observation begins to accompany you, you will notice that it is not critical: it is simply a slight degree of consciousness. It is not a critical consciousness, a judging consciousness, but an awareness. Through this awareness you simply see more. You recognize, let us say, something that you said before, or you see that you are doing something that you did before, or that you are behaving like this or like that, or having these thoughts that you had before or these feelings that you had before. This awareness does not accuse you: it says nothing but merely shews you what is going on in yourself. No doubt it may make you feel uneasy but this uneasiness does not come from Observing 'I'. The Work 'I's behind Observing 'I' may make you feel uneasy. Many other things could be said here, but the main point is to comprehend that self-observation must not be critical any more than a light that you flash over a dark room is critical of what it falls on. The object of self-observation, as it is said in the Work, is to let a ray of light into oneself. The next thing that is said is that when light is let in in this way many things begin to change of themselves. It is the light of consciousness that begins to change things. For this reason it is said in the Work that the light will cure us. Have you ever thought what it means, this extraordinary phrase: "the light will cure us"? When I first heard it said to me by G. it had such an emotional effect upon me that I was unable to speak to anybody for some time afterwards. I knew it meant something I had never understood and yet seemed to understand for the moment. We all think we can cure ourselves. I think perhaps I understood that we could not cure ourselves but that there was something that could cure us if we could gradually reach it. The next thing I understood much later was that no light could be in me unless at all costs I kept this Work alive in myself, all the ideas, all the thoughts, all the memory of it, and that this was my task, because by doing this I might be able to increase the light, and so, instead of taking thought for myself, I had to take thought for the Work, and everything else would follow at the right time. Then I understood better what it meant that we should not work for results. So our task is always to increase the light of the Work in ourselves and to keep it alive amongst ourselves.

INTRODUCTORY NOTE ON ESOTERICISM

I want to speak briefly about esoteric schools and the idea of esotericism in general. There is an immense amount of literature connected with esoteric schools that have existed at different periods of history. Ordinary history, as you know, is nothing much more than a history of crime and violence. If you open any book on history you will find nothing of esoteric history. On many occasions Mr. Ouspensky said to me that the overcoming of violence was our final aim and that all negative emotions which engender so many evil consequences not only among individual people but in a national sense spring from Man as violence. Now violence is not a thing that can be overcome right away like that. I will give you an example of what I would call the beginning of violence. In the Sufi School of esotericism which came in after Mahomet and worked on the Koran and, in fact, gave an entirely different explanation of the Koran, there was a so-called mystical poet called Sadi. As a youth Sadi was very religious in the ordinary sense and on one occasion when the Koran was being read to a class he said to his father that he had noticed that many of the boys went to sleep and he thought that this was very bad. His father said to him: "So all you have got from this reading of the Koran is nothing but finding fault with others. I assure you, my son, it would have been better had you been asleep like those boys you criticized." Now perhaps you will not see that this is the beginning of violence. Perhaps you do not see what I mean. Is intolerance the beginning of violence? Is feeling you are better than others the beginning of viclence? If you think that you are better than others, superior to others in the wrong way, do you think that this can bring about violence? Here lies a very deep research, a very long path of understanding. You remember the old esoteric symbol of the lion with its paws cut off of which we made a plaster cast at Tyeponds which we put up in one of the rooms. I often wonder what the military who took over the place thought of this plaque.

Violence always comes from thinking one can do. Now violence always breeds violence. That means that everything you do from violence passes into the world both as a triad and an octave that can only produce the reaction of violence. We see to-day violence up against violence everywhere. We see the law "a tooth for a tooth" exemplified in every direction of life. We see violence creating violence, violent machines creating new violent machines. Christ said: "Ye have heard that it was said of old time, an eye for an eye and a tooth for a tooth. But I say unto you, Resist not him that is evil." It is impossible to understand this saying except on the scale of ourselves. On the scale of life it is a different matter as far as we are concerned. But on the scale of ourselves it is something that we can begin to comprehend practically once we understand that violence always arises from the feeling of superiority, that we are better than others. Sadi thought he was better than others. He congratulated himself on his virtue. You will always be violent if you feel intolerant of others in the wrong way, if you take if for granted that you are better. More consciously, you may see where you are better without feeling the violence of intolerance. Now later on I will speak about different schools, the remains of which are incorporated into surviving literature. But I will only add that all thinking one can do becomes violence very easily. Do you remember the 11th Chapter of Genesis where it is said at the opening: "And the whole earth was of one language and one speech." This means that there was a time, which I remember G. used to speak about, when people under the influence of esotericism were all one and so had a common speech. In this connection G. once said in France that when esotericism had a central control for a short time everyone was taught to write towards the centre of government, geographically speaking, and seemed to indicate that this is the reason why we write as it were from left to right and other nations from right to left or from below upwards and so on. I only understood the idea that there was some central government quite different from anything we know, in which all nations were under one jurisdiction and, as it were, always wrote towards it. Whether he meant this seriously or not I do not know. Now to return to this ideal state of humanity. You will see what happened. They began to think they could do. They identified with their knowledge and understanding as Man inevitably does when he begins to sleep. And so the account goes on to say: "And it came to pass as they journeyed from the East that they found a valley and they dwelt there." This means that they went away from esoteric teaching—that is, the East—and went to a lower level, the valley, which means a lower level of understanding. Then they began to build. Notice how they built. "And they had brick for stone and slime they had for mortar." You know already that stone means truth on a certain level. But they made brick instead of stone—that is, they invented truth. They substituted human-made truth for esoteric truth and so they built a city and a tower and came under the wrath of God, which means the laws of esotericism. They said they would build a tower to reach to Heaven. This means they thought they could overcome esoteric truth or the Word of God, as John calls it. They passed into self-worship, the worship of their own understanding, and so thought they could do. However, the explanation of this parable will be given later on in a chapter on the Gospels.

Nowadays Science has given Man the idea that he can do. But psychologically we are all connected with some other medium, with which this Work is concerned, and to which we can become gradually more sensitive. The object of this place down here in Gloucestershire is to keep alive the teaching of the Work—that is, esotericism—in spite of all that goes on in the world of violence. This is a place that is like an oasis. Whether you appreciate this oasis or not depends on your understanding of the Work. Here we think differently, here we talk of different things, here we keep alive something that does not depend on the pendulum of violence.

Birdlip, December 2, 1944

LAW OF FATE AND LAW OF ACCIDENT

INTRODUCTORY NOTE ON THE WORK TEACHING ABOUT LAWS

The Work teaches that the Absolute is under one law—the law of its own Will. From it proceeds creation by the first trinity of forces which create the first order of worlds under 3 laws. This is sometimes called World 3. In tracing the Ray of Creation to our Earth we have next our Galaxy under 6 laws, our Solar System as a minute part of our Galaxy under 12 laws, our Planetary System as a whole under 24 laws, our Earth as part of the planets under 48, and our Moon as part of our Earth under 96.

You must understand that the part is always under more laws than the whole. It is necessary to see this clearly by finding your own examples—for example, the soldier is under the laws of the Captain, the Captain under the laws of the Colonel, etc., and the whole army under the law of the General. Does Man put himself under more laws in war? Does the general movement of things tend to-day to put Man under more and more laws? Will this make it possible for Man to reach his Essence more easily or will Man tend to become more of a machine, more mechanical? Are ants and bees under more laws than we are? Have they any individual chance of development?

The more laws Man puts himself under the more can it be said he is under the Law of Accident. In all that follows you must clearly grasp that Personality is under more laws than Essence. Essence is under planetary laws at the note *Fa* in the Ray of Creation, or rather the note *Si* in the Side-Octave, both notes being at the same level in scale. Behind Essence lies Real 'I' which is under 12 laws and corresponds diagrammatically to the level represented by the Sun. That is, Essence is above Personality in the Scale of Being, and Real 'I' is above Essence. Psychologically, Essence is internal to Personality and Real 'I' internal to Essence. What is more internal is higher in scale. So you can either say internal or higher, both terms having the same meaning.

563

LAW OF FATE AND LAW OF ACCIDENT

Recently a question was asked in London about Being attracting one's life. A concrete example was taken in reference to the assassination of one of our ministers in Cairo. The question took this form as far as I understand it: "Why was the chauffeur shot? Was it a result of his Being? How does the Work explain such an incident?" I find this question very interesting to discuss once more and the following commentaries refer to this problem.

In the first place, the Work teaches that one's Being attracts one's life, therefore from this point of view it was the Being of the chauffeur that attracted his death at that moment. We have therefore to speak about what Being means first of all, and in order to do so we must pass at once to another teaching of the Work—namely, that a man can be either under the Law of Accident or under the Law of his Fate. The question then takes this form: "Was the death of the chauffeur due to his Fate or was it due to Accident?" Now if the chauffeur had been under the Law of his Fate, then his death was due to his Fate, but if the chauffeur was under the Law of Accident his death was accidental. Now people will say that if our state of Being attracts our life, it follows that everything that happens to us is Fate and therefore inevitable and, as it were, predestined. But we must understand what Being means as we are. Our Being is a mixture. It is composed of Personality and Essence. That is, our level of Being, as we are in life, is not one thing but different things, and the different parts of our Being are under different laws. That part of our Being that is essential is under the Law of Fate: that part of our Being that is Personality, particularly False Personality, is under the Law of Accident. And this mixture of Essence, Personality and False Personality constitutes our general level of Being at the moment. False Personality is under 96 orders of laws, Personality is under 48 orders of laws, Essence is under 24 orders of laws. Our level of Being is therefore a very complicated thing. When Personality is gradually made more passive—and that means it does not take so much charge of us—our Essence begins to grow. This means that we begin to grow into our Fate. You must not think that Fate means something fatal in the sense of deadly. It means something quite the contrary. It means that when we feel more essential we know far more about what is our real life, what we should do and think. In other words we begin to know who we are quite apart from what we have been taught to be or have imagined ourselves to be. The hypnotism of life, as you all know, is a very powerful force, and the great and changing events of life always exert this tremendous hypnotic force on us. We may vow never to do this or that—or, let us say, never to make war again—but when the event comes along, when the drums begin to beat, we forget our resolutions and become identified with the event. I remember on one occasion

Mr. O. said that hundreds of thousands of people remembering the last war are perfectly certain that they will never allow themselves to engage in another war. He said this was quite right but that when the event of another war began to act on them they would forget and would see everything from another point of view. Asked why this happened, he said that it was due to two things, one that Man cannot remember and the other that Man is mechanical, a machine acted on by outer life. I remember arguing with him on one occasion and saying that so many people remember the horrors of the last war that if another war did occur practically nobody would fight. He said very seriously: "Nicoll, you don't yet understand what mechanicalness means. You do not see deeply enough what the Work teaches. You think that Man has Real Will and Real Memory. You are arguing from the point of view that Man is already conscious. The tragedy is that Man takes himself as conscious and does not see that he is mechanical. What does mechanical mean? It means that something is driven by something else. Man is driven by outer circumstances, by life. Life is like a great belt that turns the machinery of Man. People never understand this, people always think they can do and when they do something contradictory to the opinions they previously expressed they do not see any contradiction owing to the action of buffers. Buffers are the most terrible things in us: their action is to ease the shock of contradictions. I assure you that when the next war breaks out everyone will forget all they thought and felt previously." I said to him: "Supposing another war does break out?" He remained silent and looked at me and then said: "What do you think?"

Now when we are under the general law of our Being we are under very mixed laws because our Being is not united into unity. We have, as it were, some 'I's under the influence of 96 orders of laws, those especially belonging to our purely invented side, our ridiculous pictures of ourselves, or self-worship. Then we have other 'I's under 48 orders of laws which belong to our Personality, and finally we have a few 'I's very close to Essence which is under 24 orders of laws. Essence is our more real side. Behind Essence lies Real 'I' which is under 12 orders of laws and in the cosmic scale is on the level of the Sun. Let us study again the side octave from the Sun that creates organic life on the Earth. We are part of organic life, this big machine that is created for cosmic reasons to transmit the influences coming down from the upper part of the Ray of Creation so that they can pass through the narrow place called the interval between *Fa* and *Mi*, the place of missing semi-tone, so that they can reach the termination of our particular Ray, namely our Earth and our Moon. No one can properly understand what happens on this Earth and all its tragedies unless he has a clear idea that we are part of a living machinery not constructed for purposes personally beneficial. This machine called organic life was created by the Sun—that is, by influences that are conscious—not only to supply the missing part in the great Ray but also to make it possible for Man on Earth to develop upwards in the scale of Being through Esoteric Teaching. Man can ascend in this side-octave from the Sun. The Divine Intelligence of this level of the Sun has done two things which seem at first sight completely contradictory. It has created organic life at the point where it had to and at the same time it has made it possible for Man as part of organic life to ascend in this side-ladder. This ascending depends on the inner development of a particular man, whose level of being is characterized by the possession of Magnetic Centre. A man can therefore remain asleep in the great machinery of the Ray of Creation and be simply used by it or he can begin to awaken and realize that there is another possibility that he can follow. (And the more he follows this possibility, the more he will help humanity in general.) For this reason the Work teaches that Man is a self-developing organism and you will now see clearly why he can either serve life as an end in itself or take life as a means to another end.

Now in this self-development and the method the Work teaches in regard to it, you will first of all realize that the False Personality must be observed and separated from. Through the 'I's that form this powerful thing called False Personality or Imaginary 'I', we are especially under the Law of Accident. In the Work terminology we are under the influence of the Moon which is under 96 orders of laws. If Man begins to wean himself from the continual reactions of False Personality in him he begins to move inwards away from his external re-acting side. A great many mechanical reactions that he formerly indulged in, taking them as himself, will no longer have the same power over him. This is only possible through long and sincere self-observation, through the applied knowledge of the Work. But this internal movement will also be accompanied by the beginning of a liberation from what does not belong to him—namely, a liberation from the Law of Accident. When he begins to work on his Personality, on thinking that he knows, he then begins to move still further away from the Law of Accident and therefore in the direction of the Law of his Fate. Why is this so? Because he is moving towards the more real part of himself. He is throwing away or separating himself from outer skins that do not belong to him. He is, as it were, casting off his various dresses. Mr. O. once said that Man as he is psychologically can be compared with a person wearing an immense number of overcoats and that the action of the Work is like discarding coat after coat. The more dressed up one is the more one is under the Law of Accident: that means that anything can happen to you, quite apart from your Fate—it means that you are not in touch with your Fate. You are only in touch with invented and imaginary ideas of yourself. Here we come to the question of people who have what is called strong Personality. From the Work point of view such strong Personality is a great weakness. Such people insist on their rights. They are certain they know what is what. They are sure they know what is right and wrong and they can produce a very strong impression as long as things go in the way they expect. But when things go differently they collapse because they have nothing real behind them. They have no flexibility, no real intelligence, no power of adapting to different conditions. Often an apparently weak man is much stronger than these people of strong Personality who feel they can get a move on. They do not see their inner weakness nor how much superstructure they are carrying which is not themselves at all.

Now let us return to the question of the chauffeur. Here we probably have a man simply under the Law of Accident. He has to join up, he carries out his orders, he is shot. He is just an ordinary mechanical man. He may have thought more deeply about the meaning of things once or twice or more probably he has shrugged his shoulders and done what he is told. Now supposing this man had thought a great deal and supposing he had realized his situation and supposing that he could remember himself. Supposing indeed he was doing his job consciously and not mechanically. This would mean at once that his centre of gravity of consciousness was no longer in the external side but more internal—that is, nearer to Essence. His Being would then be more under the Law of his Fate. If it was his Fate to be shot at that moment he would probably know it beforehand. If it was his Fate not to be shot at that moment then he would not be shot. He might perhaps become seriously ill a day or two before this situation arose or he might break his leg or he might get up too late. It is along these lines that you all have to think about this difficult problem of Accident and Fate. "Many people," said Mr. O. on one occasion, "are dead already by their Fate but are alive by Accident. We can meet them in the street, in the club, in the restaurant. But many people are dead by Accident who if they had been under the law of their Fate would still be alive. You know how many people are dead. They usually occupy high official positions. They have what is called strong Personality—that is, they possess an enormous quantity of very powerful buffers. They receive honours or distinctions but yet they are dead and may indeed have died long ago. The Law of Accident keeps them alive. They are, so to speak, accidentally alive and they always cling to life although they are already dead." On another occasion, Mr. O. said: "Some illnesses are accidental and some fatal—i.e. under Fate." I often thought about this strange term Law of Accident. I wondered how accident could be a law. How can a law be accident? I gradually realized what it meant by realizing what it might mean to be under the Law of Fate. I understood that when we are under the Law of our Fate things go more as they should with us. I understood that a coal-heaver would not be made to be an artist, and vice versa, and I began to see that what is called the Law of Accident is really made up of laws that should never act on us, laws that we were not created to be under, and which for us take the form of accident. As it were, we get caught into orders of laws that should not affect us. It is as if a fire is burning. It is under its own laws but if we insist on casting ourselves into this fire we put ourselves under the Law of Accident because we should not cast ourselves into fires. This is very well worth while thinking about deeply.

Now to come back to the original question—was it Accident or Fate? We might say it was probably Accident but as we do not know this man it is really impossible to say. We must understand that things happen on this Earth both by Fate and by Accident. Things happen rightly and wrongly. We cannot judge by what happens. We are not living on a conscious planet but on a planet very far down in the scale of the Ray of Creation. God's Will is not done on this Earth, as the opening of the Lord's Prayer teaches us, nor is it done in the Earth of ourselves. We are not progressing. Things are not necessarily getting better. People are not becoming more conscious. And here we have to think what the Work teaches and learn how to take up new attitudes to our meaning on this Earth. Consider for example the Law of Accident manifested in bombing, and consider many other things and then try to think what the Work teaches. You cannot have ordinary life attitudes and do this Work. You must think in a new way. You must repent—. that means literally change your whole way of thinking about existence on this planet.

After this was read questions were asked and comments made.

*   *   *

I will take the first comment: "What you say about the chauffeur perhaps having been shot by Fate seems to give a very gloomy view of Fate." The idea is that Fate is something fatal and the word fatal naturally suggests something unpleasant, something terrible. I think the first thing we have to free our minds of is that the Law of Fate is *fatal* in this sense. It may be a man's Fate to be a great success, to rescue his country from revolution or uphold it at a time of disaster. We must not think that Fate is disastrous. Yet the word by our usual associations always suggests something evil and we must endeavour to see Fate in quite a different light. For example, a man may be preserved through many dangerous accidents by his Fate. By his Fate he is not allowed to die before his time. In this sense Fate means nothing fatal or deadly but on the contrary a preservative force. In this example of the chauffeur, when it was said he may have died by Fate at that moment, you must understand that I have not the slightest idea whether this is true or not. How could one possibly know unless one had studied this man over a long period and known all that it is possible to know about him? We know scarcely anything about one another or about ourselves and so we cannot possibly decide as to whether Fate or Accident is acting on a person at a particular moment. Certainly we can realize with regard to ourselves that when we are very identified or in bad negative states we are more exposed to the Law of Accident. Now by "Accident" is not meant merely physical accident such as being shot or being smashed in a car accident. The centre of gravity of the meaning of Accident is that something happens to you that does not properly belong to you. You may, for example, become tied up with the affairs of someone who has no real connection with you and as a result get involved in a way that has no real relationship to yourself. Supposing somebody advises me to take a ticket for a lottery and I do so and find myself the possessor of a hundred thousand pounds. Do you think this would belong to Accident or Fate in my life? I am convinced myself that it would belong to Accident and it would do me no good and in fact interfere with my right life. In fact, Accident would become fatal in the ordinary sense. On one occasion Mr. O. said: "When people begin to feel this Work they begin at the same time to move in the direction of their Essence which is under the law of their right destiny—their Fate. You cannot expect to win lotteries, to bet more successfully and so on. You cannot expect to be more lucky in the ordinary sense." He was talking to someone at the time who had brought off a lucky bet and had asked whether this was due to the Work. He said it was simply due to Accident. He said to me afterwards in private: "You know, Nicoll, suppose you were very lucky—do you think that this Work would make you still more lucky? On the contrary you must be prepared to find you probably lose this accidental luck." Now the moment of birth is fatal, but the moment of death is not fatal. Essence causes our birth and Essence is under the Law of Fate. When we are born we are pure Essence. We have acquired no Personality. It may be our Fate to die early, but once Personality begins to surround Essence and once False Personality begins to invent itself, we are acted on by the Law of Accident. We are born into a world of sleeping people and very early we learn to fall asleep ourselves. If we could keep awake we would remain in touch with Essence and so with our Fate. Essentially—that is, by Fate, a man may be an artist, a musician, and so on. If the Essence has been developed in a previous recurrence the man may feel his Fate more strongly than he feels the life-influences that are forming his Personality. But ordinarily we become surrounded by Personality through imitation and suggestion so that we lose touch with ourselves and so pass away from the Law of our Fate. Then anything can happen to us because we are then more or less under the Law of Accident. We begin to do and say things, we begin to imitate other people, and all this may have little or nothing to do with us and may put us in situations that do not properly belong to us. We become surrounded by an enormous number of great coats. These we have gradually to strip off. We have to learn what it means to say: "I am not really like this: this is not 'I'." This is the work of inner separation. This leads in the direction of Essence and so towards the development of our essential life which is under the Law of our Fate—that is, our real destiny, our real meaning—and from this the real individuality begins to be formed. This path is only possible through self-observation and inner separation. Every one of you must have noticed that you have in you 'I's that you wish to separate from because they lead you into all sorts of accidental and indeed meaningless situations which more deeply-placed 'I's in you know are quite useless and which always lead you in the wrong direction. You begin to know that these 'I's mislead you. When you realize this you begin to understand what Accident means and from your growing dislike of these 'I's you know a deeper consciousness by means of which you recognize these wrong 'I's, and you then prefer to remain continuously in contact with 'I's belonging to the 'I's that form this deeper consciousness. When you say to yourself genuinely: "This 'I' that is speaking through me at this moment is not really 'I'," then you know you are aware of something deeper and begin to understand what the real or more essential part of you is which belongs to your Fate, to what you really are. You then begin to understand practically something about what Accident and Fate mean in yourself.

Birdlip, December 16, 1944

COMMENTARY ON INTERNAL CONSIDERING

All internal considering is due to the presence in ourselves of 'I's that internally consider. One side of self-observation is to observe these 'I's. If you simply try to observe internal considering without trying to observe the 'I's in you that love above all things to make accounts, you will not be able to separate from them. As you know, we have in us a very large number of 'I's that seek to do us the utmost harm and, in fact, to destroy our lives. They seek to destroy our happiness in every way. It takes some time to see that this is so, because for a long time we are not aware of the fact that different 'I's are in charge of us at different moments. Owing to the action of buffers particularly we seem to be one continuous 'I'. It is only in the development of inner taste that we begin to feel the taste of different 'I's and so become aware of the presence of unpleasant or dangerous 'I's acting in us.

To-night I want to speak to you briefly about curious 'I's that belong to internal considering. One set of 'I's might be termed 'I's that make conscientious scruples about unimportant things. These 'I's can be thought of as very small, narrow 'I's in the mechanical part of Intellectual Centre whose whole object is to cause difficulties and confuse us. They are not the same as superstitious 'I's that make us walk to the right or the left, etc. They belong to the parrot-group of 'I's of which we have great numbers like, for example, those that give us obstinate opinions or that keep on telling us that it is no use and so on. On the contrary they are 'I's that really can do a great deal of harm to us. They have nothing to do with Real Conscience, which never makes us internally consider about anything. These 'I's that make conscientious scruples about unimportant things very often dominate people with the result that they exhaust them, take a great deal of force from them, and indeed enslave them. They cause a great deal of internal considering with reference to oneself rather than to other people. You can tell that these 'I's belong to internal considering because they have the same emotional taste. To be imprisoned by these 'I's is very harmful. Now it is useless arguing with them—the first thing that has to be done is to observe them. The next thing is to try to separate from them. You can only do this if you get behind them into better 'I's. If you support them through identifying with them, you will neither be able to observe them nor to separate from them. There is a saying in the Work that we should make important things important and unimportant things unimportant. Everything that keeps us awake is important and everything that puts us to sleep is unimportant in relation to the Work. It is a good plan to think what this means because one then begins to see what one has to work on. There are a thousand and one other factors in us that are unimportant and that keep us asleep. But these 'I's that make conscientious scruples about unimportant things are one of these factors. They may be connected with ritualistic ideas or they may have their origin elsewhere. But in self-observation we do not try to analyse—i.e. find the causes and origins of different 'I's in us—but seek only to become conscious of them.

Let us remind ourselves again about the general view of internal considering. On one occasion G. said to O. in reference to somebody of whom O. thought well: "Yes, he is very nice but he is weak because he is always internally considering." What does this mean? What is this internal considering that makes us weak in G.'s sense? Internal considering in the Work is first of all divided into two main aspects which are really two sides of the same thing. The first aspect is the feeling that one is not being properly treated, that one does not receive proper recognition or is misunderstood. This can pass into a kind of chronic self-pity, into pathetic resignation, and so on. The other aspect is making inner accounts against other people. You must understand that this is not the same as making requirements. Making accounts against other people springs from the feeling that one has not got one's rights. The psychological result of making accounts against others is the feeling that other people *owe* us. Other people are in debt to us. This produces a very bad inner state from which the development of any individuality is impossible. That is why in the Lord's Prayer so much is said about this in such a condensed way. As long as we feel that others owe us—i.e. as long as we persistently make inner accounts—we cannot start any change of being or reach any new understanding. The teaching of the Work will fall on our ears year after year and nothing will happen. In the first place, if you invariably make and cherish inner accounts, if you always feel you have a credit balance and others have a debit balance in regard to yourself, you are a very bad merchant, esoterically speaking. You will get nowhere. All these inner accounts must be cancelled. The Lord's Prayer says literally: "Cancel our debts in proportion as we cancel other people's debts."

Now if you cannot cancel what you believe are other people's debts you will not have debts cancelled for you through the action of the Work on you. This means that your whole relation to the Work will be wrong —it will be a bad relation.

Let me ask you this question: "How can we ever begin to realize our own nothingness if we are full of inner accounts, full of the idea that we are owed by everyone and everything? How will you overcome the action of life on you? How will you break your constant identification with the events of life if you think that life owes you? How will you escape from prison if you do not feel free to leave it and wish first of all to accept from the gaoler what you feel he owes you and see that everyone is properly punished who has in any way hurt your feelings?" Try therefore to see through self-observation over a long time where you are caught and held down by the making of inner accounts. When self-observation becomes a real thing, when you begin to see what you are like and what you have done, then, if you can stand this development of consciousness without self-justifying, you will begin to see the diminution of your internal accounting. You will feel a release from yourself and with this release you will feel a broadening of yourself, a change in the feeling of yourself. You may in fact really be able to laugh at yourself. Internal considering of every kind is very difficult to observe. It is only a sense of the Work that can make it worth while for you to observe it. In life it does not matter. A great deal of ordinary life-conversation consists of internal accounting against others. It is quite impossible to observe yourself if you are just in life and in life-values. Life-values do not develop this inner taste that the Work speaks so much about, the development of which leads eventually to Real Conscience in which there is no internal considering. I advise each of you to try to observe clearly one single form of internal considering so that you recognize it when it comes round again. Taste means emotional taste. Now everything in us is connected together by associations. One set of associations is emotional. If you recognize the emotional taste of an 'I' in you, you will be able to recognize other 'I's having the same emotional taste—not in a day, not in a week, but very gradually. If you begin to hate this emotional taste you begin to be free from the power of those 'I's which have been sitting in your house taking charge of you, eating your food and spending your money and spoiling your lives all this time. Indeed, you will wonder what on earth you have been doing all this time and why no one ever told you before.

You will see from what I have said that the first thing that is necessary is to begin to see that what you observe is not yourself. I will in conclusion quote to you once again G.'s words about this:

"To begin self-observation and self-study it is necessary to divide oneself. A man must realize that he indeed first of all consists of *two men*.

So long as a man takes himself as one person *he will never move from where he is*. His work on himself starts from the moment he begins to feel at first *two men* in himself. One is passive and the most it can do is to register or observe what is happening to it. The other, which calls itself 'I', is active, speaks of itself in the first person, and is in reality only an invented, unreal person. Let us call this invented person in a man *A*.

When a man understands his helplessness in the face of *A*, his attitude towards himself and towards *A* in him ceases to be either indifferent or unconcerned. Self-Observation becomes observation of *A*. A man understands that he is not *A*, that *A* is nothing but the mask he wears, the part that he unconsciously plays and which unfortunately he cannot stop playing, a part which rules him and makes him do and say a thousand stupid things, a thousand things which he would never do or say himself. If he is sincere with himself, he feels that he is in the power of *A* and at the same time he feels that he is not *A*. He begins to be afraid of *A*, he begins to feel that he is his enemy. No matter what he would like to do, everything is altered and intercepted by *A*. *A* is his enemy. *A*'s desires, sympathies, thoughts, opinions, are either opposed to his own views, feelings and moods, or they have nothing in common with them. And at the same time, *A* is his master. He is the slave, he has no will of his own. He has no means of expressing his desires because whatever he would like to do or say would be done for him by *A*. On this level of self-observation a man must understand that his whole aim is to free himself from *A*. And since he cannot in fact free himself from *A* because he is himself, he must therefore master *A* and make him do, not what the *A* of the given moment wants, but what *he* himself wants to do. From being the master, *A* must become the servant.

The first stage of work on oneself consists in separating oneself from A mentally, in being separated from him in actual fact, in keeping apart from him. But the fact must be born in mind that the whole attention must be concentrated upon *A*, for a man is unable to explain *what he himself really is*. But he can explain *A* to himself, and with this he must begin, remembering at the same time that he is not *A*."

Birdlip, December 23, 1944

ON TAKING IN IMPRESSIONS IN A NEW WAY

Of the three foods that enter the human machine—i.e. impressions in the top compartment, air in the second and ordinary food in the lowest—the Work constantly emphasizes that the food of impressions is the most important food. You must understand that from the Work point of view the food of impressions is the most important food of all. Ordinarily people can live with ordinary food and air and very few impressions, but if a man begins to work on himself he must think a great deal about what it means to take in more impressions.

One way to take in more impressions is to try to look at things without associations. This is a very interesting method.

Another way is to see everything happening in life in the light of the Work—that is, to bring the Work up to the place of incoming impressions.

Another way is to see Personality acting *in oneself*.

You will find for yourselves as you go on in the Work many ways of taking in impressions to a greater extent. But you must remember that everything tends to become mechanical. In consequence, if you can find a way of taking in impressions more fully, you must not expect it to continue to give results. One has to be clever. One has to have a number of irons in the fire, as Mr. O. once said—that is, different methods at different times.

Now if we could make Personality passive—I say "if"—then impressions would fall on Essence which lies behind Personality. This would give us a great deal of force. Everything would look much fresher, much more brilliant, much more interesting. As we are mechanical, we cease to take in *new* impressions often at a very early stage in our lives. We take in simply the same impressions over and over again. We see everything in exactly the same way and we take one another in exactly the same way. Of course, if you can manage to see a person you know without any associations you will get a shock. You see a quite different person. In the same way, if we begin to see ourselves, if we can get behind ourselves through self-observation, we will again get a shock. We will realize we do not know ourselves and are quite different from what we thought. You remember the strange esoteric phrase in the Gospels, where Christ is talking about what is necessary for work on oneself. He is really speaking about the Personality. He says: "Whosoever shall not receive the Kingdom of God as a little child, he shall in no wise enter therein." (*Luke* XVIII 17). Here we must think about the idea of this Work—namely, becoming *conscious*.

I would like to speak about Personality—that is, the acquired part of us—and remind you of a few things. Everyone has this built-up Personality with its own view-points, likes and dislikes, customs, attitudes, and so on. Can any of you see that you have a machine of this kind and that what is you is not it? In each country quite different kinds of Personality have become ingrained. A Chinese is quite different from an Englishman. Yet each will take his Personality as absolute truth, absolute right. If you can catch a glimpse of what I mean it may help you to see what Personality is in yourself. Now, as was said, if Personality becomes more passive, impressions begin to fall on Essence. This makes it possible for Essence to grow—an extraordinary experience. As long as impressions fall on Personality they will always produce the *same* effects mechanically. But when they begin to fall on Essence everything is always new and far richer and more varied. In fact, everything is wonderful. Instead of having the feeling that everything is repeating itself, everything is the same, one begins to feel that nothing is ever the same. But one condition that is necessary is that one lives more in the moment and notices those forces coming at the moment and so takes in impressions from the actual moment. If one is always living in imagination or in the past this is impossible. When we are in the Personality and only react in set, stereotyped mechanical ways to every moment we soon feel a strange staleness, a deadness in ourselves. We are making no attempt to take in new impressions. We are really in a person that has been formed in us and that we think is ourself. The most interesting thing is that people say: "How *can* I think differently? How *can* I feel differently?" when this is the whole point of the Work. If you cannot observe how you react, then of course nothing can be changed. If you cannot or will not take in any new ideas, again, nothing can be changed. If you think that you can retain your former ways of thinking and feeling and estimating things and simply add something new to yourself as you are, then again you cannot change. It is *you* that has to change and *you* are just how you mechanically think and feel about everything. *That is you.* Have you then begun to observe this *you*, this person who thinks, feels and acts as always? Are you satisfied with this acquired *you*?

Birdlip, December 30, 1944

THE COGNITIVE POWER OF EMOTIONS

(1) The Work says that emotions are cognitive. What do you understand by this? Give illustrations.

(2) The Work says that if the Emotional Centre were purified from negative emotions it would be clairvoyant. Could you try to explain what this means?

(3) Are negative emotions cognitive?

One of the simplest illustrations of the cognitive aspect of the emotions is the power of birds to build nests in the mating-season. Here the emotional state brings with it a knowledge which the bird does not otherwise possess and when the emotional state vanishes the whole maternal cycle is over. That is, of course, the emotional part of the Instinctive Centre that is implicated—not the Emotional Centre itself, which probably scarcely exists in birds. This is just as well, for the emotional part of Instinctive Centre can bear things and forget things better—in fact, completely. It cannot become negative, otherwise animal-life would die. Animals, birds, do not return to Papa and Mama, and once the emotional-moving state is over with its wonderful cognition the whole business is over. In the case of educated Man it is different; but in primitive savage tribes it is much the same. The emotional part of Instinctive Centre, when temporarily awake, has wonderful knowledge to transmit to Moving Centre—for a brief time.

When the Work says that the emotions have cognitive value it means that there is a definite state of knowing something connected with a particular emotional state. We now take the Emotional Centre itself. To understand that there is a definite state of knowing connected with emotions, let us remember that *knowing* is not *thinking*. We can know a thing in different ways, without thinking. We can know, for example, through our senses, that it is a fine day, and do not have to think it is: or we can know that another person is unhappy: or we can know that something is true. It is particularly with knowing truth that emotional states are connected. When one is in a particular emotional state one may know something that one cannot know in some other state. One sees the truth of something and then the emotional state changes and one no longer sees that truth that one saw before. This is especially the case when one passes from relatively simple emotions into definite negative emotions. Negative emotions can never see the truth that non-negative emotions can see. This explains a great deal in life. It explains why when we become negative towards one another we cannot see what we saw before—we cannot indeed see any truth about one another. I will quote one or two passages from your answers about seeing truth emotionally:

(1) "I understand by the Work saying that emotions are cognitive that one's knowing is of entirely different quality when Mental Centre is reinforced by Emotional Centre. For instance, Mental Centre knows that our being is composed of many 'I's. But supposing a man suddenly sees an 'I' which has tormented him all his life, and his Emotional Centre is flooded with joy at the realization that it is an 'I' and not part of himself, his knowledge is lifted instantly beyond all intellectual theorizing."

(2) "In the Work one may slowly receive knowledge of the idea, for instance, that 'Man cannot do', and then one day, in the twinkling of an eye, one sees one's own mechanicalness and helplessness and sees that it is *oneself* who cannot do—that is the cognition of Emotional Centre."

(3) "In doing these replies to questions I have felt occasionally that one is tapping along with the stick of one's mind, as a blind man taps his way with his stick, tapping away against some wall of knowledge and getting some sort of guiding response—and then suddenly one taps and gets no response, the wall has fallen away and one is faced with a void. It is no good thinking any further because one has nothing to think further with and one's mind begins to go round and round in a circle. One leaves it. Then, often some time later, with no further thought given to the question as far as one is aware, one finds suddenly that one knows something about it without knowing whence the knowledge came. Does Intellectual Centre continue working in some part of itself without

one being aware of it, or when one's mind stops its tapping can Emotional Centre work?"

As regards this last example and others to the same effect, I would say that when you put your thoughts together in order and think from the Work from different sides, a moment often comes when all these efforts at thinking are joined together into a new meaning. This is the work of the emotional side of us—whether the emotional part of Intellectual Centre or the Emotional Centre itself does not matter here. When people only have confused and scattered ideas of the Work —i.e. when they do not work on the knowledge-line of the Work—the Work cannot act on them properly because they do not seek by their own efforts to bring together the ideas of the Work through any concentration of thought. You have all heard that you must build the Work up in your minds first and that then it acts as a new transmitting machine. Remember that this Work is to make us think in a *new way*. If you never really make this effort the Work remains at a distance from you as something on the blackboard.

When it is said that the emotions are cognitive it means that through certain feelings you know certain things. Ordinarily people think the emotions are blind in regard to knowledge. The object of this Work is to awaken the Emotional Centre through changing the Mental Centre. As it is, glued to the senses and the world, the Mental Centre misleads the Emotional Centre and so cannot awaken it. When the tree of the Work is planted in the Mental Centre the Emotional Centre begins to recover itself, to awaken. The Work is not about life and the world but about a certain way of thinking about life and the world. For this reason μετάνοια, or change of mental thinking, is the first step necessary to restore the Emotional Centre to its proper working and to its different forms of clairvoyance. As long as you think in the same way as you always think, as long as you do not think from Work-ideas, from knowledge of the Work, your Emotional Centre will act as a rule from the way you think habitually or mechanically. This is one of the first secrets to grasp. The ideas of the Work are designed to awaken the Emotional Centre. But if you think in terms of making internal accounts, if you think in the ordinary way—that is, from the senses—if you imbibe the opinions of others only, the Emotional Centre must remain practically dead. The mental key is of the wrong shape and cannot open the right emotions. (I advise you all to think about the Ray of Creation and the Side-Octave from the Sun.)

As regards clairvoyance, this is a very big subject to discuss and I will make only one or two comments. Clairvoyance is a certain kind of unusual cognition. It is really of two kinds: one kind is knowing something about somebody or something entirely unconnected with oneself, and the other is knowing something about someone personally connected. Clairvoyance really means clear seeing. One can think of it as the cognitive, emotional seeing of the truth about something or someone. The Emotional Centre in us, however, is only very rarely clairvoyant and usually in such a mixed way and so often wrong that the result is useless. To purify it the acquired negative part of the Emotional Centre must be lessened in its power and not made to take the chief place in our emotional lives. Roughly speaking, as we are, it is central in us, particularly in regard to such inner life as we have and what sense of ourselves we have. The purification of the emotions begins with work on the self-emotions arising from the False Personality. The impurity of our emotional states is due largely to pretence, to meritoriousness, to falseness, to all sorts of forms of shewing off, to self-deception and insincerity. We have a quite wrong sense of ourselves, believing in our merit, believing that we can do good from ourselves, that we are conscious, that we have Will and so on. All this makes the emotional life little short of disastrous. In fact, it could easily be said that it would be better if we could have our emotional life cut out altogether.

I will quote several passages from your answers about the purification and clairvoyance of Emotional Centre:

(1) "I have heard it said in the Work that only Essence can be clairvoyant—never Personality. And young children are sometimes clairvoyant and lose this faculty when Personality forms . . . "

(2) "Is it possible that Emotional Centre with its finer hydrogens is capable, when purified from negative emotions, of transcending the laws of space and time, which is what clairvoyance appears to mean? Thus at times Emotional Centre can visualize something happening at a distance, particularly if someone with whom it has a strong emotional connection is concerned."

(3) "If Emotional Centre were purified, would one see one's life more as a whole and with more understanding, with a sense of the pattern of which all the apparently unrelated bits are a part? And, since it would then be looking from a high level, would one see oneself as one looks against a higher level of being and consciousness? Would the fact that Emotional Centre was so far purified give one strength to bear it?"

(4) "If Emotional Centre were purified of negative emotions one would, I think, be above the line of passing time and from this level would have insight into many things that are obscure and inexplicable at our present level. Time would be quite different. Events would exist together instead of as a disjointed series and many things apparently unconnected would be connected. The meaning of cause and effect would become a coherent whole. In such a state one would be receptive to influences from higher centres and I imagine one would see and understand things objectively and at their real value."

(5) "If the Emotional Centre were purified of negative emotions and one ceased to be identified with oneself, one would be able to see more deeply into one's own life and into the lives of others—the centre would then work with much higher hydrogens and one would start to become conscious in higher centres."

Let us now speak of the cognition of negative emotions. You must all understand that cognition means knowledge and that you can have evil knowledge or good knowledge. Negative emotions have their own kind of knowledge, particularly in regard to how to hurt people and wound them. When you are in a negative state towards someone you know as a rule how to hurt that person most and say wounding things. Negative emotions, which are acquired through imitation, form an extraordinary mess in the Emotional Centre which is born pure. Since all emotions have a cognitive value, even negative emotions have their own cognitive-value which enables you to see the worst side of everything. Suspicion, for example, is a negative emotion and is often very clever. It is always wrong but at the same time is right on its own level. *Remember it is always wrong.* In fact, all negative emotions on their cognitive side are always wrong. They see only one side. When followed very much they lead to hell—i.e. towards the Moon, towards an inferior, a lower way of taking everything. Seeing only the evil and never seeing the good, interpreting everything on the lowest level, is, as you know, called in the Gospels the sin against the Holy Ghost, in the passage where Christ is said by the Pharisees to be healing people by means of the devil. (*Matt.* XII 32.) Some people imagine that they do not see the worst side of things and pretend to a kind of goodness, to a kind of pretence of being cheerful or optimistic about others, whereas all the time they really believe in what their negative emotions cognitively give them. It is a quite different thing to observe a cognition that comes from negative emotions about another person and actually not believe it as portraying the whole person. You must see the cognition that comes to you through your negative emotions and acknowledge its presence and then work against it—and this requires a lot of work and a lot of Self-Remembering. Pseudo-optimism, pseudo-cheerfulness, is quite useless and in fact only intensifies the power of negative emotions in the world. Each person is given his own negative emotions, as it were, with their cognitions, with their false knowledge, and each person, if he or she wishes to work, must in some way lighten the burden of the total fog of negative emotion existing in the world, which is governed by negative emotion. But they must do it genuinely and especially by seeing their own negative emotions and so "forgiving others" in the sense of completely cancelling their debts. In every case negative emotions can only see half-truths—for instance, a person who is negative and who reports what someone else said may actually report what the person said but leave out one or two things and also leave out the way in which it was said, the intonation, and so on. So he or she makes a dark picture, a lie. You will remember talks about lying and how the first form of lying is always putting things to your advantage, slightly twisting what happened, as when a person says: "I says to her ... she says to me," etc. Now if a person is negative and therefore ungenerous, he or she may describe something that happened in regard to a person disliked and the result will be truth in a sense, but *half-*

truth. You know it is said in ancient literature that devils are very clever and ingenious but they only know half-truths. Goodness always looks stupid in comparison with the cleverness of negative 'I's that are lying. I wonder if you have ever noticed negative emotion in the faces round you, noticed the expression in their eyes, and noticed how they are only watching. Think for a moment from what they are watching and what they want to catch. Think of the collection such 'I's will make in your life-album of incidents. Perhaps you all know that when you are negative and suspicious everything that is said only pours oil on the fire. I remember when I once had to deal with some insane people, who are wholly under the power of negative emotions and negative thinking, how the slightest movement I made was always interpreted in favour of their negative ideas from which they instantly deduced all sorts of things that were partly true. Negative 'I's are really insane 'I's in us. A person in negative emotions always notices very quickly what you have neglected but takes no cognisance of what you have done. In this respect his negative emotions give him a certain cognition, often very deep and subtle and *yet always wrong*. The curious thing is that negative emotions always can find proof, and if you join all these proofs together then you will be overpowered by life. You are really stitching together a pattern of life in which you eliminate everything that really goes against these proofs and, as you know quite well, you are ignoring the good side and simply holding on to the cognitions of the unpleasant side which have their own truth. The result is that you come under the truth only of negative emotions and, as I say, such truths are false, because they do not take in all sides. Perhaps sometimes you may catch a glimpse of this side of your being which is negative, and what it is making in you every day. It is not a god but a very nasty little worm, a very tiresome little spoilt child, a most unpleasant thing to become aware of. People glorify negative states. They feel it is right to worry and be identified. However, this is not true. One must do one's best to climb out of this pit, if possible. It is possible. But it is not possible if the Work has no real essential hold over you, for otherwise you will feel justified in your negative and painful life-emotions. And not only this—but these negative emotions will feed you with their own cognitive side, so that you will always be able to prove you are right.

I will conclude by quoting some of your observations of the cognition of negative emotions:

(1) "In myself I have observed that negative emotions stimulate into unusual activity 'I's of an unpleasant nature: suspicion, feelings of not being valued highly enough, resentment, etc. make one abnormally sensitive to the possible meanings of another person's words, intonations, emphases, glances, hesitations, and so on. To some extent such negative emotions are indirectly cognitive, but not likely to be accurate."

(2) "Spiteful 'I's for instance can be extraordinarily clever at finding just the right thing to say that will hurt. If we could be

half as clever as they are, in finding in our ordinary life-contacts just the right things to say, we should make a very different thing of these contacts and connections. But negative emotions are not cognitive in relation to one's life as a whole—they are completely blind there."

(3) "Negative emotions like jealousy and hatred can develop a certain cunning and knowledge of people but merely to advance their own ends. A person who is jealous or hates someone might know a great deal about their victim, perhaps even more than someone who loves mechanically, which is so often just a projection of self-love."

(4) "As long as we are joined to a person by negative emotion, we cannot possibly know that person. We see him through a distorting medium. I have often noticed the reluctance I feel to admitting in people I dislike even such good as I know them to possess."

(5) "I am just beginning to see how very blind and stupid, but at the same time how incredibly clever in a crooked sense, a negative emotional basis can lead one's actions to be. I am beginning to see that when I start from a negative starting-point, the crooked lawyers in me can produce easily an apparently very well reasoned case, which is false from start to finish."

Birdlip, January 7, 1945

COMMENTARY ON MEMORY

On one occasion Mr. G. said, in so many words, in speaking of the First Conscious Shock: "Man should remember himself and he was born to do so. If you ask me what the Work is about at this stage, it is about Self-Remembering. At this place in the three octaves, something is missing in the present state of humanity. Therefore it is necessary now to give the shock of Self-Remembering—which should be given naturally. The trouble is that even when people begin to understand what Self-Remembering means, they forget to remember themselves. It is necessary to create a memory for Self-Remembering and for this reason one must make many alarum clocks to wake oneself up. People may even wish to remember themselves but they forget to remember that they have to remember themselves."

On another occasion he spoke about the different kinds of memory that we have, and in his earlier teaching Mr. O. explained to us that we must try to observe different kinds of memory in ourselves. He said each centre, each part of a centre, and each subdivision of a centre had its own kind of memory. This means that each 'I' has its own memory because 'I's are arranged in a certain order and live in these different parts of centres. We have, for example, very trivial memories which really belong to small 'I's in small parts of centres. We remember how we lost a bus or a train years ago and so on. Now Mr. O. said that all memories are necessary but he spoke about the education of memory, saying that if we can only remember very small things we cannot remember big things, and that if we always lived in small 'I's we could not, for example, remember the Work. He said that every part of a centre is useful except the negative part of Emotional Centre. He added that the negative part of Emotional Centre is unfortunately divided into smaller and bigger parts just as every other part of a centre is. The bigger or more internal part of the negative part of Emotional Centre is capable of remembering insults all one's life. This is not trivial memory: on the contrary such deep negative emotions make a man wait for years to have his revenge. The reason why it is more persistent is because it is in bigger 'I's in the negative parts of the Emotional Centre. Small 'I's forget: bigger 'I's remember more persistently. Some people have very deep-seated negative memory that destroys their lives. You know perhaps people who say they will never forget or forgive. It is curious how they take a certain pride in saying this, but it is like a deep ulcer in them and will always bind them to life and hold them down, and prevent any new way of thinking and feeling.

Now let us stop speaking about unpleasant forms of memory with which most of our lives are filled. Let us try to think of obviously different kinds of memory. Since every centre and every part of a centre and every subdivision of a centre has a different kind of memory we should expect to observe different kinds of memory in life. For example, some people have a very good memory for tunes but cannot remember the words of a song, whereas some people can remember the words but not the tune. Here obviously are two different kinds of memory. Again, some people may remember ordinary tunes and some may remember whole operas. These again are different memories of which we might say that those who remember ordinary tunes remember in a smaller part of a centre and those who remember whole operas remember in a bigger part. Again, some people remember figures very well, impersonally or personally: they remember impersonal things like the National Debt, or, more personally, the rate of interest on some investment, or, still more personally, the fares to somewhere. They figure out things and calculate. This is a quite different memory from mathematical calculation, or from higher Mathematics. It is connected, but Mathematics is in a higher part of the centre. A capacity for figuring we might put in the formatory centre, but a capacity for Mathematics we must put in at least the emotional part of the Intellectual Centre, and a capacity for higher Mathematics probably in the intellectual part of the Intellectual Centre. We will remind ourselves later on as to what has been said about the different parts of centres and their sub-divisions.

Now some people have a very good memory for faces, probably with no names attached: on the other hand, people may remember names very well. You may have a very good memory for what has happened in your lives as regards purely external events, whereas other people do not have this memory clearly but remember their psychological states, how they felt, what they thought. Some people cannot remember a book, but can remember the ideas contained in it, and so on. Sometimes there are very highly developed forms of memory as in youthful prodigies who can remember, let us say, a whole column of a newspaper read out to them once, or who have an extraordinary memory for historical dates. Generally speaking, prodigious memory of this limited kind is a bad sign because it becomes the precocious development of one small part of a centre at the expense of the development of all the other parts. There are many examples of different kinds of memory but it is impossible to give them here, but I would advise you to see where your memory is good and where it is bad. All memories have their uses. The main point is to realize there are many different kinds of memory and that these different kinds of memory have different qualities. Mr. O. once said somewhere that some people took pleasure in saying that they were absent-minded like the professor who always forgot his umbrella. He was speaking of the idea of Balanced Man in whom all centres work equally—that is, not one-sided man or small-part man. He said it would be necessary, if this professor came into the Work, for him to learn never to forget his umbrella, because it meant that there was something missing in him.

Now in using these different kinds of memory we should realize first that there are different kinds of memory and that we should be able to call them up when necessary. For example, I may not remember a great many things at this moment, but I should be able to remember when called upon. I want to say something here about memory that you may not understand. Memory does not mean always remembering everything, such as what bus to catch, how to cook a goose, how to add up figures, how to drive a car, what you read last year, or what you learnt at school. Memory is something we call upon at the appropriate moment. A man with a good memory means a man who has a good available memory that he can call upon at the right time. It does not mean a man who is able to remember everything all at once. At this moment, for instance, I do not remember my memory. It may so happen that I am thinking of nothing, remembering nothing. If some small parrot-'I' says: "You do not remember anything"—and how extraordinary it is that so many little mechanical 'I's tempt you in this way—one should learn to pay no attention. Attention always means use of force. For this reason memory can be compared with a great library, or, to use the Work-expression, with a great number of phonograph-rolls, all arranged in a certain way. Our centres are stored with these phonograph-rolls of every kind, and, when we remember, one of these rolls turns and speaks to us. In this library of phonograph-rolls, or books, a man with a good memory knows in which department he can find what he wants. You all know quite well the state in which you feel that you could remember something but cannot for the moment. This means that you must find the way to enter the library and go to the right department and right floor, because memory is on different floors—that is, there is higher memory and lower memory. So memory in general is like a library: this library is divided into many floors and departments. A man with a good memory knows in which department, on which floor, he can find the book he wants. This may take a little time, but if he has taken in his impressions to a certain extent consciously, he will be able to find the book he needs eventually. If, however, he has taken in his impressions mechanically—that is, without any interest or affection—he will not be able to find the way in his library, although, curiously enough, his library is arranged quite correctly. What arranges his library? It is best to answer this question by saying that his library is arranged, but he is deranged in regard to it. Just as all his centres and parts of centres are there already and arranged in the right order, so is all his life recorded and arranged in the right order in him, but he is not in contact with it. At the moment of death we sometimes remember everything, see everything, know everything. We see what it has all amounted to. It is all there in the Time-Body both rightly arranged and wrongly arranged. Also, when we have moments of awakening, we see how things are rightly arranged and how wrongly we are identified with certain things which are not important. Unless things were rightly arranged we could not see this, we would not know that we had wrongly arranged them. But we are not speaking of great memory, of fully conscious memory, of this Book of Life that is opened at death. When it is opened everything is there in its right order and from that we are judged, by ourselves.

Now let us take emotional memory. As you know, emotional memory can be divided into the memory belonging to the negative part and the memory belonging to the non-negative part of Emotional Centre. I have often thought that this is one of the most striking examples of different kinds of memory. When we are negative with a person it is extraordinary how unpleasant and apparently long-forgotten things present themselves in the sphere of our consciousness and wish to escape through our mouths—even things that we really thought were over and done with long ago. On the other hand, when we become sane again, we cannot understand how we behaved as we did. We feel quite contrary feelings which often take a stupidly exaggerated form and express themselves in quite useless sentiment, which of course makes it much easier for us to be negative again because we feel we have justified ourselves. It is only False Personality that has justified itself. The only remedy for this is either to see the same things in yourself—that is, through self-knowledge—or to bring together consciously all you know about the good side of a person and confront your negative feelings with that. We always seem to see people either one way or another way and this is the case even with people who have a picture of themselves as being very tolerant. These two kinds of memory in the Emotional Centre should become a matter of continual conscious experience to all of you. Never believe in your negative states and their memories because they are always wrong, because they are one-sided. And remember also that with such memories, if they become active and control you, you destroy your own development because no one can develop through negative emotions and their memories. They have to be let go without argument, just as you let go a thing that has a bad smell. This purification of the Emotional Centre and its memories is very difficult and long work, but if you will keep the ideas of the Work clearly before you and remember that negative emotion can only breed negative emotion, if you remember that violence can only create further violence, if you remember that nothing real can ever grow in negative parts of Emotional Centre, nothing except lies and falsity, if you remember that no one can reach even a trace of Real 'I' if he is venomous, full of hatred and self-pity and depression, then perhaps very gradually, keeping all these things in mind as well as the whole idea of the Work, you will be able to have shorter negative states. This is the dirt that has to be cleared away from us before anything else can happen. This is the dirty mind that has to change. But first one has to observe one's negative states and you will often find people who assure you they are never really negative—even those who are all the time enjoying their negative emotions to the full. I will remind you of what Mr. O. once said about negative emotions. He was talking about false schools where rules were given that were impossible to keep. He said, in so many words: "It is quite easy to say in a school that people have no right to be negative, but saying that means that Man can do. A man who under all circumstances does not become negative is already a Conscious Man. What I say to you is this: I say that you have a right *not* to be negative."

Now if you are foolishly sincere and simply express your negative thoughts and feelings in every situation you are not being Sly Man. One can always plunge into any situation with all one's ordinary negative ways of taking it. What we have to learn in the Work is to take situations in a more conscious way so that we get through them without becoming completely identified. As you know, we identify with our negative states very easily. Here we have to remember ourselves, to remember what the Work is teaching us. We have to remember that we have to endeavour not to react mechanically, and to try to think what it means to be cleverly sincere. To be cleverly sincere one must be sincere to one's understanding of the Work. This can help a great deal and this is where memory is consciously applied. "I must remember myself in this situation—" this is an example of work on oneself. It is not the same as being cautious or wary in a life-sense. It has quite another origin. Being cautious in a life-sense is going with your mechanicalness. You are mechanically cautious, but the above example is about acting consciously against one's mechanicalness—against oneself.

Now as regards memory in the Moving Centre—here lie all kinds of extraordinary memories, memory for walking, for skating, for writing, for speaking, for balancing, for bicycling, for eating, for sewing, for knitting, for doing everything with your hands and with your feet. These memories are acquired, but some are born, such as the memory for sucking. The Work teaches that centres are born blank like smooth wax and are impressed by impressions from life. The great exception is, of course, the Instinctive Centre, which is fully developed at birth —otherwise digestion, etc. would have to be learnt. The Instinctive Centre attends to the inner work of the organism and is itself the representation of the organic life cosmos in Man or what is ordinarily called nature. The cleverness of this centre is beyond all computation. It is, for example, a ten thousand times better chemist than any actual chemist or physiologist. Without this starting-point Man could not exist on the Earth. He is given this first of all and also a small development of the Moving Centre, but nothing else. This is not quite correct, because he is also given Higher Centres fully developed, that are always at work in him, but he is not in contact with them. They represent higher cosmoses in Man.

Now in the Instinctive Centre lie memories of sensation. Some people say they can recall their sensations. This may be true, but from my own observation I do not remember the actual sensation but something disembodied. For example, if I say to you what is the difference between eating strawberries and plunging into ice-cold water, you will know the difference, but the sensations are disembodied, ghost-like. When you are eating something that gives you a particular sensation of taste, smell, consistency, you are reminded of other similar sensations by association. This is memory of sensations. Or when you eat a thing said to be lamb and it is not, you know it is not. This means there is memory for different sensations but I do not think this memory is easily recallable voluntarily. Sensation works in the present moment only, just as all the senses do. Thought, for example, is different. You can recall the memory of a thought you had yesterday, but I would say you cannot recall in the same way a sensation. Thought is independent of the senses, which only work in the present moment of time and, in fact, make the present moment of time, but some trains of thought are timeless and you have to come back to your senses to know what time it is. If we could recall sensations in their totality we should never move away from agreeable sensations, but in recollection they are very thin. People forget their sensations, such as those due to war, very easily. If you could recall fully the sensation of being warm you would never be cold. Certainly it is possible to create warmth and some Yogi schools teach this first of all, but it is done through the mind and not through recall.

Let us now speak of the connection between memory and association. In connection with this enormous subject we must remember that all associations are connected with memory. The lowest level is automatic:

the highest level is through corresponding ideas. Say you swing your arm round and suddenly begin to talk about cricket, how you used to bowl for your XI. You do not know why you talk about cricket, but the movement as it were rings up memories of cricket. This is automatic. This side of our life is constantly at work only we do not notice it. For example, if you sit in a certain position, you may become negative: this is because you have been negative before when sitting in that position. Some other time we will speak more fully about associations, which are one aspect of memory. But I must say here that all that has been written above and all that follows belongs to the study of the human machine. The Work teaches us that we must know our human machine and catch glimpses of how it works. When we take ourselves for granted or take ourselves as one big 'I' always the same, it makes it impossible for us to work on ourselves. We are like a city full of different people, some of whom are very troublesome as long as we take them as 'I', and this city is full of used and unused roads. The realization of this does not lead to the loss of the feeling of oneself, but rather leads to the loss of the wrong feeling of oneself—or, to take the Work-phrase—we must realize we are a house in disorder and nobody is in charge.

Then take the formatory part of the Intellectual Centre, the moving part. Here lies the memory for words, phrases, all our ordinary orientation to life, small plans, catching buses and so on. All these are different memories in sub-divisions in which live different 'I's that attend to these matters and have been trained to do so.

Next I want to talk to you about memory in the higher parts of ordinary centres and how it differs from memory in smaller parts—or memory in bigger 'I's in contrast to memory in smaller 'I's. In the first place it is impossible to remember oneself in small 'I's and it is merely a waste of time. In fact it is worse than a waste of time because it drags the whole Work down to a very small level. The work cannot fall on small 'I's which cannot understand it and which are turned towards life and are necessary for life. So if you go about in your daily life and simply suddenly try to remember yourself because some little parrot 'I' tells you to do so—one of those little nagging 'I's that give you an entirely false sense of duty—then simply laugh at such nonsense. The act of Self-Remembering must have a certain emotional quality. It is owing to the emotional quality that one is put at once into higher parts of centres, into bigger 'I's. These can remember the Work, they can understand it. No one can work continuously but only at times. But it is possible to keep awake a little all the time and at least to observe oneself. Self-observation should accompany our ordinary life and can do so. But Self-Remembering is on a quite different level. Self-observation can lead up to Self-Remembering when one notices one is forgetting one's aim. Now in Self-Remembering all the memory of the Work enters, not necessarily consciously but by a high level of association. 'I's that are in higher parts of centres have a far more comprehensive memory than that of little 'I's that stand, as it were, close to the ground and have a very limited vision. These bigger 'I's can take in two or three things together and relate them because they have a wider vision. That is why the memory of these 'I's is quite different. They can, as it were, take in the whole of a subject, whereas little 'I's can take in only one small part, and for this reason they continually argue inside one and catch hold of little contradictions. It is a great misfortune to be judged by other people, by little 'I's—and this is after all the general human situation. You get into bigger 'I's either through an emotional state or through attention. Directed attention which has to deal with the Work-ideas can put you into an emotional state— or even a book that contains B influences. This makes it possible to remember yourself because it puts you into a chain of conscious associations, voluntarily acquired, or rather acquired by choice. Here the memory of everything is quite different because everything is in the right order. It is a very wonderful thing when this begins to happen to you—that is, when you begin to touch real Self-Remembering. Of course, if you worry about Self-Remembering or do it as your duty merely, you will not reach this state because you start from the wrong place. It is the whole feeling of the Work that makes it possible to remember oneself. And it is also the whole memory of the Work that makes it possible. But this memory is not the same as the ordinary memories we use for life. It is like going into another room. If there is nothing there then there can be no Self-Remembering in a real sense. If you remember your origin and feel it emotionally enough you may touch the level of Self-Remembering, and then you may remember many other things that long ago you have forgotten. This is special memory where things are joined together by similar emotional states, by a similar taste. And here you often find many things that you may have thought have been no good, things you have tried to do, things you thought you had failed in: you find them there in this special memory. But you can find nothing there that you thought you did well and deserved credit for. Remember that each centre feels, and that every division of a centre feels, and all these feelings are of different qualities and call up their memories. This is why so much insistence is laid on evaluation of the Work, because evaluation is feeling and it is through feeling the Work that we get into contact with 'I's in ourselves that can work and can self-remember and can lead to the state of Self-Remembering. Feeling for the Work develops through feeling when you have wrong feelings about the Work. No one can feel rightly, but people can become more conscious of when they feel wrongly. By inner separation, by non-identifying, and by dislike of wrong feelings, or discomfort about them, it may be made possible for right feelings to enter. When we have experienced some moments of right feeling we remember them afterwards in ordinary life in an inverse way—namely, through feeling that we have not got the right feelings. This action of memory is the most interesting of all. If we were not given occasionally inner perceptions and experiences a little above our ordinary level, we could not grow. The point is, we do actually have traces of experiences beyond our ordinary level. This is one of the most remarkable things about our human existence and points to our having something more in us than we are. If you will think of the Side-Octave from the Sun you will see the explanation.

Now you will see why, in the Work, memory is taken as one of the most important of all things and why the purification of memory is so important. To keep the memory of useless things alive is not the right use of memory. Memory must become selective. On one occasion Mr. O., in speaking of what he would ask for if he had three wishes, said: "One thing would be to be able to forget what I would like to forget and to remember what I want to remember." Now we forget things by reducing their importance and we remember things by increasing their importance. Some things we must starve in ourselves and some things we must feed, and the Work teaches us what we have to starve and what we have to feed. But one of the most important ways of altering memory is by cancelling debts through seeing the unpleasant things we attribute to others as also existing in ourselves and this is one of the great uses of self-observation. This checks the growth of unpleasant memories and also changes us. This kind of work on yourself is always possible at any moment wherever you are, and begins as soon as you reach the stage of being able to notice when you are taking in unpleasant impressions either from outside or from memory.

★   ★   ★

Part II.—In the first part of this Commentary it was said that everything is arranged in the right order as regards memory and that everything is there—all that you have said and done and thought and felt and sensed. Everything is all there and in the right order and in the right scale—that is, the important things are arranged on one floor in the house of memory and the unimportant things are arranged on a lower floor. But it was also said that we have our own wrong arrangement of memory. This means that we have a wrong memory although there is a real memory already stored up in us in the right order. To understand this, we must realize that we are between the external world coming in through our senses and the internal world which is governed by Higher Centres. Although we are not in contact with Higher Centres and cannot possibly be at present, yet because Higher Centres are continuously at work in us they arrange our life in the right order, whereas our Personality arranges everything in the wrong order. We have, therefore, two memories, our own memory and, deeper and far more internal, our full memory. When we observe ourselves and begin to doubt our way of remembering our lives, when we begin to move in a more internal direction, we inevitably come up against an entirely different form of remembering our lives. We begin to realize that our way of remembering our lives is entirely wrong. We think of ourselves in a certain way. But behind this personal thinking there is another thinking because of the action of Higher Centres which are all the time re-arranging the incidents of our lives in another order and on another scale. So there are two memories—one that we have access to in an ordinary sense and another that we have not access to at present. Let us call these two memories external and internal. In the external memory everything is arranged as you think it should be from mechanical Personality, from your buffers, prejudices, attitudes, opinions, and self-love, self-interests, identifications, worries: this is your external memory. But you have also an internal memory in which everything is arranged quite differently. All your Personality life-memory is recorded in this internal memory quite differently and in the right order. When Real Conscience begins to awaken you begin to feel this interior memory in which everything is rightly arranged for you, so that you see everything in a different light. This begins when Imaginary 'I' begins to die —that is, when False Personality becomes weakened and one no longer has the same feeling of oneself. In the interior memory everything is recorded, but on the right scale and in the right order: in the external memory everything is recorded on the wrong scale and in the wrong order, according to your False Personality, from small grievances, etc. You all remember the Work-parable which compares us with a driver, a horse and a carriage. You remember that the driver is asleep in a public house: this means of course that he is full of imagination about himself and full of ideas of boasting and so on. And outside this public house stands his horse and carriage in very bad condition. The driver must first awaken and leave the public house and stop spending his money there. Now, from one angle, this driver, who is drunk in the public house, is a man with an entirely wrong memory of himself. When he wakes up, he ceases to boast of himself. He no longer feels that he is anybody at all and he feels he has some other task. You probably have all noticed how you boast, how you justify, how you keep up your ordinary feeling of yourselves, your merit, your individual excellence, your superiority, your thank-Godness, and how with all these self-intoxicated feelings you cannot really touch the Work nor understand what it is all about. You hear very often that Personality must be made passive without seeing where this acquired artificial thing, which has its own quite wrong memory, is concerned. When a man is very much under his Personality and feels very strongly his own virtues he is comparable with this driver sitting in the public house intoxicating himself with his own imagination about himself. And this intoxication will give him a certain kind of memory for himself and this memory will be a deranged memory—not an arranged memory. Yet at the same time there is always more internally a memory of everything that is being recorded for you which is arranged in the right order. You all know how we invent, how imagination works in the sphere of memory, arranges things in its own way, and perhaps some of you know already how deeper self-observation makes us gradually acquainted with this false memory and makes us gradually realize that it is entirely acquired, entirely invented and has no relation to facts about oneself. One is not the person one imagines oneself to be, nor is one's past life what one has imagined it to be. Only self-observation carried out with real affection can shew you this. You can adapt to the Work and if you are clever you can give every appearance of working but you are merely adapting. And on one occasion Mr. O. said that it was quite useless to adapt to this Work as you would adapt to any situation in life. If any of you think you can merely adapt to the Work you will find sooner or later that you are no longer in the Work and, in fact, that you have never been in the Work. Now this change of memory necessary in the Work can only come about, as was said, by self-observation done sincerely and done according to the directions that the Work gives us. If this is done then a new kind of memory of your past life begins. You become a witness of a very strange effect—namely, that the whole of your past life begins to be changed for you. The reason is that every particle of memory begins to be ordered in the right way. You begin to know for certain that there is another interpretation of your past and it has always been there only you have not been conscious of it. And this means that there is another memory that has been acting on you without your knowing, and that has never tried to speak to you in any violent form. You realize with a certain, shall I say 'agony', that it was not so, that it never happened like that, that it is not true. And this word that I use is not wholly a painful thing. All enlargement of consciousness is a kind of agony but has its own sense of release from prison, its own feeling of freedom. I would say that our ordinary memories based on how we have always taken things, how we have thought certain things were right and certain things wrong, constitute one of our greatest imprisonments. Are we not imprisoned in our personal memories? What does transformation mean? All psychological transformation means to take things in a new way and unless we can take things in a new way how can we escape from our own prisons which so much depend on memory of the past, and on the way that we are taking everything at this moment—quite mechanically, thinking it is the only way to take everything. Once more I remind you that this Work is about thinking in a new way. Have you tried to remember in a new way? Everyone is a result of his memory. Unless the Work acts on you now like a ferment you will be carrying on your life in this Work in the same way that your personal memory has laid down for you. And so the past will create the future and the future will be the same as the past. Why should this be so? It will inevitably be so because your reception of life and its incidents and events will always produce the same mechanical results. And so the tapestry of your life will continue to be woven in exactly the same way as in the past. If you have no self-observation, if you cannot act more consciously at a particular moment when things are difficult, you will continue to lay down in yourself the same pattern. You may flirt with the Work as many people do, you may think it is interesting, but remember that the Work Octave starts with evaluation as *Do,* and application of the ideas to yourself as *Re.* Certainly this is a big step. Remember that you are the subject of the Work, you yourself. The Work is not something outside you. It has to come into you, or, you have to put it inside yourself and begin to live from it and view everything that you do and think and feel from the power of the Work. When this begins your whole memory of everything, of yourself, of other people, of your past tribulations—and remember that everyone makes so many internal accounts in life that each person secretly feels that he or she only has tribulations—will begin to alter. This is psychological transformation. You may have heard that this Work is sometimes called the Good News, the εὐαγγέλιον. What is the Good News of this Work? Why is this Work Good News? Think what this means. Think, for example, of the phrase: "We have a right *not* to be negative." Is this Good News? Is it Good News to you to realize you are not the person you supposed yourself to be and that you need not be bound down to this Imaginary 'I', to this False Personality? Is it Good News to you to think that there is another meaning to life that will explain everything and that you have in you by creation possibilities of reaching Real 'I', something so utterly full of meaning when you begin to touch it that none of the events of external life can drag you down? Is this Good News or not? Or do you prefer to remain glued to life and all its tragedies, all its continual uneasiness, all its feelings of dissatisfaction? Does it give you something to hold on to when you realize that this Work can bring you to a new feeling of why you exist? Now unless you change your memory you will not change your habits of feeling and thought. The present feelings and thoughts you have are mechanical and are based on your mechanical memory. Like everyone else you take all that for granted. The trouble is that you think it is right. So the memory of your habits of thought, of opinion, of feeling, make you go forward into life and its changing events always in exactly the same way. You see neither the idea of Self-Remembering, nor the idea of the continual mechanical making of internal accounts. You do not see your negative attitudes, or your negative emotions, or your definite forms of identifying. You see neither the fact that you have many different 'I's nor the fact that you are a definite psychological machine always reacting in the same way. What an extraordinary thing it is to realize this machine in oneself, in which one sits passively and which drives one through life by itself. It is very Good News to hear that there are forces with which we can make contact that can alter and ultimately transform this machine that we take as ourselves.

Now every moment of consciousness, every moment of insight, through self-observation in the light of the Work, every sudden moment of seeing what a fool one is in different ways, not only alters the future but alters the past. It begins to re-arrange the memory of the past in a different way—that is, in a way that corresponds to the internal memory where things are rightly arranged in value, in scale, in importance. Have you ever thought how you act on such very small truths that are nothing more than opinions as a rule, and how little attention you pay to the truths this Work teaches which are of a quite different order? We always have amongst us the problem of the person who feels that he or she has done his or her duty. This is, of course, a self-complacency, or call it what you like. But when such people meet the Work it is useless to fall back on all that kind of memory. The Work is something new and no matter what you have suffered in the past or what distinctions you have gained, or what efforts you have made, or what life-rewards you have obtained—or, in fact, whoever or whatever you are—this Work is a new starting-point and is about something quite different, a second education that refers to our real meaning on this planet. As you have heard, no one can interpret life in terms of itself. Life taken in terms of itself is meaningless. Think what this means. Do you believe it? Can you see life in a more whole way? Perhaps you have been personally lucky, but can you see the whole matter more deeply? Can you find any sense in life taken in terms of itself? Certainly people often do not realize their own unhappiness, but I am not talking of this—I am talking from a Work-idea—namely, that Man is asleep and that everything happens inevitably in consequence. If you think about this deeply enough, can you really say that you can interpret life in terms of itself? The Work says that everyone who has Magnetic Centre already knows, perhaps without knowing it, that life cannot be explained, cannot be interpreted, in terms of itself. There must be something else added to life to give it right meaning. And here the Work comes in with its own ideas of life on this Earth and what Man has to do with his life. Only when he gets another kind of knowledge about his meaning on this Earth can life become a means of work—that is, a teacher. Life is not the teacher but the Work is the teacher in relation to what happens on the Earth. This is Good News. This enables us to take life as a means and not as an end. So all our troubles, all our tribulations, all the continual disharmony of everything begins to have a new meaning. Is every unpleasant event going to make us negative? Is every crisis going to make us identified? Is every trouble going to make us increase our internal accounts? Is every feature of life going to drag us down? Is every difficulty going to make us lose force? Do we expect life to be always as we wish? Or is there an entirely different range of ideas and work that can eventually meet all these different situations that mechanical life creates every moment. We have to make a boat in which we can sit and not be swamped. We have to make oars and also a rudder. Or, to take another illustration, we have to make a raft to cross a very difficult stream. But we cannot make either the boat or the raft: we have to find one that is made for us and get to it. Conscious humanity has always worked on mechanical humanity and given boats, rafts, arks, in which to cross. If you feel this Work enough, if you really want something to carry you through life, then you have already something made for this purpose. Getting into this boat or raft or ark depends on creating a new memory. If you can remember this Work, if, for example, you can remember not to be negative when it is very easy to be, you are getting into this vessel, and you will find it supports you from this continual drowning which takes place every day. Work-memory is very different from life-memory. I remember G. saying one night: "Remember, remember, remember, remember why you are in the Work." Why are you in the Work? Why are you here? I have often thought about this and I thought very much at the time when he said it. I realized that one could get nothing of the Work save by wanting it quite genuinely. Certainly many mixed motives may exist but nothing is recorded in the memory save through affection, and so no real Work-memory can arise in a person unless there is affection for it. What you love you remember and love never sleeps Many other sides of us may sleep.

Birdlip, January 13, 1945

THE DOCTRINE OF 'I's

I

Let us return to the fundamental teaching of the Work and take as an example the doctrine of 'I's. "How many 'I's have we got in us?" O. was once asked. "Have we 20 or 30?" O. replied: "We have hundreds of thousands of 'I's in us, only because of the action of buffers we do not see them as distinct but retain our belief that we have only one. 'I' that always acts and feels in the same way. This is Imaginary 'I'. It is this imagination that one has one 'I', this Imaginary 'I', that prevents us from changing."

On another occasion he was asked whether 'I's weren't imaginary and he answered in so many words that 'I's were real beings in us, real persons, but because we did not see them we had the imagination of having Real 'I'. "The 'I's are real," he said, "But the Imaginary 'I' is imaginary. Each 'I' is a small living person in oneself."

Just as people are divided into No. 1, No. 2 and No. 3 Man so these 'I's in a person are similarly divided. Each 'I' has a thinking part, an emotional part and a moving part, but its centre of gravity may be more in the sphere of the thoughts or of the emotions or of the actions. Each 'I' is a distinct being that takes charge of us and speaks through our telephone calling itself 'I'. Some of the 'I's are very harmful to us, some are indifferent and some are useful. A question was asked recently as to whether all our thoughts came from different 'I's. The answer was "Yes." But not only that; all your moods, all your feelings, your actions, your words, come from different 'I's in yourself. As we are, we

594

have no individuality, no Real 'I', no big 'I' that controls all the other 'I's and arranges them in the right order. At first it is more easy to observe 'I's acting on your thoughts, giving you certain kinds of thoughts. You observe that you are thinking in a certain way about someone. This is an 'I' that is thinking, that you are taking as yourself. Or say that you are thinking about your life: this is again an 'I' and you are taking it as yourself. When you do not see this trick that is constantly being played on you, you take all these thoughts as you. You think: I am thinking this. Or you say: This is how I think. You do not see that something is thinking for you and that you are not thinking at all. You hear the thoughts of these 'I's as if it were you who were thinking them. In fact, you think that you think. Now better 'I's can see worse 'I's but worse 'I's cannot see better 'I's. What is higher can see what is lower, but what is lower cannot see what is higher. When you begin real observation of your thoughts you can begin to see certain kinds of thoughts that you do not wish to accept, say, about other people, or about yourself. Now if you think that these thoughts are you or if you say: "I think this," then you make one of the greatest mistakes you can make in this Work. You give these thoughts power over you because you identify with them, so you simply go with them without realizing what the Work is continually teaching—i.e. that you must practise inner separation. If you take everything that happens in the sphere of your thoughts as 'I' then you cannot practise inner separation. Why? Because you take everything going on in your thoughts as yourself. How then can you separate if you take everything as yourself, everything as 'I'? How can 'I' separate from 'I'?

Now as regards the sphere of the emotions—here again many 'I's exist in us that bring about changes in our emotional states. Just as 'I's transmit thoughts into our minds so do 'I's transmit feelings into the sphere of our emotions. These 'I's affect the emotional state direct and scarcely touch the thinking. Some of these 'I's can exhaust us, make us lose confidence, make us depressed, low-spirited, and so on. Yet they are 'I's acting on us and nourishing themselves at our expense. If we could always remember ourselves these 'I's could not have any power over us. But as a rule we have given them so much power that we never even challenge them and they walk in and out of our emotional part as if we belonged to them. Now although they are difficult to observe directly, after a time in the Work you will always be able to detect their presence by being aware of a drop in level or a sudden loss of force. If you are not quick enough, 'I's of this kind will get in and take possession of you and it may take days to get rid of them. We have to learn to walk in ourselves very carefully. It is no use arguing with unpleasant 'I's. That is why the practice of inner separation is so much emphasized in the Work. One moment of being asleep in some difficult situation will let in 'I's of this kind. Next moment you are in their power and they will make you see everything and feel everything in their own peculiar way. If someone in the Work at such a moment gives you a right shock you suddenly see and feel everything quite differently and wonder what you were up to. This means that the 'I's have changed and different 'I's are now in charge of you. All our work lies in separating from wrong 'I's. It begins first with the thoughts and then leads on to the emotions. This means that a struggle begins in oneself between the different 'I's, between being in wrong or in right 'I's. The power of this Work can give us this power of separating from wrong 'I's. Life cannot give us this power because life encourages very many wrong 'I's. This is why we are taught to observe ourselves in the light of the Work. The Work is a system of observation and comes from Conscious Humanity—that is, from those who have gone through this battle of 'I's and attained their goal. When we are in bad states of thinking and feeling, if we make no effort to recall better states we are dragged down. And yet we need not be dragged down. What drags us down is our choice. We have the power of choice internally, say, of thinking in one way or thinking in another way. Sometimes when we can do nothing with ourselves for the time being, we can at least retain the power of not completely consenting to our state, of not believing it entirely, and, as it were, being patient with ourselves and realizing we are all wrong, and yet not seeing how to get out of the state. Then you may be sure that you will after a time get into a better state again. But if you fully consent to your thoughts and feelings, if you say 'I' to them, in a total sense, then you will lay down in yourself something which next time it will be far more difficult to separate from because, so to speak, you have signed your name in full on the cheque. When you realize beyond any doubt that you have different 'I's in you, when you can hear them speaking or notice them working in your emotions, and yet remain separate from them, you begin to understand the Work on its practical side. You begin to understand the first line of the Work— i.e. on oneself.

Birdlip, January 21, 1945

FURTHER NOTES ON 'I's

(Answers to questions arising from the previous paper)

(1) *What is an 'I'?* An 'I' is a definite personality in us, a small being with an intellectual, an emotional and a moving part. You must understand that 'I's are quite real people in us. On one occasion O. said: "You all think that 'I's are not real. You think they are theoretical. I assure you that they are quite real and live in the House of your own Being and continually control you." He then quoted the Parable of the House in Disorder in which there is no Master and where each 'I' uses the telephone in the name of the Master.

(2) *Is it not desirable to identify with 'I's which seek the Work? Do not these 'I's become 'Deputy-Steward', proceed to 'Steward' and finally become Real 'I'?* It is not desirable to identify with anything, but I will let that pass. It is desirable to go with Work 'I's and listen to what they say, especially when one is in the power of negative 'I's. By means of self-observation through the Work and what it teaches, a number of 'I's become separated from the rest and these form Deputy-Steward. This development of consciousness through self-observation leads gradually to the higher stages of Steward and Master. If a person does not nourish Work 'I's they become feeble and may even leave us for ever.

(3) *Can our 'I's be divided into groups of similar 'I's with which most of us are familiar? Can they be dealt with as groups or must each separate 'I' be sorted out and worked on individually?* Yes, 'I's are divided into different groups because they inhabit different sub-divisions of centres. 'I's that occupy very small sub-divisions of centres are very small 'I's. They may be useful for life but they cannot understand the Work. For this reason the Work teaches that we must value the Work and feel it as something distinct from life and greater than life, because through this emotional valuation we are at once in the presence of bigger 'I's. It is impossible for a long time to see 'I's individually but it is possible to see that one has a number of different personalities. These personalities are composed of many 'I's but they each constitute a definite group as, for example, in my own case I have a large number of 'I's that belong to my medical personality. O. once said: "Try to see quite definite personalities in you. You have a social personality, a professional personality, a domestic personality, and so on, but each of these personalities is made up of a great number of small 'I's."

(4) *Since 'I's are represented in each centre, can fidgeting be said to be done by an 'I', and if so, does this also imply that habit is accompanied by intellectual and emotional fidgeting?* Yes, certainly, fidgeting is done by an 'I' that is chiefly in the small sub-divisions of Moving Centre. Yes, it can be accompanied by intellectual and emotional fidgeting. It may be a rather powerful 'I' acting on 3 centres equally. This requires observation. Observation begins with noticing the different work of the 3 centres. If you notice that you are intellectually in a fidgeting, uncertain state, you may notice that you make certain movements and so on, but often mere fidgeting is a small automatic 'I' in the Moving Centre—for instance, a person may be always scratching his head and this sort of fidgeting may belong to a very small practically automatic 'I' in the Moving Centre and not interfere with the work of the Emotional or Intellectual Centres. We all have all kinds of mechanical tricks even when we are deeply concentrating.

(5) *Are all 'I's acquired?* Yes, they are all acquired and they are acquired in all sorts of ways. It is usually said that they are chiefly acquired through imitation and education but they are all acquired because they belong to the Personality which is acquired. The Work

says that it may be true that there is a trace of Real 'I' in us, but that is all that it says. But Real 'I' is not acquired: it is already there as a possibility from our birth. We do not make Real 'I': we seek to approach it. Then *we know who we are*.

(6) *Are there 'I's in Essence?* No, it cannot be said that there are 'I's in Essence although some 'I's that we acquire are very close to Essence —i.e. we have more essential 'I's. On the other hand, we have 'I's that are very far away from Essence and that belong chiefly to False Personality. If our Personality were the expression of our Essence and fitted in with it, so to speak, we might say that our 'I's were all connected with Essence, but this is not the case as we are at present. Through the pressure of education and environment our Personality may be very unlike our Essence and when this is the case it is not unnatural to expect that we may have an unusual, degree of inner disharmony.

(7) *Suppose a man or woman has in their Personality useful 'I's such as hospitable 'I's, helpful 'I's, 'I's which are skilful in handling tools etc., but that they act 'to be seen of men.' Suppose after work on themselves they were able to do the same things from themselves . . . would those 'I's become essential in them?* We have all sorts of useful 'I's acquired through our upbringing. You must remember that Personality must be formed and may be formed better or worse. Good training is necessary for everyone accompanied by good ordinary discipline. We all have to learn a trade or profession. We have to learn manners and so on. All this is acquired. The action of the Work is such that it chooses those 'I's that are useful and lifts them up, so to speak, so that they no longer act quite mechanically but can be used deliberately—that is, consciously. The Work makes a kind of Ark in us into which everything useful goes. We cannot do this ourselves. The action of the Work does it and arranges everything in the right order.

(8) [a] *Is Essence the seed from which Real 'I' can grow?* Yes, in a way. It is better to say that behind Essence lies Real 'I' and through the development of Essence we contact Real 'I'. The object of this Work is for us to become more real, to get rid of false, unreal 'I's. This can only be done through inner sincerity and long observation and through the influence of the Work acting on one over a long time, and the latter depends on struggling to keep the Work alive in one over a long period. All this leads on to the development of Essence, which puts us in contact with Steward and Real 'I'. You must conceive Steward and Real 'I' as being above us on a higher level and as it were awaiting us, being, as it were, more internal, deeper, beneath the surface on which most of our psychic life takes place. Whether you call it a movement upwards or a movement inwards, it amounts to the same thing. All this Work has to be done by ourselves. We are in the position of having lost our way and having to find the way back again. Everyone is created perfect —that is, with Real 'I'—but we descend into this world both literally and psychologically and lose our way. There is some reason for this, and one of the explanations of it is that we are created as self-developing

organisms. It is an experiment. Every man and every woman is an experiment based on this idea which must be constantly reflected upon, constantly held in mind.

(8) [b] *Is Real 'I' the individual limit of potential development which lies above every man—the shape he could become—different for everyone, or the same?* Yes, it is the ultimate reality that we can attain. Behind Real 'I' lies God. But surely this question is a little formatory. Certainly everyone is an individual creation and so Real 'I' can never be the same. The trouble is that we try to imitate other people and it is just like a daffodil trying to become a tulip. There is not a single snowflake that is not quite different from another snowflake in its form of crystallization although the general hexagonal pattern of the snow-crystal is the same.

(9) *Is there any difference between 'I's and inner consciousness?* I can see no connection between these two factors in this question. 'I's are 'I's and inner consciousness is inner consciousness. If you mean by inner consciousness the power of self-observation, through this you can see 'I's in yourself, but the question is like saying that if you have an electric torch in the dark and see a wall in front, is the wall the same as the torch?

The Work says that by true self-observation we let a ray of light into ourselves. Through this ray of light we may see a thing in us, but an 'I' is not the same as a ray of light and of course a ray of light does not mean physical light but the light of Consciousness, which it is the object of the Work to increase beyond everything that you can imagine at present, so that you can see yourself at a glance and everything going on in every centre.

* * *

I will now comment on one or two observations that were made in the sub-groups on points in the paper:

(1) *There was something said in the paper that I thought was very encouraging. If you really see a thing, even if you can't do anything with it, it will recede.* This is quite right. And in seeing this you catch a glimpse of what the Work is about. You catch a glimpse of what self-observation is and why it is taught so strictly. The Work says that self-observation is a method of change of Being. This is a very important thing to understand and it may take years before one catches a glimpse of its meaning. On all this depends inner separation. I ask you this question: how can you separate from anything in yourself unless you observe it? If you cannot see yourself at all and never observe what is acting through you at different times—if, in short, you take yourself as one—you cannot change. If you can only see what you did not do, and never observe what you did, you are certainly very externally-minded and have not awakened the power of observing 'I' or the inner sense that we are all given. We are given this inner sense so that we can fulfil our meaning as self-developing organisms. All inner development would be quite

impossible if we had not this sense that is turned inwards towards our psychic life but merely possessed five senses turned outwards.

(2) *'I's are living but may be induced to die.* 'I's are certainly living and are quite real entities. Whether they die or not is another question. The Work merely teaches that if they are not nourished they get weak, but if, like the shades of Hades, they drink your blood, they become alive and begin to speak. 'I's may be absent from you for a time and revisit you—but that is another question. But it applies especially to higher Work 'I's in oneself. Our ordinary 'I's are constantly with us. You know, they are called 'the poor'.

(3) *It would be interesting if we could discover what there is in one. One could have a most varied life, with most varied 'I's, some quite valuable.* Yes, this would mean having reached the level of Balanced Man who can move freely about in himself and in whom all different sides of himself are to some extent developed—i.e. he has no longer his centre of gravity in one centre as have No. 1, No. 2 and No. 3 men. For example, if I am very much identified with my life as a doctor I shall not be able to move freely in myself and will have only a very one-sided development. When you are identified with your professional side or your birth side, or whatever it may be, you cannot become Balanced Man. I often think myself that one of the best phrases one can use in regard to understanding what Balanced Man means is to "be able to see what it means not to be identified with your life." Your past life should not catch you always and hold you down. Here you all have something practical to work on for a long time.

I will now comment on two further questions which have been sent in since the above was written:

(10) *Is an 'I' which passes straight into Emotional Centre one which is so well known to Intellectual Centre, from habit, that it no longer needs to pass to Intellectual Centre first?* This question is very formatory. I would simply say: Do you really know about an 'I' so distinctly? But you must remember that some impressions fall on the Emotional Centre and this means that it is necessary to observe how the Emotional Centre reacts in face of life without any self-observation. We have to employ the Intellectual Centre to observe ourselves and not let an impression fall directly on the Emotional Centre without the moment of consciousness in which one sees where it is falling. Observing 'I' starts in the Intellectual Centre where our consciousness, broadly speaking, lies. It is a question of what you let through. You can take hold of a red-hot poker by accident and yet observe the reaction before it happens automatically. It is a question of Instinctive Centre and the slight possible control of it, and the same applies to the Emotional Centre.

(11) *How does an 'I' affect the Emotional Centre direct? Can an impression pass directly to the Emotional Centre without passing through Intellectual Centre or the network of associations? Is a negative emotion invariably preceded by a*

thought? Is a negative emotion preceded by a thought? I would say that it is a question of attitude. If you have not yet seen how you react from attitude, which is mental to begin with, and accompanied by practically no thought and yet *is*, then the impression will fall directly on the negative part of Emotional Centre. Remember that the Work teaches that our impressions come in through the Intellectual Centre and then pass to the other centres. It is necessary to make a conscious point at the place where they come in. If you allow an impression to go right through then it will follow its own habitual path. We will begin to check the effect of external impressions in the Mental Centre first of all. For instance, need I, if I feel cold, shiver and complain? If I am more in control of myself I need not react in that way unless I wish to. If I am not quite mechanical the point of incoming impressions that fall upon the mind will be capable of a kind of selection so that they do not ring up automatically the same reactions. The point of the Work is to make a conscious point at the place of incoming impressions, and this demands the power of observation so that one is separated from the continual effect of life coming in and reacting always in the same mechanical way. It is a marvellous thing to realize that one need not take a life-event always in the same way. But for this to begin to take place one has to be able to see the event and at the same time see one's mechanical reaction to it. When the Work intervenes between these two things, the external event coming in through the senses and the mechanical reaction that would ordinarily take place, when there is this moment of conscious choice which the Work seeks to establish in us, then we begin to understand what the Work is about practically. This is called moving *Hydrogen 12* to the point of incoming impressions. This means also beginning to live more consciously in the midst of life.

Birdlip, January 27, 1945

SELF-REMEMBERING

In a conversation recently held here the talk turned on Self-Remembering. It has often been said that unless you believe in something higher you cannot remember yourself. There is a certain emotional feeling always connected with Self-Remembering. You cannot just in cold blood remember yourself. It is necessary to get into a certain state, whereas one can observe oneself without getting into this particular state. Yet the two actions finally meet. Through Self-Remembering we come under new influences which otherwise cannot reach us. If you feel the extraordinariness of your own existence, if you feel the miracle of your body, of your consciousness, of the world that surrounds you, if you begin to wonder who you are, then you are in the state necessary in this Work and must arise from inner choice. Here then we have people who begin to understand the Work at a certain stage and begin to apply it internally to themselves and begin to realise its meaning from something internal in themselves. And here a man no longer works for a reward, but from inner choice.

Birdlip, February 3, 1945

THE DOCTRINE OF 'I's

II

Recently we have been talking about the doctrine of different 'I's in us and how, unless we can see we consist of many 'I's, we cannot shift from where we are. Before we go on let us remind ourselves how different 'I's arise in us and what the Work teaches on this subject. The Work teaches that we are born with Essence alone and in small children we have manifestations of undeveloped Essence. Essence comes down to this level of the earth in order to grow, but it cannot grow by itself beyond a very small point. Notice, by the way, that small children do not have negative emotions, which are defined by their persistence. A child grows up among sleeping people and begins to form Personality which gradually surrounds Essence. A small child never says 'I'. When it begins to say 'I', Imaginary 'I' begins. Many 'I's are laid down by imitation, etc. and the growing child begins to say 'I' to all of them. I suppose it could be said it begins to say 'I' by a kind of imitation, by a kind of imagining itself 'I', and it hears adults always saying 'I'. However, many other interesting things enter. Now we speak of ourselves as adults. We have inevitably, and even by design, acquired a wrong feeling of 'I', that is, Imaginary 'I'. If Essence is going to grow in us further everything connected with Imaginary 'I' must become passive. Therefore it is understandable that the Work says that unless a man can divide himself into two he cannot shift from his psychological state. Dividing yourself into two means to divide yourself into an observing side and an observed side. Unless a man can observe himself he cannot change. Such a person will remain always the same man, the same woman. Also, you all know that as long as a person takes himself or herself as one person, as always being the same 'I', he or she cannot change.

Recently there was a conversation about lying. The Work has many things to say about lying. For example, the deepest thing the Work says about lying is that it destroys Essence. A person who always lies destroys his or her Essence. Now Essence is the only part in us that can grow and bring us to another level of being and so to another fate, to another position in the scale of being. A liar cannot grow. Everyone

606

has in them a great number of 'I's that lie and these 'I's are always connected with the tremendous activity of self-justifying 'I's. A person should be uncomfortable when he or she lies. The Work says there are two forms of lying—that is, lying to others and lying to oneself. At the same time the Work says that lying can only be defined by a relationship to some system of truth. If you have never been taught anything about what truth is it is difficult to see how you can lie. A small child who knows nothing does not lie and cannot lie, but when he is taught something he may begin to lie in regard to what he has been taught. You can only lie in connection with some truth. If you have never been taught any ideas of right and wrong about truth and falsity, how exactly can you lie? As soon as a man was capable of conceiving the idea of things forbidden and things allowed he gained the capacity of lying. Now you can lie in this Work, and lying in this Work destroys your possibilities of development. You can both lie to other people and lie to yourself, and I would say the centre of gravity of the Work teaching in this respect regards lying to yourself as the most important thing, but the Work begins by saying you must not lie to your teacher. You may not wish to speak to your teacher about something but if you are asked to tell what happened and you lie—and this is always known—then you are in a dangerous position, not only towards the Work but towards your inner possibilities of development. Now the system of the Work is a quite clearly defined thing and you can all know quite well what it means to lie to the Work. You may lie in life but to lie to the Work is quite a different thing. You are then lying in reference to a definite system of truth. You realise that any development of the psychic life is only possible through a system of truth taught you, which you begin to follow. You have to begin to live this Work, not merely to think of it, or talk about it. The Work is a definite system of teaching of forms of truth that if you begin to live them practically will lead you in a certain very desirable direction. This living of the truth of the Work means work on yourself. It means that you want to follow what the Work teaches. But if you lie to yourself internally, as when you say you are not negative and you are, then you block the influences of the Work in yourself.

All development depends in the esoteric sense on relating yourself to a system of teaching which does not lie in life. The Work is something extra. It is the second education. A man may be a naturally good fellow in life but this is not the idea of the Work, because the idea of the Work and of all esotericism, including the Gospels, is to bring you face to face with an entirely different way of living in life. And it is only through this entirely different way of living and of understanding that the aim of esoteric teaching on this earth is fulfilled. For example, through social training you may not express negative emotions publicly by reason of your training, but this is nothing to do with the Work. You have to get an entirely different relationship to the whole idea of negative emotions and one that is not governed by external appearances.

Internally, people who have learnt not to express their negative emotions in life may be infested with negative emotions. For this reason it is so important not to lie to oneself. On one occasion O. said: "Lying destroys Essence because Essence can only grow through truth. A man must cease to deceive himself before he can begin to grow. The worst form of lying is pretence. Everyone pretends to be what he is not. The source of all lying of this kind lies in the imagination". On another occasion he was talking about life in general and said: "Nothing in life is what it pretends to be." At that time he was talking about the League of Nations; he said: "It is not what it pretends to be, just as so many other apparently excellent organisations are not what they pretend to be. How can you expect sleeping people to create organisations far beyond their own level of being?" I was very much struck by this, as I thought, sweeping statement about charitable organisations, etc. in life. On one occasion we were passing a church with people coming out and he said the same thing—namely, to the effect that a church does not do what it pretends to do, to make people like Christ. And I was reminded of what G. once said about Christianity that there was only one Christian, called Christ.

Now let us take lying on a practical level, and let us take in particular that form of lying that begins with Imaginary 'I' and becomes connected with False Personality. We are told in the Work parable that the human race on earth are like sheep under the charge of two farmers who are magicians, and whose object is to prevent the sheep from escaping from their power, and that, being very mean, not wishing to use any expensive methods of retaining the sheep, they hypnotised the sheep and told them they were lions and eagles, and, in fact, supermen. This is a parable about the power of imagination, connected with Imaginary 'I' which eventually creates the False Personality. The False Personality is entirely pretence, entirely imagination, and its origin is from the Imaginary 'I', that is, the imagination that we have a real 'I' in us. With this form of imagination, which keeps us as sheep asleep, we gain the most extraordinary ideas about ourselves. We think we *can do*, for example, we think we have real will, we think we can decide our own lives and we can never see that *everything happens*, even our own lives. We form in ourselves a kind of secret imagination and although life itself does not correspond to this secret imagination we still cling to it, feeling we are lions, eagles, supermen etc., and never realise what we actually are like. The imagination that we have 'I', the imagination that we are doing everything from ourselves, the inability to see that we are mechanical and that everything happens to us, the non-realization of this Imaginary 'I' and all the fantasies that it builds up in the False Personality, and this inability to see where we really are, this inability to see what our lives have been, all this keeps us fast asleep in a continual self-lying, a continual pretence, a continual self-hypnotism. This state of ourselves is described in another Work parable as a driver sitting in a public house and spending all his money on drink, while his horse and carriage in which he can go somewhere real are standing out-side, neglected. You remember that this parable says the first step is to awaken the driver. What is this drink that the driver is drinking? It is imagination about himself, and we only have ourselves, to drink, literally to see the strength of this imagination. What does everybody begin to do when they begin to drink literally? They begin to boast—or they begin to reveal their secret self-imagination—how wonderful they really are and how no one has appreciated them and so on, because everyone has this secret self-romance connected with Imaginary 'I' and False Personality, and this constitutes one of the most hidden sources of making internal accounts.

The first form of lying we have to study in ourselves, the Work says, is that in which we always tend to tell about something that happened to ourselves to our own advantage. When you have to report what you said and what the other person said in some Work conversation you will find that it is practically impossible to put the matter rightly. You will tend to put the whole report to your own advantage, by leaving out some things you said and slightly over-emphasising other things you said. Of course you can do the same thing the other way round by deliberately putting yourself in a very bad light through wretched self-pity which hopes for a reward. However, people are quite certain they can speak the unbiased truth both about themselves and other people. Certainly there are more truthful 'I's in us and less truthful 'I's. But what is the whole object of this being truthful in the Work? It is not based on moral grounds. It is based on the possible development of something called Essence that can never grow through pretence or falsity. All those 'I's that lie habitually, all those 'I's that protect the central kingdom of the False Personality and justify everything, twist everything, turn everything to their own advantage, prevent this inner development of Essence from taking place. For this reason, the Work teaches, it is so important to tell the truth to your teacher, because by this exercise you learn how to tell the truth to yourself. And if you cannot tell the truth to yourself you cannot get beyond the sphere of the Imaginary 'I' and the False Personality which cannot give you any inner development. So it is not a moral question but a practical one. If we begin to see more now the falsities in our past lives we begin to alter them in the past. We can see lies in the past, but we only see them through work on ourselves in the present. If our observation of ourselves has become increased now in the present and we begin to see all sorts of false attitudes, false intonations, false ways of conceiving of our own value, false blaming, etc., we are mercifully able to see the same things having operated in the past. That is, we change the past from the present moment of work, because life is a compact thing lying coiled up in ourselves and when we die we take this coiled up thing with us. Sometimes I have thought we can change the past more easily than the future. This is partly because when you begin to awaken a little more to what you are like, the past comes forward and enters your consciousness, whereas the unknown future does not come forward in the same way. Always in the future lie further temptations but you are not tempted by the past in the same way except by habit. It is marvellous how the Work opens up your past in exactly the right way when you have begun to lift yourself in the present moment to the level of the Work. Now you begin to see what your lying has been in the past, and you begin to understand that what is called lying in the Work is not always what you thought. It may not be expressed by lying in words—call it, if you like, pretending. A person can lie with a single gesture, a single look, a single intonation, a casual mannerism, a sigh, a heartbroken expression, an illness, by a hearty manner, by being always fit and well. We all know how marvellously we have behaved and we all know what intolerable conditions we have been subjected to. The Work says we all lead an imaginary life with ourselves. Now this romance may take a great deal of strength from us and in all cases it prevents us from any real self-observation. It has to be torn out of the heart. The self-emotions are tremendously powerful. Sometimes these self-romances clustered round the Imaginary 'I' are sad and tragic. We all know one another's hopeless looks. When we are based on this inner self-romance we are very weak, whether the self-romance is about being strong and cheerful, or being misunderstood, or never having had a chance, etc. It is all self-hypnotism, and it is always a deep source of our making of internal accounts because we do not see this form of imagination which has such invisible power over us. We do not see the 'I's that use this form of imagination that gives us a false centre of gravity and makes us completely misunderstand the significance of our lives and what has happened in our lives. It prevents us seeing our lives as they are, and asking ourselves this rather terrible question—why has your life been like this?

After a time we may begin to get a Work conscience. This makes us very unhappy, not in a soul-destroying way of self-pity and pseudo suffering, but in a much cleaner way. This is the beginning of that force that can make you see your own lying. It is not an acquired life conscience from your upbringing, but the beginning of real conscience which can change one's life. It is the birth in you of something quite new, and though its action is very gentle it is absolutely authentic and you know and you recognize its authority. This is the beginning of awakening from sleep. This conscience knows nothing about your being an Englishman or a Chinese or a rich or a poor man. It is the same in everybody once it is awakened. It is nothing to do with customs you have acquired, the schools you went to, the professions you follow, or the social position you hold. For it you do not exist as a personality. The work teaches that this real conscience which is always the same lies buried in everyone and that the Work awakens it eventually. This conscience serves the *Work*. It leads to contact with higher centres. This conscience can never awaken as long as Imaginary 'I' and False Personality and all the forms of lying connected with them are dominant,

because this conscience leads in the direction of Real 'I', which is totally above the level of Imaginary 'I' and False Personality and all their pretences.

Remember also lying that harms others in the Work. This is too big a subject for here—but remember *how* you treat another in your mind.

Birdlip, February 8, 1945

COMMENTARY ON CONSCIOUS LOVE

Some time ago I received a letter in which a question was asked about a phrase occurring in the 1st Epistle of John. The passage is about love—actually about conscious love. Now all conscious love depends on throwing out what is bad and selecting only what is good. Mechanical love is of a quite different order. The passage in question was as follows:

"There is no fear in love; but perfect love casteth out fear, because fear hath punishment; and he that feareth is not made perfect in love." (1 *John* IV 18)

In the Gospel of John and in the Epistles of John we find love emphasized—not emotional love, as the conversation with Peter shews in the last chapter of the Gospel of John, but a different kind of love, which is connected with the idea of a goal, an aim, a gradual perfecting. In the above passage the phrase 'perfect love' really means, in the Greek, love that has reached perfection as it were through long trial and error. John followed the way of Bhakti Yoga. There are different kinds of Yoga—Jnana Yoga, which has to do with work on Intellectual Centre, Bhakti Yoga, which has to do with work on Emotional Centre, Hatha Yoga which has to do with work on the Moving Centre, and many branches of these three different lines which belong to Man No. 3, Man No. 2 and Man No. 1. In the 4th Way that we are beginning to study a man must work first in two rooms, and then in three, and finally in a fourth room if it is opened to him, because in the 4th Way it is necessary for a man to reach some state of balance in which all his centres begin to reflect the Work. But here in the writings of John we have evidence of the Way of Bhakti Yoga and the awakening of conscious love as distinct from mechanical emotional love and physical love. The object of this Way is to get in touch with Higher Emotional Centre directly through love. Of course we cannot understand what this love is from our ordinary idea of love, which is turned outward towards physical objects. John is speaking of another kind of love, just as the Work speaks of another kind of love possible for us, which is conscious love. But this kind of love is very far from us and to imagine

611

we possess it already is the greatest foolishness. We have to realize the illusions of love and how we ourselves cannot love and how indeed we both love and hate at the same time. For this reason John says: "He who hateth his brother is in the darkness" and also: "If a man say, I love God, and hateth his brother, he is a liar". Further, he says that whoever has not this love of which he is speaking is dead. He speaks indeed of this love as a new birth, calling it being begotten of God, and says: "Whosoever is begotten of God doeth no sin because his seed abideth in him and he cannot sin because he is begotten of God." All love, he teaches, comes from the love of something higher than oneself or the world. He says God is love and the only way in which love can be made perfect is to know and acknowledge the existence of God. It is in this connection that he says: "Herein is love made perfect", and that in this kind of love there is no fear. And that is why he also adds: "If a man say, I love God, and hateth his brother, he is a liar". He speaks often of how this love conquers the world and all its fears and cares and anxieties. He is speaking of something that can be awakened within us that is stronger than anything in life. He is speaking of something that changes the signs in us and reverses them so that what was active becomes passive and what was passive becomes active. In this connection you will remember the teaching in the Work about Personality and Essence, about how Personality is active and Essence passive, and how a man must undergo a complete reversal within himself so that Personality becomes passive and Essence active, so that he is born anew.

We are given no hint of the method of the school to which John belonged but we can see that it was a Bhakti Yoga school, and we can also see how in the 3rd Epistle someone called Diotrephes had entered this school and was apparently trying to teach some other method. John says that he loved pre-eminence. Now pre-eminence belongs to ordinary love which is self-love. Everything we see in the Gospels about love is obviously not about self-love. When the disciples quarrelled about pre-eminence they were told that to be great in the sense of the Kingdom of Heaven they must become servants. The world and its psychology in us is contrasted with the Kingdom of Heaven and its psychology, something utterly different. When this Work speaks of Imaginary 'I', False Personality, and so on, it is seeking to begin to bring us into another orientation, into a new psychology of ourselves which is ultimately called in the Gospels the Kingdom of Heaven. It is of this love that John is speaking, and not the love of the world, and of this love he says: "If any man love the world, the love of the Father is not in him. For all that is in the world, the lust of the flesh, and the lust of the eyes, and the vainglory of life, is not of the Father, but of the world." And he adds, speaking of the individual man and his attachments and identifyings: "The world passeth away and the lust thereof, but he that doeth the will of God abideth for ever." If we could all of us catch this rope of which the Work speaks and hold on to it, we would be better able to understand both what John means and what this Work means.

When the valuation of this Work is great it makes us strong inside, apart from what happens in life. We no longer have to prove ourselves in life, to satisfy our fear, to keep up our False Personality, our reputation, because we begin to obey something quite different—i.e. in our case the teaching of the Work. And this keeps something eternally young in us because we all have in us something that can always remain young and alive. But this means that we turn in another direction for our nourishment, and, passing through the doorway called self-observation, we begin to find what it is we really want and what we can really get. After a time we begin to catch glimpses of what this love means of which John speaks, and which the Work calls conscious love, because as we cease to play with ourselves and invent ourselves, so do we cease to play with and invent other people. And instead of trying to meet them and get to know them from the outside inwards, we begin to feel and know them from inside outwards. We begin to feel a common existence which is without passion, and simply is what it is without further definition. When we realize this point of inner experience we begin to understand what conscious love is, however dimly. But unless we have separated ourselves from our invention and pictures and falsities, we cannot reach this point, which is indefinable. We reach this point only through something stronger than life. If the Work, if the Gospels, if all esotericism had not something stronger behind it than anything in life, we could never reach this point. But you must understand that in the reaching of this point endless struggles are necessary, endless failures, confusions, and uncertainties, because it is we ourselves who have to win to this point by inner choice. In all ages in the past, very many have reached this point, and they communicate their strength to us. Let us hope that we ourselves may reach this point where we come to realize that love that has become perfected casteth out all fear. Certainly, taking ourselves for granted, taking ourselves as one, never letting the Work into ourselves to break us up, we cannot expect to reach this point. Only Real 'I' can love consciously. All this Work is about how to reach Real 'I'. It is all about what 'I's we have to leave behind from our own choice. Let us try to make a stronger feeling of the Work in ourselves and all that it is connected with throughout the ages, and not simply be creatures of the moment.

THE DOCTRINE OF 'I's

III.—COMMENTARY ON REMARKS MADE ABOUT "THE DOCTRINE OF 'I's" (II)

For a long time we all try to base this Work on our own self-evaluation instead of on the evaluation of the Work itself. We try, as it were, to add the Work on to what we are already. This is building on the sand—to use a metaphor from the Gospels. No one can add the Work to what he is at present because that would be starting from nothing real. The Work can only start from what is genuine, therefore it obviously cannot start from what belongs to False Personality. No one can eventually take the Work on the surface of himself—that is, on the side of Personality—but at first it cannot be helped. When the meaning of the Work penetrates more deeply we realize that we cannot take it as something just added on to the surface of ourselves. The Work is a radical thing that seeks to alter us radically in ourselves. Something was said about lying in a recent paper. Some 'I's are more sincere and some 'I's are less sincere in regard to the Work, and most 'I's hate it. A person may take hold of this Work purely from Personality without seeing its deeper implications. Then he regards it as an alternative to life and sees the Work as being against life and, in fact, sees it as an opposite to his ordinary life. He will then never understand that life can become his teacher. He will think merely that to be in the Work he must somehow or other give up his life and, as it were, go into a monastery, where he gets rid of external life. But this is not the idea of the 4th Way, which lies in life, and is applied, if it is applied, to oneself in the midst of life. The Work says nothing about giving up life, but it speaks a great deal about changing your relationship to life—that is, to your life-personality, to yourself in life and to others. Supposing that through self-observation you begin to notice that you have 'I's in you whose ambitions and motives you begin to dislike. Quite suddenly you come to the point of understanding what the Work is about. That does not mean that you have to give up life. It means simply that you begin to approach life from a different viewpoint. You may, in fact, do everything better in life than you did before. You become more careful, not only towards life but towards yourself. Your Karma begins to change from that moment. The Work very rarely speaks of Karma. Karma is the tangle of cause and effect that you lay down in yourself by your actions. The idea of Karma is introduced into the Work in connection with the laws we are under. The Work says to begin with that we are under the Law of Accident, or the Law of Fate, or the Law of Will, but it adds later on that we are also under the Law of Cause and Effect, which comes between the Law of Accident and the Law of Fate. If a man could do what he does

consciously and without identifying he would change his Karma—
that is, the line of personal cause and effect in his life. He would then
begin to pass under the Law of his Fate which is a deeper cause and
effect, and by changing his Essence he might come to the point of
changing his Fate and begin to come under the Law of Will. Of course,
if we would *will* this Work and all that it teaches, we would transcend
the Law of Accident, the Law of Cause and Effect and the Law of our
Fate. The Law of our Fate is determined by the quality of our Essence.
In Essence lie stored up things we know nothing about that belong
to previous Recurrences. You know that if Essence is changed we do
not have the same life again, but if Essence remains the same, whatever
Personality we build up for ourselves in life, we are destined to the same
cycle of experiences due to the level of our Essence. We will attract the
same life more or less and be subject to the same trials and tribulations,
the same difficulties, in fact, the same life. The idea is quite simple to
understand. It means simply that what you are really, most fundamentally, will always attract the same experiences because you will
them unknowingly. The object of the Work is to change Essence itself,
where Real Will lies. If you have no power of self-observation, if you
cannot see through your 'I's, if you take yourself for granted, you will
not change your Essence. Supposing you go with 'I's in your False
Personality, and all the hopeless tangle of inner accounts that they
make, if you have always wanted comfort, or fame, or wealth, or praise,
you will naturally have, as opposites corresponding to these four things,
a horror of misery, or obscurity, or poverty, or blame. Let us take
blame and its opposite *praise*. Let me ask you this question: Do you think
that what is most real and genuine in you—that is, Essence—can
possibly grow through the desire for praise? I fancy it is not difficult to
understand that it cannot do so, and here lies a very interesting side of
self-observation, namely, to observe how much of your ordinary
happiness depends on being praised. Or again, take *fame* and its
opposite *obscurity*: have you noticed in yourself the 'I's that wish for
fame, all those 'I's that wish to be better than other people, those 'I's
that wish to shew off? I advise you to be rather amused by them because
you will never overcome them. There is a certain inner laughter about
oneself that is extremely useful in this Work. These 'I's that invent our
lives and carry on this picture of ourselves are the 'I's that we have to
try to see because they keep our life in a continual lie, a continual outer
restlessness, a continual self-justifying based on 'What a good boy am
I'. I remember on one occasion when I was exceptionally full of self-
justifying O. saying to me in the presence of my wife: "Well, Nicoll,
is it true or not true?" and I suddenly realized it was not true and I felt
an extraordinary quietness in myself. I realized what lying meant, what
lying 'I's were, how I was lying, and from this I gradually began to
realize that all restlessness is due to lies, due to falsity, and that I was
not like this lying 'I' but that I was something else that the Work was
trying to shew me, that I had something real in myself, and all that I

was continually trying to do and say was all pretending and keeping up some fiction that I had thought to be myself. This was one of my moments of understanding what this Work is about. I began to understand what all this teaching about False Personality meant, I began to see what Imaginary 'I' meant and that there was something behind all this pseudo stuff that the Work was trying to reach and make one conscious of, and it was not a loss but a gain. You must realize that this was only a moment of understanding but it had about it a taste that one cannot forget. It was then possible for me to understand how most of our 'I's tell lies, and how by means of lies they try to fight with real life and also with ourselves and wish only to keep something going that is not ourselves.

But how difficult all this is, and what a long struggle begins from this point of insight. Have you ever noticed yourself talking away, full of righteous indignation, full of grievance, and suddenly noticed the whole thing is lies? Or have you ever come to the point of really seeing that your suffering is all lies, and experienced that extraordinary inner calm that results through seeing the truth about yourself? Because just as all lies make us restless, so does truth make us calm and at peace with ourselves. Here we all are marching into life surrounded by false and lying 'I's, 'I's that pretend, 'I's that are full of invention of ourselves, and deception and deceit, and we meet other people in a similar situation and we expect to get into contact with them or understand them, or, more horrible still, to help them to save their lives. Is it not really rather laughable? Is it not a case of the blind leading the blind? For this reason it is so necessary to see 'I's in ourselves and see how they lie. Just go with one of those invented 'I's for a moment and let this 'I' talk, and in a moment all is in an uproar inside you and before you know where you are you probably have identified with this 'I'—you have said 'I' to it and it has you in its full power, and you rise from your chair and go and see the person concerned and just say all that this 'I' wishes to say—and perhaps all the time you are thinking you are behaving consciously.

Now this Work says we must try to live more consciously both towards ourselves and other people, and the way to begin to do this is to become conscious of our 'I's, especially our negative 'I's. How wonderful it is to be in a state of consciousness in which you can see 'I's wishing to behave in a certain way or to say certain things, if the power of the Work is such in you that you avoid them and do not say what you could so easily have said mechanically. And even although these 'I's are thinking in you, you have the power of not going with their thoughts because you have other thoughts that are stronger coming from the Work. And how often in this connection you may be able to do it for a short time but afterwards when you are more asleep these 'I's that you refused to go with come back suddenly and attack you, and you write a letter or you ring up or you go and see the person and the whole matter is as before, and you add to the chain of your

Karmic cause and effect. Yet because you have separated from these 'I's for a short time things may not be quite so bad, especially if while they are discharging themselves you have a sense of dislike of them, a consciousness of them, even when you cannot control them. This is the whole point—this slight disbelief in them. This is the beginning of separation from them. And then after a time, when you become more experienced in the Work, you discover you have to do many other things before you have paid enough by effort to escape from the power of such 'I's that wish continually to keep your life down to one level. You may find you have to work on something quite different, your laziness, your lack of power of concentration, your lethargy in taking in new impressions. You may find you have to make efforts about all sorts of small things you have ignored. You may find you have to learn something that you ought to know, such as not to forget your umbrella, as O. once said. The reason is that everything hangs together in our psychology and its make-up. Everything that widens us helps in our general work on ourselves. In the 4th Way we are supposed to be able to understand all sides of life to some extent, to know something about everything, not to be ignorant people. The Work says we must work against ignorance in all its forms. All esoteric teaching says this. If we live in a few small parts of centres our basis is wrong: we are too narrow, and then work will be very difficult—a narrow jealous matter, full of envy. The Work is supposed to broaden us in every sense and to make our whole view of life broader and more intelligent. Working from too narrow a basis is not likely to lead to any results. Mr. O. once said: "What is the good of your trying to study the special knowledge of the Work when you have no ordinary knowledge that can be got from life?" At the time he was speaking about Balanced Man as the first stage to aim at—that is, the man whose centres all have some development, through effort, and he was emphasizing how in the Fourth Way, which lies in life, people must know about life, know everything they càn about what is going on, so that they can take in impressions from all sides of life. He was talking about ignorance and about what a curse it was, and how it was impossible for quite ignorant people to meet with the 4th Way, or, if they did meet it by accident, how it was impossible for them to understand what it was about, and what absurd things they made of it. He said to me about a young man who came into the Work: "He is quite ignorant. He learns this Work and thinks that he knows something, but he has nothing in him with which to compare it. He does not see that the knowledge of this Work is quite different from anything he could have learnt from life, and he has never learnt anything from life. He has nothing to make contrast with, nothing to make a struggle with in himself. A man must be in life and know about life before he can see what this teaching is about, otherwise he will take it all for granted as if it were life. That is always the difficulty with young people and often with older people who know nothing and come into the Work. They hear about the Work before they have tried to learn about life and this is the wrong order." He was speaking about how the Work must make a struggle within oneself, and was emphasizing how unless the Work makes a struggle it has no power to act on you. The Work then just goes into False Personality. Certainly, the Work in older people goes into False Personality, but it should eventually create a struggle. A person who has Magnetic Centre to begin with, and can observe himself or herself, is capable of seeing how the Work may lie in False Personality, and at first increases their ambition and self-love and makes them seek some kind of pre-eminence: But because the quality of the Work is quite different from the quality of anything belonging to False Personality, if there is Magnetic Centre, after a time a separation begins to take place between False Personality and those 'I's that wish to work. When this happens the Work has begun to act on a person and, if that person by reason of many unknown actions in the past has to a certain extent earned the possibility of inner change, then those 'I's that lie gradually become more and more observable and the great process of inner separation begins. Speaking generally, Personality becomes more passive and the real essential side begins to develop with all its accompanying insights and mental and emotional perceptions, that gradually pass towards a realization of the influences of Higher Centres. But as long as we take ourselves as one, this is impossible.

Birdlip, February 17, 1945

COMMENTARY ON ACQUIRED CONSCIENCE

(1) The Work teaches that we all have Acquired Conscience which is different in different people and nations, but that we all have Real Conscience which is buried. Do you think that Acquired Conscience is based on self-love and do you think that Real Conscience is not?

Let us speak about *acquired conscience*. Everyone has a different acquired conscience according to his or her upbringing. Suppose you have been brought up to think that a person who wears brown boots and a top hat is 'beyond the pale,' then you will have acquired conscience in judging him. I mean that you will call this Conscience. And if you yourself wear brown boots with a top hat you will be deeply pricked by your acquired conscience. Meeting such a person you will tend to have nothing to do with him.

Let us glance at the difference forms of acquired conscience that exist nowadays and have always existed. Understand that acquired conscience makes us divide things into right and wrong according to its nature. We say that brown boots with top hats are impossible. But let us look more deeply into this question. Say that you meet a man who is very interesting, and after being a long time with him you suddenly notice that he has a top hat and brown boots. Instantly your buffers will come into action and instead of taking the person as himself you will take him as an example of bad taste. In a recent conversation we were talking about this subject and how large a part tradition plays in this question. Tradition forms an acquired conscience in us and is stronger than individual contact with a person. Tradition makes you not yourself. You have traditional 'I's in you that are acquired, which makes it very difficult for you to become a real person, a real individual, free to communicate with everyone, and so it narrows down your relationship to people. You may privately think political agreement is a good thing but your traditional 'I's will prevent you from accepting it. We see many examples of this to-day. This means that your acquired conscience, traditional in this sense, prevents you from behaving intelligently as an individual. You are then collective and not individual in your judgment of things. You are really sacrificing your individual judgment to traditional conscience. But this is not Real Conscience: it is acquired conscience. A man stands on his honour, his tradition, his patriotism, and so on, and all this is acquired conscience, something he has been brought up to believe in, and such a man is not capable of direct individual thinking in connection with an actual situation. He will not give up his acquired conscience, which is various in different nations, whereas the Work teaches that Real Conscience is the same in everyone and not various, and through it agreement is possible. You can see and will see many examples of the action of acquired conscience now and in the future, such that you cannot understand how people can be so silly as to behave as they do. Then you will notice how this acquired conscience prevents any further development of the human race. To get into contact with Real Conscience one has to become more conscious of one's own mechanical reactions, and you can take this idea down to its final issues as regards your social life and so on. Yet behind all this infinite confusion acquired by tradition, upbringing, etc. there lies Real Conscience through which all people can come into relationship with one another once the acquired conscience is observed and worked against by a process of giving up its purely mechanical reactions to others.

Now acquired conscience is always connected with the self-love, which continually puffs itself up into all forms of vanity, all forms of making difficulties, of duty, etc. based on prestige, tradition, honour, nationality, and so on. In this way self-love incites continual antagonism, war, violence, and so on. That is why the Work lays such emphasis on False Personality, on invented things, on false behaviour carried out in the name of so much that is really meaningless. As a Scotsman I meet a man who belongs historically to a clan that has always been at war with my clan. I get on with this man very well in conversation, think him intelligent and like him, until I find out that he is one of this accursed clan that by tradition and honour I must hate. So I rise from the table, throw my wine in his face and go and fight a duel with him. This means that I sacrifice my individual understanding to my acquired traditional conscience. This of course is *sin* in the deepest sense of the word—i.e. missing the mark. Instead of seeing the man individually and understanding him, I become suddenly blind, violent, and sacrifice myself to the 'I's that belong to my acquired traditional conscience. In other words, I lose all possibility of individual development through my own intelligence and understanding. Recently I was reading novels written a hundred years ago. I came across the idea that a person who knits is quite to be looked down on, whereas a woman who embroiders is all right. Notice carefully that this will make an acquired conscience in a person brought up in those times and such a person may meet a woman whom he likes very much and suddenly discover that she knits and then may have nothing more to do with her. Is this acquired conscience or Real Conscience?

Now let us take some examples. One person says:

> "*An Englishman's word is his bond* hypnotizes people into feeling that all English can be trusted. If an Englishman were accused of breaking his promise he might say: 'Don't you know I'm English?'"

All I can say is that it may be so. But brought up to this idea a man will not be able to get in touch with his Real Conscience. Nor will he be able to see how often he does not fulfil his picture of himself in his domestic life, his marriage-vows, and so on. In this connection let me quote the following example in which you have a certain kind of acquired conscience, developed by the surrounding influences, exemplified by the idea of a sporting conscience which is certainly an acquired conscience. The example is as follows:

> "A sportsman's conscience would not allow him to cheat at games but in business affairs he would have no such scruples."

Next we have a very good example of how acquired conscience is based on self-love and how when the self-love is hit we feel miserable:

> "Our idea of what we should or should not do comes solely from what we want thought about us—we make pictures of ourselves and are most offended if other people do not believe in them. We think it is awful to be late because we don't want to be that sort of person, from vanity point of view—not from external considering at all . . . We say we are 'conscience-stricken' if we have been lazy, selfish or uncharitable or lost our tempers in *public*. Acquired conscience does not seem to mind if these things are done in private! . . . Acquired conscience always *justifies* if anything goes wrong, and we are found lacking in our own estimation, because we can't bear our self-love to be hurt."

This shews how our acquired conscience is connected with our self-love and is not Real Conscience, which has scarcely anything to do with self-love. We feel we have made fools of ourselves socially and so have depleted our self-love. However we have to know what it is to feel that we have been fools and made mistakes without always trying to justify ourselves and get back to where we were before, socially speaking.

One person connects this acquired conscience with the scribes and Pharisees that Christ so constantly attacks. The reason is that acquired conscience is only turned outwards and is only distressed when one has made a fool of oneself externally in the opinion of other people of one's own social rank, whereas Real Conscience is turned inwards and has scarcely anything to do with this outwardly turned conscience. As long as your lie has come off and is well-applauded it will not bother your external conscience but your internal conscience will know that you have lied and possibly harmed a great many people, however well you have carried it off. You must all understand that the awakening of the Real Conscience undermines the Personality little by little, and first of all attacks or makes uneasy the False Personality and all these pretences and façades and external appearances that we spend so much force on keeping up until the Work begins to dissolve us.

One persons asks: "*Is Fashion an example of acquired conscience?*" Well, answer this for yourself. You can be in the fashion without being controlled by the fashion. If you only feel yourself rightly through obeying fashion you have no centre of gravity save self-love and you are turned round by fashion instead of fashion turning round you. The difference is between what fashion does to you and what you do in connection with fashion. This seems to me an important idea.

Several people connected acquired conscience and self-love with internal considering. I quote one example:

"I have observed acquired conscience in connection with internal considering—for example, wanting to do the right thing— and as internal considering means 'looking after oneself', it must be connected with self-love."

One person shews how acquired conscience is based on fear:

"I think acquired conscience is based on fear, fear of consequences, fear of loss of prestige, possessions or position, fear of social ostracism, fear of criticism or of ridicule, fear of not being thought well of (this particular fear seems to be based on self-love)."

This is quite correct. Acquired conscience is based on self-love, and self-love is based on fear. Self-love is orientated outwards towards what people think of you. If they flatter you your self-love is gratified, and if not you feel depressed. You are afraid of having your self-love wounded, having no basis of truth in yourself. I listened the other day to the remark of a countryman in the road who was wearing a peculiar cap with earpads in the frozen weather here. His wife shouted out to him: "People will think you are a fool, wearing a cap like that." And he said: "I think *they* are fools for not wearing caps like mine." He did not follow fashion but made it individually. All self-love is based on fear of other people's opinion about you. Self-love can never be abolished completely in us as Christ shewed in his words: "You must love your neighbour as yourself"—i.e. there must be self-love and love of neighbour equally. You cannot help being wounded through the self-love or gratified by something you have done well through self-love. O. used to say about this that if we have done something well we can give to our self-love just one tiny moment of satisfaction and not more, but a person who is full of self-love and nothing else is always afraid and naturally so if you come to think of the reason, because his centre of gravity is outside himself, paradoxically, because he wishes to gain applause and praise to gratify himself and has nothing internal that he follows apart from the attitude of other people towards him. Certainly an individual cannot develop purely from self-love but only from a very well-harnessed self-love which is more free from vanity, but which may retain some pride. You know how often people do things from self-love and call it individuality—for instance, they insist that they are in love with someone and carry the thing through from self-love, and immediately they have attained their ambition the whole thing collapses. You must remember that self-love is extraordinarily obstinate and unintelligent and has a great deal to do with acquired conscience, tradition, buffers, pictures, and so on—i.e. it is based on keeping up appearances. But all this has nothing to do with Real Conscience from which springs Real Love. It is imagination that plays such a tremendous part in the unhappiness of life, as the Work teaches so often.

Here I will speak briefly about aim in connection with acquired conscience. The danger is that we may follow an aim made by acquired conscience. Such an aim is wrong. An aim cannot be formed from the dictates of our acquired conscience which belongs to the acquired side of ourselves—i.e. the Personality. And here we have to think very deeply about what this means. A real aim in the Work has nothing to do with this acquired conscience that dictates to us all sorts of unreal aims. The aim may be right but the basis may be wrong. I should like you to think, for example, of making an aim from acquired conscience and then reflect what it might mean to make an aim from what the Work teaches. You know the Work takes the place of Real Conscience, until the latter is slowly awakened. If we always want to cling to what we are and if our only idea of right and wrong is derived from our acquired consciences we will often make quite wrong aims and submit ourselves to useless efforts. Acquired conscience may tell you that you ought to be more sociable and enquire after other people's health and so on. Now if you really try to do this as an aim it will go all wrong because it is not real but has as its basis a matter of reputation, of being thought well of, and so on. Such an aim only tortures you because it leads into nothing real internally. Now you might have the same kind of aim, but from a much deeper level. You might, for example, be told by your better emotions that you must not be so difficult, or something like that. This comes through self-observation and through a much deeper realization of your situation. Simply to externally consider from False Conscience is nothing to do with realizing the necessity of external considering from a deeper level. The reason why you do things is quite different when you act from acquired conscience from when you act from Real Conscience. When you do a thing from Real Conscience, from Consciousness of yourself and what you are like, its action is to develop Essence. You make, as it were, Essence understand why certain things are necessary. But if you act from acquired conscience for the sake of internal considering as to how you stand with other people in order to make a better position for yourself, then it will not develop Essence because the Neutralizing Force is quite different. You will then do a thing for the sake of some form of merit and not from insight into the good of what you are doing for its own sake. You may be meritorious, an excellent person, and yet inwardly you may be nothing but a sham or practically so. What we learn of good from the acquired side of us by education must be shifted from that outer basis and become a genuine sincere thing which we wish to live, not merely imitate, which we wish to be and not merely pretend to be. In all this lies a great deal of very sincere self-observation which takes a long time and our only guide is the action of the Work on us and what it teaches once it has begun to influence us. You must remember that all our concealed hatreds and contempts, which we do not manifest for fear of our reputation, exist in us in the psychological world of ourselves—that is, the real world of ourselves—which means that we find ourselves in our own psychological world as we have made it, and if we have had a great deal of hate we will find ourselves surrounded by nothing but hate. But we will speak of this later. I will only say that we have been taught very often that we have to neutralize things in ourselves, and one of the great methods is to see ourselves and not continually blame other people. This seeing of the truth about oneself leads to inner peace and causes Essence to grow, so that next time we are different and our lives attract a different fate. But the thing must be real, not done for the sake of outer merit or praise or from some picture.

One person quotes Browning—a passage from 'Paracelsus':
"Truth is within ourselves; it takes no rise
From outward things; whate'er you may believe
There is an inmost centre in us all
Where truth abides in fulness; and around,
Wall upon wall, the gross flesh hems it in,
This perfect, clear perception—which is Truth.
A baffling and perverting carnal mesh
Binds it and makes all error: and to know
Rather consists in opening out a way
Whence the imprisoned splendour may escape
Than in effecting entry for a light
Supposed to be without."
All I will say about this is that it is quite correct to say that truth is in ourselves and that it is quite easy to say this, but it takes long and

difficult work to understand the reality of this truth in ourselves because we are full of pseudo-truth and we continually spend all our money, all our force, in keeping up this pseudo-truth about ourselves which makes us all restless. Let me remind you of what was said in a recent paper that truth makes us quiet and gives us peace, whereas pseudo-truth makes us uncertain, worried and tense. Acquired conscience is noisy, so to speak, whereas it is necessary to listen to Real Conscience. We solve lots of problems, as we suppose, through following acquired conscience in which we satisfy ourselves and in a way justify ourselves. After a time we become tired of acting from this acquired conscience and wish to listen to something deeper—that is, we do not seek to get rid of the pain we feel, by some manifestation of the acquired conscience. Do you remember what is said in Isaiah—that God dwells "in the high and holy place, with him also that is of a contrite and humble spirit."? (*Isaiah* LVII 15).

Can you understand what it means to realize the significance of this phrase "I am not like this," or "I am in this lie," or "I am in this invented person that has taken charge of my life all these years"? If you can understand what this means you will begin to understand what the Work is about. The object of this Work is to awaken Real Conscience, which is the same in everyone. This cannot be repeated often enough. In self-observation we can come to the point of saying: "I am not this 'I' that is speaking, that is behaving like this, I am not this person that I have imagined myself to be, I am not in all these external things, these honours, these positions, these pretences, these virtues, these things I try to do, these fictions that I keep up. No, I am not these things that have taken charge of my life. I am not these 'I's." "Well, then," you say, "What am I?" You cannot tell yet what you are save by seeing what you are not and getting gradually, by means of inner work, away from this great fiction that you have kept up, only you must do it with a certain amount of humour, with a certain capacity for real laughter at yourself. Then gradually more real things will cluster round your sense of yourself and this may be shewn by the fact that you suddenly find yourself able to think, able to read, able to reflect. The reason is that you are carried a little from the mill-race of life, this excited life that you have been crowding into to give you happiness, which so few can give up. For most people think that to give it up means death. On the contrary, it does not mean death, but life. You remember this phrase in the Work—*no one is happy*; but to what extent do we go to invent this happiness, and in this connection how we follow our acquired conscience thinking it will give us happiness, whereas it is exactly the thing that makes us wretched the whole time. It is like a kind of Juggernaut that crushes everything real in us and to which we sacrifice our lives.

Now you may think that this is a little solemn. Actually it is not so, but, like everything else in the Work, must be taken with a grain of salt. Let me simply say that our ordinary life-'I's are not the 'I's that will give us any inner peace or stability and that, as the Work teaches, we have to separate from those 'I's belonging to the False Personality and this False Conscience in order to touch anything deeper and more genuine. When you can observe an 'I' in yourself that is always leading you astray into false ambitions and false aims, into rivalry, into contempt of others, and when you can catch a glimpse of this 'I' having acted in you all your life, an 'I' that you had to follow and obey—then it is a very wonderful experience to be able to say to yourself "I am not this 'I'," and to begin to separate from it.

If we had Real Conscience the whole world could unite and all police, law, war, military control, and so on, would cease, because Real Conscience, which is buried in all of us, is one and the same, and if all people had Real Conscience they would understand one another and speak one common tongue, one common language. In this Work we try to study a language that will bring us together, that we can all understand, and its object is to awaken Real Conscience. But as long as we have artificial, acquired conscience, which is different in practically every case according to the upbringing, the nation, the country, and so on, there is no possibility of any common understanding, and so everything must always go on just as it has always done and, I fancy you will all see, as it will go on, even worse than ever, in the future. Here are people getting into their traditional 'I's and fighting with each other on every side, and no one is trying to understand anything, and no one can understand anything, and so the whole chaotic plot of life, which is due to Man's being asleep, will continue as before and even worse than before. But amongst ourselves we must try to form a nucleus of people who wish to work on themselves, on acquired conscience, on False Personality, and to separate from this terrible factory and meet each other on a deeper level, where it is possible to meet one another without all the insults and confusion and misunderstandings of ordinary life led by sleeping people who take themselves for granted and in every department of life behave purely mechanically. Is it not extraordinary to feel that every person has in him, as the Work teaches, the common basis of a mutual understanding which has been overlaid layer by layer by the acquired conscience and the powerful outer layer of False Personality with which everyone identifies most of all? Remember that the object of this Work is to break through this false pseudo layer that causes so much damage to ourselves and to everyone else. We know that it is difficult to respect a person with no mind of his or her own, a person who is simply composed of acquired opinions, buffers, traditional attitudes and prejudices. With such a person there is nothing but acquired conscience which may be better or worse, useful for life or otherwise, but there is nothing really individual. If we converse with such a person there is no thought, no ideas, nothing alive, no power of anything new. In fact, we know exactly beforehand what gramophone rolls will turn to the particular stimulus applied, and how the same opinions will be expressed over and over again without change.

Acquired or false conscience is in this way a rigid fixed thing, a mechanical thing, whereas Real Conscience is quite different. It sees everything in its true light and so judges it differently in each case. It is relative, not absolute.

Birdlip, February 24, 1945

COMMENTARY ON THE MEANING OF AIM IN THE WORK

The idea of "help" in the Work is difficult to understand. At certain moments we are all helped by life when things go well with us. In connection with this idea of help O. once said to us long ago: "Life is too easy for you all." I think he meant that we did not understand what "help" in the Work-sense meant. When life is difficult we usually feel in some way offended or depressed. Then the help of life is withdrawn from us; we feel upset; things are not going rightly according'to our form of expectancy of life, of how we expect life should go according to our imagination of it. In that case we are a function of life, of external circumstances. This is one meaning of the Work-phrase: "We are machines driven by life." But the Work is not exactly about this mechanical relation to life. It is not about the mechanical stability or balance that we have in life but about a new balance that can only be created by work on ourselves. This idea of the Work is very difficult to grasp for a long time. I often think we none of us grasp it deeply enough. Have you got something in you that can resist the ups and down of life or are you simply a creature of external circumstances? It is fairly evident that the Work is teaching us a new way of balancing ourselves, when, for instance, it says we must not identify as much as we do, which means that we must not take life as it presents itself to us by its ever-changing events. Now supposing you identify very much when things are good and when things are bad—i.e. you feel very excited when things are good and depressed when things are bad. Then you are a function of life—a machine, in the Work-sense. You are simply in the sea, going up and down with the sea, and you have no boat to sail and direct in the way you wish to go in spite of the weather. Supposing I find that external events do not please me very much and I begin to object to this and that? Then supposing it occurs to me that this is an occasion when I should work on myself and that I should not express my negative emotions and that I should be very careful and not react mechanically in the light of all I have been taught in the Work. You will agree with me that here a new set of ideas comes in—namely, the ideas taught by the Work. In that case I will begin to apply the Work-ideas to myself and to a small extent will cease to be a machine, a mechanism driven by life and its external ever-changing events. Supposing I do this once—then it will be easier for me to do it again when more or less the same circumstances arise. This is tasting the Work and its quality, but if I never taste the Work in this way nor its quality, and expect merely that because I hear the Work everything is going to be better for me henceforth, then I have a very naïve idea of what the Work means. To think that the Work is going to make everything immediately better for me is a very superficial conception of it, a very superficial conception of esotericism and its teaching, because the object of esoteric teaching is to produce a profound change in the person one is, a profound change in the level of being. There are many things in this Work that you cannot understand with your head but only with your heart. It takes two centres to understand anything. You may work very hard on the formatory side of the Work and try to work out each idea endlessly in formatory language, and while this is not entirely wasted it is absolutely necessary to have a practical feeling about what the ideas mean—i.e. an emotional perception of the truth of the Work. You may talk and write a long time about what identifying means without any emotional perception of its meaning: or you may have many thoughts about what lying means and yet never emotionally perceive what it means. This is because you have not applied this perception to yourself and have not seen lying or insincerity or whatever it is as an absolute fact.

*　　*　　*

Now to-night I wish to speak about *Aim* once more. You can never make aim unless you see what the Work is about—namely, about yourself and your relationship to Higher Centres or Real Conscience. All aim in the Work must be connected with the Work—work on yourself first of all, work with others, and with the whole meaning of esotericism, i.e. the Work itself. You should start with the first line of Work in connection with aim. Let me ask you this question: Where do you think you should work on yourself in connection with the ideas of the Work? Have you yet got some fairly clear conception of your life and what you should try to change in your life in view of what you have been taught? Unless you start here at this place you will never have an aim of any practical use in regard to yourself. *What is it that you think you ought to change in yourself?* Now this question is very interesting and I want to dwell on it for some time. You may, from acquired conscience, from buffers, from pretences, from False Personality, have an idea that you should change something or other. What I want to point out is that if you are guided by your acquired ideas and opinions you are following the wrong mentor. You must start from what the Work teaches because the Work replaces Real Conscience for us as we are. It teaches what Real Conscience would teach us if it were awakened in us. By having our own ideas of what we ought to do, or be like, or aim at, we are bound to go wrong from the point of view of the Work because we are acting from our own ordinary knowledge and not from the Work-knowledge. We will then interfere with the action of the Work on us and submit ourselves to all sorts of useless privations and endeavours. Real knowledge is quite different from what we call knowledge. Esoteric knowledge is a special knowledge that we have to learn and gradually understand through an emotional development which gives us an emotional perception of its meaning. All this has to do with what kinds of effort are required to change our being. Our ordinary ideas, our ordinary knowledge, will not change our being and probably will only increase our fixity in our present state of being. If you think that you know already, then you will not take the knowledge of this Work seriously. If you are quite sure you know what is right and wrong, you will not be able to change. A person must awaken eventually to the authority of the Work and must begin to view himself in the light of what it says. You may think, for example, that many of your negative emotions are correct and you will not call them negative emotions. Yet the Work teaches that all negative emotions are wrong, no matter what causes them. The Work does not look at the causes of negative emotions but at the fact that you are negative. On one occasion O. said: "Why do you always explain your negative emotions by the causes that gave rise to them? The whole point is that you are negative and that is what you have to work on." Now you all know how negative emotions prevent all development and make it impossible for the Emotional Centre to communicate with Higher Centres. If we could communicate with Higher Emotional Centre, for example, our lives would be utterly different. We would find an entirely new set of rules whereby to live, all far more subtle than those which we follow in life. We would find, for example, that where we always take a situation in one way, there are 100 or 1000 ways, all quite different, and that there is no stereotyped way of taking the events of life. This is one of the greatest things to understand in connection with aim and in connection with how we behave. We behave in a rigid, stereotyped way and so we tend to make rigid, stereotyped aims. There is a certain gaiety in realizing we need not take things always in the same way.

But before we can reach this beginning of inner freedom we must realize that *life is events* and notice how we react mechanically to each of the different events in life. Looking out through our limited senses we see life as a number of objects but we cannot see it as changing events. I often think that this is one of the first difficulties we have in understanding what the Work is about. We cannot see events because they can only be mentally and emotionally realized. For example, we can see a table, a chair, a tree, a person. These objects are not events, necessarily, but supposing the tree falls on the table and kills a person sitting at it and smashes the chair: that is an event. All these physical objects which are not events are suddenly related in one event. A person is not an event but merely an object. But supposing you hate this person when you see him it makes an event. Events gather together objects into a certain relationship. A table by itself is not an event, but if breakfast is laid on it it participates in an event for you, and if the egg is not boiled properly it becomes a negative event. A whirlwind that suddenly lifts off the roofs of houses is an event, but if you stare at the roof it is not an event. A thing that you have in your possession to look at sometimes, such as a gold watch, is not an event but an object. But if it is stolen it becomes an event. You get up in the morning and stub your toe on the carpet and then the carpet becomes an event. In other words, an event is something that relates a number of objects together in a certain way. This is a very inadequate description of events but you must try to see what is meant. It is towards these events that we must try to acquire a conscious behaviour. That is to say, we have to see our lives as events and not objects, because it is very easy to stare at everything like horses and trees and not understand that unless they are related to you in some way they do not constitute an event. This is getting off the purely sensual level and noticing that objects are not events.

Now in making this connection with the 1st line of Work you should be able to observe events to which you react in a particular way, because it is in your reactions to life as events that your personal work lies for a long time—i.e. in the way you take events happening in the world of external objects. (If you cannot understand the difference between objects and events you should think of what is happening in this war—how in the event of war all kinds of objects are re-grouped and how in another event they would be grouped quite differently. For example, millions of people are abroad who were formerly at home. The objects are the same but they are related quite differently through the event of war.) We find it very difficult to believe in events as distinct from objects. For example, we find it difficult to believe that we ourselves may be next moment in a violent temper because of some event in which we are included. We do not see that an event has happened—actually a triad of forces has suddenly acted on us and we have been incorporated into it as by a whirlwind in which different 'I's have charge of us as long as the event lasts. After the event has passed we wonder what has happened because all the objects around us are as before, but while the event lasted they conducted different forces within which we were included.

Now when we make aim we always neglect events. We do not take into consideration how difficult it will be to keep that aim in view of the different events that may happen to us. We expect a tranquil sea on which we can steer a direct course. Therefore when our aim is very superficial and momentary, formed in a moment of enthusiasm, we find that it is absolutely useless and leads nowhere. However, instead of becoming offended and beginning to blame the Work, we should begin to understand what it means to be Sly Man or, as the Gospels call it, 'φρόνιμος' or wise man (wise really meaning clever). You will remember that the wise virgins were not wise but clever and this word in the Gospels meaning clever or mentally awake is the same as the word 'sly' used in the Work. A superficial aim will lead nowhere, especially if it is from acquired conscience which has behind it merit, vanity. These aims turned towards external life are of no use in the Work. They do not touch the esoteric level—that is, the level of Real Conscience.. To begin to have a real aim you must already know that you cannot keep it and, as it were, not tell yourself what this real aim is. Real aim comes from something deeper in you, something emotional. As it is said in Matthew: "Let not thy left hand know what thy right hand doeth." (VI 3). In the language of Parables 'left' is the weak side—i.e. the Personality—and 'right' means the deeper and more real side of you. Now if you make an aim with your left hand and tell yourself you will get some advantage from it, some merit, some praise from other people, that you will be better thought of (even in the Work), you will not be doing it from your right hand or your real side. For this reason real aim must always be something you never quite put into words and let your False Personality know about, and you must not expect to attain its object right away. You will have, in fact, probably to follow a devious and apparently contradictory path to fulfil real aim and above all you must not think that because things go wrong your aim is useless. But the most important thing to understand is that in real aim you cannot go directly towards it but like a sailing-ship at sea which endeavours to sail to a certain goal, you must tack one way and then another way according to the wind.

Now a real aim depends on an *emotional perception* of something you dislike in yourself and which you wish to change eventually. It depends on a certain integrity of feeling that persists in spite of downfalls. Thus great patience is necessary in connection with any real aim. A formatory aim is quite different from real aim and although you begin with formatory aims you must realize they cannot be kept and so must admit you cannot do, in this sense. Real aim can only arise from long observation and real evaluation of the Work, because unless the presence of the Work is constantly with real aim—i.e. unless you rely on the Work as well as yourself to keep it—it can lead nowhere except into False Personality and the feeling of merit. Real aim always nourishes you, nourishes your understanding, and then you see how it can change and yet remain the same, how it can tack from one side to the other and never go in the direct way which our natural impatience demands, because all real aim is connected with our own self-development—i.e. with the development of Essence in us, with the development of understanding in us which is the greatest force we can create—whereas false aim cannot develop our understanding and very often simply contracts us and turns us into Puritans, as it were, into a rigid keeping of some little internal decision. You can do nothing by suddenly cutting yourself off from what you have been by some arbitrary act. It is only by modification and transformation that you can change your life. When you have real aim you see the difficulties of keeping it. When you make a little formatory aim it is quite different. We are told to make aims with the object of seeing that we cannot keep them—i.e. so that we can see second force or force of resistance. But when we come to make real aim we are more aware of second force and the difficulties that will stand in the way of our keeping this aim. I would like to say here that real aim is a *silent* aim—something that you never tell anyone else or even tell yourself in so many words—and this kind of aim is of such a quality that you are not dismayed by the constant apparent breaking of it, or the contradictions that arise in connection with it when apparently you are going in a different direction from what you intended. I have given you the image of a sailing-ship setting out to cross the Atlantic, from East to West, let us say, and probably this ship cannot ever really go directly to the West but must go N.W., S.W., and even occasionally in the reverse direction for the time being, yet at the same time if it keeps to its aim it will eventually get where it intended. It does not lose hope, it does not despair, because there is a certain deep intention of getting eventually where it wants to go.

* * *

Now what do you think real aim is as distinct from artificial aim? As I said, real aim can only spring out of long observation and real valuation of the Work. There is a phrase that O. used to use: "*The Work will find a way for you.*" This is a very good phrase to remember but it demands that you have a constant relationship to the Work in your soul, in your depths. It is the Work that changes us because the Work brings us a little closer, little by little, to Higher Centres, which are always telling us what to do and how to live our real lives and which we cannot hear owing to the traffic of life in the mechanical parts of centres. The great aim was given in the Gospels: "Seek ye first the Kingdom of Heaven," i.e. seek another actual level of being, promised to us both by the Gospels and by this Work. I remember again another phrase that G. sometimes used: "I can work," which can help you, especially when you feel defeated by having to tack North or South. But if you ask me to define what real aim is, I leave it to you. We have to make an aim. We do not know exactly what our next step in development is, but if the aim we make is sufficiently genuine the influences of the Work will greatly modify it in the right direction, and here you will be astonished how different what you thought you had to do is from what you have to do, and also you will be astonished to find how much help comes to you as long as you do not throw up your hands in despair. But if you will the Work, if you have goodwill to it, if your idea of Good begins to be connected with esoteric teaching, then you will be sure of getting a response that is right even though the request is wrong, provided the request is sincere. Remember that we cannot use this Work for life as our primary object but we can use life for the Work. It is difficult to see what this means, because we do not realize what is *first* in us. If we could make the Work first then everything else would be added to us and we would find what really belongs to us in life and what does not belong to us, but this state would be like something that is passive becoming active and something active becoming passive. It would mean that we began to live the Work in life. For this reason we should connect everything we do in life with the Work, even artificially at first. This is called, as far as I remember it, doing everything in the name of God. You should not do the Work for a short time and then pass out of it and come under life as an antithesis. You should try, even artificially, to act so that whatever you do in life has some connection with the Work, and not make the Work the opposite to life. G. once said: "Bring all things into the Work. Do not go into life as a relaxation from the Work but connect your relaxation in life with the Work." This may sound strange and yet it contains a very important idea. Some people will say: "If I am negative it is in the Work,"— yes, of course it is. If you speak against the Work, remember it is in the Work. If you go off the deep end in some way or other, remember it is in the Work. If you are in the Work, whatever you do is in the Work. If you cannot feel this, you will divide yourself into life-'I's and Work-'I's, which will appear to be at enmity with each other. If you are in the Work you cannot be out of it, whatever 'I' acts in you, so do not make this opposition between Work and life, and remember that the Work is not exactly ignorant of human nature. All that you do from the point of view of this not having anything to do with the Work, and all that you do from the idea of its being connected with the Work is all in the Work. You cannot live now in the Work and now in life because that will make a split in you. The idea of Balanced Man is that he includes everything, but in the right place, in the right order, in the right arrangement. Remember that even the bad animals were taken into Noah's Ark and included in the whole thing. No one can develop without this bad side: no one can simply be good without the power of being bad. It is a question of right arrangement, right order, right balance. Even 'I's that are not in the Work are useful and are in the Work, if you understand what I mean. How, unless we had many doubts, could we have any strength? How, unless we are continually tempted in the Work, could we reach any new level of understanding? Even negative 'I's are useful, provided we know how not to identify with them. Considering all these things you will see how real aim, which has to take into consideration second force, and has to be made cleverly or by means of Sly Man in oneself, is not quite what we expect and will not instantly bring beautiful rewards to us, beautiful instantaneous results. We may map a course out as a mariner does, but the master of a sailing-ship does not expect to go directly to his goal, although he intends to do so in spite of all weathers, all contrary winds. I would like you all to think what real aim is in contrast to temporary but quite useful aim, and unless you have an idea of a higher level of Humanity, the Conscious Circle of Humanity, a far better state of Humanity than we see on this Earth, then it will be difficult to make real aim. All the concepts and ideas of the Work are necessary to make real aim, and one thing above all others is necessary—that we are dissatisfied with our level of being and feel that there is the possibility of change.

* * *

Now to recapitulate. Real aim must be based on long observation of oneself and what the Work teaches about how to reach a higher level of being. The first difficulty is that we do not remember ourselves, that we are not conscious. We do not drive our own carriage but are in a public-house drunk with our imagination. Then follows the teaching of identifying, of how we are many and not one, how we say 'I' as if it meant anything, how we are full of inner accounts, full of internal considering, of how we lie, how we spend our force in self-justifying, in pretending to be what we are not, how we are full of pictures of ourselves which have nothing to do with our real selves, how we react to attitudes, how we speak from acquired opinions and never think for ourselves, how imagination creeps into everything we do or say or feel, how we are fast asleep in life but are carried along by mechanical reactions, how we are creatures of mental, emotional and physical habit, how we never see and attack our own ignorance, how we never take in new impressions about anything, how we are governed by vanity and pride and self-complacency, and finally how we are not awake but so asleep and hypnotized that we follow every event of life and make no inner stand against it—and there are many other things that the Work teaches we have to observe and see the truth about. And then we have to understand that we cannot start from all this, that we cannot add the Work to all the mess in ourselves, but we have to go down and realize we cannot do, realize how ignorant we are really, how much we say all day long that has no meaning, how we react to things and think we are actually conscious —all of which leads to the realization of our mechanicalness, the realization that we do not exist at all save as puppets jerked by strings. Now how can such a puppet make an aim save to be a greater puppet? If a puppet makes an aim it will be mere puppetry. The puppet thinks he knows how to make an aim. Standing over this puppet is the Work which tells us what kind of aim to make, and you can be sure that this aim is always against this puppet. Now all real aim is psychological: remember we live in a psychological world of thoughts and feelings and desires. This psychological world is extraordinarily complex and marvellous. It has all sorts of combinations and patterns, wrong arrangements and right arrangements. All the Work teaches at first is about getting this psychological world into a right arrangement. Suppose you are full of hate towards someone and you try to get your psychological world right. Is it not impossible? Do you all understand that you live in a psychological world and not in a physical world and

633

that you react to the events in the physical world psychologically save when the physical world blows you up physically? The Work is to get the psychological world rightly adjusted so that it transmits Higher Centres. We may in life conceal our psychological thoughts and feelings but the Work is another force not of life, and from that we can conceal nothing that is psychological. Real aim has to do with the psychological world and how we handle others and ourselves in it. In this world we have to make entirely new associations, an entirely new pattern. The object of the Work is to make this new pattern in the brain—to think in a new way, not as everybody thinks who is poised in life. Unless you think about the Work and what it means, unless you see esotericism and its aim, unless you understand that Man is a self-developing organism and can only develop by an entirely new kind of thought, then no new patterns are made in the brain and so all the undeveloped part of the brain is unused—i.e. that part that can connect with Higher Centres. If you take things as you have always taken them, nothing new can form itself, but if you take life from what the Work teaches and take yourself in a new way, you will make a new pattern, new associations in the frontal lobes if you like, and these will connect with Higher Centres. If your aim is right this will happen gradually, but if your aim is a life-aim, a purely ambitious aim, you will not form any new patterns, but just ordinary commonplace ones. That is why I said that a real aim nourishes your understanding of the Work and a purely life-aim does not, but if you include a life-aim in a Work-aim then the case is different, then new associations can be made and through new associations a new feeling of oneself is created—in fact, through a new set of associations one feels oneself a quite different person—i.e. one becomes psychologically a different person provided one can die to the old associations.

It is always interesting to reflect that Higher Centres are always trying to change us. We are self-developing organisms in the sight of Higher Centres. Contact with them can only develop us in the right way because everybody is created a different self-developing organism with his own destiny. The object of this Work is to put us in touch with Higher Centres. From this point of view it is interesting to reflect how we think we can develop ourselves from our own ideas of what development means and how different the influences of Higher Centres may be. We think we must go along this line but from the standpoint of Higher Centres we may be going in quite the wrong direction. For this reason we have to start with the Work as an aim because it is given by conscious Humanity—i.e. people who have reached Higher Centres. One thing can be said here—i.e. that we always have to develop in the direction of our own most inferior functions, our most unused side, the most despised side of ourselves, and not along the line of what we are best at. Remember we have to become balanced. If you can think well you have to feel more, if you feel too much you have to think more, and so on.

COMMENTARY ON INNER FREEDOM

(2) What do you understand by being more free? Sometimes this Work has been defined as something to give more inner freedom. Is inner freedom doing what you like as you are now?

As regards the last part of the question: "Is inner freedom doing what you like as you are now?" most people answer that it does not consist in doing what you like. At the same time I would say that it takes a long time to realize this. It takes a long time to understand that doing what we like does not give us freedom but on the contrary is really a form of slavery until we attempt more consciously to go against doing what we mechanically like. We then begin to see that doing what we like is not really what we do like. When we are governed by our passions, by our mechanical impulses, by our having our own way, we are not really quite comfortable in ourselves. To follow self-will does not lead to any real satisfaction eventually. In a matter of this kind we have to start from a very sincere basis and not from a theoretical one— i.e. from actual self-observation as to what happens when we simply do what we like, say, from our lazy side, or from our sensual side, or from our jealous side, or from our negative side, and so on. I speak like this because it is so easy to say theoretically that one does not really like to do as one likes. We are always doing as we like. For example, we are always avoiding efforts that in a kind of way we know we should make, and until we can genuinely acknowledge that by doing simply what we like at the moment we are not at peace with ourselves and that something deeper lies in us, until we see that this is quite true, we do not quite understand what the Work is about. This point has been realized all through the ages and is one of the most extraordinary things in past experience. Is it not extraordinary to realize that people have always thought in all ages that they cannot simply do what they like? How can we account for this factor running through history unless we admit that other influences are acting on us than those of our self-will, of our appetites? Here lies one of the turning-points in our understanding of the Work. Here lies a realization that something else acts on us than just having our own way. But I repeat that it must be internally realized that this is the case and that pure self-gratification does not lead to any inner harmony.

Now as regards not doing what we like—we are first of all under the external laws of the country which prevent us through fear from doing many things that we would otherwise do out of self-will. This is the first check but please note that it is a purely *external* one. A man who obeys the law out of fear is not by any means a *good* man. Probably most people do not feel any other check in themselves and would, if there were no such thing as external laws and the fear derived from them, behave in a quite impossible way because there is no internal goodness of

Being. So first of all there have to be external restraints built up by the law, to make any civilization possible. But there are also internal restraints that can act on us through the influence of the Work. These are connected with Real Conscience. In other words, we must learn to distinguish between the two kinds of restraints. For example, through the development of "inner taste" we realize the unpleasantness of negative states. But there is no external law about negative states. The police do not arrest you for being negative (but it would be a very good thing if they did). All negative states in their full culmination lead on to violence, even to revenge, even to killing. Then, of course, the external law steps in. The Commandment "Thou shalt not kill" is first of all a literal one and refers to the actual law. But the psychological meaning is quite different and, as you know, psychologically we kill a great many people and otherwise mutilate and harm them—that is to say, if we really did what we liked we should be arrested by the police in this respect. The external laws therefore to a certain extent prevent us from doing what we like, but the internal influences of the Work that can begin to act on us if we emotionally feel the Work restrain us in a quite different way from doing what we like. As the Work grows richer in understanding and more subtly connected we begin to hesitate about many things that we were unaware of before. We begin to build up a new orientation to everything and to everyone, a new house, a new inner architecture. When this begins we know that we cannot behave in certain ways, think and feel in certain ways, as we did before, with impunity. The whole approach to ourselves and the whole approach to and conception of other people begins to become a much finer and far more interesting thing. When this happens we begin to float, as it were, to lift ourselves off the ground, to learn how to sail. From all this arises Second Body—i.e. some organized body that Consciousness begins to occupy, which is psychological, quite apart from our physical body and its reactions. Then we begin to have life in ourselves, to live in life and not simply to be our reactions to life. We begin to live in our lives, and no longer to be simply of life, of the world, of mechanical reactions to external events, external things. Our *psychology* begins to be of the Work and not merely of life. Then we know that we cannot do as we like or as we did like, but have to follow, have, in fact, to like, another range of ideas, another meaning of ourselves, another mode of living in our lives, instead of being simply our lives. If you simply do as you like mechanically you are on the Earth, as it were. There is nothing to distinguish you from the Earth, from life and its incidents. When you raise yourself up through the influences of the Work you learn to touch the Earth differently. In fact, you come to the edge of the Earth where it meets the sea, and then, so to speak, you begin to live in a different medium, to sail above the Earth, to be in some vessel that is not of the Earth, a vessel that is real so that you suffer if you step out of it. This journey, this voyage, has been often represented in esoteric myths, and this is the best way of understanding what the form of Second Body means. This is a psychological body, a psychological room, that lifts you off the sensual Earth of yourself, and to maintain this body, to keep it in repair and to develop it, you have to like another set of liking, another set of values, a new set of ideas. The Work says: "Work against dislikes." Also it says in another connection: "Try to like what you dislike, and dislike what you like." As I said, the best example is just to take negative emotions—which we like—and think deeply about your relation to them, because when you realize that whenever you are negative it is your own fault, whatever the external cause, you begin to have a completely new orientation formed in you—a new psychological body. You will no longer take your pound of flesh, because if you do, if you like that, you will be right down on the Earth of yourself again and all Work-force will leak from you at once. Every atom of increased consciousness will disappear and you will be right down in the clangour and confusion of ordinary life. You will lose this Body of the Work, this Boat, this Ark.

Now several people say that we must put ourselves under more laws to become free. This is exactly what the Work says. The Work says that a man must put himself under the laws of the Work—i.e. under more laws—in order to reach any development, which is freedom. All freedom in the esoteric sense is due to inner development, both on the side of Knowledge and on the side of Being. This forms in us a new level of understanding. *A higher level of Being is always freer than a lower level.* To get to a higher level of Being you must put yourself under more laws than belong to your present level of Being. We can either live mechanically according to the laws belonging to our level of Being or we can begin to live in a new way more consciously according to the laws of a higher level of Being, and this is the object of the Work which teaches us what we have to work on in ourselves to reach a higher level of Being, not by simple obedience in a blind way but by an intelligent perception of the new Knowledge that the Work is speaking about—that is, through understanding it, which is the most powerful force that we can create in ourselves. The Work is not a series of literal commandments to obey like the Decalogue, but a series of new ideas, new insights, to make us think and see in a new way, and gradually come ourselves to the truth of them from ourselves, from our understanding.

You know that as one ascends in the Ray of Creation one comes under fewer laws. It is very important to understand this idea and this is why it is so often said that you must understand something about the meaning of the Ray of Creation. Let us suppose our Being is under 48 orders of laws and we do just as we like. Now a man under 48 orders of laws is very far down the Ray of Creation and in a very bad world, as surely you can plainly see, for this is not a good world. Such a man can come under, to begin with, 24 orders of laws, even while he exists on this Earth, and ultimately under 12, but in order to get this new freedom—because obviously to be under 24 orders of laws is to be in greater freedom than under 48 orders of laws—he must put himself for the time being under more laws to get under fewer laws—i.e. he must obey the Work according to his growing understanding of it, and live more and more according to what the Work teaches. When he begins to see the necessity of this emotionally, he is already very close to a change in his level of Being, but this change will not take place as long as he sees the Work as something external, as merely a series of rules, or statements. When he begins to see the truth of the Work for himself that is the first stage. The next stage is when he begins to apply his will to it, when he begins to will what he understands of the Work in himself—this is the second stage. Then he begins to pass under fewer laws by having kept more laws. This is the direction of freedom according to the Work, and according to all esoteric teaching. On the other hand, if he only obeys his own impulses and only gratifies his appetites and self-interests, he then, so, to speak, looks downwards and not upwards, or, if you prefer, he looks outwards and not inwards, and so he tends to go down in the Ray of Creation to the level of the Moon—i.e. he becomes a victim of his own appetites and self-will and puts himself more and more in prison and becomes more and more exacting or useless. There are many obvious examples of this, such as people who resort to drugs and so on. They obviously pass under more and more laws, simply by doing what they like, and become incapable of making any effort. Now all growth is through effort only. Esoterically speaking, it is only possible through *right* effort and for this reason we have to be taught by some genuine esoteric system *what kinds of effort* we have to make to grow. We cannot just grow by ourselves, by our own ideas. We can only grow through quite new knowledge, new ideas, and quite new conceptions of our feelings of ourselves and what we are. Here all the Work-teaching about making Personality passive comes in, because as long as we are under the full influence of Personality we are not by any means free and perhaps if we have any trace of real Magnetic Centre in us we have probably realized this even before we met the Work. To become more free means a change in the level of Being, upwards—that is, inwards. It means a deeper understanding of ourselves and of other people and of the meaning of life and why we are down here. If we are capable of growth and if we feel a genuine desire to come under the influences of the Work, then this change in the level of Being will increasingly take place. It may start from a very small seed, a very small but genuine experience which has impressed us. Then this point has to struggle with swarms of bad 'I's, wrong attitudes, wrong states. Yet if this seed is planted it will grow eventually, provided one gets sufficient help, a continual reminder of the ideas of the Work. Then after a time it will grow without very much external help. And the direction of this growth upwards or inwards is towards inner freedom, because growth means *ascending* the Side-Octave, diagrammatically speaking, towards the Sun, and so passing under fewer and fewer laws by freeing oneself from Personality. All these ideas must be connected in your minds by private thinking about them, in order to understand what greater freedom means.

Now let us turn to the first part of the question: "What do you understand by being more free?" One person gives this example:

"One may have considerable worldly ambition, and in pursuit of it be constantly tormented by fears of the adverse effect one has on others who might forward that ambition. If then one can be brought to see the vanity of such strivings and that this ambition leads to nothing but anxiety and distress, and if, in obedience to a higher law, one can completely let it go, its power is broken and one becomes immediately free of it and its resulting worries."

Yes, this is quite true. The more identified you are with life, the more fear you will feel, the more you feel that you depend for existence on external things. The more identified you are with what is outside you, the more fear of loss you will suffer from. If your centre of gravity is completely outside you, say in money or possessions, etc., the more bound you are to external circumstances and so the more a machine you are, driven by external circumstances and dependent on them. For example, if your whole happiness depends on one person then certainly you become a function of this person, which surely cannot be right. I do not see how the idea of Self-Remembering can ever be understood if one's life is a function of some other person. Similarly, as one person says: "One can be in the power of a person to whom one has a negative attitude." This is right, only see it for yourselves. One can be wholly in the power of someone one hates. But is this Self-Remembering? No, it is to be purely in the power of the world, purely on and of the "Earth", purely in the power of the senses, of what one sees externally. I repeat that Self-Remembering has nothing to do with this. The feeling that you get from hating may seem to you a very strong feeling of 'I' but this feeling is not you. It is on the contrary an 'I' that delights in hating and being cruel, whose domination you have passed under, and to whom you have dedicated your existence.

One person quotes something that was said in one of the previous papers about inner freedom. The passage was as follows: "The nature of freedom is utterly unknown to those who do not possess conscience, for they make freedom consist in doing exactly what they please." This is quite true and I will only add that if it is a question of Real Conscience you are not tortured by it but you are aware of it in a kind of gentle way, whereas if it is a question of Acquired Conscience you are tortured by it. Real Conscience is never violent but its action is so gentle that most of us cannot hear it. We have to stop the traffic of life in us and begin to hear it—and it is far cleverer than we.

Here is one good answer that is very practical. There is an old Stoic saying that we are all tied in life as it were like a dog to a cart and that we have to accept things—i.e. not to be dragged by the cart but to run with it. I quote from the answer:

"I remember hearing it said in the early days of my entering the Work that Man's position can be likened to that of a dog tied behind a cart and being dragged along by the cart because the dog resisted the chain that was leading him. If the dog had not resisted the pull of the chain but had run along with the cart he would have had greater freedom of movement. This is how I understood the first step to inner freedom—to see our real position with regard to the truth about ourselves and the laws we are under."

Yes, but a little more insight is needed. If we always object to everything and always expect what we do not find we shall be very identified with life and very much hurt by it—and so dragged along resenting everything. That is why the Work says that one of the very first things we have to do is to become passive to life—which is a very difficult thing to understand because we think we *can do* and we always think that things should be different from what they are. To practise not objecting to anything for a short time every day is a very good exercise and teaches you a lot about yourself and non-Work 'I's. To be more passive to life means to be more passive to Personality.

One person asks: "Is there some degree of inner freedom in directed attention?" Yes, you are more free simply because you are in more conscious parts of centres which are under fewer laws. Different parts of centres are under different laws.

At the conclusion of one answer a quotation from Francis Thompson is given :

> "Sole fully blest to feel
> God whistle thee to heel
> Free
> When his wings pen thee."

Yes, if you substitute for God the Work and realize what it really means to be called to heel by the Work. The trouble is that we indulge in all kinds of emotions and do not for a moment connect them with the Work or imagine that they have no bearing on the Work. You must all remember that it takes a long time for the Work to penetrate even as far as a few 'I's in us and that the majority of 'I's have never heard of the Work yet in ourselves. We have to teach the Work to "all the heathen", as the Gospels say.

Several people speak of doing what one likes as doing what one 'I' likes. For instance, one person says:

"At this level 'doing what we like' means following the impulse of the 'I' in which we happen to be at the moment. This however is not freedom, because second force in life will probably prevent us from following that impulse for very long, and even if life is kind to us for a while we shall soon be in another 'I' which wants something quite different. At this level therefore 'doing what we like' is really meaningless because there is no permanent 'I' to like."

This is a good answer. Each 'I' has its own will and each 'I' has its own power over us at the moment and here comes in a paradox. One 'I' may do something that it likes and another 'I' comes along and dislikes what this 'I' has done. All these different wills form contradictory lines and directions and provided we have very strong buffers we do not notice this and feel quite tranquil. It is a very dangerous state to be in when we see no contradictions in ourselves and do not feel a certain daily pain, or "heat", as the Work calls it.

I quote from another answer:

"I understand by 'more free', freedom in part from mechanicalness, from the power that people and events exercise over me; from Internal Considering, making accounts, from useless self-accusations and a host of other wrong psychic functions. Freedom from Attitude qua attitude, from Habit qua habit.

Inner freedom is not 'doing what you like as you are now'. That means the slavery of impulse, the will of the moment. The idea I have of Inner Freedom is that it is not achieved by the indulgence of the will of the moment but by a willingness to be guided by Will born of the perception of the Truth. As perception grows, Will grows and Inner Freedom is more fully felt."

Yes, this is quite right. If we begin to obey the ideas of the Work by seeing their truth and eventually realize what good lies in them, then we begin to be more free from the momentary wills of different 'I's—doing what they like. This means a more internal movement into ourselves and this is only gained by self-observation which moves us back from the outer pretence of ourselves. Self-observation increases Consciousness and increased Consciousness means a larger view, a wider sense of things—a more *whole* view.

One of you quotes something once said by Mr. Ouspensky: "You can do as you like so long as you remember yourself." This is quite true, only have you tried it? If you like to remember yourself more than anything else, then you can certainly do what you like, but you cannot expect this to happen just in a moment. You may understand just a little of what this means practically after many years of the Work and even then you are only just beginning to understand why this was said. You will *not* be able to do just what you like *if* you are in the third State of Consciousness. To do just what you like is mechanical: to be in a state of Self-Remembering is conscious.

COMMENTARY ON THE DIFFERENCE BETWEEN
THE OBJECT AND THE THOUGHT OF THE OBJECT

The object is physically rendered to us by the senses. Please understand that what we call physical is rendered by our senses. I see a person, I touch him and I hear him, and then I call this person a physical object—that is, the senses give a physical object. If you have no eyes, nor ears, nor sense of touch, this so-called physical object will vanish. This is the first point to understand—namely, what we mean by the physical world which our senses render to us and which we take as reality. Yet please note that if you had not the senses there would be no physical reality.

Now a question was recently asked in connection with the following quotation from a paper: "This Sufi teacher points out that whether a person takes pleasure in disliking the thing itself or in the thought of it, it is the same thing, and vice versa." The question was about understanding the difference between disliking the object and disliking the thought of it—no difference could be understood. I will remind you here of something said in this connection a long time ago. You are eating something, let us say, with great relish, and enjoying it as a physical object, and then you are told it is a stew of snails, and instantly you feel very sick. Here obviously the thought is different from the physical sensation. Now our thinking is different from our senses, and on another plane, another level. You can see a person or you can think about him. How you think about him is psychological and belongs to your inner psychological world, and you can go on thinking about this person you dislike quite apart from seeing him. When the Sufi teacher says that taking pleasure in disliking a thing and taking pleasure in the thought of it is the same thing he means just what he says. I would ask you first of all: Do you know an example of taking pleasure in disliking some object or person? Remember that a person is an object and remember that the Work teaches a great deal about how we take pleasure in disliking things. The question is subtle because we always imagine we do not take pleasure in disliking people and for this reason it is necessary to find for yourself some real example of your disliking some physical object or person. You know that if you dislike a person—i.e. an object—it gives you great pleasure to hear that someone else dislikes in the same way. This is pleasure in disliking and this pleasure is reinforced by the agreement of others with you. Is not this a common thing if you are frank with yourselves? But the pleasure of disliking somebody or something is not the same as the pleasure you take in thinking about it. When a person, looking at another person as an object transmitted through the senses, says: "Oh, how I hate a man like that," he takes pleasure in disliking the object when it is before his eyes, and afterwards, if he thinks about this person when he can no longer see him with his senses, he takes pleasure in thinking how he dislikes him, then it is, as the Sufi teacher says, exactly the same thing. He is taking pleasure in disliking the object when he sees it and taking pleasure in thinking about the object when he does not see it, and so the effect is just the same. In the one case, he is taking impressions of dislike from the visible object and in the other, he is taking impressions from the thought of it, so in both cases he is taking in negative impressions and psychologically it is the same thing in its effects on him.

If a man wants to overcome his pleasure in disliking a person he must also overcome his pleasure in thinking how he dislikes that person. The Work teaches that we must learn to handle one another rightly in the domain of our thoughts—i.e. in our psychological world —to which we have gradually to become more responsible. It is the re-ordering, the re-arrangement, of our psychological or inner life that is the object of this Work. It is how we think about others that is so important in this Work. If you take great pleasure in thinking evil of others, in thinking negatively, and attain a feeling of satisfaction from it, then your psychological world from which starts the function of second and third bodies is in a great mess and you may crystallize out psychologically in a quite wrong way. A man may for a long time not be able to overcome momentary dislike through the senses but if he is working he knows quite well he will have to get rid of thinking and feeling the same way internally. That is, he must realize that he cannot take pleasure in unpleasant thoughts about others which is the great source of our inner life as it is. If our psychological world of thought and feeling could be got into better order—i.e. the way in which we think and feel about people in our privacy—and if we could cease to take pleasure in hatred and negative criticism in general; our external relationship to one another as physical objects registered by our senses would alter completely. There are external reactions and more internal reactions. For a long time we may react mechanically—that is, we may react externally—and cannot change this, but if we have any insight—i..e self-observation—we will not necessarily let our internal side agree with our external side. Unless we see that we have an internal life of thought and feeling to which this Work is directed with the object of building up a psychological body or organization, rightly arranged, then we do not understand what the Work is about. The object of self-observation is to let a ray of light into our inner world, which is in chaos. The object of this Work is to build this inner world of chaos into an ordered world. An ordinary man behaves internally just as he pleases. He may be very polite externally. It does not occur to him that how he thinks and feels privately about other people matters. But the Work says it does matter and so it begins with self observation, whose object is to make us more conscious of what is going on in ourselves in each centre. After a time you may reach that stage where you behave much better inside than you do outside. You cannot change the external until the internal has changed. For example, I cannot expect to change some negative reaction unless I see internally what lies, what wrong thoughts and feelings, are produced in me. Then I may wish to change my inner state because through inner taste I dislike what is going on in me. Through an increase in this dislike of my internal life and so gradually strengthening it through self-observation and by sincerity with myself, my inner state may become strong enough to control my external and mechanical, reacting life. This is where a man begins to work on himself without shewing much external change. For example, I cannot pretend to myself that I can alter the reactions of my False Personality just like that, but if I observe them in the light of the Work with any sincerity I begin to dislike them. Then I begin to struggle with my thoughts and feelings privately—i.e. I begin to work on myself, on my inner life. Mechanically I may take pleasure in disliking some person whom I see visibly in front of me but after a time I take no such similar pleasure in *thinking* how I dislike this person. The reason is because I begin to be aware of my inner or psychological life—i.e. the life of thought and feeling that I have become aware of through self-observation and which, so to speak, I am trying to arrange in a right way in the light of the Work. When I am in that state of insight I will continually suffer from myself—from Nicoll and his mechanical reactions. Then I will in a certain sense have to endure this external, mechanical, reacting person, that hitherto I have taken as myself but which the Work has gradually shewn me I must separate from. At the time my Personality reacts I will no doubt feel quite justified, but from this deeper and more internal part that is beginning to awaken I will feel uncomfortable and will certainly take no pleasure in going with the thoughts of Nicoll, or with his feelings that have been called forth by some momentary irritation.

And so gradually by the growth of something internal to Nicoll, in my case, I may sometimes actually feel that something in me is beginning at times, but only at times, to be stronger than this machinery that dislikes a person right off, like that. I will no longer be so prone to agree with Nicoll and with the judgments of Nicoll. To be alone with oneself and indulge in negative feelings and enjoy unpleasant thoughts about other people will no longer commend itself to me as a good way to live in myself. When I am alone with myself I will have to review myself as to what has been going on in my centres and examine myself from the standpoint of what 'I's have charge of me in the momentary heat of my mechanical intercourse with life, when I have been completely identified with each passing event, each typical circumstance. The pleasure of reacting mechanically will no longer give me satisfaction although it may give Nicoll great satisfaction. And when I examine myself in this way when I am alone with myself, I can only do so rightly when I review myself from the standpoint of all that the Work teaches about being identified, about being negative, about making internal accounts, about judging, about lying, about self-justifying, and above

644

all about remembering to remember oneself. When I submit myself to the Work in the solitariness of myself in this way, I will dislike thinking with pleasure of people that I hate. I will not take pleasure in my thoughts although I may find it difficult not to take pleasure in disliking the person when I see him. It has been said by some philosopher of nó mean standing that religion consists in what you do in the solitariness of yourself. To get up in the morning after having indulged in all sorts of unpleasant thoughts and feelings about other people is not a good way to start the day. And a good many of us know this by inner taste. But the strengthening of this internal side which wishes to grow if we have any Work 'I's in us depends on this inner sincerity with one-self that the Work speaks about so much. For example, if I can never see I have lied I would agree with Nicoll—namely, my external side, my False Personality—and if I justify myself I cannot have any depth in my observation and the internal side of me cannot possibly grow, in which case there can never be anything stronger than Nicoll. I do not mean, as I explained, that I can deal with Nicoll straight away, but I can begin to suffer from him myself privately. And I will suffer in the right way, and please note this, only if I observe the reactions of Nicoll in the light of the Work. If I begin to do this, I will find it possible for me to separate from a great many thoughts and feelings that Nicoll takes pleasure in but which something more deeply placed in me takes no pleasure in at all. To dislike oneself is useless and only gives rise to illness and depression. But in my case to begin to see and dislike the reactions of Nicoll, to separate from them and so not to regard myself as Nicoll can give results. That is why the Work empha-sizes so much that we must break ourselves up into different parts and not take ourselves as one, as a unity, which Imaginary 'I' causes us to assume. You cannot change yourself if you take yourself as yourself and all attempts to do this will lead into a dangerous situation. You have to be able to say to yourself: "I am not this 'I', I am not that 'I'." Or again you must be able to say: "I am not this thought that comes to me," or, "I will not take pleasure in thinking or feeling in this way." It may only be possible to do this for a short time, but I can assure you that if you manage to do it only for a short time, and only from time to time, gradually something more internal will develop in you that may be able actually to take charge of you occasionally and control the reactions of the external, mechanical side. Some people think that change is something that takes place finally and irrevocably by a few moments of work and they get upset if they do not get results. But this is a quite wrong conception of what work means. The whole point lies in how you recover from falling, and it is always interesting to notice how people recover from a bad state because here lies the Work at first—in this learning to walk instead of always falling, because we are like little children learning to walk and if we never fell we could never learn.

To resume: it is on our thoughts, on how we think and feel, that the centre of gravity of our work falls and so if we take pleasure in thoughts as to how we dislike, it is the same thing as taking pleasure in disliking the object transmitted by our senses. Confronted by some object that you take pleasure in disliking there may be such a mechanical reaction that you cannot prevent it, but you can prevent the thoughts afterwards as to how you dislike this object. And it is here at this point that all the Work lies. Here for example, lie such thoughts as: "Can you find anything similar in yourself to what you take such pleasure in disliking in this other person? Have you noticed how you behave? Have you noticed what impressions you give to other people?" and so on endlessly. We are trying to build up a psychological internal order in ourselves arranged by the influences of the Work, a delicate organism built up so to speak of thoughts and feelings, of right connections, of right associations, a psychological organism that begins to put us in touch with Higher Centres—a psychological body. When we begin to realize this we cannot afford to indulge in such things as taking pleasure in thinking how we dislike other people. Why? Because in that case we are building up a negative psychological organism that will conduct everything in the wrong way, in which there is no truth and nothing good. Many people crystallize out in their negative emotions. I advise you to avoid such people.

The point then is to see clearly the difference between a sensation and a thought. You see in front of you a person you do not like because of his clothes, his voice, or his manner and you take pleasure in disliking this object while looking at it—that is, while your senses transmit his image to you. Afterwards when you no longer see this person you take pleasure in thinking how you dislike this person. The Sufi teacher says that the *effect* on you is the same. The two things are different, one being an object and the other a thought about the object, because to see a person who is present and to think about a person who is absent is not the same thing—a different centre is being employed —but the dislike in both cases is the same.

Birdlip, March 17, 1945

COMMENTARY ON NEGATIVE EMOTIONS

When the last paper was read down here on "The difference between the object and the thought of the object" a question was asked as follows: "Is it helpful to try not to express one's dislike of a person even though one dislikes the person in one's thoughts?"

I think it would be helpful to talk of this subject once more. But first of all we must review what the Work is about and what we are trying to do in the Work. It is useless acting on some small phrase in the Work unless one understands the meaning of it. For example, why should I not express my negative emotions freely? Now in life this is quite legitimate, but in the Work it is not so. If you are under life with its very small chances of development, where, so to speak, the dice are heavily loaded against you in regard to any inner development, there is no reason why you should not react to everything mechanically according to your level of being. But if you seek to be in the Work you come under another aspect of things altogether. You begin to have a new responsibility and cannot behave just as you wish to. When this moment occurs to you, when this realization of the meaning of the Work begins to become apparent to you, you are no longer able to do just as you please from your self-will. This means that you cannot react mechanically in the way you always did. You begin to feel responsible to another system of behaviour, which you must begin to obey. Otherwise the Work can have no effect on you. How can the ideas of the Work have any effect on you if you simply go on behaving as you always do, which means reacting mechanically? Everyone has his or her own mechanical way of reacting to things but the object of the Work is to change this mechanicalness. When you have a point in the Work you begin to feel uncomfortable when you behave mechanically. You begin to dislike this continual mechanical reaction to all events, to all people, and in short to everything, and when this begins to happen in you, you are beginning to pass under the laws of the Work. You begin to understand that you cannot live as before. You begin to realize you have to do something about the matter yourself. What do you have to do? You have to begin to try to do what the Work teaches. This is an extraordinary experience to realize—namely, that you have not only to behave but to think and feel differently. You must remember here that everyone thinks he or she behaves quite rightly. It takes some time before one realizes that one does not behave rightly and never has done—that is, it takes some time to realize that one's ordinary way of behaving internally and externally is not what the Work wishes. And so gradually one comes to the rather shattering moment of realizing that what the Work is teaching all the time applies to you yourself and to the way that you behave and think and feel. It may take years before this shattering moment of realization comes to you. You may talk about the Work, you may be interested in it and feel in a sense that you are in the Work and yet not notice that you do not live the Work in your daily life. There are very considerable reasons why this moment of realization is not touched for some time. One is because no one is allowed to understand this Work until he is ready to understand it. But when the ideas of the Work become emotional and begin to relate themselves to you yourself and to all that you have observed in yourself, then you may have a moment of realization of what the Work means practically in regard to yourself.

Now you know that the Work says in general that we should not express our negative emotions and that the more we express them the more they feed on us and are nourished by us. Now suppose a person simply hears this remark and repeats it to other people without realizing what it means and what connection it has with Work-ideas. I think this question is so interesting that I will spend some time in explaining what it means. Taking this saying of the Work apart from the whole context of the Work, we can easily imagine it is nothing but some kind of commandment that we are told to obey. Let us invent this commandment and call it the eleventh commandment. I believe the eleventh commandment has already been invented: "Thou shalt not be found out," so let us say that we take the commandment: "Thou shalt not be negative" as the twelfth commandment. The Work says we must not be negative and that we must not express our negative emotions. Now a person who follows this commandment, so to speak, literally, a person who flatters himself that he obeys it—which of course he does not—is nothing but a fool. He is taking the Work on a very external level. He may not express negative emotions in public but he will express them in private, either to the private circle which he thinks are his friends or in his private thoughts. He will then think that the whole idea of not expressing negative emotions consists in obeying an external commandment. Let us try to grasp why the Work teaches that negative emotions must gradually be eliminated. The Work says that as long as we enjoy chiefly negative emotions we are cut off from all contact with Higher Centres. I assure you that at a certain stage of the Work even a moment's indulgence of negative emotion towards others will cause you to lose force and even destroy for the time being everything that you aimed at in the Work-sense. Negative emotion cuts us off from all possibility of help. As was said once, to become thoroughly negative is like an explosion in a delicate chemical laboratory through which everything that is being made, being gradually created, is destroyed. I suppose some of you know this already—namely, that at all costs your mechanical reactions that produce negative emotions, your judgments of others and your vanities in connection with yourself, must be mitigated and separated from in order to keep any degree of inner psychological health.

Now when you become aware that you cannot afford to be negative then it will no longer be a commandment you obey in this respect but it will be a matter of deep understanding. And then indeed life and its events will become your teacher. You will no longer think of obeying some external rules, some commandments, but you will see the reason why. And then you will hesitate to plunge into the welter of negative states whether expressed externally or no.

Let us quote again the question with which we started: "Is it helpful to try not to express one's dislike of a person even though one dislikes the person in one's thoughts?" Here the centre of gravity in this question lies in the word 'helpful'. In what sense is it helpful not to express one's negative emotions externally? The answer is that if you express them mechanically they tend to increase and form a habit—i.e. a habit of negative emotions. From the standpoint of the ideas of the Work and what we are aiming at this is obviously something that will interfere with our possibility of reaching a new level of being—i.e. it will not help us in this respect. As regards the other part of the question about disliking people in our thoughts, it will be the same thing if we continue to feel negative towards other people, even though we obey the commandment of not expressing these negative feelings. In fact, it might be better to express them. To think negatively about others is just the same as behaving negatively. To have an enormous number of negative thoughts about others and to attempt not to shew them externally is a very good thing provided that you know that your task is to alter these negative thoughts by hook or crook in yourself. And this, of course, is quite impossible if you take yourself for granted, as always right. If you have had long self-observation and have become aware of a great many very unpleasant things in yourself, you will then be in a position to neutralize your negative thoughts about others through seeing the same things in yourself and so putting yourself in the other person's position. At this moment of writing to you these things I notice I am very negative towards a certain person down here but by putting myself in this person's position and also by seeing how this person must think of me I find that it is possible to get free entirely from negative thoughts about this person save when I fall asleep in myself and allow my mechanical negative thoughts to pass unchallenged in my mind. In this respect it is interesting to notice how you can be negative with a person—when you are asleep—and how the whole situation is changed when you are awake. I think this is one of the first things we realize when we alternate between life and Work—i.e. when we are in life things appear one way and when we are in a sense of the Work things appear quite differently, so much so that at times we cannot imagine how we behaved or spoke or felt as we did. The explanation is quite simple—we were asleep. Now this is a necessary experience and in fact gives you the whole practical method of working on yourself. People who imagine that having heard this Work for a short time they are henceforth going to behave in some beautiful way are simply fools. We can only learn to walk by falling. We all have more conscious and more mechanical moments but it is by the contrast that we learn. Let no one in this Work imagine that he or she has reached a stage where they cannot be made negative. In fact, the Work introduces us to the whole technique of dealing with negative states whether expressed or felt. And here lies a very up and down country that we have to stagger over with a certain confidence that we may reach another state of ourselves. But this up and down country cannot be traversed by anyone who imagines that a short issue to his intentions is granted him. The source of negative emotions is very deep in us all and there are some very sore places in us that without help we could never avoid. For that reason we must have a sense of what the Work teaches and why it teaches what it does teach. I know that when I am in a negative state, whether expressed or not, I am all wrong, and that I will be cut off from my best thoughts and best emotions. I no longer obey the teaching of the Work about negative emotions as a commandment. I know very well, I understand why this great teaching about negative emotions is given by the Work, and that it is no external commandment but one of the deepest things that could possibly be said in regard to reaching a better range of feelings and understanding. The satisfaction of being negative, even with a very good cause, no longer gives me any happiness. I know very well if I am negative beyond a certain point I will cease to have any inner happiness or peace of mind, which is what I aim at. I know it is useless to have my happiness depending only on people or external events. I know that the source of my understanding of the Work does not lie only in external conditions and I have experienced more than once that moment of understanding which one of our English mystical writers, Thomas Traherne, described when he said in a moment of Self-Remembering, when he felt that he had really reached his innermost being: "You will not believe how I was withdrawn from altering and minding outward things." This means to be passive towards life.

I remember once in this connection how O. in a private talk to a few of us said that we have to become passive to all that happens to us, whatever it is, and that this was the most difficult thing because if taken wrongly it led in quite the wrong direction. Just doing nothing is useless. O. said it was the most difficult thing to understand. It had nothing to do with Quietism. He said that the Work-phrase 'realizing that other people are machines' came close to the idea but it was impossible to see that rightly unless we had first seen that we are machines. Now we are nearly always negative with other people because we take them as conscious beings doing things consciously, and we also think we are conscious and do everything with conscious purpose. None of you will be able to reach this viewpoint, and do not try to do so artificially. Nothing is more easy than to regard other people as machines, leaving yourself out; nothing is more easy than to see how another person is a fool, leaving yourself out. If you can see yourself as a fool and see the fool in other people without blame, you may reach this passive point which is between the swing of the pendulum, the point from where real understanding comes. This is why everyone in the Work must work on themselves, especially when they express negative emotions or think negatively about others. Just as you can see your own foolishness without being negative so you can see the foolishness of another person without being negative about it. You can see what a thing is like, you can see what you are like, without negative emotions coming in. Will you agree with me that when you are negative with another person it is either due to a feeling of superiority or lack of understanding of the conditions of the other person? But however we think of this great question, the fact remains that negative emotions are useless and lead nowhere except into hell and ultimately to violence, and that one of the

650

great teachings of the Work is that we must free ourselves from negative states as regards ourselves and other people. And here I will remind you that the more negative 'I's you have that express themselves openly or privately in your thoughts of other people, the greater danger you are in that those negative 'I's you have nourished will turn against yourself. All negative 'I's that attack others are in us, and when we try to raise our level through inner work we will have to meet them all one by one, because they will turn on us with the same ferocity that they turn on other people.

Now I will add one thing here: people think they have no negative 'I's. They have a picture of themselves as being tolerant. They do not see what goes on in the background. Remember that the Emotional Centre should never have a negative part by birth and that all negative emotions are acquired from the example of our parents, teachers, and all those we are brought up amongst. Remember, also, as long as the negative part of Emotional Centre is active in us there can only be either no connection or a very faint connection with Higher Emotional Centre. The object of this Work is to purify ordinary centres for the reception of the influences of Higher Centres. First we must change Mental Centre and think in a new way and then change the Emotional Centre and feel in a new way about one another. This is the task that the Work lays down in so many words and it is a useless task to try to understand unless we feel there is a higher level attainable.

Now as regards the Work-teaching that if you do not express negative emotions they get less, this has given rise to a great deal of discussion. It was taught at the beginning of the Work, before anything was said about thinking negatively about others. Some people used to say it was much better to have a row and get it over, and that by expressing their negative emotions they felt better afterwards. I will leave this for discussion. I would only say this: there is a way of expressing negative emotions consciously and it is quite different from expressing them mechanically. I am certain that the expression of negative emotions mechanically only leads to a worse situation, but for the time being you are relieved. You must remember that those expressed negative emotions travel round to people and excite their negative emotions in response and eventually come back to you. We have to deal with our negative emotions and feel responsible for them. It is here that working on one's private negative thinking about a person comes in. Some people say little or nothing externally but they think and feel a great deal internally and even take a pleasure in registering a cause of fresh negative emotion although they appear smooth outwardly. In that case there is no real conscience against negative states. This is a bad internal situation and there is so much filth in their minds that they enjoy secretly. Here comes in all the close and sincere observation that is necessary in the Work, and the seeing of your own unpleasant 'I's that you project on to other people. Remember that we have a right not to be negative and this is quite different from being told we have no right to be negative. Observe yourself sometimes from the standpoint of your negative states; be sincere and admit you are in a negative state; then say to yourself: "I have a right not to be negative." Here all your understanding of the Work will come to your aid and maybe the whole negative state will vanish in a moment. This is a moment of Self-Remembering because in all Self-Remembering we put ourselves under the influences of the Work, which come from Higher Centres in which no negative states exist.

NOTE:

After this paper was read Dr. Nicoll said that one question was interesting: "Would it be helpful to try to act outwardly as though liking a person while inwardly disliking the person?" Dr. Nicoll said this would be a wonderful thing if we could act but that only conscious people could act because acting is doing in the Work-sense. What we call acting is something that will break down instantly because we are acting from self-love—i.e. from some picture of ourselves. He said, for example, you are determined to act very pleasantly towards someone and you come into the room and say most politely: "Will you have some more tea?" and the person says that she never takes tea and you feel offended and upset and say to yourself: "Well, I've done my best." This is the only kind of acting we can do at our level. There is nothing genuine in it and it will be a source of fresh and very vigorous negative emotion. But if through external considering you are genuinely concerned about another person, then perhaps your acting will be from a deeper source. You can always test your so-called acting by noticing the point where you become offended. Then you see the difference between acting from internal considering and acting from external considering. O. said: "*Only a man who can do can act. Acting is doing and only a conscious man can act.*" This means that only from real being, Real 'I', can a person act in the real sense—i.e. beyond himself, beyond his Personality.

Birdlip, March 23, 1945

COMMENTARY ON THE FOOD OF IMPRESSIONS

We live by impressions. Impressions are the most important food of all the foods that enter the human machine. We have three mouths on our faces—the eyes, the nose and the mouth. It is necessary to reflect on this and think what it means. All these three foods give energy to the body but the most important is the food of impressions. No matter what a depressed person eats with his mouth, or what air he breathes, it will not cure him until he gets that letter that he is waiting for in which it is said that he has passed his examination, or that somebody loves him, or that he has won his law-suit. Now a letter is not air, nor physical food: it is a series of ink-marks on a paper that convey to him certain meaning that transforms his state. This is one of the things we have to understand about the food of impressions. For example, what you hear somebody say about you can depress or exalt you; or again, when you see the number of the horse you have backed go up on the board you will pass from depression to rejoicing.

Now do you think we live chiefly in a world of impressions and depend upon them? What you hear, what you read, what you see, constitutes impressions—and also what we think to ourselves inwardly. Our real life is this world of impressions and how we receive them and how we react to them, and it is in this world of impressions that we have to learn to live in the right way, this very delicate world that we are continually concerned with and concerned about. A telegram may completely alter a sense of the future. A telegram is neither the food of air nor physical food like a beefsteak but it is a totally different kind of food which the Work calls impressions. When a person smiles at you it is an impression and it may warm your heart and your whole being, whereas when a person frowns at you the reverse result may be felt. Impressions are psychological and yet the Work says they have a certain materiality, a finer materiality than the materiality of air or a beefsteak.

Now I am taking the whole question of impressions from a certain angle in connection with the idea that the Work teaches: *that impressions are the most important food of all.* You must understand that this is a commentary on the food of impressions and that I am speaking about the class of impressions that make it possible for us to exist normally. Being exposed to constant bad news, constant negative criticism by others, constant fault-finding, all these form a class of impressions that will not give us the right force for normal life—I mean, under ordinary conditions of life. We all remember when someone has said something pleasant to us, and we must all have noticed how sometimes a single look or word can make us feel much better. In this delicate world of psychological impressions we are like clumsy hippopotami, both to ourselves and to other people. For a long time we try to get impressions from others that will make us content with ourselves, having no strength to work against the wrong feelings of ourselves produced, for example, by flattery, by compliments, by successful moments, etc. When we are in that state our psychic life is far too delicate and not rightly based. What is it we crave most, mechanically speaking? We crave most attention, and this belongs to the satisfaction of the vanity. This certainly gives a very powerful stimulus, so much so that if a person's psychological existence is based entirely on vanity he or she will feel depressed if there is not a constant mention of him or her in the papers, and so on. To live by impressions of this kind is to live the life of this most powerful thing in us called False Personality. To live the life of pure internal considering and of making accounts gives a very unsatisfactory basis to our existences as it depends entirely on how people behave towards us, and this means we have no centre of gravity in ourselves, so that strictly speaking we do not exist except as functions of the praise or blame of other people. Adversity will hit us very hard, whereas success will raise us to an entirely wrong feeling of ourselves. We are then like dogs that depend so much on the praise or blame of their mistresses or masters, and if a number of people meet together having these dogs in themselves you may be quite sure that these dogs will begin to yap at one another. You will be in a room full of dogs all yapping, all wishing to call attention to themselves, all jealous of each other. And I can assure you that this is the situation of the majority of people in life, when they meet together in a so-called friendly party. Unfortunately one or two of these people may have cats or tigers or bears on their laps, or even snakes, and in that case the friendly party will be extremely troublesome to anyone present who has any sensitiveness of the inner state of other people. Now we should not allow the dog or the cat or the other animals to take in impressions and so determine our psychological existence. We should try to receive impressions more deeply than these animals can, these animals in us that we so carefully carry about. The question in the Work is: "*On what do impressions fall in you?* Do they fall on your dog that always demands attention and praise—or on your cat that pretends to be affectionate, or indifferent, or on your snakes that hiss the whole time?" It is for this reason that we are told in the Work to watch where impressions go, on what 'I's they fall, because all these animals are different 'I's in us that are very undeveloped and are not really properly conscious to us yet and belong so to speak to the not yet conscious side of us—i.e. to this 'other person' in us that we do not notice yet, owing to our pretences of ourselves, but which other people perhaps have noticed already. The object of self-observation is to make us more conscious of what is in us. Unfortunately we move about in life imagining we know ourselves and not realizing we have another side that has to be made conscious gradually before we can begin to grow. Living merely on the surface of ourselves we can never penetrate more deeply into the background that prevents us from receiving influences of a finer order, influences, in fact, that alone can begin to make us grow, because it is this dark, unconscious side of ourselves that stands between us and the influences of Higher Centres—i.e. the healing influences that come down from the Side-Octave of the Ray of Creation. Unless we realize what fools we are we will always imagine we are not fools, or if, for a moment, we feel we have been foolish, say socially speaking, we will at once heal the breach by a terrific discharge or exudation of self-justifying so that we once more retain our curiously inadequate idea of ourselves, which we do not see as being inadequate or indeed as being nothing but a kind of scarecrow that we imagine to be a perfect man, a perfect woman.

When impressions begin to fall on us to a deeper level, we begin to live in an entirely new world. If you want to live in a new world you must go deeper—you must get away from the surface world of yourself and this is certainly in one sense painful but in another sense extraordinarily full of meaning and new satisfaction. You then begin to realize what this means: "I am not this 'I'," and this already means a certain degree of Self-Remembering. Now the Work teaches that we must have constant impressions in order to live. We must have the impressions of all foods, all the fruits of the Earth, because we are a microcosmos or small world living first of all in the macrocosmos or big world of nature (our first big world—i.e. the first cosmos above us called in the Work 'Organic Life'.) We are given the power in the marvellous organization of our senses to taste the impressions of this big world of nature. We are given the power of tasting butter and jam and bread and pears and apples and caviare and fish and meat, and of smelling grass and the sea. Have you ever thought that we have these powers already in us? You taste a peach or a strawberry and think that the difference of taste lies in the two fruits. Do you not see that the difference lies in your power of tasting differently and that you have the apparatus already made in you for taking in these two different impressions of taste. Think for a moment, because people find some difficulty in seeing what is meant here, and moreover people find it difficult to see that we are a microcosmos fitted into a macrocosmos and prepared for it. They find it difficult to understand that we are related to the whole cosmos in general by our construction. They find it difficult to see that we are born in a Universe to which we can respond and which responds to us if we find out the right request to make. One reason is because people take themselves as completely isolated, not seeing that they are constructed to live in the Universe and therefore must be a part of the Universe and so in some way correspondent to it. We have eyes that respond to the vibrations of light, ears that respond to the vibrations of air. In short, we are constructed to take in impressions.

Now let us confine ourselves to the first cosmos we live in—namely, Organic Life, or the Earth, without which we could not exist. It supplies us with food and air and with certain impressions. We are speaking at the moment of taste derived from the products of nature. All these are necessary for us because we have the apparatus ready. We have an extraordinarily fine apparatus of taste, smell, touch and sight, for appreciating what the Earth produces, and this fine apparatus must be satisfied reasonably with the fresh products so important for health—namely, those impressions that fall directly on the Instinctive Centre. You will perhaps see the argument. The argument is that we have got in us the powers of tasting and smelling different things created by nature and so producing different impressions, and since we have these powers in us, such as the power of distinguishing between the rich taste of a strawberry and the equally rich taste of a raspberry, therefore one side of our life of impressions must be satisfied by the products of nature since we have born in us the necessary apparatus for receiving impressions from these different objects. I think this argument is understandable, and belongs to the general argument in the Work that we have more in us than we use. For this reason you will see that all scientific attempts to make synthetic foods, powders, and so on, from which we can get no right impressions of taste, are entirely false and, in fact, not at all scientific. Since we are constructed to live first in Organic Life on the Earth as small living cells in this vast organism, we require to be nourished by it and not by any substitute for it. Now this constitutes our first or instinctive life of impressions. Food is an impression first of all, then a substance or physical food. The impression gives appetite but the food-substance gives nourishment. To try to replace synthetically the food-substance without the impression of taste and the pleasure that results is to ignore the most important food— namely, impressions. (I would like you to discuss this as it is a very important idea to grasp.) Ask yourselves why nature provides so many interesting tastes and smells in food. Also ask yourselves why people become tired physically when they receive tasteless food for a long time and what the difference between an appetizing and an unappetizing meal means in regard to exciting the right activities of Instinctive Centre—the work of the stomach, etc.

★   ★   ★

Now I want to bring in here in this connection what the Work calls the supreme food of impressions. Let us suppose we are governed by tastes. We have heard about inner taste which can discriminate between good psychological food and bad psychological food just as our physical taste can in regard to literal food. The supreme physical impression that we can give our whole machine is that of Self-Remembering, the finest taste of all tastes possible, the taste of some-thing akin to 'I'. The Work says that a moment of Self-Remembering supplies every cell in the body with food of a kind that it does not ordinarily get. The Work says that when you remember yourself you give a shock to the whole of you. Every cell receives force and new energy—i.e. a new food. This is called the First Conscious Shock where all our work lies for many years and this is always what we forget to give ourselves although we have heard it 101 times. Instead of remem-bering ourselves we insist on arguing with ourselves or on thinking about everything or even thinking about what Self-Remembering means. You have often heard that if you do not know what Self-Remembering means, you should try to stop your thoughts even for a few seconds, to stop everything for a short while, and to be nothing, no one. If you can do this, you will notice that you feel quite different, as if you had turned on the light. Or if you think this image too strong, as if you had suddenly noticed where you are, suddenly come to your senses, or, as someone once said to me: "It is as if I suddenly took

656

my head out of the water." When such an experience is undergone you may notice also that you suddenly see the room you are in, or the window seems to transmit more light, or you hear sounds more clearly, or you can read the paper without your glasses. This means that the cells in your body have been enlivened in some way, have been stimulated. They have received new food that springs out of this act of Self-Remembering. However our self-hypnosis, our continual identification with our quite useless chains of thought, our powerful pre-occupations which we think so important and of course never lead anywhere, our continual internal considering, our account-making and the entire mass of our negative emotions, make it very difficult for us eventually to attempt to self-remember. In the strain of life we never remember ourselves. To do so we must have some force coming not from life but from another direction to enable us to make the attempt. We have to step out of ourselves, out of the train and bus of mechanical life in order to do so. We have to step out of the finely interwoven and usually unpleasant pattern that we insist on thinking is our life, and we find no reason why we should and perhaps have no idea what it means to step out of the stream of our daily life for a moment and attempt to expose ourselves to influences that come from an entirely different direction.

Now I want you to think what it means when we nourish our machine by the wrong feeling of 'I' as we all do. We are told that if we could attain the right feeling of 'I' in Self-Remembering every cell in the body would have new life. And so by contrast does not this teaching imply that when we identify with the wrong feeling of ourselves we will be giving wrong force, wrong energy, to the cells of the body? Can you understand that if we are very negative and evil-minded we feel ourselves through such feelings into which we put the feeling of 'I', so that we give our body very bad food from this highest source of food which comes from our psychological state, from impressions coming from different 'I's that we are identified with, and not simply through impressions coming from the senses which have their own importance and value but are on another scale? I remember O. saying once that we all have 'I's that can make us ill when we identify with them and so get under their power. It may be necessary however to meet these 'I's and fight with them eventually, because sooner or later we have to fight everything in us that is against the Work and the harmony it seeks to make in us, by the process of perception and inner separation, by seeing what is true and what is not true, what has good-will and what has evil-will to the Work.

I am intentionally leaving this paper unfinished in that I have not drawn together the various aspects. The paper is a commentary on impressions and as it stands impressions coming through the senses are first spoken of and then impressions coming from the feeling of 'I'. The highest impression is the feeling of Real 'I'. This does not come from outside but is an impression from inside. At the same time all external impressions coming in change in their intensity according to what 'I' you are in to receive them. If you are in some state of Self-Remembering external impressions may be intensely beautiful, whereas if you are in negative 'I's the most wonderful meal or most beautiful day means nothing to you. When a thing means nothing to you, you get no impressions from it. The more a thing means to you the more impressions you get, and vice versa. But all this is a question of long observation and interchange of views amongst you. But everyone should ask himself or herself: On what food of impressions do you nourish yourself? If you are negative internally as a rule you will take in unpleasant impressions and feed yourself on them, or if you are depressed you will take in only depressing things from the news-papers. And this will infect the whole of the human machine. Or if you are fearful, nervous and so on, you will take in impressions accordingly. Usually from the stream of our inner life we get very small inner impressions or, as it were, stale impressions. However if you make an effort, you decrease 'entropy' and take in impressions. You must ask yourselves what entropy means. It means, in short, a state where everything becomes equalized and there is no inter-change of energy, and so everything is stale. When you make effort you go against your staleness. For example, when you deny yourself something you increase its attraction and then your entropy is decreased. The idea of Self-Remembering is to decrease entropy enormously by having a very distinct sense between you yourself and external life. All identifying increases entropy—i.e. runs us down—so that there is no difference between us and life, as it were. If you can see life as an illusion in the right way, as Yoga systems teach, you will feel an in-creasingly powerful difference of potential between you and life, and this will decrease entropy. But if you are immersed in life everything will come into an equilibrium and you will cease to take in impressions beyond the minimum necessary.

Birdlip, March 31, 1945

THE REASON WHY WE HAVE TO
OBSERVE OURSELVES

Let us begin by taking this idea that is taught us in the Work that Higher Centres are always speaking to us and telling us what we should do but we cannot hear them. We may be quite sure that, since the object of the Work is to connect us with Higher Centres and their messages, one of the first things we are taught—namely, to observe ourselves—must have connection with ultimately getting into contact with these Higher Centres in us which are fully formed but which we cannot hear. I mean, that there must be some reason for self-observation, and I think that it is right to say that if we simply try to observe ourselves merely because we have been told to do so we will not be observing ourselves in the right way. We will not understand why we should, or what deeper meaning lies in this practice. We shall then be inclined to say: "Why on earth should I observe myself? with what object? for what reason?" If we have not a wide enough grasp of the ideas of the Work and what the goal of the Work is, if all these ascending scales shewn in the Ray and the Side-Octave, all these teachings about higher level and lower level, fewer laws and more laws, and all that is said about Personality and Essence and so on, mean nothing to us conceptually and simply lie scattered about in our memory, having no co-ordinated and emotional life in them, then of course self-observation will be merely a dreary task imposed upon us. But surely we have to get a much more subtle and interior idea of the Work. Let us consider self-observation in the light of why we are told to practise it. We are told to practise it because it can lead to becoming more aware of the influences of Higher Centres. We cannot hear these influences because there is a kind of thick substance lying between them and ourselves. What is this thick substance? It is all that part of us that is unconscious to us, which we do not realize, which we are unaware of as existing in us. As you know, it is often said that the act of self-observation lets a ray of light into our inner darkness. This darkness is what I have just called the thick substance which will not transmit the influences of Higher Centres. A man, a woman, must come to terms eventually with this dark side of themselves, and this is only possible through long and intelligent self-observation carried out for a definite reason and not merely as a mechanical task. Remember all self-observation must be a conscious effort. You will agree that we all have in us 'I's of which we are quite unaware. We live in a false personality, not in a real one. We are full of pictures of ourselves, for example, and owing to the action of buffers which prevent our seeing contradictions we feel quite at peace with ourselves. But the object of the Work is to stir up a struggle in us, a struggle with this false contentment and complacency. And what is the method used? The method is self-observation, whereby we gradually become more conscious of what is in us and begin to lose these beloved pictures of ourselves, these forms of imagination. You remember how the driver is in the public-house, drinking. This means he is living in imagination, in pictures, in imaginary ideas about himself —in Imaginary 'I'. The first thing is that the driver must awaken.

Now we can think of the situation in the following terms: We each have a dark side to ourselves that we know nothing about—that is, a side that is not conscious to us but yet acts. Into this darkness a ray of light must enter through self-observation carried out according to what the Work teaches us to observe, to look for, to become aware of. This dark side of ourselves must gradually be connected with our idea of ourselves and, as it were, a pattern has to be made, a mingling of these two sides. And unless this ray of light enters this darkness this cannot be done, and in consequence we can never feel the influences of Higher Centres because these influences are damped down and obliterated by this dark side, this *other side* of ourselves, which as a rule we see only in other people and do not attribute to ourselves. So we tend always to blame others and accuse them, let us say, of evil thoughts, or suspicious behaviour, or bad talking, or unkindness, or lying, or indifference, or infidelity, or unreliableness, or meanness, and so on. That is to say, this other side of ourselves of which we are not conscious we tend to see in others, and, as you can understand, this is one of the great causes of human unhappiness and the constant friction in which almost everybody lives in regard to one another. In order to alter this state of affairs the Work begins with self-observation, with letting this ray of light or ray of consciousness into this inner darkness. Here the teaching of the Work is quite emphatic and cannot be misunderstood. When we study our tendency to blame others, and register it and deliberately begin to try to observe the same things in ourselves, we are undertaking one of the first and most important steps in personal work—i.e. in work on ourselves. Unless we do this, we can get nowhere. If we attempt to get somewhere without doing this over a very long period we are like people trying to see through a window that is covered with black paint. This black paint has curious properties because in some indescribable way it is ourselves. It is a kind of living darkness in ourselves which can only be cleared away by the increasing light of consciousness through self-observation. The increasing light of consciousness is the result of long, quiet, sincere self-observation, long private noticing of oneself, of one's actions, of how one speaks, of one's thoughts and how one is thinking, of one's emotions and how one is feeling. It is clear then that the initial task in the Work is to become more conscious of this dark side of ourselves, and this means we lose little by little all our ordinary ideas of ourselves which we feel at first as a loss of Personality, as a kind of weakening of ourselves. But yet if one does not allow oneself to get negative—and this is very strongly emphasized, the danger of negative states being continually mentioned—then one begins to realize that in the new and strange feelings of oneself that begin to visit one there is far more real strength and understanding than anything in the pseudo 'I' that previously ruled one. We will indeed find that quite new thoughts, feelings, insights, and meaning begin to come to us and the reason is that traces of higher influences begin to be faintly heard, so much so that where formerly we only saw one thing, one way, one meaning, one choice between what we thought was right or wrong, we now see a dozen or more meanings and choices. Where we thought there was only one step between *Do* and *Re*, and *Re* and *Mi*, in some previous barren, rigid, and stilted understanding, we see whole inner octaves extending between these notes. All increase of understanding lies in seeing finer and finer differences, subtler and more beautiful meanings, all interwoven and full of a magic quality of their own, which we realize are quite different from our previous heavy, crude kind of thinking and feeling whereby we formerly lived. But these finer visitations of understanding cannot enter our consciousness and become a continual internal source of meaning that never dies and is inexhaustible, unless we make this dark side of ourselves increasingly conscious and, as I said, this making conscious of the dark side of ourselves, or side in darkness, inevitably leads to a complete change in our idea and estimation of ourselves. Indeed, we may feel we are losing sight of ourselves, and where we used to be so sure and convinced and so ready to do and act, to speak, to criticize, we now feel a great uncertainty because we see so much more in every situation than we saw before. It is not a negative uncertainty but a positive uncertainty. It is not a feeling of helplessness but a feeling of strength because we see so clearly that where we were so sure before we then were very weak, because the certainty we felt was the certainty of a fool, the certainty of ignorance, which can only be a weakness and which no doubt continually led to wrong results and completely useless frictions which we were sure were due to others, and had nothing to do with our own completely untrustworthy reactions. How certain we used to be—but now we see how mechanical we used to be. How we used to think we understood everything and could do, and now we realize that we had no understanding and, in fact, everything simply happened mechanically to us according to the nature of our machine. How much we used to attribute to ourselves and pride ourselves on and how much now do we see that it was all done by this machine that we took for granted as ourselves.

Now in seeing this other side of ourselves, this dark side, into which the Work tells us that we must penetrate and make it increasingly conscious to ourselves by self-observation, you must remember that the doctrine of 'I's is of the first importance in this process. We have to see this dark side but not to identify with it. We have to make it conscious but not take it as ourselves. This is a matter of great difficulty and we have to remind ourselves and be reminded constantly of this point that is so important. Remember that everything we are taught in the Work itself fits together and you cannot do this Work, say, with one idea of it without taking in the others in conjunction. For example, you cannot take self-observation apart from the doctrine of 'I's, without doing yourself great harm. The reason is that if to everything you observe in yourself you say 'I' and so identify with it, the result will be complete confusion. You will become what you observe and this is fatal. We have to take our 'I's objectively. We have to see different things in us as we see different objects in the room. We do not take the table, chair, the book, as ourselves. You must never say: "What I observe is 'I'", but you must know that this 'I' that you observe is in you. Now all this belongs to not identifying. Self-observation carried out with the idea of not identifying with what you observe is the keynote of this system practically, and it is a very difficult thing to carry out. In fact, it may be a long time before you see what this method taught in this system really means. You know you must divide yourself into two, an observing side and an observed side—i.e. you must not identify with what you observe. This is the same as saying that you cannot change if you identify with everything that goes on in you—i.e. with every mood, every thought, every sensation, every form of imagination. And again this means that we have to take ourselves objectively. We have to take our psychology and all that lies in it objectively as we gradually observe it and gradually become more conscious of it. What does it mean to take a thing objectively? I do not take the table I am looking at subjectively—i.e. as part of myself. I take it as an object that is not me and that I am distinct from. This is taking a thing objectively. But the Work teaches that we have to take the things in our inner life objectively. I notice, for instance, an evil, malicious thought in my mind. It is quite useless to burst into tears and say: "How evil and malicious I am." That would be taking the 'I' that thinks like this subjectively as myself. It would be identifying with it, saying 'I' to it, and this would be quite useless and would lead nowhere. On the contrary I must see this thought and try to see what 'I' or group of 'I's it comes from and watch what they are up to, what they wish to do and to make me say. Then I will be observing these 'I's objectively. Of course, if I consent to them I shall become them and they will rush out of me and do all the harm they can. If I try to keep them back by force, taking them as myself, I shall soon lose the battle because then part of my force will be going into them—i.e. part of my feeling of myself. This will always happen if I cannot feel they are not me and that they come round at intervals and try to persuade me that they are me and beg me to say 'I' to them. If you touch them they will at once take force from you—that is, part of your feeling of 'I' will run into them. You then have, as it were, no magic circle that you can draw round yourself and stand in internally. This is why it is so dangerous to go to sleep for too long—i.e. not to work at all or think about the Work or what one is doing in it. Sometimes people allow themselves to be for a comparatively long time unaware of the Work. They step out, as it were, of any magic circle that they might have begun to draw round themselves and then all sorts of 'I's fasten on to them like so many leeches and then before they know where they are some ruffian 'I's get hold of them, having as it were drawn some blood from them and so claiming a blood-relationship. That is why it is so important to have aim in connection with some 'I's that one knows only lead to trouble and useless suffering. About certain things one must keep inner silence, the Work says. What does it mean to keep inner silence? Unpleasant 'I's may be chattering inside you and persuading you to argue with them. If you do argue with them you no longer keep inner silence. You can speak to negative 'I's if you are very careful how you do it—i.e. if you see them quite objectively in you and if you are not astonished that such 'I's exist in you. I think as we get to know this dark side in the increasing light of consciousness we none of us can be astonished at the 'I's we find there whose existence we must accept but with which we must not identify.

To resume in brief: the meaning of self-observation is to make this dark self increasingly conscious and to mingle it gradually with our previous imaginary idea of ourselves. This brings about a complete change of the feeling of oneself and begins to dissolve Imaginary 'I'. At the same time, while the process of this annihilation of our attributes is taking place, we begin to feel influences reaching us from another source of meaning. These influences could not reach us before because there was this thick darkness intervening. We can think of this dark side as the 'other person' in us that we tend to see in other people. When you begin to make this other person, this dark self, more conscious to you, it is no longer projected on to other people and your whole relationship to other people begins to change. In fact, you see other people for the first time and you release them. However, you must realize that this applies to each of you. Do not start with the idea that your neighbour should change and release you. You must release him.

Birdlip, Easter, March 31, 1945

AN EASTER MESSAGE

(from Dr. Nicoll at Birdlip to the Group at Quaremead, Ugley.)

I had thought of coming down for Easter and now find that it is not possible. You are having very good meetings and stimulating one another just as reports stimulate me. We were speaking to-day, at a place you all know, about what Easter means, what this concrete symbol of death and resurrection signifies. We were taking it from a small understandable level and not in the great terms that it implies in the case of Christ. I asked: "What does it mean to die to something quite small and how could we understand that there always follows a resurrection from what we die to?" Supposing that you in a quite real way do not go with some negative thought and its resultant feeling, supposing you really sacrifice this from yourself, from your own will, from your own understanding, will there be any resurrection? Does it mean that the same thing will recur again in the same form? Surely that would not be resurrection but recurrence. The idea of resurrection is that the quantity of force that would have gone into this thing and has been genuinely sacrificed from one's deepest will, reappears in a higher form —that is, on another level—and begins to create another form of insight, of understanding, of feeling, of thinking, just as an egg can become something quite different, on a quite different level.

Now I am not speaking to you sentimentally or religiously but

663

practically. The idea of sacrifice runs through all esotericism and is implicit in all the Work teaches. But the Work very rarely mentions the word sacrifice, speaking instead of transformation. If you genuinely forego something it has a chance of transforming itself. Now, to speak more coarsely, we often receive eggs, but never take the trouble to hatch them into chickens—in fact, we usually eat our eggs—i.e. identify. The egg is an excellent symbol of a new life. G. used to call the French Institute an incubator in which we ourselves were the eggs and the friction was the heat that could transform them. Of course, looking back, one can see that this was so. One can see that all these frictions, these difficulties that we felt so acutely, were the means whereby we could have transformed ourselves if only we had practised the Work—i.e. if only we had lived the Work and not made inner accounts and identified with our inner states and above all if we had remembered ourselves. Easter is not something that comes once a year but something that comes every day: the idea of non-identifying, or dying to some typical mechanical reaction, is a daily possibility, and if it is done in a spirit of a kind of gaiety, it will gradually result in energy being transformed daily and passing upwards to another level which after a time will become a distinct experience to you.

Would you call this kind of Work-effort increasing entropy or decreasing entropy? Are you making more energy or losing energy if you work on yourself? Everything you do mechanically, just like everything that happens in the Universe, tends to increase entropy and bring about eventually a sort of stalemate, a sort of equalization of everything. But every effort of work increases force, as you can see quite plainly in the Octave that starts from Self-Remembering, whereby higher energies are produced in us. The sacrifice of Christ was to decrease entropy for humanity. Meeting physical danger can be thought of as entropy because it is a sacrifice of physical life. A man may do enough that way and then come to the point where he has to decrease entropy in other ways by other kinds of work on himself. All kinds of mechanical sacrifice, if done in the right way, lead to an evolution, and just as Napoleon chose his best and bravest generals to be princes and governors in order to prevent the downfall of society after the French Revolution, he was actually choosing the most sacrificial types on that level. But this is not enough for the full evolution of Man which is a definite path marked by definite stages—in fact, a way that has to be traversed by everyone who seeks to evolve internally and so fulfil his real meaning of creation. Just in the same way mechanically we have to pass through stages of ordinary development and become Good Householders as a necessary starting-point. But when it comes to psychological development which the Work is speaking about—which takes us on the level of Good Householder—we have to have new knowledge and begin to make efforts in a quite different way. In the paper that follows you will be able to see something of what this means.

Now I will stop, because I will write about entropy more fully in connecting the science of the West with the wisdom of the East, which is one of our tasks. But I will ask you only one thing: if you always follow the easiest path, if you are always ruled by pleasure, self-love, and self-gratification, do you not increase entropy and become staler and staler and heavier and heavier and more and more difficult and tiresome and exacting and small-minded? That is to say, you come to a state where only very slight differences work in you, very slight differences of potential, and eventually you will certainly be quite dead psychologically. But if you practise dying to things in yourself gradually you will become more and more alive. This certainly sounds very paradoxical. Now if you have an aim and try to keep it, if only for a short time, will you increase available energy or potential in yourselves? Yes, you will, if you are sincere in your efforts, because you will be going against your mechanical selves in a particular direction—you will be making Work-effort which gives force.

Now I will only add that all this is to do with the idea of Easter, with the idea of a sacrificial rite, with the idea of killing something which rises again transformed, different from what it was. Remember here ascending octaves, and remember triads that end up worse than they started and triads that end up better than they started. We are going to speak of these next time in connection with entropy.

Birdlip, April 7, 1945

THE CONCEPTION OF ENTROPY IN SCIENCE AND THE CONCEPTION OF EFFORT IN THE WORK

As you know, one of our tasks is to connect the science of the West with the wisdom of the East. This means for us practically that we have to connect the ideas and general structure of the Work by making parallels with similar scientific ideas that exist at present. We have already mentioned the word 'entropy' (and I will say here that it seems to me a most confusing word, the original Greek meaning being, as far as I can make out, 'turning in'). Science uses this word in the following sense as applied to the Universe—namely, that the Universe is gradually running down, the sun is getting cooler, the rotation of the earth is becoming more sluggish owing to the friction due to the tides, and consequently the moon is becoming more and more distant, and the ultimate picture is a dead world, where no interchange of energy will take place such as obviously exists at present, in that the heat of the sun warms up the earth and the other planets surrounding it. Now you know that the Work teaches that we live in a growing Universe and not a dying one. However let us not dwell on this for the moment but try

665

to concentrate our attention on entropy from a psychological point of view. You must bear in mind one thing clearly: that entropy increases in any interchange of energy between two things such as a hot kettle and a cold kettle of water placed side by side. Gradually the kettles become of the same temperature and then entropy is at a maximum, there being no further interchange of that form of energy called heat. Similarly if you have an electric battery and connect the negative and positive poles with a wire you soon exhaust the current. The battery gets played out and no energy travels from one pole to the other.

The next conception of entropy is that it has to do with disorder and order. From this point of view an increase of entropy means an increasing disorder of the particles forming the thing concerned. For example, a metal clock is a machine which has order, an orderly arrangement of its parts, but supposing you put this clock into a temperature of several thousand degrees all the metal will melt—i.e. all the atoms and molecules will begin to be in disorder and the clock will cease to exist as an ordered machine. The clock disappears and is replaced by a disorderly motion of all its parts in terms of molecules and atoms. Schroedinger uses a good example among others of what increasing entropy means which I well know, to the effect that if you leave your books and papers on the table without tidying them up, you will get increasing entropy—i.e. increasing disorder—and certainly one can get into that state in which maximum entropy takes place and everything is in a total muddle.* So I am going to take entropy from the standpoint of order and disorder and try to connect it with what we might term psychological entropy.

You know probably that if you do not arrange your thoughts now and then and make an effort to formulate them, your thoughts pass into increasing disorder and this means increasing entropy. Since the less arranged and the more disordered any state of nature is means physically increasing entropy of the state, we can, I think, transfer this idea to the psychological realms and perhaps thereby understand it better. For this reason I suggest that formulation of one's thoughts, which the Work so often insists on, can be compared with an effort in the direction of decreasing entropy in oneself. On the other hand, never getting anything clear in one's mind, never saying: "Now what am I up to?" or "What do I really think?" or "What does this mean?" can be compared with an increase in entropy—i.e. increasing disorder in one's psychological or inner world. Schroedinger shews how life and its material basis is very highly organized and shews an order that is not found in ordinary physical systems—i.e. in ordinary matter. It is perhaps unnecessary that this should be pointed out because we must have all had the same idea when looking at a seed changing into a plant. But it is a real step forward for science which rarely faces all the facts. Life is characterized then by a very high degree of order which is handed on by the germ plasm or seeds with ordered results

* *What is Life?*, by Erwin Schroedinger (Cambridge University Press).

such as plants, trees, human bodies, and this is quite different from unorganized matter such as stones, grass, metals, and so on. Put quite simply it means that scientists are becoming aware that there is an ordered force at the basis of life which arranges material particles in a definite way and hands on this order from generation to generation and so is quite distinct from the average rules that apply to non-living matter.

Now regarding the subject from the psychological point of view I would like to ask you this question: supposing that you satisfy every desire, supposing that you identify with everything, supposing, in short, that you never work on yourself in any way, do you think your psychological entropy will increase or decrease? You agree with me that it will increase—i.e. you will get more and more hard to please, and reach in every direction a kind of satiety—you will be, so to speak, 'fed up' with everything. This I am taking as the psychological equivalent of physical entropy as when a hot and cold kettle reach a common temperature and no further interchange of heat takes place between them. You must all use a little imagination here to catch what I am trying to say. Of course we have many psychological sides to us which are satisfied in different ways and the question really is very complex. But you will agree that, taking the Instinctive Centre, starvation decreases entropy whereas overeating increases it, bringing on a state of satiety. Now the Work teaches that we have to make effort on ourselves in many different ways. Will you agree with me when I say that effort tends to decrease entropy and simply doing as you want increases entropy? We took the example of formulating one's thoughts. This requires a definite kind of effort. Do you feel fresher after it or not? Do you feel more available energy or not? I think you will all agree with me that you feel more energy, you feel more alive. This means that you have decreased entropy in you and so have more available energy to give out or use. But supposing you are bored to death, fed up, sated with food and sex and laziness and so on, or supposing you simply live as best you can without even trying to understand your job or take hold of anything, and just drift—then I think you will agree with me when I say you are increasing psychological entropy. Now I will connect this with going more and more to sleep in the Work-sense. I mean that increasing psychological entropy can be thought of as equivalent to increasing psychological sleep. You know what happens to us all unless we work. We get to a state where we let everything go, in which we can make no real effort of attention and cannot concentrate but really dream instead. We cannot apply ourselves to anything and so cannot take in any new impressions. We never try to learn anything new and instead of being horrified by our state of ignorance we just drift along in the stream of life. The keynote of this Work is to rouse us from sleep of this kind, therefore I think it permissible to say, in the parallel I am drawing between physical entropy and psychological entropy, that the keynote of the Work is to decrease entropy in ourselves by certain definite efforts and certain shocks which ordinarily we should never think of making. Now all efforts involve a certain sacrifice. Supposing I sit down to get hold of some difficult book, what do I have to sacrifice? I have to sacrifice my great desire to be lazy and do nothing. This means that the energy that would ordinarily be employed in being lazy and comfortable and sleepy is forced into a new channel by my effort and leads to the taking in of quite new impressions. Will entropy be increased or decreased? Certainly it will be decreased so that I will have more available energy to use afterwards. Now I will bring in the Work-phrase that *whatever you do mechanically is lost for ever and whatever you do consciously remains with you.* Making an effort is relatively speaking doing something more consciously, and it will give you force. It will decrease entropy. Going with yourself mechanically, drifting from day to day, will take energy from you and increase entropy. In fact, you have no right to say you are alive. You have no right to say you are living your life. You should rather say your life is living you. I mentioned the word sacrifice and said that all effort involves sacrifice of something as, for example, when you are negative with someone and make the effort not to identify with it. This is a sacrifice. It is a sacrifice of energy that would otherwise go into being negative, and if at the same time you remember your aim in connection with your particular and most dangerous form of negative emotion, energy will go into keeping your aim and to those 'I's that wish to grow. This is a good kind of effort to make, and we are only taking one or two examples of those efforts taught by the Work on its practical side.

Now let us take some of the great symbols of sacrifice that exist historically in the past, chiefly as religious symbols, and let us think of them in connection with the idea of effort that decreases the state of entropy and gives new force, new energy. There is first of all the symbol of Christ on the Cross, which gave a tremendous force to the world at that time. There is also another symbol belonging to the same period and more easy to understand, to begin with, the symbol behind Mith raism, the religion that spread over Europe before Christianity over-came it. In the symbol which you can see on plaques and statuary at the British Museum and elsewhere you find the god not on the Cross but mounted on a bull into which he is driving a knife and from its blood come wheat and other things useful for life. This is the symbol of sacrificing the animal side, and the underlying idea is to decrease entropy, to transform energy from a lower level to a higher level because if you always satisfy your instincts like an animal you cannot expect energy to transform itself into anything on a higher level. Now in the Work we have another symbol, so to speak, which meets us at the out-set—namely, the First Conscious Shock. You will see that this is transformation of energy brought about by shock or effort. The Work does not begin with the instincts and appetites but with thoughts, feelings, forms of identifying, forms of imagination, negative emotions, internal considering, and so on. The Work says that these are the first efforts or sacrifices before anything further can be done. The Second Conscious Shock lies in a different place but of this we are not going to speak because we must first know what the First Conscious Shock is and this takes years and years of continual new experience, new insights and new ways of giving it to ourselves. The Work does not start with the Bull of Mithra, the animal instincts. It starts with the psychological man rather than the animal in him. If the psychological man changes, then the animal will begin to change, or rather you will begin to see how the animal must change and become no longer a savage beast but a useful creature with whom you can live in reasonable peace and without the feeling of contradictions. Certainly a time comes when we have to know our animals and have to go right into them to discover what they mean. But this belongs later and at present we have to begin to see this 'other side', this psychological man or woman, that we do not think we are, this imaginary person that has to be broken up.

Now you will notice that the First Conscious Shock gives increased energy—i.e. decreased entropy—because energy called $H\,48$ becomes transformed into the energy called $H\,24$ which is 30,000 times more powerful, 30,000 times quicker, 30,000 times more understanding and subtle, and this again is transformed into $H\,12$ which is still higher and infinitely more subtle and full of meaning, infinitely more receptive and understanding, infinitely richer and more sensitive. So you can see that the idea of decreasing entropy is shewn in the Work in terms of this First Conscious Shock, which increases energy in us and so diminishes entropy or satiety or sleep.

Now to return to the idea of sacrifice, which I connected with effort. You know the Work says there are endless useless forms of sacrifice. People think they have something to sacrifice and even imagine they are sacrificing themselves when they are not doing anything of the kind. For this reason the Work speaks very harshly about sacrifice at first. I have heard sentimental women at the earlier groups of Mr. Ouspensky asking what they should sacrifice and heard the reply: "What do you mean by sacrifice? You have nothing to sacrifice. It is all imagination." On the other hand I have heard him say: "There is only one thing you can sacrifice at present and that is your suffering." And I fancy many people hearing this reply went away like that rich young man in the Gospels who was so identified with his possessions and his merits and his legal sinlessness and who, asking Christ how he could gain eternal life, was told: "Go, sell that thou hast, and give to the poor, and thou shalt have treasure in heaven: and come, follow me." (*Matt.* XIX 21). Yes, here indeed we have something to sacrifice and I think you will agree with me that it begins with sacrificing our pictures of ourselves, our imaginary 'I' and False Personality, our eminent virtue and extraordinary merits that we so much cling to and with which we are so identified. But the Work teaches us more than this, if you reflect on it. Take this startling phrase that we have to sacrifice our suffering. Your self-pity increases entropy so rapidly. Have you noticed it? Do you have more energy to work through self-pity? Do you recall what Christ said when the disciples asked him: "Lord, increase our faith." He told them the parable about simply doing what you have to do without any sense of unusual merit or suffering or any self-pity:

"Who is there of you, having a servant plowing or keeping sheep, that will say unto him, when he is come in from the field, Come straightway and sit down to meat; and will not rather say unto him, Make ready wherewith I may sup, and gird thyself, and serve me, till I have eaten and drunken; and afterward thou shalt eat and drink? Doth he thank the servant because he did the things that were commanded? Even so ye also, when ye shall have done all the things that are commanded you, say, We are unprofitable servants; we have done that which it was our duty to do."

(*Luke* XVII 7-10)

This is interesting, for here one might say by *faith* is meant that which decreases entropy and frees energies which otherwise would suffocate us by flooding into the channels of self-merit, self-pity, appetite, sloth, and negative states. Only if we were to use this idea the question would be: "Lord, how can we decrease our entropy?" Do not we derive much of our ordinary sense of 'I' from making efforts with suffering? Then this is a bad sense of 'I' to work from. How indeed we often feel we have toiled and how much we feel we have suffered in silence. We never get the appreciation we feel owing to us. Also we sing many songs to ourselves. All this increases entropy and all this is the field of sacrifice that we are told to enter and work in, to begin with, because, as I said, it is the psychological man that has to change first. And it is a wonderful thing when the psychological man or woman begins to change in you. It is wonderful because you feel an entirely new access of energy. You begin to escape from the limitations you have unconsciously set for yourself. You begin to pass beyond those barriers that your attitudes have fashioned, to escape from this narrow little place in which you have so tightly and respectably lived. You begin to see the other side, this dark side. You begin to let this ray of light into this inner darkness. You begin to open other rooms in your house. You begin to be able to move about inside yourself. All this increases energy and decreases entropy. But you must find examples for yourselves from your own work and observation, and you must each find a clear example that you can be quite certain about and of which you can see the practical result without quibble or argument. The trouble is that people go on in this Work without getting a clear example through self-observation of, say, a negative thought, and so live in obscurity as to what it is all about. For this reason Mr. Ouspensky used to say: "I want examples, not theoretical talk. Give me a good example of self-observation or a moment of work on yourself, a moment of real effort consciously made." This is quite possible for everyone.

And to do this is far better than to write long theoretical essays on what self-observation is or should be or what mechanical reactions mean or what sleep means. Once you have got a good Work-memory for actual work done by yourself on yourself and from yourself, you will then have no difficulty in understanding that every genuine Work-effort increases energy and so decreases entropy. Perhaps you will understand how it is that all great religions with real esoteric teaching behind them have always as their aim certain kinds of efforts that a man can and should make in his life-time and without the making of which a man is not a MAN at all in the esoteric sense. I fancy that that hot kettle we spoke about, if it could give itself shocks, would get hotter and hotter—i.e. increase its energy while it still gave out energy. Kettles cannot do this but esotericism says that Man can, by giving himself the right shocks at the right times, and so reach an entirely different level of energy—not mechanical man who runs down early in life and becomes a long dead person, but a man seeking to become conscious and a man who by deliberate choice puts himself in the way of inner development, inner transformation, in accordance with a teaching that has come from those who have gone this way already.

Birdlip, April 14, 1945

THE WORK-IDEA OF YES AND NO

There are many things in the Work that we have heard but do not yet understand. Some people think that when they have heard a thing they know it and understand it, confusing knowing and understanding, and when they hear it again they tend not to listen or become impatient. They say: "Oh yes, we've heard that before. We have heard over and over again that we have to observe ourselves. We have heard that we have to remember ourselves. We know all that." So when they hear these words, these phrases, they become bored and pay no attention to what is being said. It is like being told that if you want to ride a bicycle you must balance yourself on it. You may hear this repeated often enough, but do you imagine you *understand* how to ride a bicycle just by hearing and knowing that you have to balance yourself on it? Just in the same way to observe oneself in terms of what the Work teaches takes long personal work and practice. And to realize by practice, what to "remember oneself" means, takes far longer. Simply to know lies in the external memory but to be able to practise and understand what you know is quite a different thing. So to begin to understand what self-observation is, and why it is necessary, is quite a different thing from just hearing and knowing that one should observe oneself.

To-day I am going to speak of something the Work teaches that many of you have heard before—i.e. that many of you know in your memory, but probably only in your memory. Remember that what you have only in your memory is not yet a part of yourself—of your being. You may know a lot in your memory but it is quite external to what you are. It is merely like a note-book with written words, not living. Let us take the Work-idea of Yes and No and recall what is said about this. The Work says that Formatory Centre—i.e. the mechanical part of Intellectual Centre—which we ordinarily use and call *thinking* can only work in terms of Yes *or* No. Through constantly using this lowest part of the thinking centre everything is divided into Yes or No. You know how people argue from Yes or No. One man says a thing is so and another man says it is not so. One man says a thing is true and another man says it is not true, and so on. All the world is divided like this. You have only to listen to most forms of ordinary conversation to realize that it is based on this division of Yes or No. The Work says that in Higher Centres this contradiction of Yes or No does not exist because in the consciousness belonging to Higher Centres there are no contradictions—i.e. there is no Yes *or* No—but there is a union of the two which the Work calls Yes *and* No. Obviously our ordinary thought and language utterly fail here. They cannot comprehend or describe that state of consciousness and understanding that belongs to Higher Centres. But if we cannot grasp this you will agree with me that our ordinary language is based on a sharp division of Yes or No, and our ordinary thinking is similar. This means that we always exclude one side of a problem in favour of the other side. So we have to take sides all the time and are regarded as weak if we do not. So we divide ourselves into opposite camps as the whole world does, and we continually hypnotize ourselves by saying that a thing surely must either be true or not true or that a person is either good or bad, and so on. All this is the work of the formatory part of the Intellectual Centre which can only think by means of opposites—that is, by comparison—and has no idea how to draw the opposites together and find a *third* solution which is neither Yes nor No but Yes and No.

The whole thing lies in this third solution. It is sometimes said that this Work is imitating the work of Higher Centres. Now, since all opposites are united in a harmony in Higher Centres and there are no contradictions, it is clear that thinking only by the aid of that lowest instrument of thought, the Formatory Centre, will certainly not be imitating Higher Centres. What is this third solution? It is not composed of either Yes *or* No but of some combination of Yes *and* No. We are told that this "Yes and No" is the language of Higher Centres and this must mean in some way that Yes and No are united into a third thing, a third solution unknown to us, which is neither Yes nor No, but some harmony or union of two opposites, so that each opposite vanishes or loses its identity and a new thing appears that we cannot comprehend. Let us call this third thing X. Then Yes + No. = X. Our ordinary solutions to problems are Yes or No. We do not know X. I sometimes think that Sly Man knows this X and how it is rightly reached. But we can be sure that if ever by accident we stumble on this third solution to some problem we will probably get a sudden force from Higher Centres, which deal only in X, no doubt much to our surprise. But if we solve our problem only by either a heavy Yes or a heavy No, no doubt we will not get any help—not being clever enough. You remember how often in the Gospels the *clever* person is mentioned, the five clever virgins, the clever man who built his house on a rock, and so on—the word being so badly translated as "wise". Yes, I am sure there are clever and right solutions to things which escape our heavy one-footed formatory thinking. And, since the Gospels have been mentioned, think only of the parables. Are they in terms of Yes or No? Are they not in another language—in fact, in the language of Higher Emotional Centre? However, people get impatient with them and say: "Why cannot they say exactly what they mean in plain, sensible, downright language—that is either Yes or No?" But are we sure that what we call plain, sensible, downright language is either so plain or so "sensible" as we suppose? Does it express all sides, or full meaning, or full truth, or is it one-sided and inevitably so? In any case, we can grasp that the language and ways of thought and connections of ideas in Higher Centres are quite different from our ordinary forms of speech and associations, and infinitely more comprehensive and inclusive. We make a dogmatic *Yes* or a dogmatic *No*—but experience shews us that this one-sided solution is always useless, always wrong. We have therefore to be far more careful—or more *clever*—in leading ourselves out of some inner or outer problem. It is not a flat denial or a flat affirmation that will help us, because we will miss all the many intermediate stages lying between these two violent extremes—all these inner octaves of finer meaning that we seek to become more conscious of in our daily life, all these sources of new meaning. I was going to say new and undreamed of meaning. But I fancy that often these finer meanings, finer solutions, are just what we do dream of without realizing it, not understanding the marvellous language which is so similar to that of parables. There is always so much meaning passing through us that we do not realize. The reason is that the activities of the Higher Centres are continually passing through us, only we cannot hear, cannot contact them—not having a fine enough receptive side. The Emotional Centre, purified of negative emotions, begins to hear them. But when we are identified and negative it cannot. So that is a good reason to work against states of negativeness and identification. By the way, just think of the solutions you make to problems when you are negative. There is nothing very clever about them, is there? Or again, when you are violently enthusiastic. In both cases you try to solve things through one or the other opposite—through No or Yes—in accordance with how the pendulum swings, from side to side. I am sure myself that such solutions are valueless and in fact are not solutions at all. But we all have many 'I's that think they are, and these 'I's tempt us to make impossible violent decisions that we cannot keep and by which we only torture ourselves. No, it is only when the pendulum is just one side or the other of the middle point that we can see where solutions may lie—and not when the pendulum has swung to its full extent in one direction or the other. The truth is that we are not usually conscious save in the extremes of the pendulum where we identify most. But by self-observation we become slowly more conscious in the middle region of the pendulum-swing and here something can be done. Here we have, as it were, to create a conscious pendulum, restricted in its movement, that swings a little one way and then a little the other way—and this by an effort of mind, by a pressure of will. This restriction is possible only when you no longer for one moment believe in the extreme violent swings of the mechanical pendulum—that is, when you absolutely reject all violent and excited decisions of any kind. One must not listen to the 'I's at either extreme of the pendulum. This we probably can all agree to from our own personal work on ourselves. But what does this to and fro movement of the restricted pendulum mean? It has to do with Yes *and* No.

Now suppose you are entirely unconscious of your reactions—that is, that you have absolutely no power of self-observation and are quite asleep. Then you will say Yes to all moods and all impressions. You will equally say Yes to an impression of dislike or of like. You are then doing no personal work, because you are asleep. You are precisely a machine—as the Work teaches. There is then no question of Yes *or* No; and certainly there is no question of the more difficult Yes *and* No. The subject can have no interest for you. Now suppose I am working on myself and I notice an impression of dislike. I see someone and mechanically react by dislike. Let us take this from Yes *or* No. I can say Yes to the mechanical reaction that this impression of this person makes in me, in which case I will probably think how I dislike him after I no longer see him as an external object. Now suppose I do not care for this inner state and wish to do something about it. I then can say *No* to the impression—that is, to its effect in me. Then when I see the person I say *No* to the mechanical reaction in me that the sight of him causes—and also I say *No* to any negative thoughts that come when I do not actually see him. This may work very well in some cases. It may be enough. The matter dies away. On the other hand, I may find myself still bothered with negative thoughts in spite of this *No* that I have said to myself. I then try to think generously of the person, to try to appreciate him, to be kind, and so on, and so get rid of opposite ideas and feelings. This may work a short time. Then I find that I am still bothered with him and seem unable to adjust myself. Now what have I been doing so far? I have been prac- tising the method, as it were, of Yes *or* No. That is, I am trying to solve the problem by identifying with one or with the other of the opposites. I am not trying to bring them together—that is, to practise Yes *and*

674

No. I have been trying to get a one-sided solution—or a solution on one side or the other. I have not mixed the black with the white and made a pattern of both, but have tried black and then white *separately*. I cannot explain this any further. It is very difficult to put into words. I can only say that if you can manage to use the second method Yes *and* No, you will get results that you cannot get with the method of Yes *or* No. In the method of Yes *and* No you go so far in thought and feeling in one direction and so far in the opposite—just *so* far—I mean, a short way only. This is like the to and fro movement of a restricted pendulum. A mixture or mingling results. This is quite different from mechanically swinging from like of a person one day to dislike of him the next. That leads to no mingling. The opposites are not brought together consciously. But in the Yes *and* No method the opposite aspects are brought together by a conscious act of the will.

Of course Imaginary 'I' and False Personality, which must always be right and can never be wrong, come into all this. However, when we observe ourselves in the right way and begin to include the other side, the unrecognized side, the side in darkness, we then change our feeling of ourselves and begin to know for a fact that we are both Yes and No in regard to everything. You often see people who are strongly based on Yes in regard to themselves and have no conception of No— that is, of an opposite contradictory side existing in them. They always tell the truth, they always do right and are right, they always know exactly what they are doing—in short, there is nothing wrong with them that matters. These are indeed Yes-men to themselves and they are indeed dead in themselves and to themselves. They cannot grow internally—i.e. they are *dead* in the Work-sense. When we are like that, we live in a very strange artificial relationship to ourselves which the Work never ceases to try to break down. It never ceases to try to break down this inner situation because unless it is broken down the person cannot become a real person but remains a purely invented imaginary person, and it may be quite true in many cases that this is just as well. But for a person who is not quite so sure of himself, who does not accept all his opinions and valuations without some doubt, who does not take himself for granted, there is a possibility of inner change. If he works he will gradually be shewn at the right time, by the action of the Work itself on him, where the No-side comes in—i.e. where he is not what he imagined and said Yes to. This all belongs to the lessening of the power of the Personality which until then has always been active and dominating. Unless the Personality becomes gradually passive there can be no growth of the essential side of a man. For the first stages of life Personality must be built up strongly, but for the second stage, the esoteric stage, this second education that esotericism seeks to give us, the Personality must become more and more passive and all the values we have attached to the Personality must undergo change. We can no longer be like what we were. This is not extraordinary if you think what this Work is about—namely, inner change—and how the method of self-observation, of new self-knowledge, is designed to change a man. If you wish to change you cannot remain the same because change means something different. Once Mr. Ouspensky said: "It would be very good for some of you to deliberately argue against what you hold to be right and true and good." He said: "Try to take the opposite standpoint deliberately at times and see what happens to you." He added that sometimes the result was to make you doubt your own opinions, your own *Yes*, and realize there are other points of view to which you cannot say No. And I remember once at a meeting that he assumed the position of a man who was going to argue about everything that was said in the Work and maintain it was not true, and I can assure you that many people were much startled and surprised—that is, people who had never really thought for themselves about the ideas of the Work but had simply religiously written them down in the note-books of their memory without questioning. The effect on those who had struggled from their own thinking was different. Why? Because they had let in the No-side and had come to some decision as a result and so could not be so easily shaken by doubts and contrary arguments but had found their own point of view for the time being.

Now in the Fourth Way we are none of us protected lambs, spoon-fed children, and we have to undergo all the temptations of Yes or No individually in connection with esoteric teaching and all the ideas behind it, otherwise we have no real point in the Work, as it is called, and then we are like those people mentioned in that marvellous parable called "the Sower and the Seed", which speaks of the sowing of esoteric ideas on Humanity, where it is said that those who hear the ideas a little but have no root wither away when the sun gets up. Supposing I walk into a meeting and say: "I don't believe this Work. It is all nonsense," what would some of you think? And suppose I spent, as O. did, some time in bringing all sorts of negative views to bear on the Work-teaching and did my best to undermine the whole thing—how would some of you react? You know it is sometimes said in the Work that you have to reach the stage in which you can be turned and twisted in every direction and yet you always eventually right yourself and point in the direction of the Work. Do you think this is possible unless you have met the No-side of yourself individually? One thing I am sure of, if you have simply said Yes to the Work without thinking about it, you will be overwhelmed by such a manifestation of No as I have indicated.

Now let us speak again about how we have to practise Yes *and* No in place of Yes *or* No. I have compared the practice of Yes and No with a kind of to and fro movement or friction, one movement corresponding to Yes and the opposite movement to No. You can imagine a movement of your hands going one way and then the opposite way. I told you in the example I gave that it was difficult to understand what this to and fro movement might mean and I said it could only be done consciously and with a kind of controlled restricted movement so that one only goes so far in one direction and so far in the opposite direction. This means that you cannot just feel and think mechanically about a person important for you, a situation important for you in the Work-sense. You have to control the mechanical movements of the pendulum and restrict them. This is quite different, as I said, from letting yourself go mechanically in a full swing of liking and disliking, loving and hating, or, let us add, elation and despair, enthusiasm and dejection, over-estimation and underestimation, disappointment and eager expectancy. You know how people who live in these mechanical swings are easily dashed or easily elevated and so, as it were, have no *middle part*. It is very important to create a middle part which is neither one extreme nor the other and it is in fact only from this middle part that one can grow—otherwise the opposites eat each other up, as it were, or cancel one another out. All that is strong and permanent in us must be wrested from the power of these extreme swings, protected from them. Emotional people particularly have this difficulty unless they use their other centres and become more balanced. We understand from the Work that our first aim is to become balanced—No. 4 Man—but this means far more than we can grasp at present and it means a proper and harmonious development of all centres. Sometimes instinctive types or moving types imagine they are extremely well-balanced and cannot understand the swings of the emotional type. But this balance that they flatter themselves about is no real balance: it is simply insensitiveness, a complete self-centredness, a pure selfishness or grossness of being, a lack of understanding, which cannot be commended and has nothing to do with the conception of the all-sided balanced man in the Work. For when a person lacks all capacity to think or feel he is just like an animal and is certainly not a balanced person but merely an ox or a cow. However, where such a person's appetites and comforts are concerned we may find considerable swings of the pendulum.

Now let me repeat that in this practice of Yes and No, in this conscious restriction of oneself to the middle part of the pendulum, having said Yes, you must go a little into No again until from this to and fro movement a solution is reached that is neither Yes nor No. You neither admit nor deny to yourself. This movement must become quicker and quicker until something emerges which is neither Yes nor No but is actually Yes *and* No. This is the third solution. If you can do this you will find an extraordinary result—namely, that you catch a glimpse of the person objectively as if the person were reflected in a mirror in you undistorted by your subjective attitudes. The scene then changes and perhaps for a long time you are undisturbed by the person. You are free from the person and not only that but the person is free from you. Then perhaps later the whole thing will start again and you have once more to do work of this kind if you can. Now unless you have already been able to see opposites and contradictory sides in yourself you will find this Yes or No friction impossible to understand. I say this because you have to do it also to yourself and see this dark opposite side of you that you are unconscious of. It is easy to take a negative view of yourself at times—at least it should be if you have had any power of observing yourself—but to rest on such a feeling is wrong. Negative 'I's directed towards yourself will then get hold of you. When we have reached the stage of being able to be negative towards ourselves and feel we are no good and so on, we have opened to us only unpleasant memories of ourselves. You all know that our memories are divided into two groups, pleasant and unpleasant. For example, when you are negative towards a person you can only remember the unpleasant things about that person, and vice versa. It is the same with ourselves. To give way to negative thoughts about oneself is useless—i.e. if we go too far into them —so we have to draw back from them by an opposite movement and in some way say Yes to ourselves. And this struggle between Yes and No in regard to one's relationship to oneself is in my experience as important as the same struggle with regard to other people. It is neither in Yes nor in No that the truth lies but in that combination called Yes *and* No.

Now this makes a mingling of dark and bright in us, a pattern of two opposites, a synthesis. As a result of this, we are immensely broadened and strengthened both towards ourselves and other people, although as I said in a previous paper it may seem to us as though we were losing our very identity, our very sense of ourselves. But this is exactly what we have to lose in order to change. All our values have to change, particularly some quite absurd values that we cling to in regard to our own integrity and self-estimation. For example, most of you are people who often lie, whatever your imaginary idea of yourself is—nor are any of you people who always lie. If you are going to put the question: "Am I a liar—yes or no?" you will get nowhere. The actual situation is Yes and No. It is both. In this respect you are not pure white nor pure black—but black and white. It is this stage that we have to reach and acknowledge first of all, this mingling which comes through direct self-observation and self-knowledge. From this mingling quite new things may start, far beyond us at present, in regard to inner development. But we have to reach a basis of this kind to begin with because this releases us from the Personality and shifts the centre of gravity of consciousness inwards towards that which can grow in us. This is the meaning of many phrases in esoteric literature to the effect that a man must lose himself, lose his attributes, lose all he has ascribed to himself, and it is what the Work calls making the Personality passive.

Now I will speak from a different angle about this subject. When you are in a state of real self-observation you can see different 'I's trying to take hold of you. You want to sit down, you want to rest, you want to eat, you want to smoke, you want to listen to some negative 'I's, you want to feel depressed, you want to feel bored, you want to feel wronged, you want to find fault, you want to hurt somebody, you want to get into a temper. You hear all these different 'I's speaking all round you and probably many others, and you say No to them all.

All these 'I's wish you to say Yes to them, to consent to what they suggest. Now to what do you have to say No? You have to say No to yourself and not to the others, and this is Self-Remembering. You do not say No to the 'I's but you say No to yourself. G. used to say: "In Self-Remembering which self do you wish to remember?" I do not suppose anyone will understand what I mean here but at the same time it may explain something that you may have experienced. In this state of agreement between 'I' and Myself, a state is reached in which no 'I's can touch you for the time being and although they wish you to say Yes and, as it were, beckon, 'I' and Myself have agreed together to say No, not to each 'I' individually, for that would simply lead to argument with them, which is nearly always fatal, but this agreement is rather a silence in which 'I' and Myself decide to say No to ourselves as if we could not be disturbed by any 'I's surrounding us, as if we were going to occupy ourselves with something quite different, as if 'I' and Myself were in some conversation with one another that none of these surrounding 'I's had any power over. This is the best description that I can give you at present of Self-Remembering —this agreement between 'I' and Myself. Let us not waste time asking what exactly 'I' means there or what Myself means but only recall that Self-Remembering means remembering and so contacting some self in us that lifts us above the power of the crowd of 'I's. Of course the state I describe is transitory but it is a quite different experience, nor must you expect that if you ever touch it everything is going to be quite easy afterwards. Remember that learning this Work, understanding it and doing it, is a task that lasts our whole life-time. Now I will only give you one hint of what 'I' and Myself means. There is something in us called the soul about which the Work rarely speaks but which it acknowledges. The Work says that the soul is a very small thing in us at present and is merely a point of intensity. The Work says that where we are most identified is where this point of intensity goes into some desire, some 'I'. The Work also says that this small thing called the soul must get much bigger and that this is only possible through not identifying with oneself and not always going with one's self-will, so perhaps you will see from this hint how it comes about that if 'I' and Myself are in agreement no surrounding 'I's in me have any power.

Now will you please discuss first of all this idea of Yes and No— this restricted movement consciously controlled between what we usually take as our good and bad sides.

A REMINDER OF WHAT THE WORK IS ABOUT

One of the objects of this Work, this teaching, is to observe oneself. Self-observation is a method of self-change. This Work teaches that a man, a woman, can change. Why? The Work teaches that everyone is created in such a way that they can change. We are created as self-changing beings. We can change—not anyhow, but in a definite direction. The Work says we are created as self-developing organisms —like seeds. A seed can remain a seed, but it is a self-developing organism. Can we understand this? Is it clear? Is a seed capable of some definite development? This Work, the Gospels, and all esoteric teaching, is older than history. How, then, can we put ourselves in the right conditions in order to change? A seed must be planted to develop, and have the right food, air and light. So it is with us, if we become planted in the ground of esoteric teaching. This is not a fanciful idea. It is not an idealistic idea. It is not a pious idea. It is not a sentimental idea. It is a fact. Given the right conditions, a man, a woman, can begin to undergo what he and what she were originally created for. We were *not* created merely to live in life. Life does not develop a man or a woman finally. It is the first and necessary experience. But it only goes so far—that is, to the formation of Personality. Here it stops and nothing more happens. The man, the woman, having attained to this first, this necessary, development of the Personality—namely, of the profession, the craft, the business, the labour, the civilian duty, the good householder—remain then undeveloped any further in the sense of esoteric teaching. The man, the woman, having attained to such life-positions, to such successes, to such situations, then begin to die. They have become "equal to life". It must be said that many do not get as far as that. However this is the first task—the life-task. A man, a woman, must learn, must get to know, something definite in life before anything else is possible. They must be good at something, know something, be able to do something. That is why, in this Work, it is said that a man or a woman must start from the level of good householder. This Work is not for useless people, or people who live on the being and vitality of others. Such are not at the level of good householder. The Work can only begin with people who have reached a certain attainment in life and in life-experiences and who are not evil or criminal or pathological or perverted. The Work is not for the riff-raff of life, the people who are a nuisance and a burden to others, or for those who expect something for nothing. It is for responsible people—for people who understand the difference between chaos and order and see clearly that certain things must be done, however they feel personally. There is a Work-definition of 'good householder' in the supreme sense of this stage— namely, a person who does what is necessary in life but does not believe in life. This is a curious phrase and is worth reflecting upon all one's life—for many good householders believe in life, and believe · that sooner or later life will become much better than it is now. They believe in progress, in spite of things as they are. But this impulse, this idea, really is one that takes a wrong and outward direction. Progress is possible—and here esoteric teaching, this second education, comes in. A man, a woman, can progress in themselves. They can undergo a definite development by giving up what they have come to think they are. This is where self-observation starts. In my case, Nicoll—the Personality formed by life, what life has made in me, my opinions, my bias, my conceit, etc.—must gradually be separated from—through my observing Nicoll. In your case, it is your own life-built Personality that must be observed by each of you: gradually—all the time—and also at intervals—until something separates from it. This thing that separates is what can grow. Then you no longer wholly regard yourself as yourself, as your meritorious life, your virtues. *I* begin to see Dr. Nicoll. *He* begins to see Mr. Wilshin. *He* begins to see Mr. Parfit. *He* begins to see Mr. Taylor, and so on. That is, we begin to see what is not us—what life has built up in us—what we have hitherto solely taken as ourselves. The method of this slow, gradual shifting of the feeling of oneself begins with the slow, gradual observing of oneself —noticing oneself. It does not begin with going against oneself. How is this possible when one does not know oneself? How can you go against something you do not know? So it is necessary to begin with self-observation, carried over years—in fact, all one's life. This ray of light, this ray of consciousness, arising from noticing oneself, that begins to enter into the darkness, the ignorance of oneself, very slowly brings about a change. This is the beginning of this inner development of which the Work speaks so much. Things may and do go on just the same, for a long time. But one notices them. One is not asleep to them. If they are observed often, continually, at intervals, they slowly begin to alter. You cannot alter yourself directly. You can only alter by means of certain kinds of effort. These efforts are shewn us. There is the great effort of non-identifying—not identifying, with yourself, to begin with. (What a fine fellow I am!). There is the great effort of Self-Remembering. This is the first effort of all, but very difficult. There is the great effort of self-observation. There is the great and continual effort of living more consciously towards yourself, towards others in the Work and towards the Work itself. All this in- creases consciousness. Things alter by your becoming more conscious, more aware of them, by observation, by noticing without criticism, by gradual separation from them. Do you realize that to observe oneself and then criticize oneself at once is useless? Now if a person asks: "How does one alter?" or "What does one alter into?" the answer is that everyone has something which they can become if they practise the Work, and which they are destined to be. This is perfecting oneself—a phrase in the Gospels. If they observe, notice, and non-identify, they will inevitably begin to alter into what they were created to be, which

681

is not what they are in the Personality. A seed alters into what it was created to alter into, to change into, to transform itself into. So it is with us. This is what the Work teaches about ourselves. This short paper is to remind us what the Work is about.

Quaremead, Ugley, April 21, 1945

FURTHER NOTE ON THE WORK-IDEA OF YES AND NO

A question was asked at one of the groups after the last paper had been read: "If one had memory of the swing of the pendulum and of one's thoughts and feelings of the opposite—would one be less identified?" To this question I would say: Why, certainly, this is the whole point. The paper made it clear that we remember only on one side *or* the other, not both together. It was said, for example, that when we are negative we tend to remember only unpleasant things, and vice versa. Everyone must see how he swings between opposites in the Intellectual Centre and in the Emotional Centre (and also in the Instinctive Centre). What have you done to-day, all of you? Have any of you done any work on yourselves? Have you taken in impressions of one another from a negative swing and not attempted to remember opposite kinds of impressions that you may have had at other times? Remember, you must bring the opposites together consciously. For this you must have a Work-memory, a new memory, arising through self-observation. Do not get confused by these terms, pendulum and opposites. Do you not think that you already know in a way that everything swings to and fro inside one, between hope and despair, between liking and disliking, between feeling cheerful and feeling depressed, between thinking that something is true and thinking that it is not true? All these are pendulum-swings between two opposites, going in different directions all the time, all with their different times like different kinds of clocks. You will think it very strange when you are told there has to be one clock eventually instead of these many hundreds of clocks all keeping different times.

Now every thought or feeling that comes into your consciousness has an opposite. When you identify with the thought or the feeling you are under its power and are on the pendulum, and insensibly, without your knowing how or even remembering, you will find yourself having the opposite thought or opposite feeling without seeing any contradiction. This is just where our unconsciousness lies, our living state of sleep, in which we do not see our contradictions. Mr. Q. once said that when the pendulum is swinging down it is going fastest when it passes the middle point, and then as it rises on the other side it goes slower and slower until it reverses its movement. He said: "We are not quick enough to feel this movement because we work with too slow a hydrogen and so we are conscious (in the ordinary sense) at the two opposite ends." Now it is very wonderful when you begin to understand that you need not go with your mechanically arising thoughts and feelings, and you have heard this many times from me before, but I am sure that a great number of you do not understand what it means practically. We must, it was once said, learn to rule our minds. And we were told that this takes a very long time and a great deal of work and observation. I fancy that some of us on first hearing this did not imagine for a moment that it applied to ourselves. No doubt we thought that we ruled our minds absolutely. However, when a man begins to observe himself and becomes interested in his self-observation, he very soon realizes, of course, that he rules nothing within the psychological world of himself. In this invisible world in which each one of us lives we control nothing. Our thoughts come to us we know not how. Sometimes they come in swarms. And the strange thing is that we take them as our own thoughts and play them on our own piano, as it were, as if they were true. I do not know how to describe this taking of thoughts as one's own, just as I cannot describe the miracle of realizing that they are not oneself and they need not be made one's own, that one need not believe them, that one need not go with them, that one need not take them as true, and, finally, that any thought of any kind can come to us at any moment. And, of course, in the latter case, if you are not awake (just notice what being awake means) then this thought will convince you, it will be your way of thinking for that moment, and this is just exactly what we have to separate from through non-identifying almost continually. There is a phrase: "A person is listening to his thoughts." This is a very good phrase, but I do not think it is true. I would like you to discuss this. I would rather say that we do not listen to our thoughts, but we are them. Perhaps when we get rather horrified at what we are thinking we may stop, but as a rule these thoughts come in by themselves and play our piano and we think it is ourselves playing, that it is our music. The whole position has to be reversed. To be like that is just to be a machine in which the mind rules us and the thoughts make us think them. You have a thought: "Oh, how tired I am," or "How hard my life is," or something like that. Have you got sufficient inner observation? Have you cleared and well dug a big space in your mind through the practice of inner attention and put a hedge round it and a gate so that you can hear the click of the gate and watch this darling little thought coming up the drive all ready to say: "Oh, how tired I am," etc.? I fancy that once we let it in very far every thought gets hold of us and wrings us, takes our blood, makes us react, talk, behave, in a certain way, and then, satisfied with having dined off us, it retires for a time.

Now, to return to the pendulum, you will not be able to bring opposite thoughts and feelings together consciously unless you have some distinct memories of them recorded in your Work-memory, as I call it. That is the new memory that arises in us all when we begin to practise a life of self-observation, when we begin to live more consciously, not only with other people but when we are alone with ourselves. Can you remember that you appreciate some things in a person and have often done so, when you are negative with that person and can only *mechanically* remember negative things? The bringing of these two psychic acts together, these two memories, is working, not between Yes or No, but between Yes and No. If one does this gradually one does not swing so far in either liking or disliking, knowing how treacherous the country is beyond, and how asleep one is, if one gets into it. This not going very far one way or the other requires inner awareness and a certain inner alertness. It makes everything much more intense. One sees what one has to do. It is not to be confused with indifference. Conscious restraining of the pendulum is utterly different from a state of indifference. One is conscious, the other mechanical. There are many parables and images about this scattered through esoteric literature, such as driving two powerful horses, black and white, and restraining them in the right proportion, and many other images.

Now if you do not go with a thought you are free from it for the time being. The force that might have gone into it does not go into it. In what direction should the force go? It is often said that self-observation should always eventually be carried out in connection with Self-Remembering. In fact, Self-Remembering is really taught first in the Work. The point is that the force that you withdraw from one or the other side of the opposites should pass in the direction of Real 'I'. We attempt to remember ourselves because we have no Real 'I'. Now no one can get to an experience of Real 'I' (save in an illegitimate way, by drugs, for which he has to pay afterwards) without a certain emotional state which I will simply call evaluation of the Work. When a person works without any real individual feeling, without any sense of wonder, that person's work will be on too low a level—that is to say, it will be in too small 'I's, in small parts of centres. Naturally enough, these cannot make contact with Higher Centres or Real 'I'. So if a person works on such a level only there will be nothing real, and nothing new will enter the understanding because the force that has been gained from non-identifying with inner states has nowhere to go to and so may, as it were, flood back. I have often told you that you cannot, as far as I know, remember yourselves unless you have a sense of something greater—for instance, if you do not believe in Greater Mind, you cannot raise yourself emotionally to all the conceptions of the Work which concern the Conscious Circle of Humanity, the level of awakening, the level of Objective Consciousness, the attainment of Real 'I', nor will such great diagrams as the Ray of Creation and many others mean anything to you at all. It is very unfortunate when a person is in this state. Sometimes it arises because a person has not perhaps sufficient background, has not perhaps read and thought enough about the struggle of esoteric teaching with mechanical humanity. But this belongs to another conversation—about valuation and what is most important to us—that is, what we value most, which we do not notice and do not suspect.

ON BRINGING THE OPPOSITES TOGETHER

In the last few commentaries on some of the Work-ideas we have been speaking about ordinary decisions made on the basis of Yes *or* No. In this connection we brought in the idea of the law of the pendulum. The psychological pendulum swings from one side to the opposite side. I mentioned how Mr. O. had remarked that we are conscious in the ordinary sense at the opposite swings of the psychological pendulum. We are not conscious of the intermediate stages. He said that the pendulum moves fastest at the middle point and that with our slow hydrogens that subserve our ordinary so-called waking state of consciousness, which is always compared with a state of sleep in the Work, we have not the quickness of inner perception, of consciousness, of the power of registering, of catching finer octaves of meaning, that belong to the neighbourhood of the middle parts of the pendulum. He added that in every situation that we are faced with, especially when identified with it, we do not catch the finer degrees of these situations, the finer meanings, and that if we could work with the speed of emotional perception—that is, with *Hydrogen 24*—and still more so with *Hydrogen 12*—a great wealth of new meaning and new insights would be the result. We would see far finer differences, quite different solutions to the problems with which we are confronted and we could realize what immense distances of meaning really lie between what we usually regard as continuous. But as we are, our psychological life, our inner invisible life, is ordinarily controlled by *Hydrogen 48* and it is particularly the formatory part of the Intellectual Centre that works with this slow hydrogen, this heavy petrol. As you know, the Work teaches that in the formatory part, our thinking, our whole mental outlook, is only capable of expressing itself in terms of Yes *or* No. It is taught that, by contrast, Higher Centres work in terms of Yes *and* No. This means that our ordinary thinking that we trust so much and follow so much is not really thinking. It works only with the exclusion of one side and the affirmation of the other opposite side, or vice versa. For this reason, the whole world of men and women, classes and nations, is divided into opposite camps, people on one side or the other side. So too we plague one another all day long with questions such as: "Do you believe this or not?" "Do you like this or not?" "Are you a this or a that?" There is a rather over-used phrase in the Work to the effect that the formatory part of the mind is "Third Force blind". This means it is always swinging between these opposites—this Yes or No—and has no Neutralizing Force—no Yes and No—no harmonizing force—which brings the opposites together into a combination, one that we cannot understand ordinarily. This union of the opposites, this reconciling force, is a *third thing*, a Third Force, connecting both opposites and yet different from either.

Let us recall one of the definitions of Third Force which lies between the two opposite and mutually destructive forces called active and passive. It is defined as the relating force. It is a force which partakes of both sides of any question, and brings them into a new relation, into a synthesis, and yet is neither of them. I called it in the last paper "X"—i.e. something unknown to us as we are at our level of understanding. I asked you if you did not get tired, after being a long time in this Work and following the path of self-observation, of making sudden decisions which are practically always overwhelmed by an opposite result from what you expected. We make some aim in one swing of the pendulum and cannot keep it or are surprised to notice that it rouses the opposite side. Naturally, because an aim made from one side of the swing of the pendulum is made without calculation of Second Force—the force of resistance to it. Yet at first we must make aim of this kind because we have to realize that we cannot do in the ordinary violent sense. This introduces us gradually to the idea of what it means that we cannot *do* in the greatest sense—namely, that we must have help. Now help is always coming to us from the Higher Centres which are fully developed and are always working in us, always speaking to us—in fact, always telling us what to do—and I think here I do not exaggerate. But we cannot understand this language, this help, because it is in terms of Yes *and* No, in terms of this "X", this middle solution. Our formatory part especially cannot possibly hear the messages from Higher Centres because it is always dividing everything up into two contradictory statements, into Yes or No, into two opposites, which appear to be irreconcilable. But there is a point in the swing of the pendulum, although it is here going fastest, a point right in the middle of the two sides of this swing, where utterly new meaning enters. Although we cannot hope to be sufficiently awake, sufficiently alert, internally, to hear, to understand, to catch and to register, what happens at this point, we can gradually dissuade ourselves from following the suggested solutions that arise when we are at one full swing or the other. I mean, we begin to distrust the range of thoughts and feelings belonging to these extreme swings, these opposites, in which we are usually conscious in the ordinary second state of consciousness. We begin to dislike this coarse division, this coarse language, these coarse solutions—in fact, these violent solutions to our problems. We begin to know that they are useless and that some far finer adjustments are necessary.

Now if you take an ordinary person who is very opinionated you will agree with me that he will always take one side or the other of a question of opinions. Talking many years ago of the union of opposites, Mr. O. once said we must learn to argue from opposite viewpoints. An opinionated man—and of course this means ourselves—often begins by saying: "I always think, I always say . . . " and so on. Now if our inner psychological state rests on a basis of this kind we cannot do this Work. The psychological groundwork is all wrong. Let us take pictures of ourselves. You know very well a woman, a man, with strong pictures of herself or himself, after a little conversation. They have a certain idea of themselves—open or concealed. They have certain opinions. They take such and such viewpoints, but they do not necessarily realize this. Now the object of the Work on its practical side is to let a ray of light into the inner darkness of ourselves, this not-perceived side. Light means consciousness. We have a dark side of ourselves, a side in darkness that we do not see. In regard to pictures of ourselves, what is the result of light? The result is the seeing of a part of the darkness and bringing it into consciousness. This is an extension of consciousness —an increase of consciousness. You have often heard that the Work is to increase consciousness—first of ourselves, then of other people, because that is the only possible order. A man, through self-observation, increases the consciousness of himself. He no longer lives only in the front garden, but begins to walk round his house and so perform a circle. This inclusion in consciousness of what he did not know, as in the case of seeing what we are instead of living in pictures, in Imaginary 'I', brings together opposites. The effect of light falling on pictures of our-selves is therefore to change the whole feeling, the whole idea, of our-selves. False personality, Imaginary 'I', pictures, and many other things, keep us on one side of ourselves. We do not see, we do not know, and certainly do not acknowledge, the other side. So we live in a wrong relation to ourselves and, as was said, the Work cannot start from this basis. It cannot start from a one-sidedness.

*   *   *

Let us think about this dark side into which light must gradually penetrate. We can begin with the idea of different kinds of people, according to the development of centres in them. In the language of the Work a No. 1 man is a man whose centre of gravity, psychologically, is in his Instinctive-Moving Centre. A No. 2 man is in the Emotional Centre. A No. 3 man is in the Intellectual Centre. Now there are six formulations for men and women from this angle. A person may be 123, 132; 231, 213; 312, 321. This means that a man whose formula-tion as regards centres is 123 is first of all No. 1—that is, in instincts and movements—and more rarely in 2—that is, in emotional perception—and still more rarely in 3—that is, in intellectual thoughts. He is therefore an unbalanced man, a one-sided man. What then is the dark side of him in this respect? The dark side is formed by the undeveloped and so not yet properly conscious sides that lie in 2 and 3—that is, in emotional life and in intellectual life. And so with the rest of the formulations. In every case the undeveloped functions lying in the dark side may take many undesirable automatic manifestations. We can conceive that one of the many forms of swing of the pendulum in a man may be a swing sometimes between the more developed side of him lying in the light, and the less developed side lying in what is dark to him. His task then is to observe and notice and bring into the light of his own consciousness of himself, by private insight, this undeveloped dark side, and so educate it. This will result in an inner growth, an inner development of the person. It is for this reason that I said the dark side, into which the Work tells us that we must send a ray of light, can be both good and bad. Pictures are always bad. But undeveloped functions are only bad if left in the dark. If brought forward by constant observation and reflection—and here of course the complacent man is incapable of shifting his basis—they begin to add to the life, to increase meaning and interest and give new impressions. But the feeling of oneself will change. A one-sided, one-centre man feels himself in a particular way. If his other centres begin to come forward, then naturally he will lose his former feeling of himself, and many dislike this gradual transformation, and refuse it and think it an evil thing. But the devil is always the dark side, what we are ignorant of. Some people, for example, think it wicked to read novels, and so on, in endless ways. I believe there are still sects that think it wicked to learn anything. That must furnish them with a special extra-sized devil. They are really devil-worshippers without knowing it—that is, worshippers of ignorance, of darkness, of everything strict and narrow, and unmerciful. You will remember that a great deal was said about the Pharisees in the Gospels—that is, this narrow thing in ourselves. Remember that everything said in the Gospels is psychological and applies here and now to ourselves. Have you studied your own Pharisee?

★   ★   ★

Now we can come, in this commentary, to another aspect of this dark side, the side lying beyond our small range of consciousness. I will begin by saying that in the example of having pictures of ourselves that are quite different from what we are, what contradicts these forms of imagination, of vanity, of pictures of ourselves, is in darkness—we are ignorant of it. The difficulty here is that we do not even see the pictures. People can have a picture of having no picture. We do not think we have any pictures. But when you are upset or unpraised it is as well to look at some picture at work in you. This may help it to be observed. Then a very interesting process of work on oneself begins —first seeing the picture and then observing what contradicts it. This is a harmonizing process, a bringing together of opposites, both lying in darkness and acting on us beyond our control, as everything

688

does that is not standing in recognition, in acceptance, in the light of consciousness.

This drawing together of opposite things, this making outer and inner the same, this going against one-sidedness, which prevents the action of the mechanical pendulum and places consciousness increasingly towards the centre, the middle, where Yes and No exist, strengthens the whole being. As I said, nothing can grow save through this process, which destroys all self-conceit and makes you feel another kind of person. You then, as it were, can walk round the whole of your house, front and back, and then things can begin. Why? Because you can begin to understand the language of Yes and No, in which Higher Centres speak to us, as it were, in the language of parables. I will add briefly that it is only in higher divisions of centres that all such work is possible. The lowest divisions, as formatory part, can only work in Yes *or* No. And you can only get into higher divisions of centres through valuation of the Work. These higher parts gradually pass towards Higher Centres.

I will now quote some of the Sayings of Christ found in the Gospels and in some of the recent discoveries of Papyruses, referring to making inner and outer the same. In the Sermon on the Mount given in Matthew, Christ says:

"If therefore thou art offering thy gift at the altar, and there rememberest that thy brother hath aught against thee, leave there thy gift before the altar, and go thy way, first be reconciled to thy brother, and then come and offer thy gift. Agree with thine adversary quickly, whiles thou art with him in the way; lest haply the adversary deliver thee to the judge, and the judge deliver thee to the officer and thou be cast into prison . . ." (*Matthew* V 23-25)

Then there are Christ's words to the Pharisees when a certain Pharisee "marvelled that he had not first washed before dinner":

"The lord said unto him, Now do ye Pharisees cleanse the outside of the cup and of the platter; but your inward part is full of extortion and wickedness. Ye foolish ones, did not he that made the outside make the inside also? Howbeit give for alms those things which are within; and behold, all things are clean unto you." (*Luke* XI 39-41)

Among the Sayings of Christ not included in the Gospels are the following:

"When the Lord was asked by a certain man, when should his kingdom come, He saith unto him: When two shall be one, and the without as the within, and the male with the female, neither male nor female."—i.e. active and passive are replaced by Third Force.

And again :

"If ye make not the below into the above and the above into the below, the right into the left and the left into the right, the before into the behind (and the behind into the before) ye shall not enter into the kindgom of God."

THE SITUATION TO-DAY

In regard to the general situation in the world at this moment, what does the Work teach? Many feel that everything will soon be quite different, and that various conferences, agreements and so on, will permanently alter the future. They think exactly in the way that the majority of people thought at the termination of the last great European War. It is not beyond the question to say that in this new war that has touched the civilian population so deeply people may naturally expect a better re-statement of the future and a better order arising out of the universally shared suffering. Let us examine this idea from the Work-side and see what the Work teaches about humanity on this minute planet. Let us particularly examine wrong *attitude*. As you know, scientific men, astronomers, mathematicians, and so on, take the attitude that this minute speck, the Earth, is the only inhabited point in the infinitely vast creation of millions and millions of galaxies, suns and planets. What do you think of this mental attitude? Here, on this small Earth, we are first of all an insignificant point in the Milky Way—a galaxy of billions of suns, some of gigantic size. And again, our galaxy is only one of millions of other more gigantic galaxies or sun-clusters. You know that earlier scientific thought viewed the vast Universe of celestial bodies as all turning round our minute Earth. We were the centre. Certainly, to the evidence of the senses, it seems as if the sun went round and round the Earth and all the hosts of heaven, all the constellations, all the galaxies and innumerable suns which compose them. When it was discovered that the Earth by its own rotation makes it appear that the heavens turn round it and that our Sun rises and sets, the idea was treated with contempt and hatred. People said and felt that we, on this Earth, were the most important thing, and all the rest, all the stars, served us, so to speak. Is this egotism? Is it not a wrong attitude? Is it not a remarkable form of conceit and vanity? As I said, even now scientists teach that it is improbable that any life exists save on this speck of dust, our Earth. I repeat, is this some extraordinary vanity, some total lack of understanding of our own relative importance? I see no signs of this viewpoint, this mental attitude, changing to-day. We seem to imagine apparently that we are the only real living point in the inconceivable vastness of the creation.

Now the Work teaches that the whole of creation is living and that we are almost insignificant, almost totally unimportant, and that if our Earth blew up it would not be noticed or make any difference. Sometimes people say to me that they are not interested in cosmic diagrams—as the Ray of Creation—although the psychological teaching is interesting. But this Work, like all esoteric teaching, connects Man with the Universe in which he appears. To study him by himself, apart from the Universe, is erroneous, and cannot give the right emotions. Man as a microcosmos, a minute world, represents in himself the macrocosmos or Great Universe. The one is modelled on the other. They are in correspondence and nothing is in Man that is not in the Universe. And just as the Sun is greater than the Earth, and the Earth is greater than the Moon, so are there psychological *levels*, lower and higher, lesser and greater, in Man representing Moon, Earth and Sun—that is, corresponding internally with these external sense-seen beings, Moon, Earth and Sun.

Now you know from what is taught, and perhaps know through self-observation, that pride and vanity are two giants that keep us asleep and that walk in front of us and decide everything beforehand. Here notice, please, a man who admires himself. Is he asleep? Suppose then that you are a person who is scientifically convinced that only this Earth is peopled and that the rest of the Universe is dead matter. Will this help you to deal with these formidable giants that take charge of us and actually ruin everything for us? I do not see that this standpoint can do otherwise than swell up our self-importance and keep up the unreal side, the False Personality, that characterizes our present level of being. However, sometimes we look at the stars and feel our own smallness. Science should have increased our sense of wonder. It has done the reverse. It has no message save that everything is meaningless. This decrease in meaning, and therefore in understanding, is noticeable on all sides. This results in the loss of certain emotions necessary to Man for his right development. You can call such emotions by what names you like, but they all have the effect of making a man feel that he is a very small creature—and that opens him internally to the possible action of Higher Centres in him, which constantly seek to send him messages. Egoism stunts a man internally and turns him outwards, into objects, into things, into the body, into the external sense-given world—which is only one side of a man. This is one way of understanding what the Work means when it says that to-day Man is one-sided. So Man sees the solution of everything to-day as lying only outside himself and not in self-change—in manufacturing more machines, more objects, more complex things outside himself, and not in an increase of consciousness or an increase of understanding. And so machines make war on him. You may be quite certain that the next war will soon arise from new machines, of which we can catch a glimpse already. Man with his characteristic violence, his lack of understanding and self-observation, is already busied with new destructive machines and at the same time attending conferences to produce peace. This is a lack of consciousness, an incapability of seeing contradictions in himself. This incapability, this lack of consciousness, is one of the signs of our level of being. The object of the Work—of all esoteric teaching—of the Gospels —is to increase consciousness. And this begins by seeing what you are like for yourself, penetrating the dark side that lies beyond the pretence of False Personality. This is the first point—namely, that with our present lack of consciousness, with our present level of being, it is impossible to stop war. Only by an increase in consciousness can war be stopped. Our level of being attracts our life. So humanity attracts war.

The next point is that the Work teaches that Man cannot do. Everything happens in the only possible way it can happen. Everything is going to go in the only way it can go and nothing can prevent it. Yes, but one thing must be added. If mankind awoke from sleep, then everything would go differently. Why? Because if people began to see, to awaken, to become more conscious, their level of being would change, and so another order of things would be attracted by them, and war and many other things would cease. If man lived on a higher level of himself, everything would change. One thing would be that he would cease to be violent. He would overcome his own violence.

The third point is that sleeping humanity on this Earth is *used*. The suffering, pain, illness, violence, the killing, hatreds, revenge, and so on, are being used *for certain purposes* by something outside the Earth. A man can escape from this, by certain kinds of useful suffering that awaken him. But I will not speak more of this point here.

The fourth point is that our general level of being is characterized by *lying* and that this makes any real agreement impossible. Mr. O. once said that we should study lying in all its forms—our own lying and lying in general. He said we really need instruction on the subject of lying—that is, we must realize and study lying and its terrific power. On one occasion he remarked that the formatory part, from one angle, could be thought of as being given to us to lie with. Now how can you get anything right if you and everyone else lie? Lying characterizes our level of being and so it is one of the things which must change if our level of being is to be changed. I will make some brief notes on lying to remind you of what has been previously said. Nothing is what it pretends to be. Begin with yourself. Are you what you pretend to be? I mean, seriously, do you think so? Again, look at a peacock strutting. Is it a lie? Then look at yourself. Again, all propaganda is organized lying. Officialdom is packed with lies from top to bottom. All politics is based on lying—not necessarily clever. When one speaks one lies usually. Even to say 'I' is lying, for which 'I' do you mean? The whole apparatus for lying, the machinery for its propaganda, has been enormously increased in this century. What is the radio used for? It has been extensively and often only used for the propaganda of lies. Imagine how much work would have to be done, what effort would be needed, to make humanity able to see through propaganda, newspapers, films, radio, and resist their lies. People let their very souls become absorbed in films about imaginary people and imaginary life. It is all lies. It is a very good thing, however, to resist a film by not identifying with it. Then the strange force working on the imagination does not eat you. A great many things could be added about lying, such as that all negative states are due to lies and produce only lies.

A last point that I will make is that we forget very easily. People forget what things were like once, and also new people are growing up. This makes war very soon possible again. If we were all more conscious, then war would cease. But this is impossible. It is impossible for everyone to be more conscious. It is a matter of the greatest difficulty for one person to become more conscious.

You have noticed how all people who have taken momentary charge of the world base themselves on war. All the Hasnamous type, those whose well-being depends on the ill-being of others, all dictators, ground themselves on war. It shews how deeply Man's level of being attracts war and how the disease of war is in Man, and due to his own state. Since Man's level of being is the same as it was, then everything will go in the only possible way in which it can go at that level, and no one will be able to *do* anything. G. said once:

"Everything is being done in the only way it can be done. If *one* thing could be different *everything* could be different. And then perhaps there would have been no war. Everything is dependent on everthing else, everything is connected, nothing is separate. Therefore everything is going in the only way it can go. If people were different everything would be different. They are what they are, so everything is as it is."

Quaremead, Ugley, May 13, 1945

COMMENTARY ON EMOTIONAL CENTRE

To-night let us try to speak about the Emotional Centre. The Work teaches that the most difficult centre to control is the Emotional Centre. In so many words it says that the Formatory Centre (that is, the mechanical division of the Intellectual Centre) can to some extent be controlled and also the Moving Centre which controls all our movements. Mr. O. once said that the Emotional Centre was like a mad elephant and that in India when an elephant in service went mad it was necessary to find two sane elephants and put them on either side of the mad elephant with ropes so as to teach him right behaviour.

Let us think what this means. Thoughts can after a time be controlled voluntarily to some extent. Also movements—such as looking sulky which is a muscular manifestation of the face—can be controlled to a small extent voluntarily. But the Emotional Centre is involuntary —that is, beyond one's direct control. Let us take only the voluntary Moving Centre. You can control it, can you not? You can walk faster or slower, you can smile or frown. This is due to the contraction and relaxation of muscles. The Moving Centre presides over muscles. That is easy to understand. I can extend my arm or not. I can put my tongue out or not. That means that I have direct control over the muscles that subserve these movements. But can I control in the same way my emotions, my feelings of dislike or liking? You will agree that this centre, which is the most important centre of all, is not directly under our control. So it is called the mad elephant and has to be controlled at first by the two other elephants—the Intellectual Centre which thinks and the Moving Centre which acts. Let us take the example of finding oneself with a negative emotion towards someone, and let us suppose that one's aim at the moment is not to manifest, not to shew, not to consent entirely to, this negative feeling, say, one of strong dislike. It is possible in such a case to observe the Intellectual Centre—the thoughts that cluster and wish to gain consent at that moment—and not go with them. It is also possible to relax the muscles and not get "worked up" muscularly, frown and hold oneself in a certain antagonistic posture, speak with a certain harshness and so on. This can control at least the external expression of the negative state of Emotional Centre. Of course, if you really believe in your negative emotions and are doing all this in, so to speak, a social way, the result is negligible. The merit goes into your Personality—you become a kind of fox. I mean, you become a very insincere person. But if you have come to the point of disliking your mechanical dislike, disliking having your inner chemistry made negative, in fact, hating being negative and understanding what it means to be negative—how, for example, it always means that you have no psychological courage, no idea of what is necessary from the Work point of view, no inner battle, no inner strength—in short, unless you see you have always lost the Work-battle if you become identified and negative and believe you are right—then you do not yet understand how the Work shifts the battle-area into yourself and looks eventually only at that side—this inner side—or, if you like, this psychological side.

The psychological side is the man himself, the woman herself. You may treat a person outside you well. Yes, but how do you treat the person internally, in your psychological world—this invisible world known only to yourself? After a time in the Work, if it begins to act on you, you feel far more uncomfortable through wrong feeling than through anything you may have done outwardly. The Work is not mainly about outer life, but about inner life, and here sincerity and valuation are necessary—not pious, not artificial, but genuine. You can feel a fool for having behaved wrongly externally but you must begin to feel worse than a fool if you have silently, in the privacy of your internal psychological life, your real life, treated a person in a mean and miserable way in your thoughts and feelings, though no one knows it. So it has often been said to you that it is how we treat people internally, invisibly, in mind and feeling, that counts. The commandment: "Thou shalt not murder," means, esoterically, in one's inner life. It has a psychological meaning apart from a literal one. I fancy that some of you now know what I mean and what inner wretchedness can arise when one speaks to oneself negative things about others, and enjoys them, and then plasters up one's face and appears externally as an angel. The inner and the outer must correspond. This is a long task. They must, like two clocks, keep the same time.

Now all this can be very easily misunderstood and taken in a wrong way. So I will remind you again that the point is that if you are in a negative state, *it is always your own fault*, from the Work point of view. No matter what happened, what someone said, what someone did, we have to become responsible for our negative states—ourselves. You, over there, must become responsible to yourself. Of course, if you secretly love being negative and indulging in unpleasant emotions, then I can only say that whatever else you indulge in secretly this is the worst thing of all. For example, if you are a mischief-maker and enjoy the results, then you are pretty low-down in level of being. I will remind you of the first step—namely, we are not asked to like, but to stop dislike and all its ramifications. This makes a very practical starting-point. Later, when you feel the presence of negative emotion in you, as a foreign substance, as acutely as a stomach-ache, then you will seek, for your own reasons, to work on yourself and transform your inner state for your own inner health. Then you will find it necessary to know and seek to understand *all* the Work teaches and not merely give it a casual occasional glance, as if it were a thing you could pick up and cast aside just as you like, in a trivial way. The Work must become real. But this takes many years and requires a certain inner courage, an inner bravery, an inner determination, until something new is born distinct from life. This is called *a point in the Work* and this point begins the new development of which the Work speaks when it is said that a man, a woman, is created as a self-developing organism. This development is psychological, not physical.

*   *   *

Now let us speak about emotions, about feelings. What are they? Dislike is a feeling, an emotion. Does it unite us with a person, or the reverse? Can you understand another person through dislike? This is a simple question enough but have you considered it? Now you may dislike certain 'I's in a person, and, provided you dislike certain 'I's in yourself also, it does not mean that you cannot connect yourself with that person for you may like other 'I's in that person. But if you dislike a person *wholly*, no contact is possible. I think some of you do not yet realize this and I fancy that this is because you have not yet observed different 'I's in yourself—not yet seen that you are many people and not one person. Unless you can break yourself up into *many* you cannot see *many* in others. If you are complacent and asleep enough to take yourself as being all right, as being one permanent person, how can you escape from either wholesale liking or wholesale disliking—that is, how can you escape from the pendulum of Yes *or* No in all your human relations? You probably all share with me the tendency, when we are to meet someone and have been told beforehand that he or she is an unpleasant so-and-so, to accept this withering statement too easily. Of course, this is not the sign of a person in the Work—to take people at the estimated popular value. Even before I met the Work, I did not accept labels. As a result, I often found myself liking people everyone else disliked and disliking people everyone else liked. I do not think this was sheer contrariness, a sheer love of contradicting. Is it not true that we are very easily open to suggestion, very easily even hypnotized? A weak person is easily persuaded and accepts the general prevailing standards. This means there is little that is essential—that is real—in his feelings. Standardized feelings, being told and accepting what it is right to feel in the way of liking and disliking, etc., appears to me a terrible disease, such as we have prevalent at present, that attacks the individuality. But when we come under the healing influences of the Work and learn all that it teaches, we no longer see people in any standardized way—provided we no longer take *ourselves* in a standardized way.

Now people have patterns of feeling, standardized ways of taking everything, that their built-up Personality has acquired. They keep on behaving according to this pattern and *never observe* it. So they remain in the prison of what they imagine is excellent. I am sure that in such cases, if such people were to observe themselves in the light of the Work and what it tells us to do and what not to go with, things would change completely for them. They would feel another set of influences. But how many people who regard themselves as being in the Work ever observe themselves from what the Work tells them to observe? Why is this so? It is because the *feelings* are not yet developed. Now there are two directions in which the feelings can develop. Affections can develop. That is an outward direction—into life, into objects. There is an inward direction, always at the expense of self-love. What does this mean? When we feel, for example, that we cannot do in the right way, and, as it were, ask the Work how to do, we develop the inner direction of the feelings. This inner direction changes the feelings we have of ourselves. It is the halfway to Higher Centres—the other side in us. So we have to regard what the Work says about divisions of centres.

What is a sign that we are in a higher division of a centre? One sign is that there is always a change in the feeling of 'I'. Another sign is that we can control a lower emotion. Direct emotional control is only possible through one emotion being stronger than another. All emotions belonging to higher divisions of the emotional centre have the power of controlling lower emotions. The difficulty is to get into higher divisions of the centres. For this we must discover methods, knowing how the case is. Let us take a small division in the Emotional Centre:

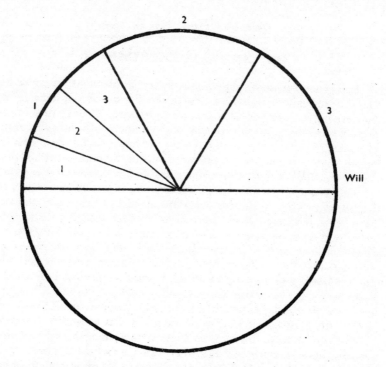

The small divisions 1, 2 and 3 are the moving, the emotional and the intellectual divisions of the moving or the most mechanical part of the Emotional Centre. 1 is the part connected with the expression of ordinary emotions. In 2 lie all our ordinary personal likes and dislikes and here is the centre of our self-love. 3 is will as the resultant of many small interests and desires. This is not Real Will which belongs to the highest division. What emotion can control the emotions arising in 2 when the court of self-love holds sway? Only emotions belonging to the large main divisions 2 and 3. By what can the large division 2 be characterized? By emotions going beyond oneself, by the feeling of the presence of what is greater than oneself, by genuine religious and aesthetic emotions. The quality of these emotions is quite different from that of the lower emotions, and can control them. In the big main division 3 lie emotions that control all the centre. These emotions can *create*, through which a man can begin to do—to have Real Will. But unless this is accompanied by an equal development of consciousness, which is the highest quality of the Intellectual Centre, the Will is not full Will. Now how comes it about that we cannot contact these higher divisions? The reason why we cannot contact these higher divisions is that we are always in small moving parts of each centre—in petty, petulant, small likes and dislikes, thoughts, etc. In regard to the Emotional Centre we are always pre-occupied with our personal likes and dislikes and so with all the manifestations of our self-love.

ON TAKING IN IMPRESSIONS

In a general sense we cannot take in new impressions unless we have new impressions of ourselves. Particularly can we not take in new impressions of other people unless we have begun to have new impressions of ourselves. To leave oneself out and begin with others is exactly what the Work does not teach. We have to begin to change in ourselves before anything can possibly change for us in the outer world of things and people and events. When one is satisfied with oneself it is difficult to understand what self-change means. So it is difficult to get new impressions. Then, since this thing oneself remains as it was, one takes in only the old stereotyped impressions of people and the world. Why is this so? It is because one's level of being is the receptive thing on which impressions fall. It can only receive what it does and can receive nothing new. I was talking some time ago to a man who has died since. He had nothing to do with the Work. I said to him that if he could see —let us say, Sir Augustus Smith—and not identify so much with him, he would probably get better in health and live longer. However, this is difficult. It always sounds strange that one has to see Mr. So-and-So or Mrs. So-and-So. Yet the most important thing in this system of teaching *inner change* is just this. Mr. O. used often to return to this theme and emphasize it. We have to do the same, for although we have heard it before we keep on forgetting it, keep on not understanding it, not quite getting what is meant. We do not, for example, easily see that we live with a person called ourselves. We take this person as ourselves. We never draw a distinction between this person and ourselves. But it is on this drawing of a distinction that the Work lays such emphasis, for, unless this separation has begun, the inner action of the Work cannot come into operation. Here are two sheets, one of cartridge-paper and the other a covering stuck to it. Before the Work can inscribe its meaning, the covering must be separated from the underlying surface. So Personality must be separated from Essence. Or, to use a different angle of approach, so (in my case) I must separate from Dr. Nicoll. But you will notice that a quite new impression of oneself is necessary for anything of this kind even to begin to happen. A complacent man is not likely to be able to shift one millimetre from his inner situation because he is satisfied with himself. So he will not be able to get new impressions of himself or of anything else. He is fastened down inside. Yes, but all of us are fastened down or stuck to something we have to get unfastened from, unstuck. It is like these two sheets of paper. One is real: the other is not. But they seem to be one, because they are stuck together. Yet they can be separated. But all this can take place only psychologically. It is one psychology stuck to another. It is nothing about things we can see or handle. That is why it is difficult. It is difficult because it is all about this invisible world in which we live, and it is of such importance where we go and what we do in this invisible world accessible only to our consciousness. The Work is about this invisible world and what separations are necessary in it and what directions must be taken in it. But naturally enough we find it very difficult to understand that it *does* matter, not so much what we think or feel, but what thoughts and feelings we identify with and say 'I' to. No one can practise this without making a certain kind of effort called Work-effort. What is this kind of effort? It starts with becoming conscious of this invisible world in which one is. But, as I said, this requires a definite kind of effort of attention and also the application of a definite kind of knowledge. So we have to observe ourselves from what the knowledge of the Work says. If you have not the knowledge then you cannot observe yourself rightly. Understand that you cannot work unless you see something of what is meant here. To take yourself as yourself, and merely *add* the Work to this crude undeveloped inner state, is useless. You will get all wrong. "A man must divide himself into two before he can shift from where he is psychologically." You must all realize that people and yourself are not merely somewhere in space and time, rich or poor, tall or short, old or young, but each is somewhere at some level in this invisible psychological world —then ask: where are you? Ask yourself and notice. I repeat that you cannot begin to do this Work unless you see something of what is meant here.

Quaremead, Ugley, May 20, 1945

A NOTE ON THE PENDULUM AND THIRD FORCE

As you know, the pendulum swings always between opposites whether literally, as in events of life, such as war and peace, or summer and winter, or psychologically, between love and hate, and so on. G. once said that Man lacked Third Force. He meant first of all that Man, who is created to become a conscious being, swings between the opposites in himself and is governed by the swing of opposite events in life. For example, war starts, and we are governed by it. Mr. O. once said some years before this war that people do not comprehend how they are governed by changing events, imagining that they are always free. They say, in time of peace, that they will never under any circumstances go to war again. "And," he added, "when a new war starts they always justify themselves and explain why they must do as they do—that is, as they cannot help doing." Now G., in teaching this Work, always emphasized that we were not yet conscious but could be so and were made to be so. Sometimes he explained this by saying that a man was not conscious in Third Force. He said on one occasion that everyone must bring the Third Force into his life in order to develop.

By Work definition, all manifestations are due to the action of three Forces called Active, Passive and Neutralizing Forces. Active and Passive Forces are on the opposites and cancel each other out, as it is expressed scientifically in Newton's first law of motion: that to every force there is an equal and opposite force. This law, of course, is not true as it stands, because if things were like that nothing could take place—nothing could move. If Newton had added that to every force there is eventually, in Time, an equal and opposite force, it would probably not have been necessary for Einstein to bring the Fourth Dimension of Time into the study of Physics. Yet Physics to-day, even though introducing the new factor of Time, has not yet reached in any deep sense the idea that there is actually a Third Force that acts between the pendulum opposites. The Third or Neutralizing Force in the Work is defined in many ways. One way is to say that it is the uniting force —that force that acts between Yes or No, Active or Passive, and makes something that is neither. You know that in statistics you have laws of averages. For example, so many people per cent. always die at 50, or 60, and on this statistical law, applying to large numbers, all insurance is based. On an average you will have so many gas molecules going one way, so many in another way, out of millions, and as a result you can make laws about the behaviour of gases under pressure and temperature. But such laws are based on large numbers and so are called statistical. If you cast a penny a million times you will get an average of heads and tails that more or less is an equilibrium. This science of statistics is really derived from the idea that there is an equilibrium in things,—that is, it is based on the law of the pendulum. But there is another force, apart from the opposites, at work in life, in ourselves, and throughout the Universe. This is the Law of Three Forces. Note carefully, please, here that average laws, statistical laws, are based only on the idea of there being two forces at work. The Work says that one of the two ultimate laws that cannot be reduced to any simpler terms is the Law of Three Forces. In everything three forces work. In the minute structure of the atom Active and Passive Forces are found, positive and negative charges, and so on—but from the Work point of view there is also a Third Force, an organizing force, a force that creates and organizes the two primitive chaotic opposite forces that of themselves can create nothing, since they are antagonists, always at war.

Now I would like to make a few comments on this Third Force, so difficult to grasp. The Work itself is a Third Force to begin with, but only when it is acknowledged and felt. Its power is to make the active Personality passive and the passive undeveloped Essence active—that is, to change the sign of these two parts of our Being. From this example you can see how a *Third Force* can alter the relationship of fixed things —just as events do in life, such as war. Everything is turned upside down. Events in life are Third Force, but they keep Personality active and Essence passive. The Work as an internal series of events changes this life-based relation—that is, alters us fundamentally through a new spirit and a new view. You cannot, of course, understand spiritual life in this sense from the facts of life. From the Work point of view a man whose mind and thought is wholly based on the evidence of his senses has his brain wrong. The spirit of life—that is, the Third Force of life—is different from the spirit of the Work. But the spirit of life —that is, the organizing principle that makes use of the irreconcilable pendulum forces, active and passive, positive and negative—constructs organized matter, whether atoms, molecules or cells, and does so on a basis that cannot be taken in a statistical sense. The cell, especially the germ-cell, is an example of this, as the physicist Schroedinger points out in his book that I asked you to read. Schroedinger is willing to admit that there are other laws in life than those deduced from the average behaviour of millions of particles whether atoms or human beings.

In most ancient esoteric writings, which all deal with the organizing spirit and never with statistics, it is sometimes said that the soul—that is, the organizing principle in a man, psychologically speaking—is almost devoured by matter in its descent into the body. The esoteric alchemists—not the pseudo-gold-seekers—called this imprisoned organizing force hidden in us Mercury. They said that if it were found lead could be transformed into gold. In the Work this organizing principle is sometimes called Buried Conscience or Real Conscience—not the acquired conscience that we follow from what we have been told by others and learnt from outside. The organizing power in creation, whether bodily or psychological, exists throughout all things. This is the Third Force and it seeks to build up by successive stages of separation something different from that in which it is lodged, so that in our case the finer matters in us are gradually freed from the heavier, more chaotic, unorganized matters. It is this Third Force that seeks to bring about the evolution of all things—to find new and better combinations and relations between the Active and Passive Forces constituting matter—or, better expressed, the opposite forces that cannot create alone and so are comparable to chaos. Organizing Spirit, organizing Third Force, which itself is buried in material chaos and works always to make something new out of it and so to free itself ultimately, is what we see right before us and yet cannot see. A person may be given new ideas, a new form of Third Force, as in the case of the Work. Do you remember the man who buried his talent *in the Earth*? The spirit of the Work is not a thing you can touch or handle, nor indeed is any form of spirit. Is the esprit de corps of a regiment a thing you can see? It is real and invisible. You remember how in the Parable of the Talents some made more of the spirit given them. One did nothing. He put the spirit given him into the Earth:

> "For it is as when a man, going into another country, called his own servants, and delivered unto them his goods. And unto one he gave five talents, unto another two, to another one; to each

according to his several ability; and he went on his journey. Straightway he that received the five talents went and traded with them, and made other five talents. In like manner he also that received the two gained other two. But he that received the one went away and digged in the earth, and hid his lord's money. Now after a long time the lord of those servants cometh, and maketh a reckoning with them. And he that received the five talents came and brought other five talents, saying, Lord, thou deliveredst unto me five talents: lo, I have gained other five talents. His lord said unto him, Well done, good and faithful servant: thou hast been faithful over a few things, I will set thee over many things: enter thou into the joy of thy lord. And he also that received the two talents came and said, Lord, thou deliveredst unto me two talents: lo, I have gained other two talents. His lord said unto him, Well done, good and faithful servant, thou hast been faithful over a few things, I will set thee over many things: enter thou into the joy of thy lord. And he also that had received the one talent came and said, Lord, I knew that thou art a hard man, reaping where thou didst not sow, and gathering where thou didst not scatter: and I was afraid, and went away and hid thy talent in the earth: lo, thou hast thine own. But his lord answered and said unto him, Thou wicked and slothful servant, thou knewest that I reap where I sowed not, and gather where I did not scatter; thou oughtest therefore to have put my money to the bankers, and at my coming I should have received back mine own with interest. Take ye away therefore the talent from him, and give it unto him that hath the ten talents. For unto everyone that hath shall be given: but from him that hath not, even that which he hath shall be taken away. And cast ye out the unprofitable servant into the outer darkness: there shall be the weeping and the gnashing of teeth." *(Matthew* XXV 14-30)

Quaremead, Ugley, June 2, 1945

WORK ON BEING

Some time ago I put to a London Group this question of which I have been reminded recently: *"Have you yet seen in your Being that which prevents you from further understanding the Work?"*

What have we all understood as being the centre of gravity of this question? What Work-idea is brought in here? The Work-idea is that one's understanding depends on the quality and level of one's Being. On another occasion it was asked: "What factor in your Being do you think prevents you from growing?" Now understanding is the resultant of your Knowledge and your Being. Suppose you do not see any reason why you should change your Being. Then your understanding of everything, including this Work, will remain at the same level. No matter how much you hear this Work, how much you study the Knowledge of this Work, your understanding of it will remain the same. Some people are certainly dissatisfied with the state of their Being and others are not. Again, many people do not understand what Being means. They take the side of their Being for granted. But those who feel dissatisfied with the kind of people they are have some idea of what it might mean to change the kind of people they are, to become different kinds of people—namely, to change their Being. It has often been said that no one is satisfied in one sense—that is, everyone wishes to change his or her circumstances, conditions of life. This is really seeing one's own Being externally as reflected in life. Since your level of Being attracts your form of life, it is clearly necessary to think in a new way about your form of life, from the standpoint of your quality of Being, the kind of person you are. This of course means a new way of thinking. If you can accept this idea, which is a definite Work-idea, a definite new form of thinking, you may be able to come to some temporary conclusion at least about what factor in your Being prevents you from understanding the Work better. A growth of Being for a person in the Work inevitably leads to a deeper understanding of the Work. The Work has more to unite with, can give more; it can influence you more; it can become more real. But if you do not work on your Being, your understanding of the Work and its influence on you will be very slight. You will live your life according to your form of Being and with an effort will remember at times that there is something called the Work. That is, the Work will remain in your memory but will not be connected with your Being yet. So you will not understand the Work much, or you will understand it a little according to what good Work-'I's you may have, and yet your understanding of it will be continually swamped by 'I's that belong to your level of Being and are in life and so are not interested in the Work and as often as not are only interested in the cares and anxieties of life, and all the forms of identification which life gives to us at every moment so gratuitously. If you are satisfied with yourself, with the kind of person you are, and have never challenged that wrong feeling of yourself, if more or less life has satisfied you, then it follows that you will have very little real desire to change the kind of person you are, to change your Being. This is always a very difficult point in the Work, a very difficult thing to grasp. A man who feels uneasy about the kind of person he is has more chance of working on his Being than a man who never questions himself but only sees, as it were, the deficiencies of others and has never had any idea that he himself may be not quite the kind of person that he supposes. A sense of the deficiencies of one's own Being is a quite different thing and I would say that both senses of deficiency are necessary in the Work. As you all know, owing to the action of buffers and owing in a general sense to our state of sleep, a man who is uneasy as regards his own Being—i.e. the kind of man he is —is rarer than possibly a man who is uneasy about his state of Knowledge.

In order to see what our level of Being is like we have to observe ourselves in the light of what the Work teaches. I know that you have heard this many times but have you ever applied it to yourselves? As I often say to you, people say: "What have we to observe?" You have all heard many times what it is you have to observe in the strict teaching of the Work. Do you, for example, observe when you are full of cares and anxieties and thoroughly identified with life? Has it ever occurred to you that this is one of the things that you have to observe? And has it ever occurred to you that this is a sign of your Being, of what you are—for example, that you are a person whose level or quality of Being is such that he or she is always full of cares and worries? Now some might suppose that this is quite easy to observe. Certainly it is quite easy to observe in another person but it is extraordinarily difficult to observe in oneself. It is extraordinarily difficult to observe that one is worrying and full of cares and anxieties, and realize that it is due to the kind of person one is in regard to one's level of Being. A person on a higher level of Being will not worry in the same way, will not have the same cares and anxieties. It is precisely this that is so difficult to grasp. Our worries and cares and anxieties seem to us to be natural, to be perfectly justified, to be right, and yet, as you know, the Work teaches that all this is not right, and it is one of the things that we have to work on. In other words, if we apply the Knowledge of the Work to our Being through self-observation, we begin to see what an enormous mass of material we have to work on. And this applying of the Knowledge of the Work to what we observe from this standpoint in our Being will lead eventually to a change in the level of Being. But for this we must have Observing 'I' in the Work-sense. In the Work-sense Observing 'I' is the result of this Work and its ideas. We no longer observe ourselves from the life point of view but from the Work point of view, and if we do this sincerely even for a short time we can no longer remain satisfied with our state of Being. If the evaluation of the Work is strong enough and is constantly reinforced by new experience within ourselves, we cannot possibly remain complacent with regard to our Being. We realize what an immense gap lies between ourselves and a man who is living more consciously than we do, a man who notices when he is becoming identified, a man who sees when he is becoming a prey to imaginary anxieties and fears, a man who is sharply aware of the fact that he is justifying himself. This gap is so great that if we ever have such a moment of insight we cannot help feeling by contrast the enormous deficiencies in our quality of Being and we can well understand at such moments that as we are we cannot expect, either in this life or in any other life, to be permitted to live amongst people of a higher level of Being. We can see quite clearly why we can never expect to pass into what is called in the Gospels the Kingdom of Heaven

—those who are on the outskirts of the Conscious Circle of Humanity—
and knowing this, realizing this, seeing it for ourselves in an
intimate private moment of self-realization, we begin to understand
what a long way we have to go before we can attain what is the
ultimate goal of all esoteric teaching. But let me add one thing here—
i.e. that if you begin to see all this about your state of Being you are
already much further on, however hopeless you may feel, than a
person who has never caught such glimpses of himself or herself,
because it is exactly this feeling of vacuum, of deficiency, of lack, that
is the starting point of work on one's own Being. For if a man or a
woman has such an experience they no longer have the same feeling
of themselves, they will no longer feel the imaginative delusions of
False Personality, of this dressed-up invented thing, through which they
ordinarily derive their sense of themselves, and if they are in the
Work, instead of feeling mere hopelessness, mere despair, in themselves,
they will feel all the strength of the Work round them, and they will
be told in many different ways that they are right in what they saw.
That is why it is so important to have the Work surrounding us with
all its strength, because otherwise to realize such things without
any help would be disastrous. For a long time a battle takes place
between what you think you ought to be and what you know you are,
and this battle will go on until you really begin to know what you
are, until you accept what you are. This, of course, as you know
from what we have been speaking about lately, means an extension
of consciousness into this dark side, which one knows and does not
acknowledge, because we know many things in a way and yet do not
accept them as part of our Being. It is partly due, or perhaps chiefly
due, to the action of the False Personality, which is always maintaining
something unreal, always striving to exist, in spite of a thousand and
one things that have been seen, observed and acknowledged privately
to oneself—but only in the atmosphere and under the influences of the
Work. All self-realization, all self-knowledge which is real, destroys
the imagination of oneself—i.e. the False Personality. The result is an
immense broadening of one's powers and not a weakening of them. It
is the False Personality that weakens us so much and renders us so
brittle, so easily upset, so narrow, and so mean in our understanding,
both of others and of ourselves.

Now if anyone takes himself or herself in hand in the Work-sense,
they must isolate themselves from the influences of life and begin to
follow the influences of the Work. A person in the Work must begin
to resist the influences of life. He or she must begin to isolate themselves
from these influences of life that are pouring in at every moment. If
people are very identified with all that happens in life, whether in their
own domestic world or in national affairs, they will not be able to feel
the action of the Work-influences on their Being. The Work carries
different influences from those that life carries. The Work is not the
same as life. Life is one thing and the Work is another thing, although

in a sense they meet. But this subject requires a very careful talk and I am not going into it here except to say that you can use life for the purposes of the Work but you must never use the Work for the purposes of life unless you understand very clearly what you are doing, and in that case you will be doing it really from the Work—i.e. you must know what you are doing. Eventually the Work must become more important to you emotionally in your evaluation than anything in life. If life is more important to you than the Work, then this alteration of signs between Personality and Essence cannot take place sufficiently. In a broad sense, Essence can only grow through the Work, through its influence, because the Work is real and Essence is the real part of you and can only be nourished aright by what is real, what is true, what is genuine; but Personality has been built up by life and there is a particular part of Personality, as you know, called False Personality, which has taken the place of any real essential feeling of ourselves. So trying to see one's False Personality is one of the most important starting-points of self-observation, because unless one can separate from this fiction of oneself nothing can shift internally. At the same time Personality itself—namely, what you have acquired from life—contains many 'I's, many factors, which also have to be changed, as, for example, a person has been brought up under a very narrow form of religion or some very narrow social teaching. It is a great mistake to think that only the False Personality must be separated from. There are many things in acquired Personality that have to be separated from, and in the Work as I teach it I advise you to notice this point. In my own case I had to separate myself from many factors that did not belong to my False Personality but were quite distinct from it and that lay in my acquired Personality through early training and upbringing. Just think how we can be taught quite wrong things. Just think about how so many people have been brought up in some kind of political belief and so have 'I's laid down in their Personality that they take for granted as being truthful. All this side of Being has to be worked on eventually and this is not necessarily included in the False Personality. Take, for example, those 'I's in your acquired Personality which perhaps have been worried about everything, or careful about everything, or anxious about everything. These 'I's by imitation will lie in Personality, in the acquired part of you, and they must be worked on just as seriously as that group of 'I's linked together by vanity that form the False Personality. Many 'I's that we have acquired by training and that exist in the Personality are useful, and with them there is no quarrel because they give us our relationship to life, our power of being an engineer or an architect, and so on. But there are many other 'I's that we have acquired in the Personality which must be separated from eventually, or perhaps re-educated might be a better word.

Now as regards this isolation from life that I spoke about, Mr. O. used to say—although he talked about it of course from many different angles—that there are four things that help above all others to isolate us from the influences of life which tend to drag us down, and keep us asleep. He said: "Knowledge of your Being, Self-Remembering, Non-identifying and Non-Considering are four supreme practices that help us to isolate ourselves from the continual impact of external life and so enable something to grow in us apart from life." How do you think that Knowledge of your Being will help you to isolate yourself from life? We have already spoken about this in the first part of the paper. I will only add that if you begin to have real Knowledge of your Being you will no longer feel the same kind of person, and so I ask you this question: If you no longer feel the same kind of person will you be so much caught up by life, so much controlled by it, or will you feel yourself to some extent isolated? How will you feel yourself isolated? You will feel yourself no longer caught up so much by life because you no longer have the same feeling of yourself that previously caught you up in life so much. In other words, your Being will change and so your Being will not attract the same life. However, I leave this point for your discussion.

I also call your attention to the last practice mentioned—Non-considering. This means not identifying with Internal Considering. Have you noticed how much of the day is spent in considering, how many of your actions are influenced by it, and how often you cannot be in what you are doing because one half of you is internally considering? Have you noticed this tremendous power that life exerts on us to keep us asleep, this factor of Internal Considering? Now as long as life is your only sphere of reality, your only field of life, the only thing for you that is real, then you will be governed amongst other things by Internal Considering. But if something stronger than life governs you, you will find that Internal Considering changes itself completely. You will find that in place of internally considering you will begin to externally consider and then a great deal of peace will come to you and a great deal of strength that hitherto has been wasted in Internal Considering. Also, you will begin to understand other people far better, and instead of worrying about everything you will have real thoughts about other people and about yourself, and everything will become much more simple and quieter. Perhaps some of you have noticed the connection between Internal Considering and the idea that one can do—but I leave this again for your discussion.

machinery we could not strip ourselves away from it. Negative emotions are acquired and are quite useless, whereas all that we are created with is useful. That is the point of which one must constantly remind oneself. They are worse than useless because they absorb and drain away so much of our ordinary force. All the finest transformations of the three foods—ordinary food, air, and impressions—are continually being interrupted and destroyed or wrongly formed by the action of the negative part of the Emotional Centre. Try to see for yourself by direct observation how a negative state drains force from you and try to see what happens when, having observed your condition, you genuinely try to separate from this state for your own private reasons and not for the sake of being congratulated or to gain merit. If you do this rightly you will feel a shock, you will experience the sensation that you have suddenly escaped from something evil, something that you did not realize was evil. Then you will begin to understand why it is said that we can detect the presence of negative states by means of inner taste. One can indeed see the negative state that one has escaped from literally lying beneath one at a lower level at such times.

Now here would be a good place to speak about negative states in illness. A person with very well-developed negative states that have never been observed and so never contended with will be inclined to have his or her general powers of resistance to illness diminished. That is one point. The next point is that a negative emotion, or, let us say, the energy connected with its manifestations, may link up with the illness and increase it—in short, it may make the illness worse or more persisting. You may suffer from something that should be merely temporary, some form of illness, some form of pain, and so on, but if it comes on a negative background that has never been faced with any courage, the condition may persist or become exaggerated. From another point of view, making bad chemistry in us, such states are, so to speak, toxic, beginning in the psychological sphere and working down to the grosser sphere of the physical matters of the body. You know how in this Work psychological matters or energies, called Hydrogens, pass by increasing condensations into the grosser matters of the body. Now remember another point. Every psychological event, whether it be a sensation or a feeling or a thought, consumes a certain amount of energy if it is identified with, whereas if you are in a state of Self-Remembering energy will be created and conserved for further use. Do you all know what it means to look back at a state with which you were identified and see it as something quite small and unimportant, and wonder how you could have consumed so much energy mechanically over it? All energy that is mechanically used is consumed. That is why it is so important to begin to think about what it means to live more consciously, for in this Work we all seek to live more consciously, both within ourselves in relation to all that is going on within us and also outwardly in our relationship to others and to life in general. Of what use is it to speak of this Work as having to do with inner transformation, with what Mr. Ouspensky calls psycho-transformism, if we do everything mechanically—that is, if *it* does everything mechanically, i.e. the machine in us? This is not living more consciously: it is just being what you are as a machine, it is simply a machine doing everything. Since negative emotions are the greatest wasters of energy and have so many other destructive effects upon us, it is of the greatest importance to try to prevent force from continually going into them. This will always happen if we identify with our negative states. That is why it is so important to try to separate from a negative state, not to go with it, not to consent to it, with the mind at least. For if both the mind and the emotions consent then there is full identification and a full influx of energy into the negative state. That is why we must try to starve our negative states because the more we nourish them, secretly approve of them and secretly enjoy them, the more energy they will insist on taking from us. A person who is a slave to his or her negative emotions is actually a slave, only the trouble is that we very easily enjoy different forms of slavery, not recognizing that we are really in prison. But it is useless to speak of all this if you do not yet know what it is to observe negative states and negative remarks in yourselves. So I tell you to observe how you talk. Some can only talk *negatively*.

Now what negative state or talk have you observed in yourself to-day, each one of you? If you are at a loss to find an answer, I can only say that you are not working, you are doing no *work on yourself*, which is the starting-point of this Work. If that is the case, then ask yourself: Why am I doing no work on myself? Then I ask you this question : Have you observed yourself criticizing someone else to-day in a negative way? Probably you will say, yes, you have. Then again I say to you that you are not working on yourself. Why are you noticing how other people behave without noticing yourself? That is behaving in a most mechanical way, in which everyone behaves in life. But we are in the Work. We are doing something extra to what is necessary in life. We are learning something that we do not learn from life and which is not necessary in life. I find it difficult to imagine that anyone who has heard this Work for some years can pass a whole day without observing some negative state in himself or herself and without making some Work-effort to separate from this state either by non-identifying with it or by what I call neutralizing it through seeing the same thing in oneself as one saw in the other person.

Now we spoke last time about work on Being and spoke about being complacent about one's state of Being—that is, being satisfied with oneself as one is. (I advise you to read that paper again and reflect on it.) Now with our Being as it is—i.e. at our level of Being—we have negative emotions. Our level of Being is characterized first of all by multiplicity of Being, by many 'I's—that is, by lack of unity. It is characterized by a state of sleep, it is characterized by the absence of Self-Remembering, it is characterized by the presence of great numbers of negative emotions which are, so to speak, continually drowning us. A higher level of Being cannot be reached if our negative emotions remain as they are and continue to exert the same power over us as they do. This is quite clear. This can be understood. Therefore study your negative states, for this is one of the most important sides of self-study. Observe them, note them down, and above all remember them so that when they come back again, as they always do, you may gradually recognize them before they can exert their full power—namely, before you can identify with them. Especially in the morning clear your mind of negative, unpleasant and criticizing states before you pass, so to speak, into external life, and at night go through your negative states and try to see them in retrospect; and if you do this genuinely, if you have come to the point of recognizing your negative condition and desiring to begin to get free from it, then you may rest assured that you will receive help from 'I's in yourself that wish to work, and they are capable possibly of passing on to a higher level of Being. But do not let the Work get cold for too long. "Eight hours' sleep is quite enough." But if you sleep psychologically for a whole week you will be in a bad way and will have to start everything all over again.

Quaremead, Ugley, June 16, 1945

THE MEANING OF FORCE IN THE WORK

Let us speak about force. When you do a thing too long you have no force. Some people have difficulty in separating their idea of force from the idea of physical force. But there are many kinds of force that act on us. From the Work point of view, when a man is completely asleep he has no force—that is, he has no Work-force. He is then in life. All force is made through some form of self-knowledge—I mean, that all Work-force is made in this way. You can be enormously powerful in a physical sense and yet from the Work point of view you have no force. In trying to understand how force is made in us we have to study first of all what makes us lose force. But again this is not starting far enough back because people who simply understand force as meaning physical force will not understand what this force that the Work speaks about means. The force that the Work speaks about is what keeps us awake, and here again it is difficult to understand what this means if one has always lived one's life completely identified with oneself and so completely asleep. Of course you do not know that you have no force if you are completely asleep. If you are simply a function of your Personality, if you are identified with what you are in life, you will not understand what force means in the Work-sense.

Let us try to speak as simply as possible about force. We have different centres in us. Each centre requires a different kind of energy

712

or force for it to work properly. There is, for example, force in Moving Centre. A man may have great energy connected with his Moving Centre and no energy for his Intellectual Centre. Now if such a man uses all his force, let us say, in Moving Centre, he will not understand what it means to have force for the Intellectual Centre. Forces or energies in us are of different kinds. If you get hold of this idea that there are different kinds of energies and forces in us, you will be better able to understand the more complete teaching about force that the Work gives. The idea of Balanced Man that I often think dominates our Work, or should do so, is that of a man who has force that can pass at different times into different centres, because Balanced Man is a man who can use all his centres at the appropriate times. A one-centred man, a one-sided man, employs his force, such as he has, mechanically, chiefly in one centre, but the Work says that we must eventually come to the point of being able to use all the centres with their right energies. Otherwise we remain ungrown, undeveloped. We have five ordinary centres, the Intellectual Centre, the Emotional Centre, the Sex Centre, the Moving Centre and the Instinctive Centre. A full man has at the right times force in all these five centres, and the force is quite different in each case. You cannot, for example, use intellectual force for lifting weights: quite different force has to be employed. Now the balancing of the machine, the balancing of the centres, depends on the right appropriating of force among these different centres. A man and a woman ordinarily live a very one-sided existence using, as it were, the same quality of force, so they get tired. But there are other centres, other forces, that can be used when one is tired in one centre. The trouble is that when we are tired in one centre we are tired, and that is the end of it. It is like walking up and down the same path. But when you are tired in one centre you are not necessarily tired in another centre. I may find myself mentally tired and unable to think or write for the time being, but if I get into my Moving Centre, let us say, I find that there is plenty of force there. However, we all have a pattern of life to which we stick too rigidly, and which confines us to a very narrow range of experience, of meaning. Every centre has its own different kind of meaning: every centre conducts meaning. But we tend to live in one pattern of meaning and do not realize that we can have other meanings that are waiting for us in some other centre or part of a centre that we have not used for a long time.

On one occasion I was talking to Mr. Ouspensky, who said that people do not study how to pass from one centre to another or from one part of a centre to another part of a centre. He said that a certain kind of effort is necessary to pass from one centre to another and that if we could find the way for ourselves to do this we should have far more energy, far more force. He went on to give one method that he had used which I cannot give you here, but later on he said that the first thing to understand is that it is possible to pass from one centre to another or from one part of the same centre to another, and that unless a person understands this he does not realize the possibilities in him. I think he meant that, not realizing that some centre or part of a centre can have force, we tend to feel exhausted when we need not be exhausted, the reason being that we live in a kind of rigid pattern of life and always do the same thing over and over again—that is, we live in very small parts. At that time Mr. Ouspensky was talking a great deal about thinking differently. He said that supposing a man begins to think differently he will at once get force because his thinking will change from one part of the Intellectual Centre to another part. But most people do not understand what it means to think differently from the way they are always thinking. I can give you an example. Suppose you have noticed that you are thinking of a person in a certain way, quite mechanically, as you always do, and these thoughts give you no force. Suppose even that you have become sufficiently sensitive to your inner life to realize that you are really losing force by thinking of this very person in this usual way. Now suppose that you apply the Work to yourself at this moment and put yourself into this person's position or even go so far as to think that you are this person yourself and that you perhaps are like him. This will change your thinking, and then you will get into a higher part of the Intellectual Centre and then suddenly you may find that you have force. You are thinking in a new way. Now this is an example of gaining force by applying the Work to yourself. After a time in the Work you will begin to get tired of your customary thoughts—i.e. the thoughts that you ordinarily go with every day—but you must remember that you can think in a new way about everything, and here you must begin by *including yourself*. It is a very marvellous experience to realize that you can think differently both about other people and about yourself, and about your past and present life. The trouble is that we simply accept our thoughts and believe that they are quite right and that they are the only possible thoughts that we can have. Why, you can think differently in a million ways. Have you noticed the rigid man, the rigid woman, who always thinks in the same set way, always says the same thing, always expresses the same opinion, like a parrot? Perhaps you may have, but I advise you first of all to notice *yourself* in this respect. Are you a parrot? Now do you understand that you can think quite differently and that you are simply using every day only one line of thinking where there are a million lines of thinking? Let us say that you are full of prejudices, crystallized attitudes, smugness, etc., with which you thoroughly agree, with which you are fully satisfied. Now if you are such a person can you expect to change, to undergo any inner development? Such a person will always be the same person, always say the same thing, always express the same standpoints, take all experience in a stereotyped way. He or she is no good from the Work point of view. Why? Because being quite satisfied does not lead to self-change.

The great key to self-change lies in observing oneself, observing how one talks, what opinions one constantly repeats, what one constantly condemns in others, what one is so proud of, and so on. You cannot change otherwise, because if you take yourself for granted as being all right you cannot change. What has to be changed in this Work, as has been so often said? It is you, *you yourself*, who must change. You have got to see that you are nothing but a mechanical parrot. *You yourself* must see that you always say the same things and do the same things and behave in the same way. That is why the Work says that unless you can begin to realize your *mechanicalness* you can never really remember yourself. And this is exactly why, if you take yourself for granted and think that you yourself can be the starting-point and that as you are you are quite acceptable and right, with the right ideas, the right forms of life, the right attitudes, and so on, you will never be able to change and you will never know what this Work is about. But if you begin to have a sincere Observing 'I'—and this is impossible unless you feel the Work emotionally and your own lack of Knowledge and Being—then after a time you will feel rather unhappy about the state of yourself, about the kind of person you are. This was pointed out recently in several papers, but I am pointing it out again now as I notice that some people cannot take this in. They start from themselves as being excellent as they are. Life has built up in us all certain kinds of people. This is our life-experience. This is the Personality. You may be very good at making shirts, or knitting socks, or gardening, or being a doctor, or being an engineer, or being a good mother, or a good father, or a fine soldier, or a good typist, or an efficient clerk, or a good business man, or a good anything you like in life, or a good wife, or a good husband, or anything you like in regard to doing your duty as taught you, and so acquired. How do you escape from all this? This is your prison. Of course, if you do not want to escape from all this, and feel satisfied, then there is no reason why you should do this Work or try to study it. That is why I said in recent papers that if you are quite satisfied with yourself as you are, you really cannot do this Work and it is no use your studying it because your buffers, your pride, your self-conceit, and your vanity and so on, will be so great that nothing can shift in you. That is exactly why it is so difficult to teach this idea of a further development that esotericism speaks about, this second education, in which Personality has to become passive. In fact, you have to realize gradually that you are absolutely nobody, nothing but a kind of invention. This again is a great difficulty and if a man or a woman cannot observe himself or herself from the Work point of view they will not be able to shift from themselves, so they will have no extra force, no Work-force, but only life-force. Life-force is that force that makes Personality and keeps it going, day by day, and this is absolutely necessary for the first development, the first education, of a human being—his or her first contact with the Earth. But there is another force called Work-force, the force of esoteric teaching, the force that you find spoken about in every page of the Gospels, the force that leads to the re-birth of a man or a woman.

Let me remind you that this Work is about *transformation of Being*—that means, becoming a new man or woman. This Work can eventually conduct to you, if you receive it, and think it sufficiently important, an entirely new valuation of yourself and an entirely new realization of your meaning in life. You will then see you are nothing as you are. This indeed is the whole point of the Work, because the Work is not about life and what it has made you, save indirectly, but it is about this further transformation that a man or a woman, having fulfilled their duties in life, can eventually undergo. But they cannot undergo this transformation unless they feel that they have come to the end of things, to the end of duty, to the end of their own excellence, to the end of science, to the end of all worldly knowledge, and yet feel that there must be something else apart from what life has made them by birth and training. I remind you here of a Work-phrase: "Life cannot be explained by life." Life cannot be explained in terms of itself, nature cannot be explained in terms of herself, and you cannot explain yourself in terms of yourself." Ask yourself: How do you think? How do you move? Can you explain it? However most people do not trouble themselves with thoughts of this kind and a great many people think that such thoughts are extremely morbid. They advise you to consult a doctor. But if you have such thoughts you have already the possession of Magnetic Centre which is a sign of Being, because a man who has Magnetic Centre, even if he has done very little in life, is even then superior in his Being to a man who is, say, a great success in life and attributes everything to himself and has seen no mystery.

Now all Work-force starts from Magnetic Centre in a certain sense. You cannot get new force without that which Magnetic Centre leads into eventually. This feeling of mystery leads you to a certain point. You cannot get this Work-force unless you feel something else apart from the visible world and visible life—from spades and bricks and accounts, and so on. If you are quite content with your food, your income, your house, your children, your excellent disposition, your immaculate virtue, your respectability, your fine career, and so on, and your prowess in general, then you have no Magnetic Centre. Sometimes when reading the newspapers I wonder whether anyone has any Magnetic Centre nowadays in high positions, in politics, and so on. It seems to me somehow that everyone thinks that he can do and all people want is more regulations, more rules, more science, to produce a perfect world. In my own case, as a comparatively young man, I realized that I did not know anything. I met doctors, I became a doctor myself, somewhat against my will, and yet all the time this feeling that I really knew nothing persisted in me. Now a man asleep in life, by which I mean a man who has no Magnetic Centre, will be quite content to become a doctor, a scientist, a general, and so on. His force will be derived from life entirely, from his successes, and he will rub his hands and tell you that he did all this or all that. This is tedious—but usual. Of course, such a man——or such a woman—will not think for a moment that he or she is all the time attributing everything to themselves. They do not see that life has made them. They will think themselves very good people, excellent people, admirable people, people doing their duty, and so on, yet I must insist on continuing to point out to you all that this is exactly where the dividing line comes between a man or a woman who can understand this Work and a man or a woman who can never understand it. It takes a very exceptional person to admit, whatever his reputation in life may be, that he knows nothing really and that he feels himself to be nothing. Some kettles are very small and are soon filled. But in this Work we are seeking people who wish to find something else than what life has made them.

Now let us come back again to the subject of force, because all that has been said is connected with the idea of making force in the Work-sense. Now no one can make any force in the Work-sense if he is completely identified, satisfied with himself, vain and proud, content with himself as he is. It is quite useless. Such people derive the feeling of themselves from their life-achievement. You can only make force in the Work-sense by not being identified with yourself. Now I will try to explain more carefully the point of this paper which is connected with the other papers recently written. You can come under a new range of forces which are very wonderful and which can give you very strange and curious feelings of power, provided that you do not identify with all that you have done in life. Of course, you have not done all that you have done in life. It has been done to you by circumstances, outside forces, outside necessity. And if you derive your feeling of yourself from all that you have done in this sense, you will never be able to get this strange force of the Work acting on you. Look at your pride, look at your vanity, look at your meritoriousness, look at your self-satisfaction, look at your virtuousness, look at your respectability, look at everything of this kind that life has built up in you, and let me ask you this question: Do you gain your feeling of yourself from all that or have you something in you that rather dislikes it and feels it is not really you? If so, you can begin to get force from the Work. But you must increase this feeling of dislike, of not accepting yourself as life has made you—i.e. you must not get your feeling of 'I', your feeling of yourself, from all that—if you want to change, because as long as you hold on to all that and take yourself as that—"What a fine fellow I am"—you will be identifying with your Personality and probably chiefly with your False Personality, and as long as this takes place, as long as this is your internal situation day by day, and minute by minute, there is no place in which the Work can enter you, because at every moment you are reinforcing this vain, conceited feeling of yourself derived from what you were or are in life. But, speaking technically, as long as life is your Neutralizing Force—i.e. as long as life is the force that makes you go, makes you do everything—it keeps the Personality active (and that of course includes specially the False Personality) and keeps the real part of you that can grow—i.e. Essence—passive. The

Work is about bringing in a new Neutralizing or Third Force whose ultimate object is to change this relationship of Essence to Personality —in fact, reverse it altogether. Many foolish things are said about giving up your life, many foolish people go into monasteries and so on, but I am not talking about this. This Way, this Work, lies in life, and the secret is not to identify with what you were or are in life. You have to start all over again. The better kind of person you were in life, the better your possibilities, if you understand what it means to make Personality passive, because it is through making Personality passive that Essence or the real part of you can grow, because Personality is like the meat in the egg and Essence is like the germ-spot that can grow at the sacrifice of the meat of the egg.

Now all Work-force is derived from the realization of this tremendous idea that the Work teaches that a new birth is possible. You have perhaps all of you noticed how many people who have been in contact with this Work are no longer quite the same as before. They find that in the atmosphere of the Work it is very little use to bring in life experience, from Personality, or especially from False Personality. They find they cannot boast of what they have done in quite the same way as people do in life. The gradual sacrifice of this meat of Personality so that the germ of Essence can grow is one reason why the Work-atmosphere must be created amongst you all—an atmosphere in which we can really laugh at ourselves sometimes. Yes, but can you laugh at yourself? Even the slight change that can take place in people who have a fairly good attitude to the Work is often very remarkable. Yes, but why does this happen? It happens because the atmosphere of the Work is different from the atmosphere of life. Technically, the Third Force of life which keeps Personality active and Essence passive is slightly changed, and some parts of Personality begin to be sacrificed, and owing to this Essence begins to grow, so people become more real to one another, because if we were all more in Essence than we are at present everything would become much more real, much more genuine, much more simple, much more true, and much more good. When you try to increase what you have been, and to feel bigger and stronger and more powerful, more important, you are going in the very reverse direction to this Work. Then you will get no force in the Work-sense. Such a state means that you are very identified with yourself—with your Personality which ascribes everything to itself. But you will not get Work-force, as I said, from this identification with yourself. You only get Work-force through nonidentifying, through self-observation, and through dissolving these pictures, these ideas, this wonderful proud imagination about yourself. The reason for this is quite simple. What prevents the two Higher Centres that are continually working in us, the Higher Mental Centre and the Higher Emotional Centre, from transmitting their force to us? They cannot get through to us, owing to our self-admiration—our Personality. All Work-force comes indirectly from these two Higher

Centres which are at a higher level of *Being* than we are—a level beyond our Personality. Remember that the Work teaches that they are fully developed and that they are transmitting messages to us the whole time. But we cannot hear them owing to our state of sleep. Is not this an extraordinary idea? Does it not seem a fantastic idea that there is something in us that is trying to change us the whole time, and cannot reach us owing to this blocking, this blackout, due to the Personality, but more particularly to the overweening False Personality?

Now if a man begins to work on himself through his own self-observation, if he begins to observe his inner sleep, his vanity, if he begins to observe his meritoriousness, if he begins to observe his negative emotions, if he begins to observe his pictures of himself, if he begins to observe his buffers and prejudices, his mechanical opinions, his stereotyped talking, his chattering, his evil talking, he (or she) will then begin to be separated from these things, because if you can observe a thing, you are no longer it (do you understand?) which is the first step in this separation, that the Work teaches. I could add many other things here that one has to observe but the ultimate issue is this: if you are identified with yourself as you are, if you are taking all your thoughts as real, and will not see that you have to separate yourself from many, many bad moods, bad self-feelings, you will get nowhere in this Work. The method of this Work is through non-identifying with yourself. You must learn not to identify with yourself—by observing yourself and separating. What is yourself? Yourself is psychological, yourself is psychic, yourself is whatever you like to call it, but it is not physical—not your body. It belongs to what you are conscious of. Are you going to put your consciousness into an evil thought or an evil mood? Are you going to put your consciousness into self-satisfaction, self-glorification, or are you going to put your consciousness into feeling that you are always right and know best? Do you not see that unless you observe yourself you cannot notice where you place your consciousness? I find myself with many feelings, many moods, many thoughts, that come to me mechanically, that I do not put my consciousness into—for instance, I do not put my feeling of 'I' into hate, or the feeling of hopelessness—I do not consent to them, I do not go with them.

Now if you do this, you will get Work-force but if you are simply yourself, taken for granted, totally identified with yourself, you will get no Work-force at all, because you will be under the Third Force of life and not the Third Force of the Work. There is spirit and matter —to use phrases that do not belong to our system. A man must develop spiritually and this means in the Work psychologically. You all are given bodies, of different sizes, and that is not your fault, so do not pride yourselves on them. But the Work is talking about a psychological inner development where truth counts for so much. Suppose you are trying to build up this second body that we all have to build up in this Work, a psychological body. This body is based on truth, on sincerity. Now suppose you have a negative emotion against someone. This means at once that you will have wrong connections in your psychological body that survives after death (if it can). So you have a psychological body all wrongly connected, because all negative states make you lie. If you notice, when you are negative you are always lying. Have you yet got the strength to see that you are lying by tasting negative emotion? Don't you begin to understand that this Work is to build up truth in us, not moral truth, in the orthodox sense, not truth from a particular kind of orthodox belief, but real truth, through inner sincerity? That is why the Work starts with self-observation, uncritical and absolutely sincere. This builds up gradually in us a transmitting instrument, a psychological instrument, that can conduct the influences of the Higher Centres, because the Higher Centres that are always working in us can only reach us when there is truth in us. For that reason many of us have to go through what you might call very disturbing experiences to get rid of our False Personality, our meritoriousness, our vanity, our prejudices. Prejudice is quite useless. It conducts nothing. Meritorious feeling is even worse; to ascribe to yourself your excellence in any form will make it impossible for Higher Centres to come through to you. I would advise some of you who call yourselves Christians to read carefully the Sermon on the Mount and consider what it means as far as you can. But to resume the paper, you will get no force in the Work-sense unless you work against Personality and do not identify with the kind of person that you take yourself for granted as being, because you are not what you think you are.

This is one paper on force—on Work-force. All Work-force is derived by going against yourself, by going against your natural mechanical reaction at the moment. But every man or woman must have a private feeling of the Work in their hearts, in their minds, so that even when they are alone they do not consent to mechanical negative thoughts and externally do not talk mechanically about other people in this Work. If this is sincerely done, then we can produce perhaps a real Work-atmosphere finally to which everyone contributes and if it drops people will ask themselves sincerely what they said, what they did, why Work-force has apparently leaked.

COMMENTARY ON OBSERVING 'I'

ON SEEING CONTRADICTIONS IN OURSELVES

In these commentaries that have been written recently about the dark or unconscious or unacknowledged sides of us, which result in our living always in the little parts of ourselves, not remembering the rest of ourselves at different moments, we spoke of the necessity of increasing consciousness so that it begins to embrace the whole circle of human life. For that reason it was once said in the early teaching that we must get to know every 'I' in us and it was added that why we are all wrong and cannot grow further is because we are conscious of one 'I' at a time which we take as our consciousness, as ourselves. Therefore we see no contradictions in ourselves and live, so to speak, always in a very small place at a time. As Work-memory is increased, through self-observation, we begin to distrust the particular 'I' we happen to be in at the particular moment of time. When I say that we do not trust it, I mean that we do not quite believe what it is saying, what it is thinking, what it is feeling, just at that moment. If we do not begin to understand this, any 'I' that happens to be at the moment uppermost in us, any 'I' that we take as ourselves at that moment, and which says and does and promises things for a very short time, later we know nothing about. In other words, we have to become far more conscious of this rotation of 'I's in us so that we can remember what one 'I' said and also what another 'I' said. Otherwise we have no distinct Being —which means that our Being is constantly shifting, being controlled by temporary 'I's of the moment.

Now what is that thing in us that can stand higher than ordinary 'I's, and why is it said so much in the Work that we must observe our different 'I's? The answer is that we have Observing 'I' in us if we can only use it and it can have a memory of its own because it stands outside the machinery of these turning 'I's and views them, as it were, in a detached way and makes in itself its own memory of these different 'I's that it has observed—and this memory is called Work-memory. You must understand that each 'I' mechanically getting up and having charge for the moment has its own memory but Observing 'I' has a quite different quality of memory.

Now I wish to speak to you about narrowness of outlook. We may have a certain vague memory of having acted in one way and then acted in a contrary way. We are often uneasy, and I do not like any man or woman who is not a little uneasy about himself or herself. Only when you have a vague uneasiness about your own contradictions, and things which you find incompatible with other things in yourself, you must realize that you have a certain kind of observation, a certain kind of vague consciousness of what your own life is like, but that you are identified with it and judge yourself in consequence according to your upbringing. Now the point about Observing 'I' established by the influence of the Work and the acceptance and valuation of it, is that it is something that can observe you uncritically—that is, without identifying. It observes you impersonally, it observes your Personality impersonally, and it remembers what it has observed uncritically, impersonally. Personality is composed of different 'I's and is, as it were, turning like a wheel so that at one moment one 'I' is uppermost and in charge and at another moment another is uppermost and in charge. We have a dim recollection of this already but we always take sides in regard to this dim observation of ourselves. But the establishment of the Observing 'I' in the Work-sense is the establishment in you of a level of consciousness above these different ever changing 'I's. The Observing 'I' in the sense of the Work does not take sides with anything. It merely records what you are doing, what you are saying, at different moments, through the action of different 'I's, and does not say that this is better or this is worse. Observing 'I' is not shocked by anything, it is not a kind of Grandmamma or Grandpapa in you, but it is quite pure and simple, and Mr. Ouspensky used often to compare it with a camera that simply photographs your psychological state at each moment. He said Observing 'I' must stand outside the Personality, stand outside this cage of 'I's, this Zoological Garden of 'I's, that are constantly taking charge in a kind of rotation and calling themselves 'I'—that is, *you*. The establishment of this Observing 'I', he used to point out, is something that is very difficult because such observation as we have ordinarily in social intercourse is based really on one 'I' a little bit observing another 'I' and criticizing it and finding fault with it. The Observing 'I' in the Work-sense stands outside all these 'I's that take charge of us at each moment. It is therefore on a level above Personality, and, as you know, this Observing 'I' that the Work emphasizes so much, and about which it is so constantly said that it must be uncritical and have no acquired moral values, is the most important thing to establish in ourselves if we want to change. This Observing 'I' that the Work speaks of is under the influence of the Work itself—i.e. it comes under the influence of the Work later on. But at first our task is to establish an impersonal uncritical observation of ourselves. What does uncritical mean? It means that if you observe something in yourself you do not criticize it as good or bad. You simply see that you—i.e. the machine of yourself, the acquired 'I's in you—are doing this or that at the particular moment. They are talking in this way, they are talking in that way ; they are feeling this, they are feeling that. No single 'I' in your Personality will ever include the whole of yourself in its consciousness. But the real Observing 'I' will include the whole of your life eventually. It will become conscious of all sides of yourself. It will have its own uncritical, gentle memory of all the different sides of you. Certain things in your life are incompatible with other things and so you feel conflict and distress. For instance, to a person with a very narrow outlook, many things become incompatible as a result of this very narrow outlook. A man thinks things are evil owing to a very narrow outlook. Now suppose this person becomes broader-minded many things that were formerly incompatible begin to take their place and no longer seem incompatible. But for Observing 'I' nothing is incompatible because nothing is criticized, so we might say in a rather too small way that Observing 'I' is very broad-minded. As you know, lots of people are sure of many things that they do not possess. I fancy all of you think you are very broad-minded and I always dislike it when I am told that I have to meet a person who is broad-minded. I may remind you that this is no sort of description to give me of a person who wants to come into this Work. Your so-called broad-minded person, yourself, is extremely narrow-minded. What does broad-minded mean? It is not a Work-expression. Do you think that this Observing 'I', when it is once established, and observes and records every side of yourself, is broad-minded? Yes, of course it is. Unless you come into this relationship of real Observing 'I', which is so uncritical, you will not be able to shift yourself from where you are because you will be always in the turning wheel of different and contradictory 'I's that you try vaguely with a kind of dim consciousness to reconcile with one another. You have to accept the whole of your life, all the side that is dark to you at the moment, all that side that is unconscious to you at the instant, the very narrow outlook—which of course we all deny having—as the result of your little Being, your small tedious little Being, always quarrelling and objecting and finding fault at every moment. Now the only cure for this is to broaden your Being, and that means to become more conscious of the whole of your Being, all these 'I's in you, and to be able to endure the contradictions of all of them. All this is only possible by establishing this uncritical and sincere Observing 'I'. Through its memory, through a right relationship to it, you will find that you begin to change in your whole picture of yourself, in your whole idea of yourself; because you must remember that when you die all your life appears to you with all its contradictions, because it is yourself. It is sometimes said that people see their whole lives when drowning or something like that, and this is not nonsense. But what we have to do is to try to see all round ourselves in this life before we die. Then certainly we will no longer have the same opinion of ourselves, the same prejudices, the same buffers. But this is the work of Observing 'I'. This is what Observing 'I' must fulfil in ourselves little by little.

When you have no Observing 'I', when you have no power of separating from what life has made you, when you take yourself for granted, then you must remember that you have a very small Bank balance and are very quickly overdrawn. Now what does this mean, to have a very small Bank balance? Of course, it has nothing to do with money or your literal Bank. It refers to your capacity for bearing things without being identified. Suppose you have a very high opinion of yourself, then your Bank balance is very quickly overdrawn. Let me try to explain this to some people who cannot understand about psychological ideas, psychological meaning. If you have a very great opinion of yourself you will be easily offended, easily irritated, easily upset, therefore your Bank balance will be very quickly overdrawn. That is, you will soon feel negative, feel offended. Now you should not lay up treasure in any ordinary mechanical Bank. We are told to lay up treasure in Heaven—that is, on a higher level. If you are insupportably full of your own excellence and merit, are you laying up treasure in Heaven? No, you are simply a person who is going to be very easily offended, insulted, very soon overdrawn on his or her Bank.

We have to acknowledge and accept all sides of ourselves, because only through the acknowledgement, the acceptance, the consciousness of all sides of ourselves can we advance at all. This is exactly what broadens our Being. Under the influence of the memory of Observing 'I', under the influence of this uncritical self-observation, we begin to feel loosened from all sorts of fantastic ideas of ourselves. We begin to be loosened from all sorts of fantastic attributions to ourselves of virtues and merit that we do not possess at all. We certainly then become little children. We certainly then begin to understand what the opening words of the Sermon on the Mount mean. We certainly then cease to be big, overswelling with some small pride or vanity. We begin to get an entirely new sense of ourselves, an entirely new feeling, entirely new thoughts. We cease to be the person we have imagined ourselves to be all through our lives. For this you must have a different kind of self-knowledge. Your whole groundwork becomes different. Through the influence of Observing 'I' you will be rescued from many dangers. What is our greatest danger as we get older? Our greatest danger is to crystallize out into our idea of ourselves. After a time things begin to become rather fixed in us, we begin to believe our imagination of ourselves, of the kind of people we are. What good and kind creatures we are. But this uncritical Observing 'I', if it is supported properly by the constant feeling and valuation of the Work, begins to prevent us from this early crystallization into a certain definite kind of person which is quite false. If we can give value to the Work, then we can give value to what Observing 'I' notices about ourselves, and then we shall not be in such great danger of crystallizing out into what we imagine ourselves to be, into some definite opinion of ourselves, into our own excellence, our own extraordinary merit, our own unexplained values. We are all such tiny and unpleasant creatures that it takes a great deal of self-observation to observe that we are really quite ridiculous in our vanity, in our pride. I rather fancy that some people always think that they have a marvellous gift to bestow upon other people. But what is this precious gift that people want to bestow on others? Have you asked yourselves individually what you have in yourselves worth while for anyone else to accept? I think after a time in the Work people become more simple in this way. And why is this so? Because they really begin to observe themselves instead of imagining that they are what they believe. They begin to see that the gulf between what they imagine themselves to have been and what they are is very wide. When this happens through the constant uncritical influence of Observing 'I', the whole relationship to oneself begins to change. All that you have hitherto based your value on, all your different forms of feeling superior to others, all this begins to be dissolved. You no longer build yourself up on False Personality that is your most dangerous enemy and is composed entirely of imagination. Of course, this cannot be done artificially by mock humility than which I fancy nothing is worse. You can go about looking down your nose while inside you are full of hissing serpents. No, I am not speaking of any false humility. What I am speaking about is what the Work speaks about—namely, that if Observing 'I' is established in you and you really begin to observe yourself and how you speak and how you feel and how you think and how contradictory the whole thing is, then you will have a very beautiful experience because you will no longer have to keep up the invented person to whom you are a slave. Now this can only happen in the Work because the Work must hold you at certain moments and give you strength. No one is allowed in the Work, no one is allowed by the Work, to observe themselves further than they can bear. You may be quite sure that in the atmosphere of the Work no one will suffer wrongly. A great many have not even begun to observe themselves and the reason is that they cannot do it, they cannot get beyond their idea of themselves, or rather they cannot get under their imagination of themselves. Instantly they begin to feel they are no good, of no importance, they suffocate. And yet I must remind you again of what we were told when we went to the French Institute that "Personality has scarcely any right to exist here", and I will also remind you at the end of this paper that unless a man begins to realize his own nothingness he can get nowhere. If a man or a woman begins to see through his or her self, through all their lies, and their inventions of themselves and if they do it in the atmosphere of the Work, feeling that the Work will lead them to a new level of Being, they are safe and they will undergo little by little a perfectly definite and real transformation of themselves, but if they try to do this without the influence of the Work behind them they will get nowhere and all their observation will be useless and simply lead to quarrels, arguments and negative emotion. We are all trying to study something that is very big, and we must realize that we are very small.

ON CHANGING OUR LEVEL OF BEING

Let us begin this paper by saying that a typical feature in us will always attract a typical event. In speaking about Chief Feature Mr. Ouspensky said on one occasion that Chief Feature is comparable with a number of typical features that can constitute Chief Feature. At a meeting here recently we spoke about different levels of Being and drew them as lines, as parallel lines, like the wires on telegraph posts. It was said that if we could raise the level of our Being even a little by work on ourselves, which is the only way to do this, we might get to the next parallel line above our present level and thereby avoid a number of unpleasant things that would inevitably happen to us were we to remain on the same level. If we always behave typically, characteristically, and that of course means mechanically, if we are simply machines reacting to life and to people always in the same way as we have always reacted, then we shall always be following one telegraph wire, one line of Being. We shall always be following the lowest level of our Being—that is, the mechanical level. A person who does this does not transform his life in the least possible way, so life always meets him in exactly the same way. The same things, the same situations, the same misunderstandings, the same difficulties, always meet him or her. In a way you can, as it were, deduce your level of Being from noticing what always happens to you, because your level of Being attracts your life. This means that your life is your Being, your life is an expression of what you are, therefore your Being is what you are, and all that happens to you in life is the result of your level of Being. Of course if you are perfectly satisfied with your life there is no necessity for you to attempt to change your level of Being, but I have always noticed that people who say that they are satisfied with their lives are not really so at all. They say things like this to me: "I am quite satisfied with my life, but I dislike this or that person very much," or "I did not have a proper chance," or "I am very worried about someone," or "I do not seem to get on properly in the way that I should like for I always have these recurring difficulties," or "These people do not seem to like me," or "I do not think I am appreciated properly," and so on. Yet they say that they are satisfied with their lives. What I am trying to say is that people do not see any connection between their Being and their lives and, as you know, one reason is because no one ever thinks that what happens to him in life is anything to do with his level of Being. People do not see that their level of Being attracts all these things which they regard as having nothing to do with themselves. But the Work teaches that it is your level of Being that attracts all this and keeps you constantly under its influence.

On one occasion Mr. Ouspensky said: "Can you see your level of Being at all yet? Can you see where you stand in the world of Being yet?" Now I would ask you: "Do you understand about levels of Being? Do you understand how deeply the Work is based on different levels from the Ray of Creation downwards and how everything is at a certain level of Being in this vast scheme of Being reaching up to the Being of God?" The question then arises in a practical sense: "How can we change our level of Being? What is it we have to do to change this level of Being that we speak of as all having?" The answer is that the whole Work is about changing our Being and giving us methods as to how to change it. We spoke briefly of the Sermon on the Mount as being a practical illustration of how to change one's level of Being, and we took the first saying: "Blessed are the poor in spirit for theirs is the Kingdom of Heaven". Now bliss is a wonderful thing to touch. The Work says that we must practise non-identifying, and non-identifying begins with not identifying with yourself. Now if you are full of yourself you are rich in spirit, but if you begin to observe yourself through what the Work teaches about identifying you will become poor in spirit—that is, you will not identify with yourself so much. What will the result be? You will find what for you is bliss. You will find an enormous relief, a strange kind of happiness in no longer having to keep up the idea of yourself with which you were formerly so identified. Now here you have a quite direct practical method of changing your level of Being. The Work also, as you know, speaks of many other methods which have to be applied at the moment. All the practical work, all the directions given to you constantly in terms of the original teaching, belong to methods of changing your Being. That is why I say to you so often: Do you know practically what the Work teaches that you have to do? It is a very good thing when a person reaches that stage in the Work when he or she realizes that it is about something absolutely practical and that all these phrases, these formulations, that they have to listen to for so long, are real instructions as to what they have to do to change the level of Being at which they are mechanically.

Let us take another phrase from the Sermon on the Mount: "Blessed are the meek." This means that those who are meek will get bliss, inner happiness, will get something that everyone is looking for because no one is happy internally, no one has this strange source of inner happiness called bliss. People often think blessedness is what is going to happen later on but from the Work point of view as well as from the Gospel point of view this is not the right way to take the profound idea that is indicated here. You can get a source of inner happiness if you apply the ideas of the Work to yourself. Now what does 'meek' mean in the original sense of the Greek word? It means 'not resentful'. "Blessed are those who are not resentful." Now I think you can connect this with that phrase used in the Work which says that we must stop making internal accounts. When you are resentful are you not making internal accounts? Are you not considering internally? You will notice that the Sermon on the Mount begins with the practice of non-identifying with yourself and puts it into the phrase: those who are poor in spirit will get bliss. A man very full of himself, a man completely identified with himself, is a man who will not be able to reach this different level of Being where different influences begin to act on him that will fill up this extraordinary lack of inner happiness that everyone, if he is honest, knows he suffers from. Now you will see that if a man can observe himself and cease so much to identify with himself and with his pictures of himself and with his vanity and so on, he will be able to practise being meek in the real sense of the Greek word—that is, he will not be so resentful when people do not behave to him as he thinks they ought to behave—that is, he will not make so many internal accounts against others, and, in fact, he may eventually reach the state that is mentioned in the Lord's Prayer of being able to cancel the debts of others against him completely, for this is the real meaning of the Greek word translated as *forgive* in the phrase "forgive us our debts as we forgive others". No, the meaning is far more powerful than that, far more practical. The meaning is *cancel completely*. From this we can see how close the teaching of the Work about not making internal accounts comes to what is said also in the Gospels. I remind you that this Work was always said to be esoteric Christianity—namely, the inner meaning and fragrance of the Gospels that has survived. The Gospels speak a great deal about the Kingdom of Heaven and what it is necessary to do to enter it. The Gospels say that you have to become a quite different person to have any chance of entering the Kingdom of Heaven. They also say that unless a man becomes as a little child he cannot enter the Kingdom of Heaven. Yes, but what does it mean practically? The Work talks not about the Kingdom of Heaven but about the Conscious Circle of Humanity, and by 'that it means people at a much higher level of Being than we are at as we are now. Christ lays down certain rules, certain indications, certain teachings, about how to get to the Kingdom of Heaven. These are given in the Sermon on the Mount, and we are given a perfectly clear indication as to how we may reach the Conscious Circle of Humanity, by work on our Being, by work on our level of Being as we are now. I fancy that the Sermon on the Mount cannot be understood as it is translated save through what we have been given through this Work. By means of what we have been given by this Work on its practical side we can understand more or less what the opening verses of the Sermon on the Mount, which have been so badly translated by ignorant people, really mean. As I said, we can understand what it means to be poor in spirit in the right way.

Now let me speak about the next level of Being awaiting you. What for you is the Kingdom of Heaven? What for you is the Conscious Circle of Humanity? It is no good thinking about matters very remote from you. The whole thing is very close to you—in fact, "closer than your neck-vein". Your Kingdom of Heaven, your Conscious Circle of Humanity, is your next level of Being, which lies very close to but very distinct from your present level of Being. That is why it is such a good thing to work on yourself. That is why once you begin to see this you feel that you have something that no one will ever take away from you. You begin to understand what the Work is about, what the Kingdom of Heaven is about, what the Conscious Circle of Humanity is about, on your own scale. Each one of you can become a little more conscious than you are. Each one of you, whether man or woman, can live a little more consciously than you do. Each one of you can feel the force of the Work entering you in the ordinary affairs of the day. You can *do* this Work, remember. You cannot do in life, but you can do this Work. I remember it was once said a long time ago by G. that we must remember that we can do this Work. What would be the good of teaching a system of Work that no one could do? He said: "All call out in loud voices and say: I can work." We did this and I think we all got force from it. So every one of you say to yourselves sometimes just this phrase: "I can work," because this is what we can do. I *can* remember myself according to my own level; I *can* separate from negative emotions according to my own state and my own level; I *can* stop making internal accounts; I *can* practise non-identifying; I *can* stop fantasies; I *can* stop self-justifying; and so on. And even if it is only for a short time yet you are working if you can do this and you will change your level of Being, not downwards, but upwards, not outwards, but inwards, and through this you will come under different influences, better influences, influences in other words that belong to your next level of Being, your next telegraph wire, this next level of Being close to you and above you. But you will never get up to this telegraph wire, this next level of Being, unless you practise this Work and you cannot practise it unless you begin to feel its good and so begin to value it as one of the most important things you have ever met in your life, because if you do not value this Work and if you do not see that it is about something other than what you have ever done before in your life, it will simply pass into your ordinary level of Being, your mechanical Being, and will become twisted and distorted and useless.

Some of you know that there is discontinuity in the Universe. This has been discovered and verified by experiment. In other words, there are different levels discontinuous with one another. The level of Being awaiting you just above your present line which is your evolution, your inner development, your inner growth, is discontinuous with your present level, just as one rung of a ladder is not continuous with the next. You have to jump. You cannot apply the methods of thinking that you have at your present level of Being to the Work because the Work comes down from above to you and you have to go from below upwards to it. You may argue that it is a very good thing to be identified but the Work says it is not and you have to see for yourself by inner experience through long self-observation that it is not good to identify. The Work comes down very close but it is not on the same level.

Now suppose you have been in this Work for some time and you have heard many things said in the Work and you have always taken all the things you have heard just on the level of your Being as it is now, then I will tell you at once that you have never tried to apply the Work but simply listened to it. You have never observed yourself from what this Work teaches. You have no Work-Observing 'I' formed in you. You have never seen where and how you are identified with yourself, you have never observed your pictures, your imagination of yourself, you have never observed your forms of internal considering, making accounts. You have never observed when you lie. You have never observed your forms of self-justifying. You have never observed different 'I's in yourself or even different centres in yourself. You are simply asleep at your level of Being and however earnestly you may tell me that you want the Work I will not believe you in my heart. I notice that such people say to me: "I would like to hear more about the Work." But if I am a teacher of Greek and have taught you over and over again how to pronounce some simple word and make a few simple sentences and I notice that not one of you can speak even a single word of Greek, then I will come to the conclusion that it is useless teaching you Greek. One person, however, may suddenly begin to speak some quite good Greek to me and I realize that this person has been taking in what has been said practically and has really begun to work.

So once more, at the end of this paper, I ask you again as so often: What work have you done on yourself to-day? Have you observed, each one of you, anything of what the Work teaches you about yourself? Have you noticed yourself being very identified? Have you noticed yourself being negative? Have you noticed yourself laying up a lot of accounts against others as by criticizing them, seeming superior to them, thinking they are fools? Have you noticed your forms of imagination and given them free play? Have you been full of self-pity? Have you been gloomy and depressed and useless to others? Have you spoken only mechanically and said things mechanically when you might have said things more consciously? Has the day defeated you or have you defeated the day? Have you lost force all the time or have you gained force? Have you got the feeling that you are doing something else than merely living the day and objecting to it? Have you gone to the day or has the day made you go to it? In all this you will see a great difference between living mechanically and living your life more consciously. We all suffer from our level of Being. We have to see that we ourselves have to do something, each one of us. The mechanical way in which we take everything characterizes our level of Being. We have to take things differently and the Work shews us in what way we must begin to take things differently. And even if you have behaved badly, if you have given way to negative emotion and even worse experiences, if you have reacted mechanically, you can go back and see where you went to sleep and in some way correct it, and remember next time that you have to live more consciously, for all this Work is about how to live more consciously in mechanical life.

ON BEGINNING TO LIVE MORE CONSCIOUSLY

Each one of you is under the Law of the Pendulum. Each one of you feels good and then bad, feels happy and then feels dejected. Each one of you feels affection and liking and then feels the opposite—disliking —and that curious opposite to affection for which there is no word. This is all mechanical life. This is all living mechanically. This is all living in the swing of the Pendulum of life, and as long as you do this what you gain you will lose and so you will always remain at the same level of Being. At one moment you love, at the next moment you hate; at one moment you feel enthusiasm, the next moment you feel dejected; at one moment you think you are a fine person and the next moment you feel you are not. This is the Law of the Pendulum which swings to and fro. Somehow or other we have to be no longer so much under this inevitable Law of the Pendulum which causes the tides to advance and retire, which causes the winter to be followed by the summer, the summer by the winter, and which in the case of your own heart causes it to expand and contract. The Law of the Pendulum is very well illustrated by the action of the heart. The heart has two phases called diastole and systole. The diastole of the heart is when it is receiving blood, the systole of the heart is when it is contracting and driving the blood through the body. You can see perhaps how interesting this idea of the Pendulum is as illustrated by the heart because when the heart is passive and is receiving blood it is on one side of the Pendulum, it accepts what is coming in to it, and then at a certain moment it changes its rhythm and becomes active and drives out what it has received, and this nourishes the whole body. Diastole is connected with a Greek verb meaning to put in order, to arrange, to make ready. This means that when the heart is not doing anything but receiving blood it is, as it were, arranging, putting in order, making ready for this next phase called contraction or systole. Systole means, in the Greek, drawing together of what has been received and driving it forth, as in the contraction of the heart that drives into the body the blood that it has received. I have often thought that this is a very good way of thinking about the Pendulum in a practical sense. We have sometimes moments of expansion and sometimes moments of contraction. We have moments in which things go right and moments in which things go wrong. The Pendulum of our psychology, of our emotions, of our general feelings, swings to and fro. But when the Pendulum swings back this should be surely a phase in which things are put in order, in which one consults oneself, in which one gets things arranged rightly and made ready before one goes forward again. You cannot expect always to be just the same. Yet how many people are disappointed when, having felt sómething, they find that for the time being they no longer feel it. Then of course they quarrel, feel bored and

731

so on. In other words, the negative swing of the Pendulum for most people is simply a blank. But it should not be a blank. It should be a phase inhabited by consciousness and by a sense of the Work in which one collects oneself together again and reflects, and does not necessarily think that everything is over, at an end.

Now if one can inhabit with consciousness both sides of the Pendulum swing in every centre, in every part of a centre, one's life no longer becomes discontented, a mere function of the Pendulum swinging. One learns to see things from two points of view. One learns to take oneself from two points of view and especially one learns to take other people in the same way. Instead of being very disgusted or disappointed or bored, one begins to inhabit this uncivilized country in oneself, this barbarism, with more conscious thoughts, with memory, and then one returns on the swing having prepared something, and once more re-enters into life without being depressed and without feeling hopeless. All this that I am speaking about to-night has to do with seeing both sides, the dark and the bright side, together, through conscious memory, through work, and it is only through work that you can remember both sides of the Pendulum and so gradually pass psychologically into the middle part of the Pendulum where everything that we seek in this Work lies. This corresponds to making full circle, to being able to go round the circle of life so that it is no longer a Pendulum but a circular motion which is no longer governed by opposites. (I have already told you that the motion of a Pendulum is really a circular motion seen in two dimensions. Try to illustrate this for yourself practically.) Now when you go round the circle of all experience you will begin to include the dark side of yourself in your consciousness and you no longer see any contradictions such as the Pendulum view of life gives. This means an increase of consciousness. This means seeing that summer and winter are not opposites but lie on a circle, a rhythm that is necessary. People who live very much in opposites, people who are always arguing whether this is right or that is right—as we see very obviously to-day —are in the illusion of the Pendulum.

I will quote you a very ancient saying about this. As long as you stand on a basis of rigid right and wrong you cannot make this psychological circle in yourself, as, for example, in the Enneagram about which we have not spoken much recently. The quotation is from the writings of Kwang-ze. He says: "All subjects may be looked at from two points of view—from that and from this . . . But that view involves both a right and a wrong; and this view involves also a right and a wrong:— are there indeed, or are there not, the two views, that and this? They have not found their point of correspondency which is called the pivot of the Tao. As soon as one finds this pivot, he stands in the centre of the ring (of thought) where he can respond without end to the changing views;—without end to those affirming, and without end to those denying. Therefore I said, 'There is nothing like the proper light (of the mind).' "

This thing called the Tao is really the Work. It is a reconciliation of opposites in yourself and the reaching of a new place in which the opposites do not control you. It is called the Tao in ancient Chinese esotericism. It is a Way. Tao means a Way or a harmonizing Way. For example, at one moment you think you are good and at the next moment you think you are bad, and if you observe yourself critically you will always be in this dilemma, in this double feeling.

Now I quote from a later writing on the same subject. According to Plato's report, Socrates tells his pupils that he once went to see a wise woman, the prophetess Diotima, and asked her about love. He said to her that Love was a great deity and beautiful, but Diotima replied that he was neither beautiful nor good. "What then, is Love ugly and evil?" he objected, but Diotima answered: "Do you think that everything which is not beautiful must of necessity be ugly?" "Certainly," said Socrates. You will see here that Socrates was thinking on the opposites—that is, he was thinking in the ordinary way in which we all think that if a thing is not beautiful it must be ugly and if a thing is not good it must be bad. The conversation continues. Diotima asked Socrates: "Do you think everything that is not wise is ignorant? Do you not perceive that there is something between ignorance and wisdom?" "What is that?" said Socrates. "To have a right opinion or conjecture," was the answer, "a right opinion is something between understanding and ignorance." Socrates admitted the truth of this and Diotima then continued: "Do not then say that what is not beautiful is of necessity deformed, nor what is not good is of necessity evil, nor, since you have confessed that Love is neither beautiful nor good, infer, therefore, that he is deformed or evil, but rather something intermediate."

If we are on the Pendulum all thought and feeling lies in opposites. If a man does not agree with your political views he is hateful to you. If a man does not like you, he dislikes you, and so on. This is the Law of the Pendulum exemplified in all of us at our present state of Being and Knowledge. This is how the world of war and strife is carried on —namely, by people disagreeing with each other according to the Law of the Pendulum. In this Work we must find some way of reconciling these opposites and not being on this Pendulum swing at every moment, because you will all know by now that by being on the Pendulum swing and taking up violent opposite standpoints nothing can be reconciled, no harmony can be produced, and our own lives and the life of humanity will continue as always. I knock you down and then you knock me down. One side produces the other. One opposite with which you identify instantly causes other people to take up an opposite opinion. It seems to me so important that you all begin to realize this, and especially in regard to yourselves because your own views of yourselves are on these opposites and are specially governed by False Personality. You all do many things that you do not accept, that you do not include, in your general sense of yourselves, and so you swing all the time and

to do it, but if your level drops, you will both object and dislike, and your objections will feed your dislike. But if you will stop objecting you will find that your dislike will not be fed and will not increase. This is a result that is well worth reaching, through self-observation and through work on yourself. It will enable you to pass through many difficult trials in this Work and it will also make your ordinary life much more simple. Always remember that if you object to other people and nourish these objections, you may be certain that these other people will object to you and nourish their objections. All this is to do with rendering Personality more passive and weakening the False Personality. We must all practise silence towards one another, inner silence, stopping inner talk in regard to objecting to one another. Then things will grow and develop in our Branch of the Work. What is the result? The result is that if we stop all this mechanical objecting we begin to include other people in our lives. So we shall see that this last talk about practical psychology has to do with the first part of the paper. If you like and dislike you are on the Pendulum and nothing can happen to you from the Work point of view. Now if you non-object, which is not making accounts and therefore non-identifying with people, you will begin to be much richer and wider and more sane in yourself, and after a time you will feel your disliking and liking change, but this will never happen if you object the whole time, and I mean by objecting, objecting in yourself although you do not express it.

In connection with all this I got a very interesting report from one of you who met a woman who had undergone severe mental stress and had broken down. This woman said that she had met Lucifer in her visions and that she knew him because he had such hopeless eyes, and then she said: "You know, sin is not smoking too much or drinking too much. It is something which grows big inside you and makes you think you are right." You know that in the East people who have got a little beyond ordinary mental control are often regarded as sacred, being under the hand of God. All that I can say is that these two remarks seem to touch very closely on what this Work is speaking about. False Personality cuts us off from everything and drives us straight into life—according to this woman, straight into hell, where Lucifer with his hopeless eyes rules.

ON SELF-REMEMBERING

We should remember ourselves at least once a day. It is very important to remember oneself and in every act of Self-Remembering lies one of the great inner meanings of this Work and of all Esotericism in general. If we cannot remember ourselves once a day then we should remember ourselves three times a day. That is to say, we should make a bigger effort. Remembering oneself is just as if an actor on the stage who had become completely absorbed in the rôle he was playing suddenly remembered that he was merely acting the rôle and that he was really somebody else and not the part he was playing. This would mean that he would wake up. He would no longer take himself as the hero or the king or the cardinal that he was playing. But what do we do? We are just like that actor who has forgotten that he is playing a rôle. We find ourselves fitted into the parts belonging to every phase of tragedy and comedy but we identify with everything. We do not see that we ourselves are something else, something different, and so we do not remember ourselves and so we are said in the Work to be asleep. A little while ago it was asked: Why should we not identify? It is possible to answer this question from a thousand points of view. One great reason is that if we identify we are not doing this Work. The question is like saying: Why should we do this Work? There is absolutely no reason why we should do this Work if we do not wish to. This Work is only for people who are looking for something. If we identify we cannot remember ourselves. As I said, the Work lays the greatest emphasis on Self-Remembering. It says that the most important thing we have to do is to remember ourselves and it adds that this can only be understood when we realize that we do not remember ourselves. Now if a man is identified he is not remembering himself. There are degrees and qualities of identifying. Some slight forms of identifying are trivial and unimportant. On the other hand, some slight forms of identifying lead very speedily to bigger forms and of these one has to be careful, just as one has to be careful about all small things that start up in oneself innocently, so to speak, and very speedily lead into unpleasant places in ourselves such as very unpleasant forms of negative emotion. One has to be just as careful where one walks inside oneself after a time, as where one walks in the world visible to one's senses. Through self-observation our internal world becomes visible to us— that is, we become conscious of it and learn to recognize where we are in it and what takes us down in it and what takes us upwards in regard to our experiences and the small degrees in level of Being that we all possess. Can you afford to walk in your sleep too long?

Since identifying is the enemy of Self-Remembering and since Self-Remembering is our supreme task, it is clear that we have to study our forms of identifying. With what have you been identified most to-day?

Or let me ask you another question: Have you remembered yourself to-day? Of course, we do not take our lives in the sense of parts that we have been given to play. The Work says that we start from our lives just as they are and that this is the best starting-point for the Work. We do not have to break off our lives and go into monasteries or hermitages. For instance, our lives may go on just the same as before, but if we begin to understand what the Work means we take our lives in a different way. I always find this difficult to explain to those who do not yet catch a glimpse of what is meant. Suppose you were to go on a stage where there were hundreds and thousands of actors dressed up in all sorts of costumes, quarrelling and making love and murdering and so on, and you realized to your horror that they were all fast asleep and were completely identified with their parts, which means that they were taking themselves to be what they had been cast to be in the big drama—what would you do? You would probably seize hold of the nearest one and shake him violently and try to make him wake up. You might shout in his ear and say: " Don't be so silly, don't stick that knife into that person, you are asleep, you forget who you really are." And what do you think the result would be? Probably that knife would be pushed into you !

Now if we can see that our lives are somewhat similar to parts given to actors and that each of us has a different part best suited to him, our attitude would change. What does "best suited to him" mean? It means best suited to him to wake up from. If you take your life on Earth as an end in itself you can never get to the attitude that the Work teaches. The Work takes life as a means to another end. If you take life as an end in itself can you ever cease to identify with it ?

You know how in various myths and fairy stories and esoteric legends there is the idea that the hero is sent out into the world to seek for something, and he is warned not to forget whence he came— this is one thing that he must always remember. Let me quote from an ancient hymn which contains a great deal of teaching. Here the son of kings is sent by his parents down "into Egypt", into the world, to bring back a pearl. But after he had been in the world some time he forgot that he was the son of kings, he forgot the pearl and "lay in a deep sleep ". He was awakened from sleep and remembered himself. " I remembered that I was a son of kings," he said, "and my free soul longed for its natural state. I remembered the pearl, for which I had been sent to Egypt . . . and I snatched away the pearl and turned to go back to my Father's house." In this allegory you will see that the prince remembered his divine origin, he remembered that he was not what he had begun to take himself in life.

Many ancient teachings speak of life as being an illusion. But this is not easy to understand. The Work does not speak about life as an illusion but it says a great deal about our taking life in the wrong illusory way and it constantly emphasizes that we must learn to take it in the right way. In this connection it is constantly speaking about identifying both with ourselves and with the events of life. This identifying, whose direction is inwards and outwards, keeps us asleep and makes it impossible for us to remember ourselves and in consequence makes it impossible for certain influences to reach us that can help us, consisting in certain emotions, certain thoughts, certain feelings, not derived from our business affairs, our daily existence, or life as seen, as it appears to be.

The illusion of life lies, the Work says, in Man's thinking he can do, in Man's thinking he is conscious, in Man's thinking that he is a unity. The Work says that in life everything happens in the only possible way it can happen. When you apparently act in life, when you apparently do something in life, you are doing the only thing that you could do. It is not you who are doing it. When you begin to see this, when you begin to realize your mechanicalness in this way, you are already beginning to remember yourself, you are already beginning to be separated from the machine of yourself and to approach something that lies behind the machine of yourself in the direction of Real 'I'. This is why the Work says that realization of one's own mechanicalness is a form of Self-Remembering. In this kind of Self-Remembering you are aware that what you are doing and saying and thinking is not really you. You become a spectator of yourself and you see that all that you have called you and your life is an illusion in the sense that it is all happening, and in that sense it is not real—it is not Reality. When I see that an event is entangling me and that I am reacting to this event quite mechanically, the whole business becomes unreal to me because where I thought before that *I* was doing, *I* was acting, *I* was seeing, I see it now as *IT* that is acting. In the same way in separating from one's inner fantasies and thoughts that spring from False Personality, from vanity, and so on, a person may have a moment of Self-Remembering in which he escapes from their hypnotic power and sees that they are trying to get hold of him and that that is their real object—namely, to put him to sleep again. You must remember that everything in life seeks to keep us asleep. In the Legend of Endymion it is related that the Moon kept Endymion asleep because this was the only way in which she could keep her power over him. Remember that the Work teaches that we live in a world of sleeping people in which everything happens, and that we are also asleep. The only difference is that we are trying to wake up. We cannot change life. A man must begin with himself—a woman with herself. We can begin to change ourselves. But this is impossible unless we begin to see that we ourselves are asleep, that we are identified with the tragic or comic parts given us in life, and that we have forgotten ourselves and that we do not even try to remember ourselves. Are you overcome by your difficulties? Do you feel no one has ever been in such adverse circumstances? Or, on the contrary, do you feel yourself the happiest person in the world? In Self-Remembering one does not start from this situation, this state of affairs, this domestic scene, this particular event one is in. Life becomes our teacher only when we understand that it offers us different circumstances, different experiences, different events at different moments, with which not to identify. Life is a series of outer events and inner states and they are always shifting and turning. If we stick at every point, then we are identified all the way round. We take everything personally, as being ourselves, like the actor who takes every rôle he has to play as himself. Then we are indeed asleep and being turned round like little wheels by the big wheel of life. When all traces of individuality fail, collectivity grows. We have to struggle hard not to become only small wheels driven by life, by the circle of events. The secret lies in not identifying, and in Self-Remembering. But if you take every little upset, every domestic incident, seriously and with full identifying, how then can you work or expect to work? You do not even realize you are playing a typical rôle that millions of others have played or are playing, and that you will not get free from it unless you wake up and see that you are not remembering yourself.

Now we each have a circle of different 'I's that revolve. Each plays its rôle—pathetic, silly, fine, serio-comic, tragic, and various other stock parts. The trouble is that we do not play these rôles but they play us. Really to play a rôle in the Work-sense a man must be conscious. To play a rôle consciously is an example of what the Work calls *doing*. Only a conscious man can *do*. As we are, rôles play us. So it is a good thing to observe them and not identify with them so much—to see them acting in oneself and yet not feel that one is them—to say *silently* "I am not this!" This is to begin to remember oneself as different from these 'I's. But every day we must practise Self-Remembering at first simply by stopping everything, by being not in anything, not connected with anything in life or in ourselves as life has made us.

Now remember, a man identified with himself cannot remember himself because he has no horizon above him. He is limited by himself. A man who blames everybody, a man who ascribes everything to himself, is identified with himself and really dead. Let us recall the first three levels of Consciousness: (1) Sleep in bed—(2) So-called waking consciousness, in which people live and also kill each other—and (3) Self-Remembering. It is only to this level—the level of Self-Remembering —that help can penetrate and actually reach us from higher levels of the Universe of Being—that is, from Conscious Humanity. That is why it is so important to practise Self-Remembering—to try to do it and gradually find the way to do it. If the intention is sincere and the aim intelligent and based on an understanding of the Work, the way will be found.

Sometimes when you watch a person you may wonder what would happen if he or she saw their forms of identifying in a flash—their mannerisms, their dress, their intonations, their expressions, the seriousness with which they take themselves and their position. Yes, and the same applies to ourselves.

I will tell you a story about forgetting to remember oneself. There

740

was once an island on which a number of people landed from a ship in order to rehearse a play. One person was cast for the part of a villain, another was a spy, another a noble woman, another a brave man, another a miser, another a hero, another a misunderstood wife, another a misunderstood husband, another a long-suffering person, and so on. The first day they all acted the play and enjoyed it and afterwards laughed at one another's parts. But the island had peculiar properties. As the days went on, each time they acted this play they began to feel more and more that they were actually the parts they acted. And then everything went wrong and they remained on the island and the ship vanished, leaving only a little boat behind.

Quaremead, Ugley, July 21, 1945

FURTHER NOTE ON CHANGING OUR LEVEL OF BEING

On one occasion Mr. Ouspensky said in so many words : "We must learn to isolate ourselves from life." He was speaking about the Work-formulation that there are two Third Forces or Neutralizing Forces, in their broadest definition, that we can be under, the Neutralizing Force of life and the Neutralizing Force of the Work or Esotericism. As you know, in this great formulation of these two quite different Third Forces—i.e. the ideas of life and the ideas of the Work—we are told that the Third Force of life keeps Personality active and the real, essential part of us passive and so ungrown: on the other hand we are told that if we can feel the Third Force of the Work, the position is reversed and the Personality begins to become more passive and the more essential part of us, the real side of us, begins to grow. Man was created a self-developing organism to practise a certain growth of Essence, which if you like you can call a growth of the essential individuality. In life in general this individual growth, which is latent in us all, does not take place. In certain stages of history there have been no doubt better outer circumstances for this more individual growth, this unique growth of people's individuality, to take place. From the Work point of view all attempts to standardize people, all wrong ideas of equality, are antagonistic to the fundamental conception behind our creation. Regimentation, mass-production, machine-made people—all such viewpoints are totally antagonistic to the ideas behind Esotericism in general. Man, says the Work, is an unfinished creation and he is left to finish himself, to complete himself. O. used to say that there were certain periods in history when this possibility was more likely to be achieved, but now, as you know, the Work says that we are faced by a general movement to political ideas which have as their aim a society of bees or a society of ants—i.e. a social organism in which no

741

together, for people to unite in the right way, they must learn a common language." Now you know, all of you, that we are trying to learn a common language in this Work and we are trying to study the same ideas and understand them, because the Work is full of new ideas and full of practical instructions as to how we should work on ourselves. When you meet a Work-person you are capable of speaking to him or her in a way that you cannot speak to a person in life who has never heard of any of the ideas of this Work or any other forms of Esotericism. You all know that if you talk to a person in life and even touch upon any of the ideas of this Work the person will begin to argue at once and probably become very hostile. What is the reason? The real reason is that this person in life instantly feels uneasy. He feels that in some way he is being attacked or depreciated. That is why it is so dangerous to speak of this Work to people who have no Magnetic Centre or who have not been prepared a little in some intelligent way so that they can see a little bit beyond their immediate life-interests. Everyone flatters himself, everyone has a very strong self-conceit, and everyone feels that he or she is right, quite apart from the fact that they may be very unhappy. That is why it is so difficult to speak to people about this Work because they very easily become suspicious and always become resentful. Yet unless they can shift a little bit from their life-basis and let some of the ideas of the Work into their minds, they cannot change their fixed position in life. They belong to the great machinery of life that has made them what they are. They have the illusion that they are conscious, they have the illusion that they can do independently of life-circumstances, they have the illusion that they are one person and do not see that they are many different people at different times, and they have many other illusions which you will study in this system of work. In other words, by these illusions, by their general attitude to human existence on this earth, they are completely under the power of the Third Force of life. They cannot isolate themselves from this prodigious force which takes so many different aspects at different moments and yet is always exactly the same force and always has exactly the same inner taste. For this reason nothing extra can grow in them and so the Work says that they are like seeds and that they live and die as seeds without undergoing any growth. In the language of the Work we are part of Organic Life which is a sensitive film that surrounds this earth and transmits certain influences to the undeveloped tip of the twig of the great cosmic tree which is our moon. This little twig formed by the earth and the moon is growing. From the Work point of view the moon is not a dead planet, a dead creature, but a growing one, and it is fed by all the useless suffering on the earth, all the useless pain. This is a very startling thought and sounds very strange to us. Our self-conceit is such that we even believe that this earth, this minute speck, is the only inhabited planet in the enormous Universe of Suns and Galaxies. Even from this you can see how enormous our native ignorance and our native egotism are.

Now the Work says that we are at a phase in our human existence at which it is possible to escape from serving the moon. The trouble is that through long-established habit—habit of mind, habit of feeling, habit of attitude, as well as other habits—we cannot wake up and cease to feed the moon with all our useless suffering. And having no right ideas about our existence on the earth we cannot isolate ourselves from these life influences that keep us exactly where we are and keep us at our level of Being. We might think that war would wake us up, make us become more conscious. Yet this is not the effect of war, although it may happen at certain moments of common danger, but we fall back afterwards into sleep because we cannot isolate ourselves from the Third Force of life. The picture changes and we all start quarrelling with one another—i.e. we are still governed by the blind cosmic forces under which we are and under which we should not be. Now in this Work we speak about ourselves and about self-change—about changing ourselves and coming under new influences ourselves. If we want to do this we have to isolate ourselves from the force of life and we have to do this in the 4th Way—which is this Work—without physically isolating ourselves. We have to do it here and now in the midst of our present life. Recently I was speaking about aim and said that every one of you in the Work must have some aim in connection with changing yourself. I said that people who are quite satisfied with the state of their Being are not really suitable for this Work. Do you want to change anything in yourself? Have you faced yourself with this question? Let me remind you of some of the characteristic phrases used in the Work. One is: "If you change your Being, your life changes." Now everyone probably wishes his or her life to change. Everyone feels he or she ought to have a better life. But the Work says that your Being attracts your life and that if you want to change your life you have to begin to work on yourself and change your Being which is constantly attracting this life that you made. In other words, you have to begin to quarrel with your Being, with the kind of person you are.

Now this is quite impossible unless you observe your Being from what you are taught to observe in this Work. A very great difficulty lies here because everyone is quite satisfied with himself or herself. Owing to the action of buffers in us, which are like big blocks of wood, we live peaceably with ourselves without seeing all our contradictions. As you know, if these buffers, which life has made in us and which lie in the Personality, were suddenly removed and we saw all our contradictions and became conscious at the same time in all our different 'I's, we should go mad. We could not stand such an experience. It would utterly destroy all our self-conceit and our self-complacency and our excellent estimation of ourselves. But the action of self-observation in the Work makes us gradually conscious of our contradictions and gradually undermines this curious static frozen state that we are all in as regards ourselves. Then we can begin to work on our Being because we begin to see at what level our Being is. Sometimes some of us may catch glimpses

745

of our state of Being and then we know how we feel about ourselves and our past life. At such moments we discover, or rather it is revealed to us, that we are nothing like what we suppose or imagine, and that imagination has played a tremendous part in making our life tolerable to ourselves, and pictures of ourselves have been our most darling possessions. Now such glimpses make us willing to work on our own Being and this enables us to understand what it means when the Work says that your life will not change unless your Being changes. You begin to see the connection with yourself. A man with a great feeling for himself cannot see his Being because he is blinded by his pictures of himself. But a man who has such an experience as I have described above, such a revelation, begins to get a trace of feeling his own nothingness entering his consciousness and this is exactly the germinal force of the Work acting—the regenerative or Third Force of the Work. As long as a man is entirely supported by success in life, how on earth can he feel such a force acting on him?

Now in order to isolate ourselves from life, apart from what has been said above, there are three great Work-practices that aid in this. The first is Self-Remembering, the second is non-identifying, and the third is non-considering in the sense of not making accounts against others. If you practise Self-Remembering, non-identifying and not making accounts against others, you will begin to isolate yourself from all the aspects of the Third Force of life. As a result you begin to pass under the new Third Force of the Work. This latter Third Force can change you because it will gradually make Personality more passive. But if you are always under the Third Force of life exclusively you cannot change. Your level of Being will always remain the same and you will always attract the same kind of experiences. This is what you all have to think about and try to see what is meant. Suppose that I am a poor man and I become a millionaire I will be just the same as I was as regards my Being. I will attract exactly the same kind of experiences. Why is this so? It is because life has made me a poor man and then a rich man but my Being is just the same as before. But suppose I have some experience in the Work and realize what my Being is like and no longer identify with myself as previously, then whether I am poor or rich my life will begin to change because I am letting in a new influence, a new Third Force—i.e. the Work. If you begin to see your level of Being you begin to have a quite new thing to think about and to work upon. That is why it is so important to observe yourself.

Now all this in this paper is quite fundamental and has been spoken of often before from different angles. The emphasis is laid upon the importance of isolating oneself from life because it is only through some form of isolating yourself from life that you can build anything up, that you can change, that you can, in short, do this Work. If life is very strong and hypnotizes you completely, if you always see your aim as lying outside yourself, in the world, you will not be able to isolate yourself sufficiently from the terrific power of the Third Force of life, and you will not understand what the Work is about—i.e. about changing oneself. We are all fitted into life in the very best way to work on ourselves. Our troubles, our grievances, our forms of blame, are just what we have to work on through Self-Remembering, through non-identifying, through not making accounts against other people. But unless we observe ourselves we can do none of these things.

Remember there is help—but our minds—our brains, if you like —get connected up by the senses, by the impact of the external visible world in the wrong way to receive it. First we must be efficient in life before we start this Work. Later the ideas of the Work, if received with understanding, begin to make a new set of connections and these conduct help. These new connections, these new association-paths, are our second education. This second education is what the Work is about. But if you cannot begin to stop, to alter, some of the old mechanical association-paths, you cannot make a new set of connections capable of transmitting the influences of the Work—that is, of the Third Force which opens a higher level of understanding. "We must," said Mr. Ouspensky, "believe in Higher Man. We must believe there is something, already there, higher than we are. We must believe in Greater Mind." Otherwise our minds are closed. The way is shut, and we look downwards, like the animals, at the physical Earth.

Quaremead, Ugley, July 28, 1945

A NOTE ON INTERNAL CONSIDERING

It is always useful to observe what forms our internal considering takes. Internal considering is one of the things that the Work teaches us that we must observe in ourselves. If you practise self-observation in the Work-meaning you must observe what the Work teaches you to observe and, as it were, classify your observations. It is no good simply trying to observe yourself without any rhyme or reason. I will ask each one of you here now this question: Have you observed your typical forms of internal considering? Did you think that someone ought to have answered your letter earlier or said Good-morning to you? In other words, did you think that someone ought to have treated you differently? This form of internal considering is called making accounts, feeling that you are owed something by others, feeling that you are not properly treated in general and that your peculiar excellence and value are not appreciated. All that gives rise to a great deal of bad psychological material in you and lays down many forms of association in the mind that later it may be very difficult to get free from. Moreover such forms of internal considering always lead to negative states. A great deal of internal considering arises from a kind of weakness in us.

747

We expect too much. In the Work-phrase we make *too many requirements in life*. A person who makes very many requirements is always difficult. But you must remember that the Work makes certain requirements of you all and this is quite a different matter. I may get angry with a person in the Work, not because of mechanical internal considering, but because this person is not treating the Work rightly—that is, this person is not properly evaluating the Work. When you are brought face to face with yourself in connection with evaluation of the Work you cannot behave entirely mechanically towards it and if you do behave mechanically you will find that you will suffer as a consequence. For example, if someone tells me an obvious lie, if I am angry, whether I express it or not, I am not acting from mechanical internal considering or personal feeling. It is my feeling for the Work itself that makes me angry with a person who lies to me. The Work says that you must never lie to your teacher, if he asks you, say, exactly what happened. You may be very rarely asked such a question but if you are you must remember and understand not to lie because a man who lies in this highest sense in the Work lies to the Work itself. Then the Work cannot help him. This feature, lying, which may be the person's Chief Feature, will run through everything he or she does, because there is not a single thing that we do that is not connected closely or remotely with our Chief Feature. At the same time a person may lie at some critical moment, from one centre or from one 'I', and later on feel shame because some other and better-class 'I' checks him. This is at once a sign that such persons can grow, that their Being can change.

Now just as the physical body cannot grow rightly unless it is properly proportioned and rightly connected, so the psychological body which we are trying to form, this Second Body, as it is called, cannot grow rightly unless it is properly formed and properly proportioned and rightly connected. You can all see for yourselves that lying makes wrong psychological connections and that if you are a persistent liar and always justify yourself, you are building up a psychological body that is twisted and distorted and so no good at death, when life-influences cease.

Now if a person internally considers all day long, secretly or openly, and is full of accounts against other people, two things at least will happen. One is that a great deal of force will be lost in this continual internal considering that leads to so many negative trains of thought and feeling. The second thing is that the psychological body will be all wrong. It will be deformed *in fact*. It cannot grow into its right development and so is no psychological body. Why? Because there will be no inner strength and saved-up force through which it can grow. Everything that happens in life will cause inner resentment and internal considering and so loss of force. One will be simply identified with everything in life and unable to make this inner isolation that we spoke of recently. If a person always thinks that he is neglected or badly treated he will be in a continual state of internal considering. Of course, one can easily pretend that one is tough and does not mind, but this is merely a picture of oneself and behind it internal considering goes on just in the same way. A kind of hard crust can be formed towards people. But it is precisely this picture, this hard crust, that must be dissolved and replaced by understanding. Sometimes I think that one of the things that helps us most in regard to internal considering is the constant thinking and constant reminding of ourselves that we and others are mechanical. We are machines, each of a certain kind, that behave in a certain mechanical way. Then you can say to yourself: "Well, he (or she) is like that." But this again is a very dangerous thought, especially if it is said contemptuously, because you have to see yourself. You also are like that. You are a machine and always act mechanically. You are just as difficult for other people as you think other people are for you. Everyone has a different kind of rudeness but you must remember that you also have your own form of rudeness, open or concealed. Then again, there is another closely connected thought that may help when one observes that one is internally considering and that is that we keep on imagining that people are doing things intentionally to us when they are not at all, and they in their turn think that we are doing things intentionally to them. Therefore we have to endure one another's unpleasant manifestations and realize how we are machines at present. The one thing we must struggle with is forming long unchecked trains of internal considering, trains of pitiful thoughts, because they will drag us down and make us ill eventually. A pleas.nt independence is quite different from rudeness or self-pity. A dislike of arguing is a good sign also. It is just the same as when you wish to say something to someone that is not very easy and so instead of saying it rudely or arguing you say it in a certain indirect and pleasant way and also include yourself as capable of having the same fault. We have to learn to laugh at ourselves far more than we laugh at others just as we have to learn to have more contempt for certain sides of ourselves than we have for other people. A man who has a great deal of self-conceit will only expect a great deal from others and will make many requirements, so much so that he will be incapable of enjoying his life but will only enjoy his self-conceit. Such a person is sick in his or her mind.

When you observe a train of internal considering in yourself notice what it is saying to you and if possible remember that you have had the same kind of train of thought before and probably, as you will soon see, all through your life. You must also challenge this train of thought, stand up to it inside and have, as it were, a conscious dialogue with it like this: You say to these 'I's or this 'I': "Now what are you up to? What are you saying?" And then, as it were, you make them speak. Such dialogues are very useful because you will practically always see the absurdity of these mechanical streams of internal considering that you are allowing these 'I's to form in you unmolested. It is very good to have a good row with oneself now and then. But the first requisite is that you are able to observe yourself. If you cannot observe yourself and are simply identified with everything that goes on in you, then you cannot have a row with yourself. You are not able to separate from a single thing in yourself. It is all too sacred. You will simply be yourself sacredly and solemnly and adore yourself. So then you are fixed and unchanging day by day. You are without any power of seeing what you are like impersonally. You will then be identified with yourself just as you are, with every feeling, with every thought, with everything that goes on in you, and with all your phrases and habits. You will give full acknowledgement to all these mechanical things and not see for a moment that it is exactly these things that you must observe and begin to separate from by not going with them, by not consenting to them, and, as I said above, by challenging them—that is, by asking them what they are doing, what truth lies behind them, and what your inner life means—if it means anything. You all know how easy it is to misunderstand something, especially if you are inclined to be negative. Then internal considering starts up and you simply go with it instead of giving yourself this conscious shock and saying: "What is all this that is going on about? Did things happen like that? Was what took place done intentionally? Is it simply my suspicion at work and so on?" It is this inner psychological mess that we are all in, owing to lack of any organized psychological body, that causes so many of our troubles in life. According to G., it causes something like 80% of our physical illnesses. Do you not all understand that with wrong thinking, with floods of negative emotion, with continual lying, with these constant inner forms of self-justifying, with this terrible self-conceit which makes us so big, and this state of sleep towards the kind of people we are, it is a wonderful thing that we are not all insane. We are given a physical body with a wonderful, delicate organization. The Work teaches that we have to make a psychological body and that this is our real destiny on this planet and the meaning of our creation down here. Imagine this delicate organization of the physical body governed by a psychological mess. It is remarkable, therefore, that we have any health. To build up a well-connected psychological body it is necessary for a man to begin to live the Work in himself and learn to know what he must separate from, what he must struggle with, what he must not identify with. It is not so much what we do but what our inner state is that matters. That is why the Work lays such emphasis for example on negative emotions because when people indulge habitually in negative states without for a moment seeing what enormous harm they are causing to themselves, they have no idea about their own responsibility to themselves. After a time in the Work we cannot prolong negative states unchecked. Real Conscience begins to touch us. Now we may have excellent bodies but if our inner states are allowed to express themselves without hindrance and without observation we are really comparable to lepers. This is what is meant in the Gospels by the word 'leper'. That is, we have terrible diseases internally. Sometimes these

750

psychological diseases work out into the body and express themselves in various physical disorders. This may not be the case with a purely animal man but it is certainly the case with an emotional or an intellectual man, in my experience.

Now all negative states, in which we will include internal considering, because internal considering always makes us negative, do us harm. The greatest harm that they do us is that they cut us off from help—i.e. from Higher Centres. You will remember that these are fully developed in us and are constantly at work but we cannot hear them owing to the bad state of our reception. The thunder-storms of our negative emotions render reception impossible. Yes, but have you seen any of your negative states? Are you aware of them? It is extraordinary to watch a person who is habitually negative and notice how he has no observation of himself, no consciousness of himself. As you have often heard, you cannot begin to work upon anything in yourself if you cannot first begin to observe it, and all negative states eat you and take your force. But since there is something in us that wishes to help us it may be a good thing to study how to get in touch with it. Now negative emotions will always prevent this, always form a dark cover over us. Negative states simply make us empty of all meaning except those unpleasant meanings with which the negative part of Emotional Centre can continually feed us and which sometimes lead down to those inexhaustible and horrible forms of meaning derived from suspicion which is so close to insanity. But we try to reach more difficult meanings—not such easy meanings.

After a time, when you can be alone with yourself and at the same time alone with this Work and its meanings, you begin to realize that you have no right to be negative and that you have no excuse for it. You see you have got to find some way out. You may not be able to prevent negative states from starting but you may be able to stop them. This is one meaning of what is called work on oneself. You become responsible. It is a very good thing to have some private responsible idea of what this Work is about and that begins when one begins to apply it to oneself and to the state one is in at any moment. This can be called living more consciously. It can also be called walking instead of lying down flat. G. once said: "In this Work we have good leather to sell for people who wish to walk, but people must make their shoes out of this leather for themselves." Now we can do a thing from the wrong 'I' and do the same thing from the right 'I'. To walk, to live more consciously, it is necessary to understand this. Anything done from internal considering or negative states is useless. It does not belong to what we seek to form in ourselves in making this Second Body.

A NOTE ON RECURRENCE

The Work is the finest, the thinnest, the purest force that exists. It arranges everything in the right order. Do you remember how the Work is defined in Hebrews, which is a Gnostic book? It is called the Logos or the Word: "The Word of God is living and active, and sharper than any two-edged sword, and piercing even to the dividing of soul and spirit, of both joints and marrow, and quick to discern the thoughts and feelings of the heart." (*Heb.* IV 12). All this means that nothing can be done wrongly without payment. Quoting from another source, it is said that the *voûs*, which is the mind of God, which is the Logos or Word of God, "is infinite and self-ruled". We seek in the Work to come under a discipline which is nothing to do with physical discipline but is a mental and emotional discipline, and we are taught in this Work that we have something buried in us called Conscience and that once we can get a little free from our Personality and all its tiresome manifestations and its tedious repetitions of the same thing, the same behaviour, the same attitudes, the same phrases, we can begin to touch Real Conscience which comes actually from Higher Centres. From this point of view you must all understand that we have many accounts against us for wrong behaviour for wrong thinking, and, above all, for wrong talking. Everything has to be worked out eventually.

Now I will talk for a moment on the idea of Recurrence. As you know, modern physics says that Time is curved. This means that it is a circle. It is not an extended line, but a line that bends round on itself and comes back to the same place. For this reason the Work teaches (in its secondary teaching) that our lives are curved and come back to the moment of birth. This means that if nothing is changed in our lives we shall once more enter the same circle, do the same things, feel the same things, and behave in the same way. But the Work teaches that if we try to work on ourselves and change our Being, next time we shall not have quite the same kind of life. But this depends on many things. For example, it depends on how we are brought up, on the influences acting on us from outside, from our parents, our nurses, from the literature of the day. You all know this strange phrase in the Decalogue (the 10 Commandments) "I the Lord thy God am a jealous God, visiting the sins of the fathers upon the children, upon the third and upon the fourth generation of them that hate me." (*Ex.* XX 5). This means practically that if the parents change, the children can change. It means, in short, that if I am a parent and change during my circle of life, I will help my children. For this reason there is much to hope for, if parents work and change their level of Being, because, if that happens, the children born again in Recurrence will not have the same kind of parents because the parents have changed. For example, if I have a child who dies, with the ordinary conception of Time as a straight line leading from past to future I shall not be able to see how I can change my child. Do you understand that no one can conceive what this means unless he or she understands about this circle of life and about the Recurrence of things? If no one tries to change, whether child or parent, then everything will be the same and will go round and round in the same way. Do you imagine that I cannot change my father because he died many years ago? I assure you that from the esoteric standpoint I can change my father if I overcome in myself certain things and that my efforts will affect not only myself but my father. Now this Work can change many things in people as some of you may have noticed. The more strongly you feel this Work and the more you conceive its meaning in your mind and the more you make yourself distinct from mechanical life through the force of this Work, then not only can you change yourself but also everyone connected with you— even people long ago who are not in your present time. For this reason the Work teaches that Time is one of the worst illusions that we can come under as ordinarily conceived because how can we help people a long way back? The answer is, by working on yourself now you can change not only yourself but everything, both in the past and in the future, because the future and the past *equally exist*. There is no past and no future if Time is a circle.

Now some of our circles inter-connect with other circles belonging to other people and if you want to understand what Recurrence means you must understand that. Time is not a straight line but infinite circles all turning on themselves and some inter-communicating with one another. The past is as living as the present or the future. From this grand conception we can gain hope. We can understand that what we do now affects other people, both in the past and in the present and in the future. Everything the Work says is connected together so that if a person works now on himself or herself and begins to change their level of Being they affect people not only in the past but in the future. Regret is useless but work is always useful. You must remember, each one of you, that when you do a real act of work on yourself now, you change the past as well as the future, and you change your past in relation to all those people who were connected with you in the past. G. once said: "If you want to change yourself, you must change your grandfather." What does this mean? One meaning is that by changing your attitude to your father and to your grandfather you will change them also, although apparently they are dead, and so when you are born once more in visible life, on the circle of your own life, when you meet your father and your grandfather again you will change them.

Now I do not wish to speak any more on this difficult subject of Recurrence at present, but you must all remember that everything you do now in regard to work on yourself and changing yourself will reflect itself in a million ways both into the future and into the past. For this reason we may have people who no longer exist in our time, but all people exist in Time and constantly repeat their circles. In other words, there is no Time as our senses conceive it and everything is living and everything is always present.

Now let me add one thing. In the Old Testament there are many ideas about Recurrence. There is in Ecclesiastes the idea that Time is not a straight line of past, present and future, but a circle constantly recurring, constantly repeating itself. It is said: "That which hath been is that which shall be; and that which hath been done is that which shall be done." (*Ecc.* III 9.) But you must remember that "that which hath been shall be" depends entirely on whether you work and not identify, and separate from it, because then it has no power over you. Then you will change and everything else will change in connection with you.

Recently I was asked a question: *What is the meaning of this: There are two futures, one in Time and one in Space?* A future in Time means that you are always just the same person, always saying the same things, always behaving as you ordinarily do. This future belongs to the level of Being that you are actually at. It will always attract the same things. Your future in vertical scale means that you change your level of Being and no longer identify so much with Personality, with the person you have taken yourself to be. You will begin to change yourself. Then you rise vertically in the Scale of Being and your future is then different. In terms of Recurrence, instead of circling round the same life again and again in the same part of Time, you do not do the same things, because you remember. But it is a strange idea that we can change the future and the past. It is a strange idea that I can change my father. It takes a long time to understand this conception of Time as bent, as circular, and not as a straight line. In Ecclesiastes it is said: "God seeketh again that which is passed away." (*Ecc.* III 15.) This means that what you think is over and done with is not over and done with and the Work says that you can change what was in the past by working on yourself *now*. I sometimes think that this means that you have to see the whole of your past as living and that by working *now* you can change the whole of the past and all that is connected with it. So you will agree with me that if you can catch this vision of something above the senses and the sensory mind there is hope of an extraordinary kind.

NOTE

In this paper Dr. Nicoll refers to the ideas of Time and Recurrence which are discussed by Mr. Ouspensky in "A New Model of the Universe". Chapter XI.

A NOTE ON BUFFERS

A little child has no buffers. A little child is awake although of course it is all on a very small scale. The Work says that children are born awake and that they are born into a world of sleeping people and very soon they fall asleep themselves in the Work-sense and they lose a kind of integrity that belongs to small children. In small children there is a kind of Real Conscience, but very soon this is overlaid by the action of life and the Personality begins to be formed. Personality is formed differently according to each period and is encouraged by nurses and parents. The important thing to remember is that there is omething awake in us because we are born only with Essence which is awake. Then Personality is acquired and imitation sets in and something artificial is formed. With this formation of Personality, which is acquired and which must be acquired, Real Conscience disappears. It goes underground. You know how difficult it is to argue with a little child about something which you probably know yourself is not quite true. There is a kind of sincerity in the child. But the fate of all of us born on this Earth is first to form Personality and then perhaps later on to work on this Personality and reach a new level of development. In other words, Personality must be formed before anything else can happen in the way of the true destiny of Man, which is to reach a higher stage of himself. All methods of upbringing of children based on the idea that they are natural and simple are wrong because Essence ceases to grow after a very short time. For this reason the Work has no sympathy with crack-brained theoretical ideas of children being brought up in a simple way without discipline. If Essence were capable of growing continually then such ideas would be correct. One of the striking things that the Work says is that Essence can only grow by itself a short way. After that it cannot grow, and Personality, the acquired side of a person, must form itself over Essence and surround it. A further growth of Essence depends upon the formation of Personality through experience in life and the ultimate gradual rendering of it more passive. Then all the material collected in Personality and all the energies belonging to it, if directed in a new way, nourish the Essence, so that it can then undergo its destined further development. So a man must first go into life and be in his own way good at life. For that reason we do not want in this Work people who have undergone no discipline from life or who have not become in some degree what are called Good Householders—i.e. responsible people who know something about life and can do something in life in the ordinary sense. The Work has a special name for people who have never met with life properly. They are called 'tramps'. This is a technical word—a Work-word. Such people try one thing after another and as soon as it becomes at all difficult they give it up and try something else.

Now to-night I wish to speak about buffers. Buffers are inevitably in every normal person simply because Personality must be formed first as strongly as possible in everyone. I am not speaking about False Personality but about Personality. In this psychological thing called Personality, which surrounds Essence to begin with, lie all the knowledge, all the life-talents, that you have acquired. You have gone through all the routine of learning a profession, let us say, and all this is laid down in your Personality and has made it possible for you to relate yourself to life. But Conscience such as you had as a very small creature has ceased to exist. You have of necessity to learn the ways of life and, as it were, ignore all the obvious compromises that are necessary. You have learned, as it were, to follow your job and adapt to it without going too deeply into it. In other words, Real Conscience has disappeared because if everyone had Real Conscience the world of to-day would be utterly impossible. Now what has taken the place of Real Conscience? The place of Real Conscience has been taken by what in the Work are called 'buffers.' When this concept was first brought forward Mr. Ouspensky said that buffers are just like the buffers on railway carriages in that they lessen the shock. He sometimes compared them with blocks of wood that separate the obvious contradictions in ourselves. A child he said, born into a world of sleeping people, very soon learns to have buffers because he is surrounded by people who have nothing but buffers, people who no longer see their contradictions. He said: "Buffers make things easy for us. They prevent us from seeing what we are really doing and saying. Most people who are strong in life, who have perhaps become leaders, are people who have very strong buffers. They are strong because of these wooden blocks that prevent them from seeing what they are doing and what harm they are causing. A well-buffered man or woman has no doubts about himself or herself." Mr. O. said also that people with very strong buffers usually cannot observe themselves at all and they take themselves for granted. They are kept going by their buffers, by their lack of insight into what they are really like or what they are doing. Sometimes people say: "Are buffers the same as self-justifying?" This is not the case, because a well-buffered person, a person with very thick buffers, does not even seek to justify himself. It is only a person whose buffers are not quite so strong, and who begins to feel a little uneasy, who begins to use self-justification to keep his buffers going.

In order to understand buffers therefore we have to understand that they take the place of Real Conscience and this they do very successfully in the vast majority of people. Such people will never wish this Work or understand what it is about. They think it is a very strange thing and quite unnecessary and interpret it in their own way. Now the Work speaks a great deal about two things, Consciousness and Conscience. The Work does not teach Love or Faith or Hope directly, but it bases itself on the words, 'Conscience', 'Consciousness'. The Work teaches that all the troubles of humanity arise because people are not conscious and keep on thinking that they are. If a person asks: "Why do all the evils and brutality and cruelty and madness exist?" the answer is because Man is not conscious, he does not know what he is doing. It adds that Man is under the illusion that he is a fully conscious being, and what he calls full consciousness is nothing but the second state of consciousness in the Work-conception of different levels of consciousness. A man, the Work says, an ordinary man, is in what the Work calls the so-called waking state of consciousness, but he has not yet attained the third level of consciousness, called Self-Consciousness, Self-Awareness and finally Self-Remembering. This is something you can all verify for yourselves by thought and by self-observation and observation of others. This so-called waking state of consciousness which Western psychology takes as full consciousness, the Work teaches, is the most dangerous consciousness of all. The level of consciousness below it, sleep in bed, is harmless in comparison. We do not, while we are in bed, go and kill one another in the name of liberty and justice and patriotism, but in the so-called waking state of consciousness, when a man's Moving Centre is released from sleep, all the evil events of the world take place. Millions of sleeping people kill millions of other sleeping people feeling that they are fully conscious. That is why the Work says that humanity is not conscious yet but is under the illusion that it is. That is why the Work teaches that we must try to be more conscious, and this can only begin with self-observation and an insight into oneself.

Now if we were at the third level of consciousness—i.e. the state of Self-Consciousness, Self-Awareness and Self-Remembering—we should no longer be so much under the influence of buffers. That means that we should begin to feel this buried Conscience, this Real Conscience, that we once knew long ago and have completely lost sight of. What characterizes the ordinary state of consciousness, our so-called waking state, is the presence of buffers, so that we can do the most contradictory things without any pain to ourselves, aided by the accessory capacity we have of justifying ourselves in everything we say and do, so that this state of sleep that we call consciousness is intensified. We are asleep from the standpoint of the Work, the Gospels, and all esoteric teaching. We are sleeping people pretending that we are fully conscious. We think that what happens in the world is nothing to do with us. We read of unpleasant and ghastly things taking place and we go through unpleasant and ghastly experiences ourselves, but we do not realize that this is not only because other people are in sleep but because we are asleep ourselves. We are not yet men or women, we are not yet conscious. In fact, the Work teaches that we are an experiment and that if we do not succeed we shall be wiped away as a useless experiment.

Now the action of buffers is so powerful that no one can understand it unless he has begun to see for himself the existence of a single buffer in himself. Now we must bring in the idea of the False Personality as

757

distinct from the necessarily acquired Personality itself. What are your fantasies that are connected with your False Personality? And, on the other hand, what is the reality of yourself? Is there any correspondence? If you have a moment of insight, a moment of awakening, you will get a terrible shock. You will see that all your boasting, all your self-flattery, all your imagination of yourself, is nothing to do with what you really are or with what you have really done. To put this in the mildest terms, you will find a considerable discrepancy. Yes, but how is it that we do not see this all the time? The answer is because of the action of these powerful, thick buffers in us, that have taken the place of Real Conscience. Now Consciousness in the Work is defined as knowing all together and Conscience is defined as feeling all together. Sometimes a serious moment, a serious shock, a painful episode, begins to make us feel everything together at the same time. If you accidentally overhear something said about you by someone who likes you, you will receive a great shock. If you know the person likes you you will see that this is the truth that you have never seen for yourself. This is called a shock in the Work. If the tone of voice is friendly and if you can see that the person was merely stating a fact, it suddenly invades the territory of your False Personality, the imagination that you are living in, and you feel purified, you feel that it is quite true, and probably you will never forget such a moment. Now you will ask me: Is this seeing a buffer? Yes, it is, if you can remember it, but it only is so if it has been very painful to you—that is, if the sudden realization gained from this source is a real shock to you and contains the pain of truth which cannot be denied by yourself. All truth is painful and yet beautiful in its action upon you. Merely pointing out to other people their faults has not this effect and only produces negative results. But one can also begin to see buffers in oneself gradually provided that one fights for the Work against the continual action of life. Of course, if you get right down into life, into matters of the five senses, you will not try to live differently, but if the Work has for a long time a continual, even slight, action on you, you will be brought to see your first most important buffer—that is, the discrepancy between your imagination of what you are and what you are really. You have had a picture of yourself never being deceitful and, let us say, in some moment of greater consciousness, you catch a glimpse of how deceitful you always are. What has prevented you from seeing this before? What has prevented you is the presence of a buffer. But when you begin to be conscious on both sides of the buffer simultaneously and see your picture of yourself not being deceitful and observe yourself being deceitful at the same time, your consciousness enlarges and then you will feel something coming from Conscience, something painful and yet very tolerable. Seeing a buffer is always painful. When one really begins to see a buffer it breaks and can never grow again. But, of course, when this happens you no longer have the same feeling of yourself. The province of this Work and its direction lies exactly here in one's own psychology and of course one of the objects of this Work is to make a new psychological body properly connected. I do not know if you understand what I say when I say you are all invention and that you are not your invention and that you have to pay an enormous quantity of force in order to keep your invention of yourself going. It is such a new experience to give up one side of this invented stuff and come to terms with yourself—to terms of peace with yourself. The growth of consciousness and the growth of Conscience must necessarily go hand in hand. We must know more about ourselves—that is, we must become far more conscious of ourselves, our contradictory 'I's, in order to feel more about ourselves, which is to begin to feel Real Conscience. This is not an exalting process. It is not a self-justifying process. You do not feel grander and grander but you become, to yourself and perhaps to others, far more real, and at the same time you get increasingly free from this very unsatisfactory feeling coming from the False Personality by dint of which we try to live our rather unsuccessful lives.

Now the Work says that Conscience is the fire which alone can begin to change us. The Work says in this connection that Man is like a chemical retort with many metallic powders in it which every tap of life, every external event, shifts. All these powders in this retort that Man is can be fused to form an individuality or Real 'I'. But in order that this may take place a fire must be lit under the retort and the powders gradually fused to form something permanent in a man or a woman.

Now you will see from what has been said briefly above that as long as a man or a woman is full of buffers no Real Conscience can exist in such a person. Mr. Ouspensky once said: "You must first of all have Conscience towards this Work. And this is the first thing that you must have." He said: "This Work takes the place of Real Conscience for you but as this real buried Conscience begins to come to the surface and replaces your purely acquired local conscience the Work merges into Conscience and the two become one and the same thing." This means that what we have to be taught externally by word of mouth in this Work gradually connects with something internal and similar in us and so the two become one and the same. Then the Work is in a person and not outside him. Then he obeys the Work, not because he is told to do so externally, but because he feels it internally. We are so far gone in sleep, so far removed from Real Conscience, which is the same in us all by birth, that we have to be reminded by all the methods of esoteric teaching from outside. We have to hear from without what we really know inside already. You must understand that the concept Conscience in the Work has nothing in common with the concept morality belonging to any particular period or nation. The concept Conscience is far deeper than anything acquired from without by upbringing. Conscience, the Work teaches, is something that is present in us all, but has been overlaid, and necessarily overlaid at first, because the Personality with its acquired conscience must be formed first of all.

Now I will quote from what G. taught. He was asked once how it was that we could not change. He said first of all: "No one can change, whether man or woman, as long as they take themselves as one person." And I will point out to you here that although you have heard this more than once, it is not at all easy to understand. You take yourself as one person all day long and always say 'I' as if this 'I' were some permanent unchanging thing in you. Can you bear to see that you are not one person but many different people? Have you yet begun to doubt yourself? The False Personality from which springs the Imaginary 'I' takes us as always one unvarying person and it will not allow even the idea that one has three centres to exist, far less the idea that one has many different 'I's that speak in quite different voices. But is it so humiliating to acknowledge this sincerely to yourself? Think of all the tragedies that are caused by people taking one another as conscious beings and as having one permanent unchanging 'I'. Now G. goes on as follows in connection with this question of changing ourselves. He begins by pointing out that our machines are all wrong, that they are very dirty machines that have had all sorts of wrong connections made in them that have never been corrected, never been observed, and with these dirty wrongly connected machines we try to make relationships with one another, having no idea that anything is wrong. He said:

"The chief thing that you forget is that you are not beginning from the beginning with a nice clean new machine. There stand behind you many years of a wrong and stupid life, of indulgence in every kind of weakness, of shutting your eyes to your own errors, of striving to avoid all unpleasant truths, of constant lying to yourselves, of self-justification, of blaming others and so on. All this cannot help affecting the machine. The machine is dirty, rusty, and in some places artificial appliances have been formed, the necessity for which has been created by its own wrong way of working. These artificial appliances will now interfere very much with all your good intentions.

They are called *Buffers*. Buffer is a term that requires special explanation. Buffers are like the contrivances on railway carriages to lessen shock. If there were no buffers the shock of one carriage against another would be very unpleasant and dangerous. Buffers soften these shocks and render them unnoticeable and imperceptible. Exactly the same appliances are to be found within Man. They are not created by nature, but by Man himself, although involuntarily. The cause of their appearance is the existence in Man of many contradictions of opinions, feelings, sympathies, words, and actions.

If a man throughout the whole of his life were to feel all the contradictions that are within him, he could not live and act as calmly as he lives and acts now. He would have constant friction and unrest.

We fail to see how hostile the different 'I's of our Personality are to one another. If a man were to feel all these contradictions he would feel *what he really is*. He would feel that he is mad. Moreover, a thought like this deprives Man of his self-respect, self-confidence, weakens his energy. Somehow or other he must master this thought or banish it. He must either destroy contradictions or cease to feel and see them. But if *buffers* are created in him he can cease to feel them, and he will not feel the impact from the clash of contradictory views, emotions, and contradictory words.

Buffers are created slowly and gradually. Very many buffers are created artificially by education, others by the hypnotic influence of all surrounding life. A man is surrounded by people who live, speak, think, and feel by means of buffers. Imitating them in their opinions, actions and words, a man involuntarily creates similar buffers in himself. Buffers make a man's life more easy. It is very hard to live without buffers. But they keep him from the possibility of inner development because buffers are made to lessen shocks and it is only shocks that can lead a man out of the state in which he lives—that is, waken him.

Buffers help a man not to feel *Conscience*. 'Conscience' is a term which needs explanation. In ordinary life the concept Conscience is taken too simply—as if we *had* a Conscience. Actually the concept Conscience in the sphere of *emotions* is equivalent to the concept *Consciousness* in the sphere of the intellect. And as we have no *Consciousness*, we have no *Conscience*. Consciousness is a state in which a man *knows all at once* everything that he in general knows and in which he can see how little he does know and how many contradictions there are in what he knows.

And as everyone has within him thousands of contradictory feelings which vary from a deeply hidden realization of his own nothingness and fears of all kinds to the most stupid kind of self-conceit, self-confidence, self-satisfaction and self-praise, to feel all this *together* would be not only painful but literally unbearable."

Quaremead, Ugley, August 11, 1945

MAN'S SITUATION ON THE EARTH

It is sometimes said in the Work that the most powerful force that we can make in ourselves is understanding. On one occasion, at the beginning of this war, Mr. Ouspensky was asked what view should be taken, how one should think about it. He said in so many words that we must try to understand why all these things happened. Now there is very little understanding in life and it has often seemed to me that understanding is diminishing, but when Mr. Ouspensky said that we must try to understand he meant, of course, that we must apply the knowledge and teaching of this Work to the present situation and try to understand why things go as they do. In order to do this, one must have a certain power of reflection, a certain detachment from external things. The Work teaches that we are very far down in the Scale of Being and exist on a planet which is under 48 orders of laws and that we are removed by only one place from the very lowest level of the Universe which is that level called the Moon which is under 96 orders of laws. It is necessary to reflect on what this means and to connect it in one's mind. We exist in a world which is obviously far from perfect and the Work teaches that we exist on this planet because we ourselves cannot exist on a better one. Our average level of Being, the kind of people we are, is such that we could not possibly exist in a better world. Yet the Work teaches that there are better worlds and it says the interesting thing that a better world is under fewer laws and a worse world is under more laws. This means that in a better world we are less imprisoned and in a worse world we are more imprisoned. At present we are in a world under 48 orders of laws—that is, a prison in which 48 orders of laws exist from which we cannot escape—and whatever we do in trying to change our world in an external way as, for example, by means of science, we shall still be under these 48 orders of laws. The Work teaches that the only way to get to a better place in the Universe is through self-change. But since we all, owing to the power of the senses over us, see improvement as lying only in change in external conditions, we miss the point.

Let us review for a moment the present state of the world and the present ideals that dominate people in regard to making this planet a better world. You see on one side inventions such as penicillin and many other similar things which are of benefit to mankind, and on the other hand you see the inventions of destructive agents such as poison-gas, atomic bombs, and so on. For everything that is invented of a beneficial nature, there seems to be invented an opposite of a harmful nature. Man, feeling that he can do, does not see this continual contradiction. He does not see that he is living in a world under a definite number of laws that cannot be changed. It is as if there were always the same amount of everything and if a thing is got rid of in one place it appears again in another place. There is always the same amount of air, let us say, in an air-cushion. You may push it in in one place but it will swell out in another place. This idea that we live in a contained world of this kind, a prison under a definite number of laws, is not understood. The Work says, amongst other things, that the Earth is a pain-factory from which a certain quantity of pain and suffering is demanded. People believe that medicine is going to do away with illness but what happens actually is that if a relative cure for one thing is found you will practically always find that some other illness increases. Let us suppose that small-pox as a disease has been decreased by vaccination but cancer has increased. I am not making any definite connection between these two things but simply indicating in general what happens.

Can you mention a single law that you are under? I am not talking about man-made laws but about laws belonging to this Earth on which we appear for a brief period. One of these laws is that you have to eat. If you don't eat you die. This is a law. Another law is that you have to breathe oxygen. If you do not breathe oxygen, or if you breathe carbon-monoxide from a charcoal-stove, you die. This is a law belonging to this planet. Yet, curiously enough, we do not see ourselves as being under laws of this kind and imagine ourselves as being quite free and able to do exactly as we like. In other words, we do not reflect upon the nature of our lives on this Earth. And we have the constant illusion that we can do—i.e. that we can alter everything in our favour. And because we have this illusion that we can do, we have also the equally firm illusion that we are progressing and that the mere passage of time means that we all get better and better and more and more comfortable. We regard things like wars as exceptions, just as we regard illnesses as exceptions, not seeing that they are the rule, and belong to our level of Being.

What is the way out from this prison in which these laws constantly interact and play on humanity like a set of different-coloured spotlights? The Work, the Gospels, and all esoteric teaching say the same thing: to begin to escape from these 48 orders of laws governing this planetary prison called the Earth a man must cease to see the final solution in changing external conditions but must see it in changing himself. He must begin to change his relationship to this world and in order to do so he must begin to observe himself and the world and work on his mechanical reactions to it. This is the whole meaning of the Sermon on the Mount which has nothing to do with being pious but has a far deeper meaning and a far more interesting meaning. If a man remains mechanical, if he always thinks and feels and speaks in the same mechanical way, he remains in prison, but if a man begins to try to awaken he begins to pass under fewer laws. Everything taught in this Work about negative emotions, identifying, internal considering, Self-Remembering, about vanity and pride, about making accounts, about imagination, about False Personality, and so on, has to do with coming under fewer laws—that is, under better influences—and all these things that the Work is constantly talking to you about and asking you to practise begin with observing yourself, with waking up from the state of sleep in which you are merely functions of life and merely serve nature and have no inner hope, no inner stability, no inner peace of mind. In this great prison of the world, under these 48 orders of laws, mankind as a whole is asleep. The Work, the Gospels, and all esoteric teaching seek to awaken Man out of this state of sleep. The central idea is that Man can undergo a definite change, a definite transformation, if he will work on himself aright. This is called inner change or inner development, and it is a quite definite thing that you can become aware of yourself once it has begun to touch you. Then, instead of remaining acorns which swine can eat, you begin to grow into trees which no swine can eat.

What would completely change the world at this moment? The world would change completely if everyone had good-will. Such an idea is vaguely mentioned even by politicians. Do you know what it means to have good-will? You may imagine that you have good-will. Now suppose that you begin to observe yourself and your daily actions, suppose that you begin to become responsible to yourself for your inner thoughts and what you say secretly, can you any longer have the illusion that you have good-will? You will begin to see what an immense task it is to get free from these evil places in mind and feeling. Then you will begin to understand what this Work is about and you will also understand how impossible it is for humanity as a whole to change since it is so difficult for you yourself to change in this respect. When such ideas come to us we begin really to think, we begin to reflect and to want to understand. We begin to understand, for example, why things go as they do, and why no one can do anything. But it is always possible for some people to change who wish to do so and wish to study how it is possible to change and what it means.

*　　*　　*

As regards these orders of laws that I have mentioned briefly above —in the cosmological teaching, the Work says that the world is created from the Absolute—that is, from the unconditioned, from that which is under no laws. The first and highest level of creation is produced by the 3 forces of the Trinity, active, passive and neutralizing forces. This first order of creation is under 3 laws, or a trinity of forces. The second order of creation is under 3 laws and 3 of its own—that is, 6 orders of laws. This process proceeds downwards to every level of creation. Our world is very low down and is under 48 orders of laws. But this will be explained in great detail later. To speak roughly, the Earth is under the laws of the Solar System, the Solar System is under the laws of the Milky Way or Starry Galaxy, the Galaxy is under the laws of all the Galaxies, and so on, just as in any organ in life, such as the Army, a private soldier is under more laws than a non-commissioned officer, and he is under more laws than the Colonel, and the Colonel is under more laws than the General, and so on. This is called order or scale and the Work takes the Universe as an order or scale. In this order or scale our Earth comes very low down and our Moon is at the lowest level. This must be understood not only physically and literally but also psychologically.

KNOWLEDGE AND ACKNOWLEDGEMENT OF THE WORK

In order to come under fewer laws we deliberately put ourselves under more laws—that is, under the Work. To come under better influences we must put ourselves under influences that do not come from life, but from the Conscious Circle of Humanity. Let us suppose a man never works on himself. Supposing he never makes any attempt to remember himself and although he has repeatedly heard about it —that is, knows about this idea of the Work—he has never brought himself to the point of making any effort to remember himself. This man makes no Work-effort. Or again, let us suppose he never observes himself: again he makes no Work-effort. In such a case the Work cannot have any possible action on him nor is he in any way connected with the Work internally. Why is he not connected with the Work? He makes no attempt to apply the Work to himself and to realize its truth in himself. Perhaps he never even thinks about it except in an idle or sarcastic way. Now a great deal depends on how we think about the ideas of this Work. It is only the deepest part of us that can change and unless we think from this deepest part the Work remains something external to us, something outside us. A man may have knowledge of this Work and not acknowledge it. Or again, he may acknowledge it to himself. Certainly this deeper acknowledgement must take time because there are so many layers of 'I's in us that do not wish to work or that make the Work merely a matter of memory— that is, they remember the ideas formatorily but do not feel them emotionally. For this reason the Work says that a man must value the ideas and that means that he must feel them emotionally. You have often heard me speak of this before but it cannot be spoken of enough. The Work is not something that you hear about from time to time but is something that must eventually be always with you, something that you eventually think about even more than your interests and problems in life. This takes time. As I said, it is the way in which we think of the ideas of the Work that either makes or does not make deep connection with it. Of course, if we do not value it, it cannot affect our thinking or change it. The emotions, the affections, make connections. It is our most internal thinking which counts—i.e. how we think privately in our own solitariness—behind the façade— because from here springs everything essential and from here Essence can grow—not from outer thought or life-thought. It is possible to talk about the Work quite well and yet one does not acknowledge it deeply—that is, essentially. As Mr. Ouspensky once said: "We have a great many overcoats to take off."

When the Work begins to enter a man more deeply, it sets up a continual conflict—not a violent, agitated conflict, but a quiet, almost wordless conflict. He finds that wherever he goes, whatever he does, he is aware of the Work in him. He begins to see life in the light of the Work. In this respect he begins to become different from other people who are only immersed in the things of life. Sometimes he sees more clearly and sometimes more obscurely but he is aware that something is going on in him, in his depths, which previously, before he met the Work, did not exist. Of course, by this time he knows quite well that it is useless to try to persuade himself of the truth of this Work. It is not a question of persuasion but of acknowledgement, and acknowledgement comes by perceiving the truth of it through applying it to oneself. Each of the ideas of the Work begins to expand into larger and larger meaning. He may begin actually to see that the Work is so—and yet he still will not consent to it deeply. His Being resists his Knowledge. He does not do what he knows and so as a rule does not know what he does. And yet all the time he is aware that there is something new in him that is always acting on him in a silent way, without persuasion, without compulsion. So he feels a constant heat, a pain. The Work is now in him. Now it is necessary for a man in this state to work on himself and to meditate on—that is, pay attention to—one or another of the ideas of the Work and see its ramifications. He begins to learn that it is necessary for him particularly to try to remember himself, for the act of Self-Remembering puts us in contact with influences that otherwise do not reach us. Thinking is not enough. Self-Remembering is necessary and it is not thinking. Again, he does not let himself get negative, because that spoils everything. And finally, he remembers that there are three lines of Work and that when he cannot work on one line he can always work on another.

I will add one thing that was said recently: you must begin to isolate yourself from life-influences through non-identifying in order to make space in yourself to feel this Work. If you have no room in yourself for this Work, how can it possibly influence you?

Quaremead, Ugley, September 1. 1945

FURTHER COMMENTARY ON MAKING WORK-EFFORT

In this Work all effort must be intelligent. It must have behind it an aim that you yourself understand intelligently and it must be carried out with your own consent. All real effort—that is, intelligent effort—is about developing the undeveloped sides of ourselves. Each of us has a machine that is only developed to a small extent on one side of itself. All intelligent Work-effort is about developing all the sides of the machine to which we are connected and bringing it to a right state of working. However most people have the idea that effort means simply doing something you do not want to do without understanding why it is necessary to do it. Or again, people think that effort consists only in not doing something, in refraining from something.

Now all Work-effort is based on understanding and if you make effort without understanding what you are doing it cannot lead anywhere. It has no meaning for you. A man in this Work through self-observation may come to know that he is always in one centre and does not use his other centres. If he has begun to understand the Work he will make an aim to make efforts in the direction of his undeveloped centres or parts of centres. This is intelligent aim, intelligent effort. To make an effort in a direction that has no real connection with what one needs is quite a good experience but it may have no result because it is not being done from one's own understanding and one's own insight into what is necessary for oneself. I may decide to get up early in the morning and dig all day in the field and find myself too tired to think afterwards. I may then think it is necessary for me to get up still earlier and dig harder the next day. But am I making this effort from my understanding? Such efforts are artificial, arbitrary efforts. They are quite useful at first because they give a great deal of matter for self-observation and for that rare form of thinking—i.e. "What am I really doing and for what reason?" For example, it might be much better for me not to go and dig in the field all day long, but instead to make an effort in regard to my Emotional Centre and my negative feelings, or to make an effort on my Thinking Centre and work something out in my mind that I have avoided doing. You have all heard that there is a class of effort in the Work called making effort to avoid effort. Probably some of you have noticed and become conscious of the fact that you should make some different effort, say, with the mind or in not identifying with unpleasant emotions, and instead of so doing you go, so to speak, to dig in the field. It is easier, but it is not intelligent. It is not based on understanding our own situation.

What do you have to do to change your relationship to your own centres? Now the first aim of this Work is to become No. 4 Man— that is, Balanced Man—and to cease being a one-sided man, either a No. 1 Man—i.e. a purely physical man—or a No. 2 Man or a No. 3 Man. In life everyone is one-sided, one-centred, and for this reason no one understands anyone else and everything is in the muddle that it is obviously in. Right effort will give you far more results than unintelligent effort, but you will only get to the point of beginning to understand what right effort means when you observe yourself sincerely and quite objectively—otherwise you will not be able to see how one-sided you are and how instead of travelling on four wheels you try to travel on one. At the same time, as I said, artificial efforts are useful for the purposes of self-observation and making you aware of Second Force. You have to fire off, as it were, many bullets in different directions, but after a time you will find that there is one bullet that will hit the mark—one thing that you should do. Supposing a person is very critical or slanderous and he decides to make the effort of digging all day in the field. Certainly he is not hitting the mark. He is making no effort against his too great tendency to criticize others or to slander others openly or privately. He is not taking hold of himself in the right way. He does not see that where effort should lie, for him, is precisely in the direction of not being too critical or talking in a slanderous way about others. At the same time, physical effort is necessary in this Work. G. taught that we have to break our laziness, physically speaking, and in this way go beyond what we ordinarily would avoid in the direction of physical effort, in the whole realm of pots and pans and digging and working with our hands and so on, or we will be handicapped and will be unable to work on ourselves in any other way. Now if you watch a person working physically you will often notice that the person is not working at all but simply doing what he or she has been told to do and not really consenting to it or thinking intelligently. G. said that in all physical work all centres should be employed and then it becomes intelligent and useful. But suppose I dig in the field all day and never notice what I am doing and how to use my spade but simply go on mechanically—then I am not working. This is called mechanical effort as distinct from conscious effort. The simplest way of understanding the difference is to notice what you are doing, to notice your resistance to what you are doing and to try to work on yourself in such a way that you are doing it yourself with your own consent, with your own understanding. Then the effort becomes, relatively speaking, conscious effort, and you will end up the day with force instead of being merely exhausted and possibly negative. A man, G. said, who is working physically, should try to master what he is doing—namely, to notice what he is doing and how to do it more easily, faster and more intelligently. Everything you do mechanically is lost but everything you do more consciously begins to belong to you. For example, mechanical goodness is useless in the Work, but conscious, active goodness gives you force. Doing something difficult at the moment when you feel very disinclined to do it, if it is done intelligently, will always give you force. But if you work in any way with continual internal considering, with continual thoughts and feelings that other people should do this and not you, your efforts are useless and this applies even to the small things you do here. Our task is to use parts of centres which we do not ordinarily use so as to open up this 3-storey house in which we live and in which we inhabit only a very small part. It is just this inhabiting a small part of this 3-storey house that makes life tedious and produces that curious staleness that everyone feels.

Now if you do not try to transform the day and what it brings—that is, if you do not make conscious effort towards any of the events of the day—you will not be making Work-effort. You are reacting mechanically—that is, as you have always done—to each moment of the day. That is undesirable. After a time, when the Work is beginning to touch you, you will hate feeling that you are simply doing everything mechanically. Then perhaps you will begin to know what it means to transform the day, to transform the moment, this very moment in which you are listening to this paper. We have this possibility of transforming each moment. We have this possibility of approaching life quite differently. One way is not to talk about everything—to keep silence. This Work is a discipline, in every direction, for every centre, not only when you are here, but when you are engaged in your necessary affairs of life. You can bring the atmosphere of the Work into everything that you do. But if you identify with everything and make inner accounts, this will be impossible. Life will eat you. Taking things from the Work point of view can alter your Being. If you make effort of this kind—namely, to bring the Work into what you do—you will be working intelligently and making intelligent effort. This must not of course be done heavily but with a certain lightness of touch that you will gradually find out about for yourself. You must not shew too much that you are working.

The supreme effort of the Work lies in making effort against your Chief Feature, whether you are digging in a field or listening to a meeting or cooking or travelling by train or are alone with yourself or surrounded by other people. The reason is that Chief Feature enters into the way you think, the way you relate yourself to others, it enters into your emotions and enters into your movements and the way you do your life-work as well as into your conceit and appetites and quarrels. But it is very difficult even to begin to catch glimpses of your Chief Feature and it is quite useless to speculate theoretically on what it is. I would advise you to think about what was said at the beginning of this paper—i.e. about making intelligent effort based on self-observation. I would ask you this question: Where through self-observation do you perceive that you avoid making certain kinds of effort? Where do you always get negative? At what point do you always identify? At what point do you find things intolerable? Or again, what do you feel is your right? What is owed to you before you can consent to do anything? We all have a favourable idea of ourselves but when we are stirred up by what we think intolerable in external circumstances we soon realize that we are very limited people capable of only a very little good-will and very little effort. You may be quite sure that your Chief Feature has something to do with all this. We have to make effort beyond this narrow limit in which we usually make effort. G. said that only extra effort counts and I fancy that each one of us should know by now what extra effort is, whether intellectual, emotional, or physical. If we cannot get beyond our mechanical limitations, if we only remain in the narrow sphere of ourselves, we have no chance of becoming No. 4 Man—i.e. Balanced Man. We shall have no idea what extra effort means. A man whose centre of gravity is in the Moving Centre would never for a moment think that he has to make intellectual effort and really think. He will not see where extra effort lies for him. And if he decides to make extra effort he will only dig longer in the field. But this is not intelligent effort which I now connect with extra effort.

Now I will bring this short paper to a close and ask you to think only about what intelligent effort means for yourselves in view of the fact that we seek to become the many-sided Balanced Man—i.e. a person in whom all the centres contribute their different meanings to his daily life.

Quaremead, Ugley, September 8, 1945

COMMENTARY ON INNER FREEDOM

Inner freedom is not a thing that is gained by outer compulsion. We cannot impose freedom on a person by law nor can a person gain inner freedom by being made to undergo any form of training or discipline. Sometimes when you are half-awake in the morning you catch a glimpse of what inner freedom means. You are still asleep to life and awake to some other level where all the different forms of slavery that our Personality imposes on us, all our different forms of internal considering, and all the cares and anxieties of existence, are still, as it were, beneath us at a lower level. And then the next instant you are right down in that level, and, ironically enough, we call this being fully awake. We lose this feeling of ourselves, which we had a moment previously and which is a form of Self-Remembering and belongs to the Third State of Consciousness, and descend by a very rapid lift to the second state of consciousness. You remember what G. said of this second state of consciousness which we call in the Western world full consciousness. He said: "In this state of so-called full consciousness, which I call a state of sleep, millions of sleeping people kill millions of other sleeping people. Thousands of sleeping people write books which thousands of other sleeping people read. And everything happens in the only way it can happen, as long as people remain asleep." However we do not see clearly enough the nature of this sleeping life that humanity is always leading. So we have not sufficient strength to keep apart from it internally, because we think it is leading somewhere, and so we identify with it and hope for the best. It is through the terrible power of identifying that we get caught up in it and usually by the most trivial and absurd things, and so we lose all traces of our inner freedom and serve nature—that is, this enormous machine called Organic Life—this pain-factory.

According to the great Work-principle demonstrated so plainly, so very clearly, in the Ray of Creation, a higher level is under fewer laws than a lower level. When we drop in our level we therefore pass under more laws. We pass, for example, into all our forms of internal accounting—into our personal likes and hatreds. The greater the depth

770

of sleep the greater the number of laws we are under. The greater the state of sleep the more we are dependent—for example, we desire encouragement, praise, appreciation, and seem to have nothing strong enough to maintain itself independently. We derive our feeling of ourselves from outside. I can assure you that a sense of the Work will begin to give you independence—an inner strength—and this I am going to connect to-night in this commentary with the idea of inner freedom. But to gain this you have to serve the Work and not Nature. For this reason it is said that for a man to become free he must first of all put himself under more laws than other people, and by this is meant under the laws of the Work. But these laws of the Work cannot remain forms of blind external obedience but become things that you acknowledge and understand and eventually will for yourself. Through perceiving their truth we give assent to them and through beginning to live according to them through our own assent and acknowledgement we make it possible for them to begin to change our Being. They set up within us a set of new connections in the mind and this attracts Essence, and in this way they form channels of connections which relate us to a higher level and so give us an inner power to resist the continued impacts of external life—the world of the newspapers, etc. In other words we begin to resist and eventually transform the incoming impressions of life and instead of reacting to them mechanically and being wholly identified, wholly upset, wholly worried by them, we may begin to be able to use them as material for work on ourselves.

Now the more truth you see in the Work through applying it to yourself by means of self-observation the more free you will become. Yes, but how can you expect to have any degree of inner freedom if you are at the mercy of every change, every event, every little incident in external life? If everything upsets you so easily, how can you have inner freedom? You serve life—you serve Nature. If you are always habitually worried and feel this is the best state to be in, how can you have inner freedom? If you are always steeped in powerful forms of self-phantasy, of imagination, and never correct them, how can you have inner freedom? If you are always negative, how can you have inner freedom? If you never seek to deal with the many giant forms of identifying, how can you have inner freedom? If you always justify and so support your poor False Personality, that lives so narrowly and proudly, how can you have inner freedom? How indeed can you understand what the Work is about, if you do not grasp that one of the things we have to do is to pass through the day without having been caught and fastened by everything and not without having attempted to transform the effects of any particular set of impressions of things said or done by others? We have spoken recently of the necessity of isolating oneself from life, and in this connection it was said that a person in the Work should practise Self-Remembering at least once a day and that if they cannot do that they must practise it three times a day —that is, they must make still greater efforts. All Self-Remembering is to lift you out of the whirlpool and uproar and dreariness going on in yourself and caused by life acting on you mechanically and by your looking to life as your only nourisher, your only source of happiness. If you have no conception of what Self-Remembering is, if you understand nothing about there being a higher level in yourself that you can attain to, then simply try to practise complete stopping of thought for a second if you can, because it is better than nothing. It will at least break the chain of mechanical associations for a moment and may possibly enable something else to reach you which otherwise is impossible.

At the last meeting we spoke of intelligent effort and therefore, by implication, of useless effort. We spoke about intelligent effort in connection with the idea of No. 4 Man or Balanced Man and we shall speak of this again and many times again, but one of the first conceptions that you can make in your minds of intelligent effort is that you can make effort about what the Work teaches you to make effort about. It teaches you to work against identifying, imagination, self-justifying, negative emotions, internal considering, and many other things, so please do not decide that an intelligent effort consists in giving up smoking, let us say. When I hear of effort of this kind I wonder whether the person concerned has ever understood what the Work is about. Surely it is much more important for a man to observe one of his typical forms of negative emotion, one of his typical bitternesses, one of his typical prejudices, one of his typical forms of depression or of being unpleasant to other people, or one of his typical forms of wrong criticism or of lying, and to try to work against that? To make such effort requires self-observation—that is, application of the Work to yourself. When a person says to me that he has decided that he must make aim not to smoke so much I wonder whether he has ever observed himself in the light of the Work-teaching.

Quaremead, Ugley, September 15, 1945

COMMENTARY ON INNER TALKING

One of the surprising things in this Work is to be told that you are all wrong. Everyone probably thinks that his or her outer life is all wrong, but cannot grasp that they in themselves are all wrong. For example, all your acquired attitudes laid down, your valuation of things, may be all wrong. This is a surprise. It means that you have been following quite wrong ideals, quite wrong thoughts, quite wrong viewpoints, quite wrong ideas about what you have to do or have not to do, all your life. It is for this reason that a second education is so necessary for those who wish it. I have used the term before. The Work may be compared with a second education about how to live on this

Earth in the right way from the standpoint of the Work. Looking back I can see how many people who influenced my life in the earliest days were quite wrong. Now if you always follow wrong standards that you have acquired, if you always think that these things ought to be done and those things ought not to be done and so on, you may be following something that can never give you any development or any peace or any inner freedom. One class of buffers in us can be formulated roughly as: "We never do this, we never do that." It is a marvellous experience to feel the Work and observe oneself from what it teaches and see how all one's life one has been following quite wrong aims, quite wrong ideals, quite wrong standpoints, so I repeat that this Work can be called a second education which is undergone at the expense of one's acquired education.

This second education that the Work gives you and which you must seize hold of for yourselves, each individually, can produce harmonies in you and understanding that your first acquired education can never give you. This second education is of course at the expense of the acquired Personality. You begin to examine yourself, you begin to observe yourself, you begin to see that many acquired attitudes lead nowhere and only produce a sense of discomfort, disharmony. I have often said to you recently how important it is to observe yourself from what the Work teaches you as being important, and what the Work teaches you as not being important. You may, for example, always feel it is right to be worried about everything or constantly to write letters giving your serious advice about some insoluble domestic situation and all the rest of it. This is done because you have acquired certain ingrained attitudes about what is right and wrong and may cause a great deal of unnecessary misery both as regards yourself and as regards other people with whom you correspond. Now, as regards this loosening of oneself from oneself, this possibility of becoming different from what one is, this possibility of taking everything in a new way that does not agree with what one has been told to do, with what opinions one has been taught to follow—all this is the beginning of the action of the Work on oneself. Our acquired opinions and viewpoints can give us no internal freedom, no internal development. For this reason the Work comes down as something overshadowing our small lives to teach us how really to behave, how really to think, how really to view life on this Earth. If you study this Work closely enough you will find that it gives you a complete new way of relating yourself to life, to other people, and, above all, to yourself. But if you are still holding to your fixed opinions, to your buffers, to your whole acquired way of taking life as you always have in the past, you will never understand what the Work is speaking to you about. Remember it is you yourself who have to change—it is you yourself who are all wrong, from the Work point of view—namely, from the standpoint of Higher Man. It is you who have a dirty and wrongly connected machine.

*   *   *

773

Let us study one of the things that the Work teaches us that we have to try to do. I will take to-night the subject of *Inner Talking* about which the Work says many things. Let me ask you this question: Have any of you been taught in your ordinarily acquired—your first—education anything about inner talking? Did you have lectures at school about the dangers of inner talking or ever have defined to you what inner talking means? I am quite sure that none of you has ever been taught this in life, but when you come into the Work one of the things that the Work teaches you is to try to stop inner talking because it is very dangerous. I am not speaking of people who go along in the streets muttering to themselves. That is certainly inner talking, but I am speaking about this inner talking that goes on in you all the time that is not expressed outwardly. In other words, we are talking about the inner psychological state upon which the Work lays its main emphasis. The Work is about our inner states. It is not about outer life primarily: it is about *you* internally. It is about how you are within yourself invisibly and what you go with in yourself. Here lies the point of application of the Work. One of the first things that we have to study in the Work is how to save force, and first of all we have to study how to stop the waste of force before we begin to study how to save force—that is, how not to waste force. Every psychic act takes force. Nothing can happen in you psychologically, invisibly in yourself, without taking force from you. If you are in an envious state and envying someone in your thoughts, this takes force from you. Now the study of force in ourselves is an extremely complicated question. I will remind you here that when you use force consciously—i.e. as far as we are conscious in directed attention—you do not lose force but you gain force. But every psychic act that happens mechanically takes force from you—that is to say, you waste force and it is gone without any result. One of the forms of losing force mechanically in this way is through what the Work calls inner talking.

Now the Work says that inner talking is difficult to stop and you must be clever about it and find out how to deal with it. But it says first of all that you must be able to observe it—that is, you must begin to be aware through self-observation that inner talking is going on in you. Inner talking is never dialogue but is always a monologue. Inner talking is always negative in character. A great deal of inner talking is connected with self-justifying—namely, with the attempt to put yourself in the right. You feel, for example, that someone has not treated you rightly. This will start off inner talking. The point is that you have already become negative by not being rightly treated in your opinion of yourself and have not been quite satisfied by the behaviour of someone else, and you begin to become negative towards other people, towards how you are being treated by others. You then start a chain of inner talking or rather, a chain of inner talking begins automatically in you, and you will often find that it is based on justifying yourself, putting yourself in the right towards this wrong behaviour of

774

other people towards you. However, there are other forms of inner talking, often more deeply placed, which sometimes refer to people long ago dead and are due to old laid down gramophone records in you that something starts off. I am not going to speak to-night about these older gramophone records, because if you will learn something about these forms of inner talking that are started up now you will get much better results in understanding the source of inner talking and you will then be able with this conscious strength to go back to more ancient forms of inner talking and deal with them more consciously.

The first thing that we must do in regard to inner talking is to observe it and notice what this inner talking is saying. As I said, it is always a monologue. Yet all inner talking is personal and is directed against a person. This person may be God, but then you are regarding him as a person. You feel neglected, you feel wrongly treated, you feel you have not had a chance, and so on. It is always personal, it is always directed against some person whom you either know about or do not know about, but it is always against a person, known or unknown, a person who says nothing and who apparently does not appreciate you sufficiently. You can in certain states so identify, and so internally consider, that matter itself becomes personal to you as a hostile power. You knock a cup over and smash it and it is the cup's fault. Now in all inner talking you never blame yourself. That would stop it. You may think you do blame yourself and there are some very subtle forms of inner talking which are mixed up with apparent self-blame and which are rooted in something quite different. But the more of a grievance you hold against life in general, the more you feel in general that things should have been different for you, the more frequent and habitual your inner talking will tend to become.

Now we have to cancel all sense of people owing us anything at all. This is extremely difficult. But it is one of the few things mentioned in the Lord's Prayer: "Cancel what we owe as we cancel what others owe us." When a person allows inner talking to go on and on in himself he is losing force all the time. This kind of mental mumbling drags a person down very much because it is basically negative. As you know, all negative states drain force from us uselessly and are sometimes compared with the state of a person who has opened an artery and is gradually bleeding to death without knowing he is dying. To surround oneself with something that gradually becomes more and more impermeable to the impacts of life is one of the ideas of this Work. This idea is expressed in many different ways. One is that one must isolate or insulate oneself from the effects of life upon us. This insulation is the idea lying behind non-identifying. We have to make a good container. We have to make a vessel in which this Work and all its results can lie without being completely dissolved at every moment, completely lost by the many awkward movements of daily life. In other words, one has to be able to hold on to something strongly and more and more strongly, and it is exactly this holding on that prevents a leakage and builds up what must be built up in us. This power of having a container, this power of separation and Self-Remembering, makes it possible for what is called Second Body to grow, that is, something that is not a function of external conditions. Here lies the depth of the Work and here lies the first explanation of all that the Work teaches that we have to practise in this second education. It has often been said that one can either serve life or serve the Work. If a small thing upsets you, if a mere spoken word spoils your life, you are not in a condition to develop. You have nothing whereby to develop, as it were—no force to create the Second Body. Now inner talking weakens us in this respect probably more than anything else does. It is a continual source of leakage, of force, a serving of life. What does life mean? Life means among other things what people say to us, how they behave to us, what comes through our senses, through what we see, what we hear. In the Work-sense life is this external thing that we make contact with through the eyes, through the ears, the taste, etc. The psychological senses are the eyes and the ears. They are the vehicles of sense. They convey to us impressions from the external world in which other people exist as visible, audible things. Your psychological life is invisible to the senses of other people and to the external senses of yourself. Your psychological life is how you think, how you feel, and it is to this life, this inner psychological life, as was said, that the Work directs your attention. It says: "Observe yourself." How do you think of other people? No doubt you think it does not matter, and that it is a private thing of your own. But it does matter for if you think evil of other people you are all wrong inside and you will get into a situation after a time, if you try to do this Work, that I dread to think of. All that side of you must be cleared up and made right. Here cancelling comes in. Now inner talking comes practically always from wrong thinking and wrong feeling. Just as you have a rash on your skin and feel you must be ill, so if you find yourself full of inner talking, full of unpleasant phrases that automatically repeat themselves, full of justifying, you may be quite sure that you are psychologically ill. If you begin to feel this Work as one of the important things in your life you will feel extremely uncomfortable, you will really feel ill, and you will really wish to see what it is all about and how you can stop it. You will always find that it is because you are lying, because you are not facing what actually happens, let us say. You may be lying through some phantasy that you have of yourself, some absurd picture, that in itself is a lie. And in this Work you cannot go very far with pleasing self-made pictures of your own nobility or value. When you begin to observe yourself deeply enough, these pictures, these phantasies, begin to change. You know that you yourself are just as bad or worse than the other person. Then I am quite sure from my own experience that a great deal of your inner talking will stop. You do not seek to justify yourself.

Try to change inner talking, which, as I said, is always a monologue, directed against another person, into a dialogue with another person, and give this other person an existence and say to him or her: "I do not think that I have been rightly treated," and try to make this other person reply. Inner dialogue is an extremely useful thing to cultivate. You may be surprised that this other person whom you have materialized in your mind may suddenly say to you: "Who do you think you are?" It will be a very surprising experience to have someone in you saying that to you about yourself. And this materialized person may go so far as to say: "What was it *you* said?" Now this will break up all your nice little negative enjoyment. You will feel that you have an enemy in yourself, or perhaps a friend, and that you cannot think or feel just as you have always been thinking or feeling in your own rather unpleasant privacy. Sometimes it is a good thing to put up the Work against you when you are in inner talking. Notice what your inner talking is up to. Then repeat it to this image of the Work that you have summoned up in yourself and just see what the Work says. It is calling up 'I's which are rather more conscious to have a dialogue with your mechanical 'I's which are not conscious. Let us suppose you get some answer from your Work 'I's. Instantly your mechanical 'I's will try to make an excuse. They will say, for example: "Oh, well, this is all very difficult for us." Now let us cast this difficult situation in terms of the Work speaking to you, and by you I mean your mechanical psychology that is continually wasting force in absolutely useless psychic activities. You summon up the Work. The Work says: "Why are you negative?" You say: "I am not negative." And then for a moment there is silence and then you (i.e. your mechanical inner talking) say something like this: "Well, I could never do the Work." Silence. And then you will find that your effort to divide yourself into two will rapidly die away and *you* (i.e. your mechanical side) will continue to internally talk, probably with added force. Now it is just here that a certain subtlety of self-observation comes in. I do not think that afterwards, at least for a little time, your mechanical inner talking will go quite so happily.

I will end this short Commentary by saying that when you are in attention your inner talking stops. Painting is useful. What you have to understand is that inner talking unchecked exhausts you, wastes your force, and probably makes it possible for you to have many illnesses that are unnecessary. A person too high in himself or herself will always have a great deal of inner talking because when you are too high in yourself the activity of self-justifying is constantly at work. Remember that one of the aims of this Work is to realize our nothingness. Such a realization will stop all inner talking and all inner waste of force due to it. But it is extraordinary to notice in oneself and in other people what a lot of smashing it takes, what a lot of untoward circumstances are required to bring down this inner phantasy, this inner elevation, that it takes so much force to maintain.